Perpetuating Advantage

Perpetuating Advantage

Mechanisms of Structural Injustice

ROBERT E. GOODIN

OXFORD
UNIVERSITY PRESS

Great Clarendon Street, Oxford, OX2 6DP,
United Kingdom

Oxford University Press is a department of the University of Oxford.
It furthers the University's objective of excellence in research, scholarship,
and education by publishing worldwide. Oxford is a registered trade mark of
Oxford University Press in the UK and in certain other countries

© Robert E. Goodin 2023

The moral rights of the author have been asserted

All rights reserved. No part of this publication may be reproduced, stored in
a retrieval system, or transmitted, in any form or by any means, without the
prior permission in writing of Oxford University Press, or as expressly permitted
by law, by licence or under terms agreed with the appropriate reprographics
rights organization. Enquiries concerning reproduction outside the scope of the
above should be sent to the Rights Department, Oxford University Press, at the
address above

You must not circulate this work in any other form
and you must impose this same condition on any acquirer

Published in the United States of America by Oxford University Press
198 Madison Avenue, New York, NY 10016, United States of America

British Library Cataloguing in Publication Data

Data available

Library of Congress Control Number: 2022950607

ISBN 978–0–19–288820–4

DOI: 10.1093/oso/9780192888204.001.0001

Printed and bound by
CPI Group (UK) Ltd, Croydon, CR0 4YY

Links to third party websites are provided by Oxford in good faith and
for information only. Oxford disclaims any responsibility for the materials
contained in any third party website referenced in this work.

The truth is, when it comes to all those tidy stories of hard work and self-determination that we like to tell ourselves about America, well, the reality is a lot more complicated than that. Because for too many people in this country, no matter how hard they work, there are structural barriers working against them that just make the road longer and rockier. And sometimes it's almost impossible to move upward at all.
—Michelle Obama, 2020

Contents

Analytic Table of Contents	viii
Preface	xi
1. Introduction	1
2. Modes of Perpetuating Advantage	21

PART I. MECHANISMS PERPETUATING ADVANTAGE

3. Position Confers Advantage	37
4. Network Confers Advantage	54
5. Language, Coding Categories, and Interpretive Schema Confer Advantage	69
6. Social Expectations and Norms Confer Advantage	95
7. Reputation Confers Advantage	117
8. Coordination and Organization Confer Advantage	131

PART II. UNDERLYING DRIVERS

9. External Opportunities: Scale Effects	151
10. Internal Constraints: Attention Scarcity	163
11. Interrupting Advantage	174
References	199
Index	244

Analytic Table of Contents

Preface	xi
1. Introduction	1
1.1 Structures *and* Agents	5
1.2 Focus on Advantage, More Generally	10
1.3 Types of Advantage	14
1.4 Mechanisms of Perpetuation, More Generally	16
1.4.1 Over Time, Across Generations	16
1.4.2 Flypaper and Bottlenecks	18
1.5 Not Allocating Blame, but Guiding Reform	19
2. Modes of Perpetuating Advantage	21
2.1 Retaining Advantage	22
2.2 Expanding Advantage	25
2.3 Replicating Advantage	29
2.4 Recreating Advantage	31
2.5 Summing Up	33

PART I. MECHANISMS PERPETUATING ADVANTAGE

3. Position Confers Advantage	37
3.1 Four Types of Positional Advantage	38
3.1.1 Position in a Status Hierarchy	38
3.1.2 Position in an Institutional Hierarchy	40
3.1.3 Position in a Naked-power Hierarchy	41
3.1.4 Position in a Formally Organized Competitive Hierarchy	42
3.2 The Dynamics of Positional-good Competition	42
3.3 Separate Spheres	46
3.3.1 Differing Scope Restrictions	46
3.3.2 Do Different Positional Advantages Cancel One Another?	47
3.4 Nearly Universal Means	49
3.5 Undoing Positional Advantage	51
4. Network Confers Advantage	54
4.1 The Nature of Networks	55
4.2 Network Power and Advantage	57

4.3	Network Homogeneity and Homophily Advantages the Advantaged	60
4.4	Examples of Network Advantage in Action	61
	4.4.1 Labour Market Networks	62
	4.4.2 Legal Services Networks	64
	4.4.3 A Dramatic Historical Speculation	65
4.5	Sources of Network Effects: Information and Trust	66
4.6	Distributional Consequences of Network Externalities	68

5. Language, Coding Categories, and Interpretive Schema Confer Advantage — 69

5.1	Language as a Source of Advantage	69
	5.1.1 Language Conventions Can Be Asymmetrically Beneficial	70
	5.1.2 The Choice of Language Confers Advantage and Disadvantage	73
	5.1.3 Languages as Status Markers	76
	5.1.4 Manipulating Language: The Implicit and Unspoken	79
5.2	Coding Categories	81
5.3	Interpretative Schema	88
5.4	What Is to Be Done?	92

6. Social Expectations and Norms Confer Advantage — 95

6.1	Descriptive Norms and Expectations	96
	6.1.1 Acting on What *You* Expect to Happen	97
	6.1.2 Acting on the Basis of What *Others* Expect to Happen	100
	6.1.2.1 As a Rational Response	100
	6.1.2.2 As a Psychological Tendency	103
6.2	Prescriptive Norms and Expectations	104
	6.2.1 Moral Norms	104
	6.2.2 Social Norms	106
	6.2.3 Role Norms	107
	6.2.4 Legal Norms	109
6.3	The Relations Between Descriptive and Prescriptive Norms	110
6.4	The Value of Knowing What to Expect	113
	6.4.1 Successfully Exercising Temporally Extended Agency	113
	6.4.2 Stabilizing Expectations and Its Distributional Consequences	115

7. Reputation Confers Advantage — 117

7.1	Reputation for Power	117
7.2	Reputation for Status Position	120
7.3	Reputation for Network Influence and Preferential Attachment	122
7.4	Reputation for Reliability and Trustworthiness	125
	7.4.1 Why Trust Matters	125
	7.4.2 Assortation by Reputation: Trust-based Network Construction	128

8. Coordination and Organization Confer Advantage 131
　8.1 Varieties of Coordination Problems 132
　8.2 Methods of Coordinating 135
　　8.2.1 Formal Coordination by Mutual Agreement 135
　　8.2.2 Shared Norms or Conventions 137
　　8.2.3 Mutual Adjustment 139
　　8.2.4 Mutual Alignment 141
　8.3 Structures for Coordinating: Organizations, Formal and Informal 142
　8.4 The Biases of Organization 146

PART II. UNDERLYING DRIVERS

9. External Opportunities: Scale Effects 151
　9.1 Scale Effects in Production 152
　9.2 Scale Effects in Consumption 155
　9.3 Scale Effects in Valuation 159
　　9.3.1 Scale Effects in Communication: Network Externalities 159
　　9.3.2 Analogous Phenomena 161

10. Internal Constraints: Attention Scarcity 163
　10.1 Attention as a Scarce Resource 163
　10.2 Lessons from the Internet 167
　10.3 How Attention Scarcity Perpetuates Advantage 171

11. Interrupting Advantage 174
　11.1 Responding to Structural Injustice: The Standard Prescriptions 175
　　11.1.1 Disruption, Then What? 175
　　11.1.2 Collective Action: The Motivational Issue 177
　11.2 Head-on Attacks on Mechanisms Perpetuating Advantage 179
　　11.2.1 Destroy the Mechanisms 179
　　11.2.2 Reduce the Need for the Mechanisms 181
　　11.2.3 Reduce the Differential Advantages Conferred 184
　11.3 Amelioration Strategies 187
　　11.3.1 Siphon Off the Benefits 189
　　11.3.2 Regulate the Process 192
　　11.3.3 Provide Alternative Mechanisms 192
　11.4 Who Should Do What? 195
　11.5 Conclusion 197

References 199
Index 244

Preface

The impetus behind this book is a concern with social injustice and despair at the way in which social structures can serve to bake it into our social relations. The aim of the book is to understand *how* that happens. What are the various mechanisms that might be in play? How do they work, and how might they be interrupted? Understanding is thus sought, most fundamentally, as an aid to action.

Analysing structural injustice by focusing on the mechanisms that perpetrate and perpetuate it is beneficial, twice over. First, that focus enables me to make a unique contribution to these discussions. For all the voluminous literature on structural injustice, there is precious little on the precise mechanisms by which it occurs. Such discussions as do exist tend to focus on one particular mechanism or another. There is no remotely comparable attempt at a comprehensive, systematic survey of all such mechanisms and how they fit together. My discussion, like previous ones, will start by isolating and trying to separate out the independent effects of each of the many mechanisms of structural injustice. But my discussion will also be sensitive to the larger ecology within which each mechanism works, alongside with and often reinforced by other such mechanisms and often being held (often very imperfectly) in check by some countervailing measures. When I say that some mechanism has the effect of causing 'the rich to get richer', metaphorically or all too often literally, that will therefore always be as a partial rather than global claim pertaining purely to the effect of that particular mechanism 'in itself' rather than the overall tendency of the larger system within which it operates, necessarily.

A second benefit of focusing on mechanisms is strategic. That focus enables me to skirt two vexed problems: first, how to define structural injustice; and second, how, at a high level of abstraction, to characterize responsibilities for remedying it. Proposals on both scores proliferate, with no resolution in prospect. Focusing on mechanisms of structural injustice allows me to sidestep those twin quagmires. Here is the reason. Whatever else it is, structural injustice is 'unfair advantage and disadvantage perpetuated through social structures'. And the mechanisms perpetuating advantage and disadvantage through social structures are much the same, whether the pattern of advantages and disadvantages produced is substantively fair or unfair. Hence we do not need to answer the conceptual question of 'what is structural injustice?' in order to answer the mechanism question of 'how is it perpetuated?' Furthermore, once we have answered the mechanism question, we will have a more precise idea of what needs to be done by whom in order for it to be overcome. High level, abstract debates over highly stylized models of different types of responsibility for overcoming structural injustice in general can then be replaced with much more fine-grained and tailor-made prescriptions.

This book is fundamentally a conceptual mapping exercise. The aim is to provide an inventory of the many and varied mechanisms by which social structural mechanisms can perpetuate advantage and disadvantage. I draw examples from many different places and many different periods. I offer those empirical examples purely as 'proofs of concept'. They serve simply to show that some such mechanisms are no mere flights of philosophical fancy—those mechanisms have actually figured somewhere in the real world, at some point or another.

Before mounting the larger political project of attacking any particular instance of structural injustice, of course, further empirical will be required to ascertain which mechanisms are *presently* at work in that *particular* setting. That is a task for elsewhere and later, not this book. Still, by showing what all mechanisms to look out for, I hope that this conceptual mapping exercise might serve as useful groundwork for that larger social scientific, and ultimately political, project.

I should add, finally, that my aim here is to provide a mapping of generic types of mechanisms that perpetuate social advantage. Not only may different ones of those mechanisms be at work at different times and places, as I have just said. Each specific mechanism may also work differently not only at different times and places but also as applied to different sources of social advantage (gender versus race, for example). Those, too, are questions requiring further empirical investigation before mounting a practical attack on any particular instance of structural injustice. Identifying generic mechanisms, as is done in this book, is only a first step—but hopefully a useful first step—in that larger empirical, and ultimately political, process.

****

Although the current text is of recent vintage, this book's deeper origins and many of its ideas are the products of a great many conversations over a great many years. I discussed agency and structure at length with Bob Jessop and Hugh Ward in the 1980s and structural injustice at length with Iris Young a couple of decades later. Brian Barry and I discussed positional goods with Fred Hirsch in the 1970s. I discussed mechanisms more generally with Jon Elster, Art Stinchcombe, and Chuck Tilly over the next three decades. And I discussed all those topics and many more with Claus Offe, during his 15 years of recurring visits to ANU as our Adjunct Professor. In many ways large and small, this book reflects the caldron of interdisciplinarity that was the ANU Research School of Social Sciences in its heyday.

While I have thus been unwittingly assembling resources for this book for quite some time, they gelled into a unified whole only relatively recently. One impetus was collaboration with Christian Barry on various related projects over the past decade. Another impetus was conversations with Ana Tanasoca concerning mechanisms underlying public deliberation in naturalized settings. In the early stages of its composition, the book benefited from conversational input from Amandine Catala, Timo Jütten, Avery Kolers, and Josh Ober. At later stages valuable comments on the manuscript as a whole came from Bruce Headey, Avery Kolers (once again), Kai Spiekermann, Katie Steele, and referees for Oxford University Press. I am once again grateful to my long-standing editor there, Dominic Byatt, for skilfully shepherding the project to successful completion.

This book was drafted in the semi-solitude of coronavirus lockdowns. Isaac Newton made much better use of a similar period, three and a half centuries before. Still, like him, I found the period highly fruitful.

1
Introduction

This book is deeply concerned with injustice. But unlike most books on the subject, it is relatively unconcerned to specify what injustice is or how it comes about in the first instance. This book is focused, instead, on how injustice is perpetuated over time.[1]

Experiencing an injustice is bad, even if the injustice is quickly corrected. But it is worse to endure that injustice for a protracted period.[2] It is wrong to commit an injustice, even knowing it will be quickly corrected. But it is worse to commit that injustice if it is likely to be long lasting. It is bad to perpetuate an unjust state of affairs that would otherwise fade away—sometimes as bad as creating it in the first place.[3]

Sometimes advantages and disadvantages are perpetuated through the same mechanisms by which they are created in the first place. Take the example of a racist estate agent who refuses to show any house in a white neighbourhood to any black buyer. The same racism leads the estate agent to discriminate against a black homebuyer first for one property, and then for another, and them for another.[4] The same thing that disadvantages black homebuyers in the first instance keeps disadvantaging them over and over again.

Other times, unjust advantages and disadvantages are perpetuated through mechanisms different than those creating them in the first place. Here is a common scenario of that sort: the initial injustice was perpetuated through a brute act of interpersonal power; that injustice is then perpetuated, not through

---

[1] As Haslanger (2012, p. 332) says, if only in passing: 'In considering oppression it is important to ask three separate questions: (1) Does the institution *cause* or *create* unjust disadvantage to a group? (2) Does the institution *perpetuate* unjust disadvantage to a group? (3) Does the institution *amplify* or *exacerbate* unjust disadvantage to a group? There is a tendency to focus on (1) when asking whether an institution is oppressive. But (2) and (3) are no less important to promote justice.' For an analysis of Haslanger's third category, see Hellman's (2018) discussion of 'compounding injustice'.

[2] On the notion of 'enduring injustice' see Spinner-Halev (2012, esp. ch. 3).

[3] If, for example, done intentionally and with long-lasting effects. See Barry and Wiens (2016) and Section 1.2 below.

[4] You can call it (i) a case of persisting injustice (the black homebuyer continues being refused properties) or (ii) a case of repeated or replicated injustice (each refusal is unjust, just like the last) or (iii) a case of expanding injustice (with the discriminated-against black homebuyer being deprived of an increasing proportion of houses in the white neighbourhood). Those descriptions, and the underlying phenomena, are different in important respects, as will be elaborated upon in Chapter 2. For purposes of the point being made here, however, they do not matter.

recurring exercises of interpersonal power of the same sort, but rather by its having been embedded in impersonal structures that then surreptitiously shape subsequent exercises of agency.[5] The history of emancipated slaves in the American South after the Civil War is a prime example. Emancipation brought former slaves a certain (if imperfect) measure of freedom from the brute oppression of white masters and overseers. The terms of their emancipation, however, made it structurally inevitable that they would become landless share-croppers in 'debt peonage' to credit merchants.[6]

Such structures serve to channel subsequent exercises of agency, constraining it in certain respects at the same time as enabling it in others. Structures make some courses of action easier or more rewarding, while making other courses of action more difficult or costly—and differentially so, for different groups of actors.

That is simply what structures do. When Habermas writes about *The Structural Transformation of the Public Sphere*, for example, his reference is to two developments—the eighteenth-century rise of the coffeehouse and of the broadsheet newspaper—that together facilitated political communication among the bourgeoisie and the growth of a civil society independent from courtly politics.[7] When trust-busters at the end of the nineteenth century condemned interlocking directorates, they were complaining about corporate governance structures that facilitated coordination among notionally independent corporations that were supposed to be competing with one another, thus enabling them to collude on artificially high prices and other arrangements in restraint of trade.[8] The latter sorts of structures are to be bemoaned, the former to be welcomed. But both are structures of a similar sort, created by

---

[5] There is a natural impetus to try to 'hide' the recurring effects of injustices behind impersonal structures, rather than re-enact blatantly wrongful acts time and again (Nuti 2019). In an oppressive structure, as Young (1990, p. 41) says, 'causes are embedded in unquestioned norms, habits and symbols, in the assumptions underlying institutional rules and the collective consequences of following those rules.... In this extended structural sense oppression refers to the vast and deep injustices some groups suffer as a consequence of often unconscious assumptions and reactions of well-meaning people in ordinary interactions, media and cultural stereotypes, and structural features of bureaucratic hierarchies and market mechanisms—in short, the normal processes of everyday life.'

[6] For a more recent economic history, see Ransom and Sutch (1977). For an older and more evocative social history, see Du Bois's classic account of *Black Reconstruction* which concludes: 'It was the policy of the state to keep the Negro laborer poor, to confine him as far as possible to menial occupations, to make him a surplus labor reservoir and to force him into peonage and unpaid toil' (1935, p. 696, see further ch. 14).

[7] Habermas 1962/1989.

[8] Brandeis 1914; Baran and Sweezy 1966. Having one of 'J.P. Morgan's men' on its board has been calculated to have increased the value of a firm's common stock equity by some 30 per cent in the years before World War I, in part because it 'aided the formation of oligopoly' (De Long 1991). On subsequent periods, see Useem (1983), Knoke (1993) and for the latest manifestation ('hybrid networks') Teubner (2002).

human agency and employed by human agents in pursuit of their purposes, aiding some and inhibiting others.[9]

The structures of interest in this book are all social constructs like that. Some take the form of physical infrastructure, like bridges and border walls.[10] Others are social infrastructure—social institutions, practices, relations, and the like.[11] Some parts of that social infrastructure constitute intentional agents capable of acting in their own right. Corporations, clubs, and national governments are examples of that. But even structures that are themselves intentionally inert (like bridges, constitutions, and codes of etiquette) nonetheless serve to channel the intentional actions of others.[12]

Sometimes, as in the case of the coffeehouses, these effects may be unintended. Other times, as in the case of interlocking directorates, they are far from that. The latter sorts of structures embody the ossified intentions of those who created and recreated them, working with, on, and through those structures. Those sorts of structures are of particular moral concern for that reason. But the former sorts of structures are of concern as well. Those structures have the effect, unintended but nonetheless very real, of tilting the social playing field systematically to the advantage of some and the disadvantage of others. That is worrying in and of itself.

All that is familiar from the existing literature on structural power and structural injustice.[13] What is substantially missing from that literature is any proper account of what exactly the structures in question are, and how exactly they work to perpetuate injustice.[14] Likewise, gesturing towards 'path dependency' is simply to assert the conclusion that past choices affect future ones, rather than to offer an explanation of how, exactly, that happens.[15]

---

[9] Hayward (in Hayward and Lukes 2008, p. 16) equates 'structural constraints' with 'codified and institutionalized human actions that create patterned asymmetries in the social capacity to act'. See similarly: MacIntyre 1999; Reiman 2012.
[10] Liao and Huebner 2021.
[11] Haslanger 2016.
[12] Reiman 1989, p. 203. Young 2011, pp. 53–6. The limiting case may be robots, which may or may not be intentionally inert: but they certainly have been intentionally programmed by human agents; those programmers' values infuse those robots' design and their design shapes the uses to which they can be put (Sparrow 2021).
[13] Seminal texts include: Galtung 1969, 1990; Young 2011, ch. 2; Haslanger 2012, ch. 11; 2016, 2017. For a brief overview of debates growing out of Young and Haslanger's work see McKeown (2017).
[14] Critiquing Sewell's (1992) concept of 'structure', Lizardo (2010, p. 675) worries 'whether such a wide ranging notion can be useful for actual research.... [I]f structures refer to everything, they also refer to nothing at all'. Hence we should move from the study of 'structuralism' to the study of specific structures—just as I argue we should get past generalities about 'structural injustice' and examine specific mechanisms perpetrating it.
[15] Generically, path dependency just says that past outcomes shape future outcomes by making some options either more rewarding or less costly. But how exactly they do that is an open question not answered by the sheer fact of path dependency. It could be by making some options conceptually

The standard laundry list of sources of structural injustice identifies *where* structural power resides. We are told that it is found in the political system, in the economy, in society, in culture, in language, in the physical environment, both built and natural. All that, however, is merely to name the *sites* where structural injustice occurs. What we really need to know is not so much where structural injustice occurs but, instead, *by what mechanisms* it occurs, *how* those mechanisms work, and how they can be *stopped* from working.[16] Exploring that latter set of issues is the larger aim of this book.

Focusing on mechanisms that perpetuate structural injustice serves a very particular purpose. The 'mechanism approach' aims at 'opening up black boxes, ... striving for narrowing the gap ... between input and output, cause and effect. A mechanism-based explanation seeks to provide a fine-grained as well as tight coupling between explanans and explanandum.'[17] That is the first aim of this book—to understand the mechanisms by which advantage (most especially, unjust advantage) is perpetuated.

That first aim is in service of a second, which is to understand the mechanisms perpetuating unjust advantage in hopes of disrupting them. Sometimes by calling a problem 'structural' we mean merely to say that it is not amenable to any policy solutions, anyway not at an acceptable social cost. 'Structural unemployment' is a classic example of that usage.[18] Clearly, I reject that usage. For me, a problem is 'structural' if it is sourced in structures—more specifically, one of the mechanisms I shall discuss in Part II of the book.

A problem is all the more problematic if it defies any cost-effective policy remedies, to be sure. But that is not the defining feature of a 'structural' problem. Many problems that are genuinely structural in my sense may well defy cost-effective policy remedies. But that is not true of all cases of unjust perpetuation of advantage that are properly seen as having structural sources. Many can at least be ameliorated, if not remedied altogether, in ways that I elaborate in Chapter 11.

---

more familiar, more accessible via existing networks or organizational structures or better supported by existing social norms and expectations and reputational structures. On path dependency in general see: David 1985; Arthur 1989; Pierson 2000. On the many different ways of formally modelling path dependency, other than the 'outcome-dependent' version just sketched, see Page (2006).

[16] As Reskin (2003, p. 16) remarked in her Presidential Address to the American Sociological Association, 'In explaining social stratification, identifying mechanisms is particularly important because—as the methods for distributing social goods—they are the engines of equality and inequality.'

[17] Hedström and Swedberg 1998, p. 25. See further the other chapters in that collection, as well as: Elster 1983, 1989, 2007; Stinchcombe 1991; Tilly 2001; Tilly and Goodin 2006, pp. 14–9; Hedström and Bearman 2009; Hedström and Ylikoski. 2010.

[18] In a US Department of Commerce publication, for example, Bergmann and Kaun (1967, ch. 1) define 'structural unemployment' as 'that amount of unemployment (less minimal frictional and seasonal) which cannot be removed by monetary and fiscal policy without creating continuing inflation (as opposed to one-shot, nonrepeatable price rises) deriving directly from shortages of labor'.

In discussing structural mechanisms that perpetuate advantage, I shall be discussing them in their most generic forms. Their particular instantiations of course vary wildly, and interventions aiming to interrupt their workings must of course be sensitive to those local variations. But it is equally important, if not more so, to be attuned to their generic workings. Take for example networks, the topic of Chapter 4. Those networks might take many forms: trade routes, railroad tracks, telegraph lines, or kinship or friendship bonds. But whatever the specific form, networks are all alike in distributing information and other valued resources to those within the network and most particularly to those located centrally within it, to the advantage of those within and the disadvantage of those outside of those networks.

Finally, the structures I shall be discussing have both external and internal aspects. In the network example just discussed, the rail and telegraph lines are an example of the former, the friendship ties an example of the latter. Some internal aspects are physical (sex, disability, to shift examples).[19] Other internal aspects are more psychological. Examples of that include Chapter 5's concepts, codes, and categories——what many would call 'ideologies'—through which we interpret our world. Other examples are the expectations and reputations that shape the way we interact in the world, discussed in Chapters 6 and 7. The sense of entitlement and the self-confidence that those confer on the already advantaged, and the demoralization that they instil in the disadvantaged, contribute substantially to the perpetuation of existing patterns of advantage and disadvantage.[20]

1.1 Structures *and* Agents

The very term 'structural injustice' would itself be an oxymoron if 'structure or agent' were—as it has sometimes been treated as being—a genuinely mutually exclusive dichotomy.[21] The reason is simply that structures themselves

---

[19] At least insofar as you accept—as I do—that those are not *purely* social constructs.

[20] The general observation is itself something of a commonplace, famously expressed by Mahatma Gandhi: 'Man often becomes what he believes himself to be. If I keep on saying to myself that I cannot do a certain thing, it is possible that I may end by really becoming incapable of doing it. On the contrary, if I have the belief that I can do it, I shall surely acquire the capacity to do it even if I may not have it at the beginning' (quoted in Deats 2005, p. 108). For more popular treatments see: Peale 1952; Beauvoir 1955; Bell 1976, p. 233; Manne 2020. For more academic (social-scientific or philosophical) ones see: Cook 1975; Derber 1978; Major 1987; Bénabou and Tirole 2002; Flåm and Risa 2003; Morton 2021; Gomez 2022.

[21] Although enthusiasts sometimes phrase it in this hyperbolic way, more judicious scholars merely claim that structures can sometimes cause outcomes without the intervention of any human agency. Galtung (1969, p. 170) for example writes: 'We shall refer to the type of violence where there is an actor that commits the violence as *personal* or *direct*, and to violence where there is no such actor as *structural* or *indirect*.' (He equates 'structural injustice' with the latter: p. 171.) Galtung goes on to argue

lack agency.²² Yet injustice is a wrong, and a wrong by definition requires the exercise of agency.²³

The *Oxford English Dictionary* defines a 'wrong' as an 'unjust action or conduct' by one person that causes 'injury, hurt, harm, or prejudice' to another.²⁴ Actions are not simply happenings—events that occur in the world. They are the doings of actors intentionally exercising their agency.²⁵ Those agents may be natural individuals, or they may be artificially created entities (like corporations) or formally organized groups of natural individuals (like gangs). But even artificial or collective agents act, when they do, via the exercise of agency by natural individuals within them.

Talk of 'structural injustice' purports to draw attention to ways in which unjust advantage is perpetuated by structures *rather than* agents.²⁶ The aim is to encourage us to stop looking for 'bad people' to blame, and to look instead at social structures that lead 'good people' to do bad and enable 'bad people' to do bad.²⁷

If the 'rather than' in the claim in the previous paragraph were taken literally, however, the claim would be nonsensical. Things possessing no agency can commit no acts; hence, neither can they commit any wrongs

---

that the two are 'empirically independent' of one another—'it is possible to have them in pure forms, to have one without the other' (p. 178). See more generally, Dawe (1970) on 'the two sociologies'.

²² Sociologists sometimes talk as if structure possesses agency, as when Sewell (1992, p. 2) writes: 'Structure, in its nominative sense, always implies structure in its transitive verbal sense. Whatever aspect of social life we designate as structure is posited as "structuring" some other aspect of social existence....' But that is just a classic example of what Ryle (1931–1932) calls a 'systematically misleading expression'.

²³ One of the great themes of the structural injustice literature, of course, is that the macro-social consequences of exercises of individual agency can be wrong without each or indeed any of those individual exercises having been culpable or wrong. In Haslanger's (2012, p. 318) example: 'the distribution of power may be unjust and yet the injustice not be properly explicated in terms of an agent's wrongdoing'. Yet those individual acts might have been wrong, taking a suitably broader view of the various ways in which individuals might be culpable (e.g., for omissions as well as acts, for negligence as well as intentional harms, for legacy as well as contemporaneous wrongs) (Estlund 2020). As Young (2011, p. 96) says, even if '[t]he actions of particular persons do not contribute to [structural] injustice for other persons directly', they do so 'indirectly, collectively and cumulatively through the production of structural constraints on the actions of many and privileged opportunities for some'. I would argue that, insofar as they can and should foresee those cumulative consequences of their actions together with those of others, we can and should hold those people responsible for those actions. Young (2011) clearly does not want to dwell on that, but I am not sure she would want to deny it at all strongly either.

²⁴ Qv. 'wrong (n)', 2a, 5b.

²⁵ Davidson 1980. See also the *Oxford English Dictionary* definitions of 'act (v)', 2a and 'action (n)', 2, 12, 15b. To say that 'they intend to act' is not, of course, to say that they necessarily 'intend the consequences of their actions'.

²⁶ Wendt (1987, pp. 336–7) criticizes structural theories of international relations for making this claim, which he shows to be exaggerated.

²⁷ Hayward, recalling Acton's phrase (in Hayward and Lukes 2008, pp. 10–11). See similarly Haslanger 2015.

or do any injustice.²⁸ Harms inflicted by non-agentic forces (like floods or fires) are merely misfortunes—maybe undeserved misfortunes, maybe grave misfortunes, but only misfortunes rather than wrongs or injustices, strictly speaking.

No doubt there are some important features of the natural world that truly are beyond the control of any human agent. But a great many of them can be affected at least to some extent by human agency. Someone clearing his land upstream from you increased the risk of your farm being flooded; someone failing to repair the levee did likewise. The fire threatening your home may have been started by someone, accidentally or otherwise; and someone failing to back-burn at the right time may have been instrumental in the fire's reaching your door. At a few steps further removed, the distribution of income and wealth in your society led to poorer people like you being driven to live and work in environments at risk from flooding during hurricanes, where land and housing is cheaper in consequence.²⁹ Or, working the other way around, institutional structures and social practices that suit those in the metropolitan centre might not (for reasons of sheer distance or geographical or cultural distinctiveness) suit those at the further peripheries.³⁰

The upshot is just this. The vast majority (maybe literally all) of the seemingly agency-free structures that perpetuate advantage and disadvantage actually have some sort of human agency standing somewhere in the background.³¹ 'Structure or agent' is a false dichotomy, as such dichotomies so often are.³² Instead of thinking of outcomes as being produced by 'structures *rather than* agency', we should be attuned to ways in which outcomes might have been

---

²⁸ When we speak of a 'cosmic injustice' we do so either in a purely metaphorical way or as an allusion to some sort of supernatural agency. (Defining 'cosmic irony', the *Oxford English Dictionary* refers similarly to 'events ... seemingly orchestrated by fate or providence'.)

²⁹ Young 2006.

³⁰ Such arguments obviously have application both within countries (Lipset and Rokkan 1967; Rokkan and Urwin 1982) and globally (Frank 1966).

³¹ Galtung (1969, p. 178) canvasses (but discounts in a way I would not) the possibility that 'all cases of structural violence can, by closer scrutiny, be traced back to personal violence in their *pre-history*' and pure cases of structural injustice 'are only pure as long as the pre-history of the case ... [is] conveniently forgotten'. Wendt (1999, pp. 165–84) thinks 'constitutive' structures exert causal power without (further) intervention of human agency; but, still, human agency was typically involved in putting those constitutive structures in place. In Burt's (1992) terms, there are 'structural holes' that (very metaphorically) 'call forth' other structures to fill them: but it is human agents who have created the structures that left the holes; and it is human agents who answer to call to create structures to fill them. They may do so individually rather than collectively, and in uncoordinated ways that nonetheless have cumulative consequences. Vrousalis (2021, p. 40) argues for example that the regulative function upholding capitalist institutions can be performed through the exercise of 'collective power' even if there is 'no joint agency or shared intentions on the part of the dominators'.

³² Archer 1982. Giddens 1984. On the more general point, see Goodin (2009, pp. 9–12).

produced by the interaction of agency and structure.³³ Most particularly, we ought to be alert to possibilities of 'agency *working through* structures'.³⁴ That, I submit, is what we should be talking about, when talking of 'structural injustice'—even if the hyperbolic image of structures acting on their own is (sadly for some) lost in the process.

Notice that there is a considerable strategic advantage for agents to perpetuate advantage through opaque structures rather than through direct, blatant, transparent interventions of their own.³⁵ Working through structures leaves nobody to blame and 'nobody to shoot'.³⁶ Exercising agency through impersonal, automatic mechanisms that seem to involve no obvious exercise of agency *masks* that very exercise of agency.³⁷ It is a deceptive exercise of power, and it is doubly objectionable for that reason. It is worse for being deceptive (which is arguably a wrong in itself); and, being deceptive, the exercise of power is harder for others to detect and deflect (so worse for that reason, in addition).³⁸

Often structural impediments to the exercise of your will have been placed there by the prior efforts of other human agents, often with the express intention of constraining subsequent actors like you in the exercise of their will in precisely those ways.³⁹ Those are instances in which people have deliberately

---

³³ Young 2011, pp. 18, 100. See similarly Burt's (1982) account of 'structural action' and Giddens' (1984) of 'structuration' as generalized by Grewal (2008, pp. 52–6). Wiedenbrüg (2021) provides a worked example with reference to financial crises.

³⁴ Goodin 2000a. That should be seen to include, particularly in the cases of the cognitive structures discussed in Chapters 5 and 6, 'agency not seeing how it can work given the structures'. See more generally: Wendt 1987; Ingram and Clay 2000. That point also applies in relation to 'structural power' (Hayward and Lukes 2008), 'social capital' (Coleman 1988, p. S98; 1990, p. 302) and the 'acts of artifacts' (cf. Latour 1999, pp. 176–7; Verbeek 2005, p. 154 and ch. 5 passim; Illies and Meijers 2009; Peterson and Spahn 2011).

³⁵ In Bourdieu's (1986, pp. 254–5) example, 'When the subversive critique which aims to weaken the dominant class ... is incorporated in institutionalized mechanisms (for example, laws of inheritance) aimed at controlling the official, direct transmission of power and privileges, the holders of capital have an ever greater interest in resorting to reproduction strategies capable of ensuring better-disguised transmission ... by exploiting the convertibility of the types of capital. Thus the more the official transmission of capital is prevented or hindered, the more the effects of the clandestine circulation of capital in the form of cultural capital become determinant in the reproduction of the social structure. As an instrument of reproduction capable of disguising its own function, the scope of the educational system tends to increase....'

³⁶ Hayward and Lukes 2008. Jugov and Ypi (2018) point similarly to the 'epistemic opacity' of structural injustice. This is the source of the common objection that, if no one (in particular) is to blame for structural injustice, then morally everyone gets a 'free pass' (Nussbaum 2011, p. xxi) in relation to it. See Barry and Macdonald 2016; Neuhäuser 2014; Zheng 2018a; and, for an overview, McKeown 2017.

³⁷ As Galtung (1969, p. 173) says, 'Structural violence is silent, it does not show....' Young (2012, pp. 54–5) expands upon this thought. Schilke and Rossman (2018, p. 1082) offer experimental evidence of 'structural obfuscation'.

³⁸ Goodin 1980, esp. ch. 1.

³⁹ But not always—and as I have said structures that lock in injustice without anyone intending for them to do so are not necessarily any the less morally objectionable for that fact.

created or otherwise availed themselves of structures that 'lock in' injustice, in a way that requires no further direct exercise of agency.⁴⁰

The thought is as old as Rousseau's *Discourse on Inequality*. There he wrote: 'The first man who, having enclosed a piece of ground, bethought himself of saying, "This is mine," and found people simple enough to believe him, was the real founder of civil society.'⁴¹ It is as new as the Long Island Expressway, whose overpasses were deliberately built so low as to preclude inner-city blacks riding buses from reaching the affluent suburbs beyond.⁴²

Impediments of all those sorts are the subject of this book. The structures of most interest are ones whose effects are perduring and pervasive. The US Supreme Court employs just such standards in distinguishing errors that it calls 'structural' from other sorts of error in the trial process.⁴³

One final note on method. In the chapters that follow, I shall primarily focus on structures that work in seemingly 'innocent' ways (which is to say, without the further intervention of any nefarious human agency) to perpetuate some people's advantage and others' disadvantage.⁴⁴ I am particularly interested in such mechanisms, precisely because they are so easily overlooked when focusing, as we more typically do, on the dastardly deeds of the rich and powerful in feathering their own nests.

In focusing on those more 'innocent' sources of structural injustice, I do not deny that other more nefarious agentic forces are also often at work, both

---

⁴⁰ In a rather different connection, the US Supreme Court has held that 'practices, procedures, or tests neutral on their face, and even neutral in terms of intent, cannot be maintained if they operate to "freeze" the status quo of prior discriminatory employment practices' (Burger 1971).

⁴¹ Rousseau 1755/1973, pt. 2, p. 76. Hume 1752/1760) says similarly: 'It is confessed, that private justice, or the abstinence from the properties of others, is a most cardinal virtue: Yet reason tells us, that there is no property in durable objects, such as lands or houses, ... but must, in some period, have been founded on fraud and injustice.' For contemporary echoes see: Pateman 1988; Mills 1997; Pateman and Mills 2007; Piketty 2020.

⁴² Winner 1980, pp. 123–4; see further Caro 1974, pp. 951–8. Other studies show that building new bridges (Bütikofer, Løken, and Willén 2022) and highways (Fretz, Parchet, and Robert-Nicoud 2022) differentially advantages the well-educated and highly skilled who are best situated to take advantage of the new opportunities afforded by them.

⁴³ Any sort of error in a trial that leads to the conviction of an innocent person (or the acquittal of a guilty one, for that matter) is a miscarriage of justice, of course. But 'structural defects in the constitution of the trial mechanism' are ones that fundamentally affect 'the framework within which the trial proceeds', such that 'a criminal trial cannot reliably serve its function as a vehicle for determination of guilt or innocence'. Examples include 'absence of counsel for a criminal defendant', 'the presence on the bench of a judge who is not impartial', and 'unlawful exclusion of members of the defendant's race from a grand jury' (White 1991, pp. 309–10; reaffirmed by Ginsberg 2018, pp. 1510–11).

⁴⁴ This is a familiar focus in work on structural injustice. Anderson (2012, p. 164, emphasis added) writes that: 'A structural theory supplies criteria for assessing global properties of a system of rules that govern transactions, and imposes constraints on permissible rules with an eye toward controlling the cumulative effects of individual transactions that may be *innocent* from a local point of view.' Explicating her theory of structural injustice, Young (2011, p. 63) says that 'masses of individuals ... following the rules, minding their own business, and trying to accomplish their legitimate goals can ... result in undesirable unintended consequences when looked at structurally' (see similarly pp. 52, 100, 104).

in perpetrating the injustice in the first instance and in perpetuating it in the second. Certainly such nefarious forces are all too often at work, at one or both stages. Hence cancelling the more innocent sources of structural injustice would not necessarily eradicate structural injustice altogether. The powerful and privileged still could, and presumably would, work on and through structures to enact their ill will and protect their privileged position. Even undertaking all the remedial actions discussed in Chapter 11 will not stop that from happening. Making it more difficult for them to do so—or maybe just making it more difficult for them to disguise that as the impersonal working of some autonomous structure—is the most that can be hoped for.

Nevertheless, thinking hard about these more innocent sources of structural injustice is a very worthwhile project. With those structural replicators of injustice in place, it would often be impossible to eradicate that injustice with even the best will in the world—and that fact can, in itself, serve as a cover for the exercise of ill will. Once that cover is ripped off, ill will is laid bare. Of course, those with 'ill will' will indeed try to frustrate attempts to rip off what gives it cover—but that, too, will only serve to expose its true nature.

1.2 Focus on Advantage, More Generally

Although motivated by a concern with injustice, the actual focus of this book will be broader—on mechanisms that perpetuate advantage more generally. Where the advantage is unjustly held, structural mechanisms that perpetuate it would of course be perpetuating injustice. But my focus here is on the mechanisms of perpetuating advantage, whether or not that advantage is unjust or in some other way morally wrong.

Multiple considerations commend that more general focus. One is strategic. Wrongs come in many forms. There are one-on-one wrongs, as when the thief steals your wallet. There are one-on-many wrongs, as when the feudal lord appropriates the lion's share of his serfs' crops. There are many-on-one wrongs, as when a sweatshop worker's wage is driven down by the combined demands of lots of consumers in a global market for ridiculously cheap clothing.

Some of those wrongs may be well described as 'injustices'. For others, terms like 'exploitation' or even merely 'unfairly piling on' might seem more apt. What exactly constitutes 'injustice' is a fraught topic.[45] Philosophers argue

---

[45] Among those controversies are doubts whether, or in what sense, structural injustice is 'unjust' at all (Estlund 2020). Cognate issues concern how philosophers and other social critics, being socially

long and hard over exactly how best to characterize that concept. Middle-class parents reading bedtime stories to their children confers educational advantage on them: but do we really want to say that should be ruled out by our theory of justice?[46] Best not to get bogged down in those controversies, if they can possibly be avoided.[47] And here, I think they can.

The reason that those controversies can comfortably be skirted in the present context is that the mechanisms that 'innocently' perpetuate injustice are, by and large, precisely the same mechanisms as perpetuate advantage in general. Hence we do not need to decide in advance which patterns of advantage are unjust, and which are not, in order to decide what mechanisms are of interest.[48]

Some of the mechanisms I shall be discussing may be particularly useful for perpetuating specifically unjust advantages, and be of more interest for that reason. But my goal here is merely to describe how the mechanisms operate, not to set priorities among them. Therefore those differences do not really matter, just so long as the way in which the mechanisms work to perpetuate advantage is (as it broadly seems to be) impervious to the moral status of the advantages being perpetuated.

That is the first reason for focusing on mechanisms that perpetuate advantage more generally. There is no need for a narrower focus. We must examine exactly the same mechanisms, either way. And once we have come to understand how advantage in general is perpetuated, we will know all we need to know in order to understand how wrongful advantage is perpetuated.

There is a second and substantively more important reason for focusing on the perpetuation of advantage as such, rather than focusing more narrowly on advantages that were unjust from the start. That reason is this: advantages that were not unjust initially can *become* unjust by their being perpetuated.[49]

---

situated agents, can get sufficiently 'outside' their own cultural and ideological formations to mount a critique of them (Beauvoir 1955; Kruks 2005; Haslanger 2017, pp. 164–8).

[46] Swift 2004, pp. 7–8. Becker et al. (2018) offer a formal economic model of how inequality can be transmitted intergenerationally purely by parents who themselves have lots of human capital using more of it and its proceeds to invest in human capital formation in their children.

[47] Reiman (2012, pp. 742–4) rightly complains, against Young (2011), that any account of 'structural injustices' needs to be backed up by a theory of 'justice', or else what it dubs 'injustices' might simply be 'misfortunes'. Collaborative work between an outstanding philosopher of justice and an outstanding sociologist of social mobility came to grief on precisely that point (Marshall, Swift, and Roberts 1997, ch. 8).

[48] In talking about 'patterns' of advantage that are seemingly 'innocently' produced by structural forces, I am of course bracketing out deliberate acts of wrongdoing that the advantaged may undertake in order to preserve their advantages.

[49] That might be thought to follow straightforwardly from the 'rule against perpetuities' in the common law of contract, first propounded in the *Duke of Norfolk's Case* (1682) 3 Ch Cas 122 ER 931.

There is nothing unjust about your having won a fair lottery that everyone else had an equal chance of winning.[50] But it *would* be deeply unjust unnecessarily to let the outcome of that one-off lottery determine the life chances of everyone in the community for all time to come.[51]

Lotteries may be the fairest way to allocate lumpy goods that are scarce relative to claims or desires for them.[52] But *ex ante* fairness is all that is ensured by distributing things randomly. *Ex post*, the randomly generated distribution gives some people more than they deserve and others less.[53] Ideally, therefore, there should be a periodic reshuffling of advantages that were the products of pure luck. Goods that have been allocated purely by the luck of the draw should be reallocated, from time to time, by new random draws so that people generally get to enjoy the goods for periods of time proportional to the relative strengths of their claims to them.[54]

The same is true of the advantages that one enjoys through some meritorious performance rather than pure luck. Those advantages are, by definition, deserved. But the merit embodied in any one meritorious performance is rarely so great that that single instance of meritorious performance should set you up for life. That is particularly so, where the outcome sets you up in an advantageous position over others for the rest of your life and theirs.

Initial advantage may well be hard to eradicate, whatever we do. Certainly it could be wrong to pin any great hopes on sheer flux quickly and completely cancelling undeserved initial holdings, as boosters of notions of 'democratic' wealth (from Alexis de Tocqueville to Milton Friedman) are inclined to suppose.[55] For a stylized calculation, suppose that fully half of your holdings

---

But that rule is arguably aimed less at justice and more at efficiency. See Beitz (2018) for a contemporary philosophical discussion.

[50] In practice, lottery tickets are bought disproportionately by the poor—despite the fact that the probabilistic rate of return on that investment is low (both lower and riskier than bank interest, for example)—because only a large infusion of capital will really change their lives (Beckert and Lutter 2009). White (1942, p. 141) offered the same explanation of why poor people in the US during the Great Depression gambled their money in numbers games rather than putting their money into bank savings accounts with better rates of return.

[51] Chambers 2009.

[52] Broome 1990, p. 95. 'Some things there be', says Hobbes (1651, ch. 15), 'that can neither be divided, nor enjoyed in common. The Law of Nature, which prescribeth equity, requireth that the entire right, or else (making the use alternate) the first possession, be determined by lot. For equal distribution is of the law of nature, and other means of equal distribution cannot be imagined.'

[53] For a demonstration that ex ante and ex post standards of fairness differ, see Fleurbaey and Peragine (2013).

[54] Goodwin 1992, p. 93. In a way, this is just the standard luck-egalitarian thought that the effects of brute luck ought to be neutralized through social policy. It is very un-luck-egalitarian, of course, in its use of brute luck in frequent fair lotteries to cancel the effects of brute luck.

[55] The underlying thought is found in the biblical verse 'time and chance happeneth to them all' (*Ecclesiastes* 9:11, quoted in Stinchcombe 1998, p. 269). Tocqueville (1835, vol. 2, pt. 3, ch. 17, pp. 590–1; vol 1. pt. 1, ch. 3, p. 47; vol. 2, pt. 3, ch. 21, p. 611) writes, 'in aristocracies each man is pretty

are randomly reallocated each time reallocation occurs, every five years of your 45-year working life.⁵⁶ That would be an extraordinary rate of economic volatility, of course. But even so, fully 22 per cent of your expected holdings over the course of your working life as a whole would still have been fixed by your initial allocation.⁵⁷ And that is not just true in stylized examples. Recent OECD reports suggest that something like that is true of the real world.⁵⁸

Thus, try as we might, it is hard to eradicate the effects of undeserved initial advantage. But any mechanisms that work in the *opposite* direction—perpetuating initial advantage (particularly where it is either not deserved at all or well beyond what is deserved)—are particularly odious. As I have said, even if initial advantages were not themselves wrong, perpetuating them unduly can in and of itself be wrong.

Furthermore, allowing advantages to persist over time is more wrongful (not less), insofar as the longer advantages persist the more likely they are to become socially accepted. As a brute sociological or psychological fact, it may be true that people simply 'get accustomed' to those patterns over time.⁵⁹ But the fact that it no longer occurs to people to query the justifiability of some pattern of advantage does not make what was an unjustified pattern of advantage suddenly justified. It should instead be a cause for moral concern that, with the passage of time, people come to accept what they have no reason to accept. And if those psychological or sociological facts are true, then the right

---

firmly fixed in his sphere, [whereas] in democracies, contrariwise, all men are ... subject continually to great vicissitudes'; hence 'wealth circulates there with incredible rapidity, and ... two successive generations seldom enjoy its favours.... As there is no longer a race of poor men, so there is not a race of rich men; the rich daily rise out of the crowd and constantly return thither'. Friedman (1962, pp. 171–2) writes, similarly, that we 'need to distinguish two basically different kinds of inequality: temporary, short-run differences in income, and differences in long-run income status.... The one kind of inequality is a sign of dynamic change, social mobility, equality of opportunity; the other of a status society.... [C]ompetitive free-enterprise capitalism tends to substitute the one for the other.... [I]nequality in [non-capitalist societies] tends to be permanent, whereas capitalism undermines status and introduces social mobility.' See similarly: Edgeworth 1925, pp. 102–3; Hicks 1941, p. 111; Blalock 1991, pp. 30–1; and Persad 2015. Cf. Rawls 1971, pp. 170–1; Goodin 2001; and Beckert 2022.

⁵⁶ This calculation thus takes no account of savings or economic growth over time, which may well alter the results (Miles 2022).

⁵⁷ Goodin 2001. A miniscule portion of initial holdings will remain in the very last five-year period, of course; but this is the proportion of your holdings that come from your initial allocation, averaging across all nine periods. Of course this is a lowball estimate because it only takes account of what proportion of assets in your initial portfolio remain and not of other assets you were able to add to your portfolio because of those assets.

⁵⁸ 'While two-thirds of people with low-earning parents succeed to move to a higher status, for almost half among them, upward earnings mobility is limited to the neighbouring earnings group. As a result, in an "average OECD country" it would take around four to five generations for children from the bottom earnings decile to attain the level of mean earnings' (OECD 2018a, p. 14).

⁵⁹ At the limit, people sometimes come to believe that longstanding practices are legitimate because they have existed since 'time immemorial' (Pocock 1957).

way to address that concern is to prevent the unjustified pattern of advantage from persisting for so long that people no longer think to question it.

At law, 'statutes of limitations' and the rule of 'adverse possession' similarly block wrongs from being remedied after a certain period of time.[60] But it would be wrong to think that time washes those wrongs clean. What the passage of time actually does is to render those wrongs injusticiable, simply too hard to remedy: evidence has grown stale, so the wrongs are hard to prove; counterfactuals grow increasingly imponderable with the passage of time, making the right remedy increasingly hard to reckon.[61] That makes it more important (not less) so to remedy those wrongs in a timely manner. Just as with unjustified advantage socially, so too with wrongful advantage at law: it should not be allowed to persist so long that realistically we can no longer remedy it.

1.3 Types of Advantage

Advantages are of two basic types. One is absolute, the other comparative.[62]

The absolute conception of advantage points primarily to the level of well-being that you enjoy and, secondarily, to the stock of resources available to you from which you can derive that well-being.[63] Someone who enjoys a high standard of consumption is advantaged in the primary sense. Someone with a well-stocked larder is advantaged in the secondary sense. Conceivably the two can come apart: a miser, for example, can have lots of money in the bank but no food in his stomach.[64] But usually these two kinds of absolute advantage, primary and secondary, tend to be closely intertwined.

The comparative conception of advantage points to the stock of resources available to people for the purposes of competing with one another for other resources from which they can derive absolute well-being. Call these 'competition resources', in contrast to the absolute conception's 'consumption

---

[60] Blackstone 1765, bk. 2, ch. 13; bk. 3, ch. 20.
[61] Waldron 1992; Doyle 2017.
[62] The first corresponds to the *Oxford English Dictionary*'s definition 1 of 'advantage (n)' as 'benefit; increased well-being or convenience'. The second corresponds to its definition 4 of 'advantage (n)' as 'the fact or state of being in a better position with respect to another; superiority, esp. in a confrontation or contest'.
[63] These correspond loosely to Sen's (1992) 'functionings' and 'capabilities', which Wolff and de-Shalit (2007, pt. 2) employ in their analysis of 'disadvantage'. 'Available to you' usually amounts to being 'under your direct control'. But sometimes there might be resources under the direct control of someone else (a parent or partner for example) who would make them available to you if you needed or wanted them.
[64] Ringen 1988.

resources'.⁶⁵ How much of the latter any given quantity of the former will secure for you depends crucially upon how much of the former your competitors have and are willing to commit to the competition.

These two types of advantage are themselves often linked, of course. The same resources that could serve as 'resources for consumption' could alternatively be employed as 'resources for competition'. And sometimes consuming them would itself make you more competitive, as when the less malnourished prevail over the more malnourished ones in local labour markets.⁶⁶

Envy apart, there seems to be no good reason for anyone to object to others having more absolute advantages than they do themselves.⁶⁷ It may even be to your own long-term advantage that others have more absolute advantages. Those extra absolute advantages might serve to incentivize the others to undertake activities (productive labour, or whatever) that make you absolutely better off than you would otherwise have been.⁶⁸ Or their having those extra absolute advantages at the moment might be a precondition for those absolute advantages eventually coming to be shared more widely, by you and others. Examples of that might be knowledge or technological innovations that are initially held by the few but eventually come to be shared more widely.⁶⁹

With competitive advantage, the situation is just the opposite. The more competitive advantage possessed by others with whom you are in competition, the less likely you are to win that competition. Their being more competitively advantaged makes you more competitively disadvantaged. In Amartya Sen's classic account of the Great Bengali Famine of 1944, some people's being employed by the relatively well-paying British army not only put more money in those people's pockets but also less rice in other people's stomachs, as the former bid up the price of rice with their new riches.⁷⁰

---

⁶⁵ Although of course those 'resources for consumption' can be saved for future consumption, sometimes in ways that cause them to grow while being saved—in which case we might call them 'resources for (non-competitive) investment in future consumption'.
⁶⁶ Studies showed that in twentieth-century developing countries (Dasgupta and Rey 1986/7; Dasgupta 1993, chs 14–17). Similarly 'in France and England circa 1790 ... the food supply [permitted only an] ... exceedingly low [and unequal] level of work capacity.... In France the bottom 10 percent of the labor force lacked the energy for regular work, and the next 10 percent had enough energy for less than three hours of light work daily.... Although the English situation was somewhat better, the bottom 3 percent of its labor force lacked the energy for any work, but the balance of the bottom 20 percent had enough energy for about 6 hours of light work (1.09 hours of heavy work) each day' (Fogel 1994, p. 373).
⁶⁷ Schoeck 1969.
⁶⁸ This is the thought underlying Rawls' (1971, sec. 13) 'difference principle'.
⁶⁹ Another example might be the electoral franchise (Przeworski 2009; Goodin 2010b, pp. 188 ff.).
⁷⁰ Sen 1977, 1981. I shall say more about all this in Section 3.2 below.

Morally, of course, absolute advantage—how well-off people are in absolute terms—matters hugely. But the focus of this book is on how absolute advantages are perpetuated over time. So when I speak of 'advantage' in the following pages, I will most typically be referring to comparative advantage and the edge that that gives to some people over others in the competition for resources from which they can derive absolute advantages.

1.4 Mechanisms of Perpetuation, More Generally

Some of the mechanisms that I shall be discussing are specific to the case of perpetuating advantage. Others are mechanisms that merely perpetuate existing social arrangements more generally, whether they confer advantage on anyone or not. My interest here in the latter sorts of mechanisms is simply that they *can* be used to perpetuate advantage, where advantage exists.

Those all-purpose mechanisms for locking in existing states of affairs may be all the more interesting, from a strategic perspective. Precisely because they work whether or not there exists some advantage to be perpetuated, deploying them does not in and of itself call unwanted attention to any advantages that they may serve to perpetuate. Just as impersonal structure can sometimes mask the exercise of agency, mechanisms perpetuating the status quo regardless of advantage can mask the advantage that is thereby perpetuated.

1.4.1 Over Time, Across Generations

Writers on social mobility tend to focus on intergenerational transmission of advantage and disadvantage. The key question there is what chances your offspring have of occupying a higher social class (or a lower one) than you do yourself.[71] In this book I shall be concerned with perpetuation of advantage more generally, which makes me equally (sometimes more) concerned with changes in one's fortunes within one's own lifetime.

Many of the same mechanisms that perpetuate advantage within generations perpetuate it across generations as well. Or, anyway, there are very close analogues in the intragenerational case to those in the intergenerational one. For example, a major mechanism of intergenerational transmission of disadvantage is malnutrition in childhood. People who cannot afford food for themselves and their children raise children who, having grown up malnourished,

---

[71] For a survey see Marshall, Swift, and Roberts 1997, chs 3–6.

themselves are unlikely to be in a much better position themselves when they grow up.⁷² Intragenerationally too, as I have already said, people who are malnourished are less able to compete in labour markets themselves, which means they will have inadequate means to feed themselves properly tomorrow as well as today.⁷³ Or, for another wholly different example, the less education a person has at age 20 the less that person (or their offspring, either) is likely to get subsequently.⁷⁴

The same will be true of many of the mechanisms that I shall show, over the chapters to come, perpetuate advantage and disadvantage. Insofar as the same languages, coding categories, and interpretative schema (Chapter 5) or the same norms and expectations (Chapter 6) or the same organizational structures (Chapter 8) persist over protracted periods of time, they are likely to impact people in the next generation in much the same way as they did those in the previous one.

Some sources of social advantage and disadvantage seem on their face more *ad hominem* and hence more likely to have impact within a person's own lifetime rather than across generations. One's social position or personal reputation or personal networks may often be more like that. But sometimes they may not be. Even where social position cannot formally be inherited, parents can sometimes informally pass it along. Likewise a parent's personal reputation can easily morph into a 'family reputation' from which their offspring might benefit. And in practice children often 'inherit'—in the sense of having ready use of—the networks of their parents. So even mechanisms that might on their face seem to confer advantage only, or primarily, within one person's own lifetime might well have important intergenerational impacts as well.

Some mechanisms of transmission of advantage and disadvantage are more peculiar to the intergenerational case, however. Conferring early-life developmental advantages on their children is something that advantaged parents can do for their children but not, obviously, for themselves. And that sort of advantage matters greatly. For example, one longitudinal study of de-identified tax returns of five million Americans who had moved during childhood found that 'the outcomes of children whose families move to a better neighbourhood—as measured by the outcomes of children already living there—improve linearly

---

⁷² OECD 2018a, ch. 5. See more generally: McEwen and McEwen 2017; Almond, Currie, and Duque 2018.
⁷³ Dasgupta and Ray 1986/7. Dasgupta 1993. For to see the importance of childhood malnutrition on earnings, even in a prosperous country, note that a Swedish programme providing free school lunches to all children increased their lifetime income by some three per cent (Lundborg, Rooth, and Axel-Petersen 2022).
⁷⁴ OECD 2018a, ch. 5.

in proportion to the amount of time they spend growing up in that area, at a rate of approximately 4% per year of exposure'.[75] Parents can advantage their children by moving to a better neighbourhood. But obviously they cannot after-the-fact change the neighbourhood in which they had themselves grown up.

Bequests fall somewhere in between those two polar cases. Bequests play a substantial role in the intergenerational transmission of advantage.[76] One Swedish study found that there was a three to four per cent correlation between the wealth of children and their parents, half of which was explained by inherited wealth.[77] Since 'bequests' by definition 'pass to the recipient after one's death', one cannot literally bequeath anything to one's own future self.[78] But in an extended sense, of course, one can through savings transfer some of one's current advantages to one's future self. Those who are currently more advantaged are obviously better situated to do that than those who are not. So savings, as well as bequests, are a way of perpetuating advantage over time, both intrapersonally and intergenerationally.

1.4.2 Flypaper and Bottlenecks

Advantage of the most worrying sort is, as I have said, comparative. Perpetuation of advantage can be accomplished by working on either side (or both) of the inequality representing the comparative advantage that one person or group enjoys over another.

One strategy for perpetuating advantage is negative. That consists in preventing the relatively disadvantaged from gaining any more advantage. The other strategy for perpetuating advantage is positive in form. That consists in helping the relatively advantaged retain their existing advantage. Those two strategies often operate in conjunction with one another. Analytically, however, they are importantly different.

In terms of the social mobility literature just discussed, the perpetuation of comparative advantage is standardly recognized as having these two components. Negatively, upward mobility is choked off by a combination of oppression and imposing 'bottlenecks' through which few can pass. Positively, existing advantage is protected, and downward mobility is inhibited by various

---

[75] Chetty and Hendren 2018.
[76] Halliday 2018; Beckert 2022.
[77] Adermon, Lindahl, and Waldenström 2018.
[78] *Oxford English Dictionary*, q.v. 'bequeathe' (v.), 4b.

mechanisms making privilege sticky—hard to lose, once obtained. Think of those latter mechanisms, collectively, as sociological 'flypaper'.

The former, negative strategy is perhaps the most classic—or anyway, much the most discussed—method of perpetuating advantage. The focus, there, is upon the top dogs keeping the bottom dogs down. There are myriad ways of doing so. Some are more direct and more blatant than others. Oppression by physical force is the most direct and the most blatant. Rigging the terms of the competition, creating tight 'bottlenecks' through which few can pass when attempting to rise in the social order, is among the most subtle and indirect.[79]

I do not deny the sociological importance of that strategy. But that strategy has been the focus of widespread discussion already. I shall certainly allude to variations on it from time to time, over the course of this book.[80] My principal focus, however, will be on the other side of the equation, which is often more neglected. That is the set of processes by which the advantages of those presently advantaged are *positively* perpetuated over time.

1.5 Not Allocating Blame, but Guiding Reform

My discussion in this book differs from many other treatments of these topics in one last way. Discussions of wrongs, structural injustice sometimes included, are typically oriented at least in part (typically, in large part) to allocating responsibility and blame for those wrongs.[81]

I surely do have views about the wrongs associated with perpetuating advantage. I doubt they are typically well characterized as anything so strong as 'complicity', in the ways some suggest.[82] Neither, on the other hand, am I persuaded that they are typically excused as 'unavoidable ignorance' of 'imperceptible effects' of the contribution each makes to the perpetuation of the unjust structure.[83] Often they are the product of something much more like 'wilful ignorance' of morally significant features of the situation[84]—even if

---

[79] Fishkin 2014.
[80] In particular, to the ways in which people can exercise power over others by controlling bottlenecks such as those that arise from network position (Section 4.2) or from scarcities of time and attention (Section 10.1).
[81] This is the tradition from which Young (2011) was powerfully dissenting.
[82] Reiman 2012, 2013; Murphy 2017, ch. 1; Aragon and Jaggar 2018. Cf. Young 2011, esp. chs 3–4; Sangiovani 2018.
[83] Cf. Parfit 1984, pp. 76 ff.; Kagan 2011; Nefsky 2017; Sangiovani 2018, pp. 469 ff.
[84] Young 2011, pp. 158–61; Hayward 2017. Morally, if not always legally, we can and do blame people for being 'culpably ignorant' of facts of which they could and should be aware when acting (Smith 1983; Lepora and Goodin 2013; cf. Reiman 2012, p. 750). The complaint then is one of 'negligence' rather than 'intentional wrong-doing'. See Oppenheimer (1993) for an application to discrimination law.

the wrongness of that is not then cashed out in terms of any difference that one could have made through one's own individual actions, had one not been wilfully ignorant.[85]

Allocating backward-looking responsibility and blame is, however, incidental to the main aim of this book. My orientation here, like that of Iris Marion Young, is instead forward looking.[86] I want to try to understand the mechanisms by which advantage is perpetuated in order to enable us better to interrupt them, when (as often we do) we decide that the perpetuation of those advantages is wrong for some reason (because they were wrong from the start, or because they became wrong in being perpetuated).

But my aim in this book is understanding—understanding how the mechanisms perpetuating advantage work, in the first instance, and understanding how they might be disrupted, in the second. Who should bear responsibility for doing that, and on what grounds, are separate questions best left for later in the book. It is better not to rush headlong into questions about who should bear those forward-looking responsibilities until we first have a clear idea of what exactly those agents are being asked to do and why exactly we should think that their doing so would contribute to solving the problem at hand.[87]

---

[85] Even if people are not causally responsible, in an individual difference-making way, they might nonetheless bear 'constitutive responsibility' in some way or another: for varying specifications see Nefsky (2017), Goodin (2018a), and Sangiovani (2018).

[86] Young 2011, pp. 96, 108–9.

[87] Rushing headlong into issues of allocating responsibility, albeit of a different forward-looking sort, is the besetting sin of the tradition Young (2011) inaugurated in analysing structural injustice. For the latest instantiation see Sangiovanni (2018). I return to this theme in the conclusion (see Section 11.1 below).

2
Modes of Perpetuating Advantage

On one naive understanding, 'perpetuating advantage' might seem akin to 'seizing and holding territory' in a military manoeuvre. That mode of perpetuating advantage involves a two-step process. The first step is to seize the advantage (the territory). The second, wholly different, step is to hold it.

That analogy points to a model of *retaining* some advantage that you already have. That is definitely one mode of perpetuating advantage. It is arguably the simplest way. Certainly it is the most familiar one. But that is far from the only mode of perpetuating advantage. The aim of this chapter is to map the fuller range of possible modes of perpetuating advantage.[1]

Advantage can also be perpetuated by its being *expanded*. On this scenario, people do not merely hold onto what they already have; they do that, and more. They expand their advantage, holding onto the advantages that they previously had while (and by) adding to them yet further advantages—perhaps more of the same kind, or perhaps of other kinds. The famous 'Matthew Effect', according to which 'the rich get richer', points to one version of this phenomenon.[2]

Both of those first two modes of perpetuating advantage involve people retaining in subsequent periods the *very same* advantages that they held in the previous period. With the next two modes of perpetuating advantage, that is not the case. In those scenarios, the advantages that people have in one period are not retained but, rather, are *replicated* or *recreated* in the next period. In neither of those latter two cases is the advantage that a person possesses in one period literally the very same advantage as that person enjoyed in the

---

[1] By 'modes of perpetuating advantage' I mean to refer to 'patterns of outcomes'. Distinguishing those is the aim of this chapter, whereas subsequent chapters identify distinctive 'mechanisms' that produce those patterns of outcomes.

[2] So named by Merton (1968, 1988) after the biblical verse *Matthew* 25:29, 'For unto every one that hath shall be given, and he shall have abundance: but from him that hath not shall be taken away even that which he hath.' Hobbes's (1651, ch. 10) version is: 'Good successe is power; because it maketh reputation of wisdome, or good fortune; which makes men either fear him, or rely on him.' Adam Smith's (1776, bk 1, ch. 9) version, quoted approvingly by Marx (1844b/1959, p. 15), is: 'Money, says the proverb, makes money. When you have got a little, it is often easy to get more. The great difficulty is to get that little.' For a popular contemporary discussion see Rigney (2010). For more formal discussions and surveys of empirical evidence see: Dannefer 2003; Podolny and Lynn 2009; Perc 2014; Bask and Bask 2015.

previous period. What is being perpetuated in these cases is not any particular advantage but, instead, the level or degree or kind of advantage.[3]

In the case of a *replicated* advantage, the new advantage is *just like* the old. (Indeed, it is literally a copy of it.) In the case of a *recreated* advantage, the new advantage may be different from the old but it is *just as advantageous*. In either case, the same people who were advantaged in one period are equally (albeit perhaps differently) advantaged in the next. That is the sense in which, in these two latter cases, the pattern of advantage can be said to have been perpetuated from one period to the next. Whereas in the first pair of cases what is constant across time is *who holds what*, in the latter pair of cases what is constant across time is *who holds how much*.

I shall elaborate upon, and give examples of, each of those four modes of perpetuating advantage over the course of this chapter. Given the larger theme of this book, I shall be particularly concerned to show how, in each, someone's having an advantage in one period can lead to that person's having the same or a similar advantage in subsequent periods. These, however, will merely be preliminary sketches of processes to be discussed later in more detail. Laying bare the deeper mechanisms that underlie all of these modes of perpetuating advantage is the larger task that occupies the rest of this book.

2.1 Retaining Advantage

As I said in Section 1.2, even if you are subject to stochastic processes eating into your holdings, it will probably be quite some time before those initial holdings are fully eroded. Here I want to make a stronger point than that, which is that having more of an advantage might actually make it *easier* for you to hold onto that advantage.

In one way, retaining advantages might look hard, simply because the more you have the more you have to defend against loss. But while it is true that you have more to defend, it is also true that you have more with which to defend it. Of course if you have to expend some of your resources to defend the rest, that would eat into your existing resources. But maybe no such resource expenditures would be required. If you have a conspicuous advantage in terms of the relevant resources over those who might try wresting them from you, and you show yourself willing to fight to preserve them, you will often be able to

---

[3] In terms of the distinction introduced in Section 1.3, 'level' when we are talking of 'absolute advantage', 'degree' when we are talking of 'comparative advantage'. Insofar as 'comparative advantage' always refers to the degree of advantage, rather than its source, perhaps in that sense people really do enjoy the 'same (degree of) advantage' when one source of advantage is replaced by another in either of these two ways.

preserve them without a fight or hence any expenditure of your resources. The reason is that people generally avoid getting into a fight that they are almost certain to lose. The 'law of anticipated reactions' thus enables those who have more advantages to retain those advantages costlessly across time.[4]

Another important way for advantages to be perpetuated over time is by their being tied[5] to some ostensibly ascriptive characteristic—such as race, sex, or caste—that does not change over time.[6] Then any given person retains the same advantages from one period to the next, simply because that person's ascriptive characteristics to which those advantages are tied are the same from one period to the next.

Ascriptive characteristics are supposed, by definition, to be essential and unalterable facts about a person. That is what is being asserted when attributing such characteristics to a person. For purposes of the present analysis, it does not matter whether 'essentialism' is true and those characteristics really are naturally given or whether they are purely social constructions. Either way, they are very substantially invariant across time, and that is all that matters for the present analysis. Insofar as the attributions persist over time, so too do the advantages and disadvantages socially associated with them.

Even if essentialism is true, surface manifestations are of course imperfect indicators of underlying essences.[7] That creates scope for some people to 'pass' as something they are not: light-skinned Afro-Americans as Caucasian; lower-caste Hindus as being of a higher caste, by adopting the ritual practices of that caste.[8] That can lead to people being denounced as 'not being what they appear to be', in terms of their true ascriptive characteristics.[9] My interest here, however, is less with people falsifying their ascriptive characteristics in

---

[4] Friedrich 1941, p. 592. See further Section 7.1.
[5] Directly or indirectly: procedures and criteria that are, on their face, neutral can actually have highly disparate impacts on different affective groups (Hernes 1998, pp. 81–2; Stryker 2001, esp. pp. 23–6; Reskin 2003, pp. 11, 14; Blank et al. 2004, pp. 51–3).
[6] 'Caste privilege' is familiar to students of the Indian subcontinent (Weber 1968, vol. 2, ch. 9, sec. 6, pp. 933–4; Dumont 1980). 'Male privilege' and 'white privilege' are notions familiar more broadly (McIntosh 1988, 1998; Rothman 2014). Harris (1993) goes so far as to talk about quasi-legal 'property rights in Whiteness'.
[7] Although at least as regards behavioural manifestations and underlying attitudes, there is some evidence that behaving in such a way as to signal falsely that you have a certain underlying attitude can sometimes over time lead to your coming to have that underlying attitude (Sherman 2005, pp. 277–8).
[8] It has been estimated that, in the US between 1880 and 1940, at least 19 per cent of black males (and perhaps far more) passed as white at some point in their lives (Nix and Qian 2015, pp. 4, 26). On passing among Afro-Americans more generally, see: Myrdal 1944, pp. 129–30; Hobbs 2014; Davenport 2020. On caste see Srinivas (1956). On both see Darity (2022, pp. 416–18). Note that people might attempt to 'pass' as a member of a lower status group if certain benefits have been set aside for those groups alone—a classic example is whites bribing government officials to list them as Native Americans so they could claim land set aside for 'their' tribe (Landry 2018; Darity 2022, pp. 18–19).
[9] Garfinkel (1956, p. 421) imagines 'degradation ceremonies' in general as involving the 'call upon all men to bear witness that [the person being degraded] is not as he appears but is otherwise and *in essence* of a lower species'. On the ethics of 'passing' more particularly see: Piper 1996; Silvermint 2018.

order to gain advantage than it is with the already-advantaged retaining those advantages thanks to their enduring ascriptive characteristics.

Part of that story is utterly straightforward. Insofar as the ascriptive characteristics attributed to a person are constant over time, any advantage tied to them will be likewise.[10] But there are two other parts of that story that are less straightforward. First, why is any particular advantage linked to any particular ascriptive characteristic in the first place? And second, why does that link persist over time?

The answer to the first of those two questions is presumably just that some accident of history got locked into the social structure through some exercise of power, perhaps long in the past. A stylized version of this conjectural history would go something like this.[11] The circumstances giving rise to the group's advantage, in the very first instance, were quirky and could not be relied upon to last. Promulgating the myth that the advantage was the natural product of some ascriptive characteristic that the advantaged group happened to share, rather than a pure accident of history, safeguards the group's advantage through successive turns of history's screw. In perhaps the most dramatic manifestation of this phenomenon, race-based slavery was instituted in many different places and at many different times through manipulation of symbolic power in such a way as to make it appear, to both master and slave, as the natural order.[12]

Still, how advantage arose in the first instance is, as I have said, not the concern of this book. Neither, by extension, is how the link between some particular advantage and some particular ascriptive characteristic was forged in the first instance. My concern here is instead with how the advantage—and by extension, the link between advantage and some particular ascriptive characteristic—is perpetuated over time.

Three factors unite to generate that result. The first factor is located in individual psychology. That is 'loss aversion'—the tendency for people to accord disproportionate importance to avoiding losing something that they already have.[13] The second factor is ease of social and political mobilization. Since the

---

[10] There are of course clear cases where ascriptive characteristics actually do change. Sex reassignment surgery is one conspicuous example. Even then, however, some will always ask of those with 'altered' characteristics, 'Are they *really* one of us?' If that attitude is widespread, people's characteristics might change without the social treatment of them changing. Social mobility is often like that, with the *nouveau riche* being socially shunned no matter how rich they may have become.

[11] After the fashion of Rousseau's (1755/1973) *Discourse on Inequality*.

[12] Patterson 1982, ch. 2.

[13] Kahneman and Tversky 1979; Kahneman, Knetsch, and Thaler 1990.

advantage in question automatically accrues to every member of the ascriptive group in question, every member of that group has a clear interest in sustaining the link between their ascriptive characteristic and the advantage. Tying advantage to ascriptive characteristics thus creates an easily mobilized constituency in support of maintaining that link.[14] The third factor works through power and resources. Those who are advantaged (on the basis of their ascriptive characteristics) in one round will have more power and resources with which to defend their advantaged position (by sustaining the link between those ascriptive characteristics and advantage) in subsequent rounds.[15]

Those three factors combine to explain why those who are advantaged by the existing links between advantages and ascriptive characteristics are both motivated (by loss aversion) and able (through mobilization and power resources of their ascriptive group) to perpetuate those links, and the advantages flowing from them, over time. Of course, there are others who are *dis*advantaged by the existing links between advantages and ascriptive characteristics and who thus have reason to want to disrupt those links. But for the reasons given above, they have less capacity (and, if the psychological evidence about loss aversion is correct, perhaps also less motivation)[16] to do so than those who are advantaged by those links have for preserving them.

Tying advantage to enduring ascriptive characteristics is not the only way that people manage to hold onto the very same advantage from one period to the next. But it is one very important way in which they do so, and it is a good example of this first mode of perpetuating advantage by people simply holding onto what they already have.

2.2 Expanding Advantage

Next let us consider the mode of retaining advantage that works by extending it. According to the well-known Matthew Effect to which I alluded at the beginning of this chapter, 'the rich get richer'. The variation on that theme of particular interest in the present context is that 'the rich *stay* rich by getting

---

[14] Groups with concentrated rather than diffuse interests are easier to mobilize (Olson 1965), although if the latter do manage to organize they might be able to claim greater 'legitimacy' (Trumbull 2012).

[15] Korpi 1985.

[16] Although a sense of shared grievance can be a strong motivator for collective mobilization as well (Cameron 1974).

richer'. Expanding your advantages can be a good way of safeguarding your existing advantages.

The Matthew Effect points to processes of 'cumulative advantage'.[17] Things that are 'cumulative' are, by definition, 'formed by accumulation or heaping on'[18]—here, more and more advantages, one after another.[19] Consider, by analogy, the classical physical exemplar of a cumulative process, which is a snowball rolling downhill. With each rotation more snow attaches to the snowball, thus increasing the surface area to which yet more snow can attach in its next rotation.[20] As a result, the snowball accumulates snow, not at a constant rate, but rather at an increasing rate with each rotation.[21] Similarly, it has been argued, with the psychological effects that various forms of discrimination, 'microaggression', and 'epistemic injustice' have on people in oppressed groups who are subject to them.[22]

In some models of accumulation, things are only ever added and nothing is ever subtracted.[23] That is the implicit assumption, for example, behind any macroeconomic model that employs a fixed, positive rate of capital accumulation. But of course accumulation is not always like that. Think, for example, of meteorological models of the accumulation of snow on the ground, which factor in the rates both of new snow falling and of old snow melting.[24] Even in the case of capital accumulation, realistic models need to make provision for episodes of 'creative destruction' and capital disaccumulation.[25] When it comes to 'social advantage' more generally, patterns of steady increase

---

[17] DiPrete and Eirich 2006. Note that the relative advantage of rich over poor will increase even if the poor as well as the rich experience cumulative absolute advantage over time, just so long as the rate of cumulation for the rich is greater than for the poor (Bask and Bask 2015).

[18] This is the *Oxford English Dictionary*'s first definition of 'cumulative (adj.)'.

[19] And cumulative disadvantages similarly by piling on one disadvantage after another. Young (2011, p. 96) explicitly analyses 'structural injustice' in these terms, saying: 'The actions of particular persons ... contribute to injustice for other persons ... indirectly, collectively and cumulatively through the production of structural constraints on the actions of many and privileged opportunities for some'.

[20] Washington (1775) invoked the analogy in the early days of the American Revolution, warning his commander in Virginia that their enemy's 'strength will increase as a snow ball by rolling..., if some expedient cannot be hit upon to convince the slaves' not to join the British army.

[21] As Zuckerman (1977, p. 60) puts it, 'Advantage can accumulate in two ways: by addition or by multiplication.'

[22] Psychiatrist Chester Pierce, who coined the term 'microaggression', writes that 'even though any single negotiation of offense can in justice be considered of itself to be relatively innocuous, the cumulative effect to the victim and to the victimizer is of an unimaginable magnitude' (1970, p. 266; see similarly Friedlaender 2018; Rini 2019; McClure and Rini 2020). A century before, an early American writer on 'manners' referred similarly to 'the power of littles!' (Hale 1868, p. 80, quoted in 1947/1968, p. 20). So too with epistemic injustices: 'The cumulative effects of how our epistemic system elicits, evaluates and connects countless individual communicative acts can be unjust, even if no injustice has been committed in any particular epistemic transaction' (Anderson 2012, pp. 164–5).

[23] An absorbing state in a Markov process is like that.

[24] Anderson 2006.

punctuated by occasional sharp disruptions to existing holdings are presumably quite common.[26]

There are two ways in which advantage might prove to be cumulative.[27] In one of them, people who are already advantaged might acquire still further advantage *for the same reason* they have their current advantage.[28] In the other, people who are already advantaged might acquire still further advantage *because of* their current advantage.[29]

For one example of the difference, consider these two alternative accounts of the acquisition of educational advantage. One explanation of that is the child's home environment; and the same home environment that helped or hindered the child in one year will do likewise in the next and the next. That is an example of the first sort of process of accumulation of advantage: the educationally rich keep getting richer, owing to the repeated operation of the same causal forces that made them rich in the first place.

Another explanation of the accumulation of educational advantage is that the content of the curriculum is itself cumulative, so someone who has better mastered one year's lessons will be better able to absorb the next year's

---

[26] There are other reasons, socially, why the accumulation does not tend towards infinity at the limit. One, more naturalistic, is that the resources that serve as rewards are themselves limited (Zuckerman 1977, ch. 8; Merton 1988). Another, more sociological, is that if the accumulator's 'status level is strongly influenced by the status levels of those dispensing recognition to them, the eventually the top-ranked actor is nearly matched in status by the lower-ranked actor she endorses' (Bothner et al. 2010, p. 80).

[27] Examples of both types are found in the case of racial (dis)advantage (Blank et al. 2004, ch. 11; Blank 2005).

[28] This will be the case with any multi-stage process in which the same biases figure in each stage of the process. Consider for example how the same racial stereotypes bias decisions at each of the various stages of buying a house: when a real estate agent decides whether to take you on as a client, when homeowners decide whether to sell their house to you, when a lender evaluates your loan application, when an assessor determines the value of the house you propose to buy (Korver-Glenn 2018). Another example is how 'credit ratings' are in fact used not just to decide whether to extend credit but also in deciding whether to rent you property, how much to charge you for auto or homeowner insurance, whether to give you a cell phone contract, etc.; and any errors or biases in the credit rating will affect outcomes across all those other sectors at once (Rona-Tas 2017). Stereotyping is also often 'self confirming', in the sense that 'observers, by acting on the generalization, set in motion a sequence of events that has the effect of reinforcing their initial judgment' (Loury 2002, p. 23). It leads to self-fulfilling prophecies: if you believe blacks cannot be educated, you do not try to educate them, and lo and behold the blacks you subsequently encounter are uneducated, reinforcing your original belief (Tilly 1998, p. 72). Similarly, when Gunnar Myrdal talks of a 'vicious cycle' of 'cumulation', he refers merely to a system of mutually reinforcing reciprocal causal relations, i.e., 'general interdependence between all the factors in the Negro problem. White prejudice and discrimination keep the Negro low in standards of living, health, education, manners and morals. This, in turn, gives support to white prejudice. White prejudice and Negro standards thus mutually "cause" each other' (Myrdal 1944, p. 75; see further pp. 75–8, 101, and Appendix 3; see also Blank et al. 2004, esp. ch. 11 and Brown and Wellman 2005 updating Myrdal's analysis). Self-fulfilling prophecies will be further discussed in Section 6.1.1.

[29] That is one way in which 'each outcome is another opportunity', although not the one Chambers (2009) has in mind. Something like this is involved in Kuznets' (1955, pp. 8–9) model of 'the cumulative effect of concentration of savings upon upper-income shares', as people invest in the next round what they had saved in the previous one. See further DiPrete and Eirich (2006, pp. 273–4).

lessons.[30] That is an example of the second sort of process of accumulation of advantage: the educationally rich keep getting richer, because pedagogic success in one year itself causally contributes to pedagogic success in subsequent years.

For another example of the same difference, imagine the same firm keeps getting contracts from the city government to build roads. One explanation of that—per the first style of explanation sketched above—might be that the same qualities that led to their being preferred for the first contract also led to their being preferred for the second, the third, and the fourth. Maybe they have a highly efficient road building strategy, or a particularly low-cost workforce, and can consistently make the lowest bid, for example.

An alternative explanation—per the second style of explanation sketched above—might be that they are better able to make winning bids for subsequent contracts precisely because they won the previous contract. That might be because they learned something in the process of fulfilling the first contract (about what the government really wants, for example) that enables them to make more persuasive bids for future ones. Or it might be because of something the government learned: having been well satisfied with the first road that the firm built for them, they are more inclined to contract with the same firm for the next road. Or it may be the result of sheer ignorance: perhaps the competing bid documents provides the government with virtually no useful information; and the government simply goes with the winner of the last contract once again because at least they have something (the firm's track record on the last road project) to go on with them. The details vary, but the basic upshot is the same with all these sorts of stories. The firm that won the last contract is more likely to win the next, purely because it won the last one (and because of what resulted from its winning that one), rather than because of what caused it to win the initial contract.

It is not *necessarily* the case that cumulative advantage amounts simply to keeping everything you have and adding more. Advantage can be cumulative in the sense that the accumulation of snow on the ground is cumulative: it is simply a matter of more being added than subtracted. Those are cases of the sort that will be discussed in Section 2.4. Here let us focus on cases where cumulative advantage does take the form of retaining all present holdings and simply supplementing them with more.

---

[30] Competence at reading particularly works this way (Stanovich 1986). The somewhat mixed evidence of cumulative advantage in schooling more generally is surveyed by DiPrete and Eirich (2006, pp. 285–7).

How exactly might having more advantage in one round help you retain existing advantages in future rounds? Doubtless there will be many different specific mechanisms, depending on the details of the case. But for one straightforward example, consider the case of California wineries: 'high status wineries [can] charge more for any given quality of wine'; and because those wineries therefore have more capital, they then 'invest more in grapes that can be used to produce higher quality wines', which further enhances both their high status and high sales.[31]

Here is a more general explanation.[32] As the ancient adage says, 'The best defence is a good offence.'[33] And the more advantages you have (both absolutely and particularly comparatively), the better positioned you often are to go on the offensive.

Why believe that that adage, however ancient, is actually true? Here is one reason: If you merely strive to protect what you already have, and you lose, then you lose some of your present holdings. If on the other hand you strive to secure more than you already have, and you lose, then while you might not get any more maybe at least you might not lose what you presently have. That is not always necessarily the case, to be sure. But it might be often enough for the adage to hold broadly true.

Here is a second reason to believe that old adage: Most things have diminishing marginal utility for most people. If so, it will be rational for people to be loss averse, in the way described in Section 2.1. That is to say, they will be more anxious to avoid losing any given increment of a good or advantage than they will be to gain a similar additional increment of it. One upshot of that fact is that, if you go on the offensive and try to gain some advantage in a way that would disadvantage others, those others would devote more efforts to protecting what they have than to taking what you have.

2.3 Replicating Advantage

The first two modes of perpetuating advantage involve preserving exactly the same advantage[34] from one period to the next. In the next two modes of perpetuating advantage that I shall discuss, the advantages that exist in successive

---

[31] Sauder, Lynn, and Podolny 2012, p. 271; see also Benjamin and Podolny 1999.
[32] I return to discuss this further in Section 7.1.
[33] The thought can be traced at least as far back as Sun Tzu, a famous Chinese military strategist in the fifth century BCE. The origins of this precise formulation are unknown, but a similar version is contained in a 1799 letter from George Washington: 'offensive operations, often times, is the *surest,* if not the *only* (in some cases) means of defence'.
[34] And, in the second case, adding more.

periods are different—but they are of just the same kind (in the first case), or anyway equally advantageous (in the second case).

Let us consider first the case in which advantage is *replicated* from one period to the next. A 'replica' is 'a copy'—literally a 'duplicate'—of the original.[35] A replica is 'identical to' (or the 'same as') the original, in the sense that it is a token of the same type as the original.[36] But it is not the very same token as the original.[37] A replica is just like the original, but it is not the original.

Some processes of perpetuating advantage do not retain the very same advantage from one period to the next but, instead, create replica advantages in the next period that are just like the initial advantage. Under 'Jim Crow' laws in the American South, whites were entitled to the advantage of a seat at the front of the bus. But a white man who demanded that a black woman move back in the bus was not going to get the very same advantage, in the sense of 'exactly the same seat', as when he last rode that bus. He was merely going to get the same *kind* of advantage, namely, a seat at the front of the bus.

Sometimes the reason that one's advantage in one period is a replica of one's advantage in the last is because the same causal mechanism was at work in each period producing both. Section 2.2 discussed ways in which the same causal mechanism might work, at one and the same time, both to retain and to expand a person's advantages. Here my interest is in the ways in which the same causal mechanism might work to replicate in the next period an advantage of the same kind that a person had enjoyed in the previous period.

The causal mechanism at work might, as in Section 2.1, be the linking of certain advantages to some ascriptive characteristic (race, etc.). The same ascriptive characteristic generating an advantage on one occasion will then generate a similar sort of advantage on subsequent occasions. Alternatively, the causal mechanism might be a social norm.[38] Across much of the developing world, for example, the norm is for men in the family to be served first at meals, which is definitely a nutritional advantage when the household's food is in short supply.[39] The same norm that gave the man that advantage at one meal will give that man the same sort of advantage at the next. Or yet again,

---

[35] According to the *Oxford English Dictionary*, qv. 'replica (n.)', definition 3a.
[36] In the sense of *Oxford English Dictionary*, qv. 'identical (adj.)', definition 2a: 'Agreeing entirely in material, constitution, properties, qualities, or meaning: said of two or more things which are ... individual examples of one category, or copies of one pattern, where any one of them may, for all purposes, or for the purposes contemplated, be substituted for any other.'
[37] In the sense of *Oxford English Dictionary*, qv. 'identical (adj.)', definition 1a: 'Being the same in identity; the very same, selfsame: said of one thing (or set of things) viewed at different times or in different relations. Often emphasized by *same, very*.'
[38] See further Section 6.2.
[39] Drèze and Sen 1989, pp. 50 ff. Dasgupta 1993, ch. 11, esp. pp. 334–6.

the causal mechanism might be some belief that has been rendered 'sticky' by being embedded in some social coding categories or interpretive schema.[40] Being identified as an 'old Etonian' might make you a particularly desirable employee. If so, the same categorization that helped you secure one good job would also help you secure another good job when next you go onto the labour market.

Replicating advantage is also something that happens across generations, as a simple variation on that last story makes clear. A father who enjoyed the labour-market advantages that accrued from being an 'old Etonian' can replicate those advantages for his son by securing admission for his son to Eton as a 'legacy' enrolment. The same kind of occupational advantages that being an 'old Etonian' generated for the father will be generated for the son.

2.4 Recreating Advantage

A final mode of perpetuating advantage is by recreating last period's advantage in the next period. Sometimes what is recreated is identical in form. Then it is a case of 'replicating advantage', already discussed. In this section I shall focus on cases in which the recreated advantage is different in kind but just as advantageous as the previous advantage.

Most of these cases are ones of advantage being 'transformed'.[41] Take the classic case of the *nouveau riche*, who over time (sometimes spanning generations) transform their newfound wealth into social status. They do this in various ways: sometimes by marriage, sometimes by purchase of landed estates;[42] sometimes, indeed, by the literal purchase of titles of nobility.[43]

Running alongside all of those is the strategy of intentionally adopting the manners and mores of the upper classes, with the intention of becoming (or being treated as, or mistaken for) one of them. That is, of course, just the European analogue of the aforementioned 'Sanskritization' on the Indian subcontinent, whereby people adopt the ritual practices of a higher caste or class in hopes of becoming (or anyway being treated as or mistaken for) one of them.

As Max Weber says, 'Status honour is normally expressed by the fact that above all else a specific style of life is expected from all those who wish to

---

[40] See further Section 5.2.
[41] In Bourdieu's (1986) terms, this involves the conversion of one form of 'capital' (economic, social, cultural) into another. Victorian novels are full of this sort of thing (Franklin 2003).
[42] Lisle-Williams 1984.
[43] Stone 1958.

belong to the circle.'⁴⁴ Adopting that style of life can be a way of gaining *entré* to that circle—perhaps for oneself, and certainly for one's children. A commentator on how the English distinguish between 'gentlemen and players' remarks upon the

> luxuriant undergrowth of unwritten and unspoken rules of behaviour ... [t]he observance of [which] helped to give great coherence to the gentlemanly elite. So, naturally, they came to be peculiarly embedded in the practices and attitudes of the schools to which were sent the children not only of the existing elite but of those parents whose accumulated profits thus enabled the family crossing of the great social divide to be completed.⁴⁵

Sometimes those strategies for transforming money into status seem just to be deceptive ruses. Other times those strategies look more like a straightforward economic transaction, with those who have made money transparently attempting to buy social status with that money. People there do not bother acquiring the manners or mores, affectations or accents of the upper classes. They just buy country houses off impoverished aristocrats, thereby becoming the functional (if perhaps not quite the social) equivalents of landed gentry themselves. All of those are ways whereby the *nouveau riche* transform one sort of advantage (financial advantage) into another (the advantage of higher social status, or anyway a reasonably close approximation of it).

For another example of advantage being transformed from one period to the next, consider the so-called 'revolving door' by which former politicians and public officials become lobbyists paid to peddle influence with their former colleagues who are still in positions of power and authority. The revolving door transforms one sort of advantage (political power) in one period into another sort of advantage (financial reward) in the next.

The magnitude of the phenomenon is remarkable.⁴⁶ In the US, fully half of recently retired members of Congress register as lobbyists.⁴⁷ And as the *New York Times* reports, 'A former member of the House or Senate with even modest seniority can now expect to walk into a job paying up to $1 million or more

---

⁴⁴ Weber 1968, vol. 2, ch. 9, sec. 6, p. 932.
⁴⁵ Coleman 1973, p. 98.
⁴⁶ For another example, consider the OECD's (2009) analysis of the revolving door between regulators and financial institutions and the role of that phenomenon in the 2008 global financial crisis (see also Brezis and Cariolle 2019).
⁴⁷ Lazarus, McKay, and Herbel 2016, p. 90.

a year—and much more when bonuses are paid for bringing in new clients.'[48] Similarly in the European Union, some 30 per cent of recent ex-members of the European Parliament and fully half of former European Commissioners now work for organizations on the EU lobby register.[49]

Lest there be any doubt that it is former political advantage that underlies those lobbyists' current financial advantage, consider this telling fact. Evidence suggests that, when a former member of a US senator's staff has become a lobbyist and that senator leaves office, the former staffer suffers an immediate and permanent 24 per cent drop in his or her lobbying income.[50]

2.5 Summing Up

In short, there are four distinct modes of perpetuating advantage from one period to the next. One is simply by retaining it, holding onto the advantages that you already have. Another is by expanding your advantage, which also helps you retain your existing advantages. Yet others involve replicating or recreating your former advantage in the next period. In all those modes of perpetuating advantage, the more advantage you enjoyed in the previous period, the more advantage you are likely to enjoy in the next period.

This chapter has been only a first cut at the problem, describing *patterns* ('modes') of advantage being perpetuated. What *causes* those patterns to exist is the subject of subsequent chapters. Those chapters will explore the many specific *mechanisms* that give rise to those patterns of perpetuated advantage, as well as examining a great many more examples of it.

---

[48] Edsall 2011. For just one example: Richard Gephart, long-serving leader of the Democrats in the House of Representatives, formed his own lobbying firm upon leaving Congress; within five years, it was pulling in over six million dollars a year.

[49] Freund and Bendel 2017, p. 6.

[50] Blanes i Vidal, Draca, and Fons-Rosen 2012; see similarly Strickland (2020). McCrain (2018) finds that the payoff that comes through knowing staffers in a legislative office may be of more value to lobbyists than having a direct connection to a senator. These findings put paid to the claims of the lobbyists themselves that it is the substantive expertise rather than the personal networks gained in their previous employment that matters most (Salisbury et al. 1989)—although that too would count as an instance of advantage being transformed from one period to the next, which is what this example is here illustrating.

PART I
MECHANISMS PERPETUATING ADVANTAGE

Having seen the various modes of perpetuating advantage, I now turn to examine the many different mechanisms by which that is done. In work on structural injustice, the traditional focus is as I have said on sites at which that injustice occurs: in the workplace, in the schools, in the financial sector, in the housing market, and so on. Of course I too shall offer illustrations drawn from all of those sites over the coming chapters. But my emphasis will be more on *how* advantage and disadvantage are perpetuated and less on *where*. The former is pragmatically more important. If our ultimate aim is to disrupt those processes, we must first and foremost figure out how they work. Understanding that is a necessary precondition for devising a strategy for stopping them from working.

Over the coming chapters, I shall identify several mechanisms that help to perpetuate advantage and disadvantage. One's position in a stratification hierarchy can both confer and cement in advantage and disadvantage. So too can one's position in a social network. The language, coding categories, and interpretive schema prevailing in one's society also advantages some and disadvantages others, in recurring ways. So too do the social expectations and norms that prevail in one's society. Reputation confers repeated advantages on some people and disadvantages on others. So too are those who are organized and coordinated advantaged over those who are not.

Running across my discussion of all those specific mechanisms will be a few recurring tropes. Those point to the underlying drivers that make all the more specific mechanisms work. Those will be the subject of Part II of the book. Those are what we need to try to disrupt, if we are to interrupt the processes that perpetuate advantage and disadvantage.

3
Position Confers Advantage

In discussing structural injustice, Iris Marion Young often speaks of people's 'position' in society as conferring advantages or disadvantages upon them.[1] By that, she means to refer to their location in the social structure and the prerogatives, expectations, benefits, and burdens that accrue to placeholders of that position. Those in relatively privileged positions have more and better options for working their will on the world, those in relatively disadvantages positions have fewer and worse ones. And insofar as a person remains in the same advantage-conferring position, that person will be able to use that position to replicate and recreate those advantages time and again.[2]

There are multiple ways of cashing out the notion of 'position', however. All are importantly operative in society as we know it. Different forms of positional advantage sometimes operate independently of one another, sometimes in conjunction with one another.[3] Even when working independently, they often interact with one another, sometimes cutting across one another and other times reinforcing one another.

Even where they all push in the same direction, each type of positional advantage operates according to its own distinct logic. To understand (and to combat) them, it is therefore important first to analyse each in its own right. Different positional advantages have different sources (Section 3.1) and different scope restrictions (Section 3.3.1). Abstracting from all those importantly different particulars, however, all forms of positional advantage nonetheless work in broadly the same way to advantage their possessors.

Sometimes different types of positional advantage are subject to tight scope restrictions. When they are, each operates within its own narrowly circumscribed 'separate sphere' (Section 3.3.1). Sometimes, however, one type of

---

[1] Young 2011, pp. 56–9; 2012.
[2] In the terms introduced in Sections 2.3 and 2.4. That is virtually analytic: being able to do that just *is* what is to be in those advantage-conferring positions. Being in those positions may well also enable a person to retain and expand previously acquired advantages (in the terms of Sections 2.1 and 2.2), but that is a more contingent matter.
[3] On Weber's (1946, pp. 422–3) account anyway, in China in the period of the central monarchy, how many ancestors one was permitted to invoke was determined by one's rank, which was determined in turn by one's success in passing examinations. That makes one form of positional advantage ('ancestral positional advantage') strictly a function of another ('educational positional advantage').

positional advantage is broad in its scope and serves to determine outcomes across a wide range of distributional contests at one and the same time (Section 3.4). Furthermore, even where each type of positional advantage is tightly restricted in its scope, we cannot just assume that they operate independently of one another and, in effect, cancel one another out (Section 3.3.2).

This chapter culminates in a brief and schematic characterization of different strategies for undoing positional advantages (Section 3.5). How easy that will be, and which of those strategies might be most promising, obviously depends on many things. One important factor is how pervasive that type of positional advantage is in determining a wide range of outcomes in that society. Another is how tightly that type of positional advantage is interlinked with other types of positional advantage in that society.

3.1 Four Types of Positional Advantage

Let me begin by offering a taxonomy of four different types of positional advantage.

3.1.1 Position in a Status Hierarchy

The first sense of 'position' is position in a status hierarchy.[4] The higher up you are in the status hierarchy, the more social benefits accrue to you in consequence.[5] Status is here taken to be something like 'social standing'.[6] It has various payoffs that are psychic in the first instance: respect, honour,

---

[4] This is the focus of the classic literature on social stratification (Bendix and Lipset 1953) and of more recent feminist work on 'categorical injustice' (Ásta 2018, 2019; Jenkins 2020).

[5] More precisely, people enjoying higher status within the hierarchy receive more of whatever it is that is allocated by the hierarchy. Typically, those are benefits; but logically they could be burdens as well as (or even instead of) benefits. And someone's enjoying high status benefits within a hierarchy is consistent with that person's having less benefits overall once non-hierarchically allocated benefits are taken into account (van Wietmarschen 2021).

Something similar is true of firms and other organizations, which benefit from their position in a status order within the market (Podolny 1993; Sauder, Lynn, and Podolny 2012). I shall confine my discussion here to the positional advantage that individuals enjoy by virtue of their own personal position within a status hierarchy. But of course individuals also enjoy advantage by virtue of their attachment to firms and organizations that enjoy high status within that status order, as well.

[6] This is Marshall's (1963, p. 229) preferred term for location in a hierarchy of social prestige, as opposed to merely (unranked) location in a social system. It is the latter to which Parsons (1952, p. 25) alludes when saying that a person's status is 'his place in the relationship system considered as a structure, that is a patterned system of parts'. Linton (1936, p. 113) classically defines 'a status' as 'simply a collection of rights and duties'; but surely rights and duties *derive from* a status, rather than constituting it.

esteem.[7] Those payoffs may be valued for their own sake.[8] But they are also of instrumental consequence.[9] From them flow tribute and deference.[10] The former increases the higher status person's material holdings, the latter his capacity to work his will on the world.[11] Even the most seemingly innocuous assignments of status can have significant and long-lasting material consequences. One study has shown, for example, that a person's class rank as a nine-year-old in year three of primary school has been shown to have a modest but significant effect on that person's earnings fully two decades later.[12]

The bases for ranking social status are many and varied.[13] Legally, they were set out in what used to be called the 'law of persons', specifying (in ways reminiscent of feudal orders) rights and duties arising from people's particular personalistic relations to one another: master, servant, husband, wife, and so on.[14] In aristocracies, status is assigned according to birth. In plutocracies, it is assigned according to wealth. Elsewhere it is assigned according to occupational grade[15] or educational achievement.[16] In more primitive societies, it is assigned according to physical strength. In more civilized societies, it is assigned according to wisdom or aesthetic sensibilities.

---

[7] Weber (1946, pp. 190–1) speaks specifically of 'status honour'. See further Origgi (2018, ch. 6).

[8] Indeed, social psychological evidence shows that the 'desire for status' is a 'fundamental human motive' (Anderson et al. 2015). Origgi (2018, ch. 2) similarly argues that 'reputation' embodying 'status and honour' is an end and not merely a means.

[9] Including better health: 'Were it possible to reduce the mortality rate of clerical officers in the [British] civil service to that of administrators, they would have less than half their current death rate' (Marmot et al. 1991, p. 1392; Marmot 2004, 2017).

[10] One study, for example, found that in a B-26 air crew, pilots influence group decisions more than navigators and navigators more than gunners—and that remains true even when the pilot's opinion is objectively incorrect and even when the group task is unrelated to B-26 air crew activities (cited in Berger, Cohen, and Zelditch 1972, pp. 241). See also Podolny and Lynn 2009, p. 548.

[11] 'For all practical purposes, stratification by status goes hand in hand with monopolization of ideal and material goods or opportunities....' (Weber 1946, pp. 190). See similarly: Goldhamer and Shils 1939; Anderson 2014.

[12] Denning, Murphy. and Weinhardt 2022.

[13] For a catalogue see Ross (1901, ch. 9).

[14] Blackstone 1765, vol. 1, chs 2–17; Turner 1988, pp. 22–3. Maine (1901, p. 170) defines the transformation from ancient to modern law in terms of the movement from 'status' to 'contract'; but as my discussion of the 'employment contract' below makes clear, that is not a repudiation of status hierarchy as such but merely a move from what contemporary sociologists call 'ascribed status' to 'achieved status' (achieved, there, by signing the employment contract). One form of status society may well be more objectionable than the other, but both are equally forms of status societies.

[15] Blau and Duncan (1967) is the *locus classicus* on occupational status hierarchies. Note Weber's (1946, p. 405n) insistence that 'it is incorrect to think of the "occupational status group"' as a status group per se, because 'status groups' are defined by a 'style of life' and not just an occupation. For Weber (1946, p. 193), 'An "occupational group" is also a status group' only insofar as 'it successfully claims social honor ... by virtue of [its] special style of life'.

[16] On modern society, see Collins (1979). For an earlier example consider ancient China, where 'during the period of the central monarchy ... qualification for office and rank depended upon the number of examinations [a person] had successfully passed.... The question usually put to a stranger of unknown rank was how many examinations he had passed' (Weber 1946, pp. 422–3).

What is common across all those cases is that the positional advantage conferred by social status comes from norms of deference, backed largely by internalized views of 'one's place in the proper order' and expectations about what others expect and what social sanctions they will bring to bear if those expectations are not met.[17] Hence the motivation on the part of the strong to transform might into right and power into status privilege.[18]

Those in higher status positions, conversely, are regarded as 'better' than others—often on the (typically substantially unfounded)[19] assumption that they are 'better at' something that it is in the general community interest to be successfully done.[20] On the basis of those expectations, they are afforded opportunities that are denied to others. When successful, they accrue rewards for which the others did not have a chance to compete.[21] And as those opportunities and attendant rewards recur time and again, those who enjoy higher positions in the status hierarchy accrue more and more advantage compared to those not in such positions.[22]

3.1.2 Position in an Institutional Hierarchy

A second sense of 'position' is position within an institutional hierarchy.[23] In this case, there are formal organizations that claim legitimate authority over a group of people (be they citizens or employees), and there are individuals in positions of authority within those organizations. What such individuals demand from those over whom they claim to have authority is not so

---

[17] For example, the Church of England's 1662 *Book of Common Prayer*'s Catechism has the supplicant acknowledging, among 'duties to my neighbour': 'To order myself lowly and reverently to all my betters' (Church of England 1762, p. 371, quoted in Ross 1901, p. 383, see further chs 13 and 15). See similarly: Bradley 1876; Dahrendorf 1958/1968; Hollis 1977; Dumont 1980. I further discuss expectations in Chapter 6.

[18] Echoing Rousseau (1755/1973, pt. 2, p. 76), Kemper (1974, p. 849) remarks upon how 'those who have power in society ... and ... have the means to obtain, benefits, rewards, and privileges from others by force, coercion, threat, etc., attempt to convert the power relationship into a status relationship so that the benefits they receive from others will be given voluntarily'.

[19] For example, which college basketball teams are invited to the NCAA postseason tournament is to a significant degree a function of the reputational status of the college, independently of its team's performance that year (Washington and Zajac 2005).

[20] Berger, Cohen, and Zeldich 1972. Correll and Ridgeway 2003. Ridgeway 2014.

[21] Consider for example the way in which racial desegregation of US schools led to 'category manipulation' to preserve white privilege: when forced to admit more blacks to a category of learning-disability education that previously was a white-majority category, schools recoded those white students into a different category (transforming it from black- to white-majority) and attached benefits to it similar to those they had enjoyed in their previous category (Saatcioglu and Skritc 2019).

[22] Thus engaging in what Tilly (1998) calls 'opportunity hoarding'.

[23] 'The conferring of an institutional status on an individual an act of *classifying* that individual. Classifying an individual is an act of placing them in an institutional order', imposing constraints and conferring powers on them in the process (Ásta 2019, p. 393).

much deference as obedience. People subject to their authority accede to those demands out of respect (their own, or their sense of others' respect) for the authority from which the individual derives authority. Polities, firms, and some churches all have formal institutional hierarchies of just that sort.[24] Occupying an elevated position within such an institutional hierarchy confers advantages to people in working their will on the world, and all the many other advantages that flow from that in turn.[25]

3.1.3 Position in a Naked-power Hierarchy

A third sense of 'position' is position within a naked-power hierarchy.[26] Position there is position is a pecking order, literally akin to that among chickens in the barnyard. Here, people simply yield to someone's greater capacity to bring power to bear, rather than deferring in any way (although they may do that too, once status norms based on it have been internalized). Those who are well-positioned in a naked-power hierarchy simply take what they want.[27] Others accede to that exercise of force not because they think (or think that anyone thinks) that they should, but simply because they must.[28] That is the 'law of the jungle', the jungles in question ranging from rain forests of silverback Great Apes to robber baron capitalism of the sort depicted by Upton Sinclair.[29]

Sometimes ruling elites preserve their material advantages through the blatant exercise of brute force. Think for example of the Peterloo Massacre where the British government used the cavalry to break up a mass meeting demanding expansion of the franchise, or the Haymarket Massacre and subsequent persecution of trade unionists demanding an eight-hour working day, or the Tiananmen Square massacre of protestors demanding democratization in China. Companies and governments in the Third World still regularly collude in exercising brute force against those standing in the way of their development

---

[24] Weber's (1946, pp. 196–244) analysis of bureaucracy is the *locus classicus*.
[25] According to one influential model of social stratification 'earnings are attributes of jobs and not of persons' (Sørensen 1979, p. 383), and social positions pay 'rents' to their occupants 'independent[ly] of the characteristics of the incumbents' (Sørensen 1996, p. 1333).
[26] Brute physical force is the prime example of naked power, but it is far from the only one. I nonetheless say 'naked power' here, to distinguish it from many other forms of power, some of which operate with respect to the other sorts of positions under discussion elsewhere in this chapter.
[27] Or, through the 'law of anticipated reactions', others give them what they want because they know that they can simply take it when push comes to shove.
[28] As Hume (1752/1760) says of the rule of 'usurpers or foreign conquerors': 'they have no recourse to any notion of voluntary consent or promise, which, they know, never was, in tis case, either expected or demanded. the original establishment was formed by violence, and submitted to from necessity.'
[29] Sinclair 1906.

projects, particularly involving extractive industries.[30] Other times ruling elites preserve their material advantages more surreptitiously, by weakening public security forces protecting the rest of society.[31]

3.1.4 Position in a Formally Organized Competitive Hierarchy

A fourth sense of 'position' is position within a formally organized competitive hierarchy.[32] Here, people do not simply take what they want; rather they 'win' it, under established rules governing the competition. People accede to those rules of competition either because they themselves approve of them, or because they suppose that others do and that they will be socially or legally sanctioned if they violate them.[33] Economic markets are competitive hierarchies of this sort, where some people are better positioned than others to compete on the terms laid down by the laws and norms governing market competition. Political competition is another, governed by electoral law. But there are of course all sorts of other competitions that display the same characteristics. They range from the Congress of Cardinals that elects the Pope under the apostolic constitution of the Catholic Church to sporting competitions governed by the rules of the game.

3.2 The Dynamics of Positional-good Competition

Different though those four types of positional advantage are in their source and their scope, they are strikingly similar in the basic way in which they actually work to perpetuate advantage. Here I shall elaborate the basic mechanism at work, abstracting from detail that obviously varies across the cases.

Let us start by stripping away one complicating factor. Clearly it is the case that positional advantage of any of these four sorts can often assist one in securing what I called in Section 1.3 'consumption resources'. And by helping to secure such resources, they thereby help to promote the well-being of the individual thus advantaged. But for purposes of this section's discussion I shall bracket those considerations. My interest here is primarily in how positional

---

[30] ICJ 2008, vol. 1, pp. 11, 20. See more generally Ruggie 2008.
[31] Kleinfeld and Barham 2018.
[32] As I shall argue in Section 3.2, all exercises of positional advantage are competitive in some larger sense. In the present section, I shall focus just on ones that are formally organized as such.
[33] I further elaborate on that distinction in Chapter 6, especially Section 6.3.

advantage of each of those sorts might help one secure what Section 1.3 called 'competition resources'. That is to say, I am interested in how one's current positional advantage can be used to secure and enhance one's future positional advantage.

I shall, for purposes of this stylized discussion, assume that there are two types of goods. Firstly, there are end-use goods ('consumption resources'). When consumed, those goods are the proximate source of well-being for the agent. Secondly, there are positional goods ('competition resources'). Positional goods are purely of instrumental value to the agent in securing end-use goods in competition with others for the same end-use goods.[34] Of course, as I have said in Section 1.3, certain goods in the real world often have elements of both.[35] But for purposes of the present discussion, I shall be speaking only in terms of pure cases of each.

Now, notice that all of the four types of positional advantage identified in Section 3.1 actually have a competitive (or comparative, or relative) aspect to them. That is obvious with respect to advantages flowing from one's position in a formally structured competitive setting, what I called above one's 'position in a competitive hierarchy'. But the same is true in a brute-force hierarchy. When arm-wrestling, what determines the outcome is not your absolute strength but rather your strength compared to your opponent. The same is true in a status hierarchy. People will defer to you, and do what you want, only if no one higher up the hierarchy wants them to do something different. And the same is true in an institutional hierarchy. People will obey your commands only if no one higher up in the organization commands them to do otherwise.[36]

In the classic case of positional-good competition, there is a fixed stock of some end-use good.[37] How much of the end-use good any given person gets is then a function of how much of the positional good that player has and is willing to commit to that purpose, compared to how much of the positional good other players have and are willing to commit. The person with more positional goods committed to the competition secures the end-use good.[38]

---

[34] Hobbes (1651, ch. 10) analysed 'power' in just these terms, writing: 'The power of a man ... is his present means, to obtain some future apparent good'.
[35] As borne out by Solnick and Hemenway's (2005) survey of what goods people think are and are not 'positional'.
[36] Let 'higher up' here mean just 'possesses the authority, within the organization, to countermand your command'. Obviously, such authority can be context- and content-specific, and people who are higher up the hierarchy for some purposes may be lower down it for others.
[37] Competition for status is typically like that—there is a fixed amount of it to be distributed, and 'there is no way to make status competition positive-sum' (Sankaran 2021, p. 8).
[38] Either all of it or anyway a larger proportion of it, depending on the terms of the competition.

Various social situations have been modelled on this basis.[39] In a war of attrition, the side with the most weapons and wherewithal wins the war. When employers make hiring decisions purely on the basis of applicants' formal credentials, the person with the highest qualification secures the job.[40] In the study to which I have already alluded in Section 1.3, Amartya Sen famously traced the Great Bengal Famine to a similar phenomenon: rice was not in particularly short supply that year, but many people could not afford to buy (enough of) it because others who were well-paid by the British Army as the war front moved closer bid up the price of rice beyond what they could afford.[41] And in 'attention games' where people are competing for other people's attention, as internet advertisers or dealers on the floor of open-outcry stock exchanges, those who are the comparatively showiest or shout loudest win the competition however showy or loud the others are in absolute terms.[42]

There are two features of such positional-good driven competitions that merit particular comment. One is that, insofar as positional goods are valued purely as a means and not as being of end-use value themselves, increasing the stock of those goods is socially wasteful. Any given person might secure some competitive advantage by adding to his stock of positional goods, but that advantage will be nullified if others add similarly to their stock of positional goods. As in a literal arms race so too in the 'educational arms race' of over-credentialization, a lot of money is spent pointlessly as everyone ends up being situated exactly the same with respect to the end-use good they were trying to secure as before.[43]

That points to an important social cost in letting the distribution of end-use goods be determined by people's relative positional advantages. But given my focus in this book on perpetuating advantage, what particularly interests me is the way in which position-based competition perpetuates and expands advantage for those who are already advantaged. The most important observation, in that connection, is that positional-good competition is used not only to allocate end-use goods but also to allocate positional goods to be used in subsequent rounds of the competition.

---

[39] Hirsch 1976. For a formal analysis see Shubik's (1971) discussion of what he dubs 'games of status'.
[40] Collins 1979; Goodin 1990b; Halliday 2016. Horowitz (2018) reports evidence consistent with this hypothesis.
[41] Sen 1981, 1983. Money (what Sen calls 'exchange entitlements') is just one paradigmatic case of a 'positional good'.
[42] Manzini and Mariotti 2018. See further, Chapter 10 below.
[43] This is Hirsch's (1976) main point. It is elaborated in Frank (2016, ch. 7).

The perpetuation of advantage in that way is particularly marked when the competition is of a 'winner-take-all' form. Competitions of that sort are found in markets where rewards are based not on 'absolute productivity' but instead on 'relative performance against competitors'.[44] They are found in electoral competition conducted on the first-past-the-post system.[45] And at least in part as a result of that, distributional politics is often practised on a winner-take-all basis, as well.[46]

Winner-take-all competitions typically have the effect of exacerbating inequality. The reason is simply that, in such competitions, outcomes are disproportionate to inputs. When people who originally had just a little more than others win everything at stake in the competition, that sets them up in an even more advantageous position going into the next round of competition. It does, anyway, insofar as the winnings are not exclusively end-use consumption goods but can be used to advantage in subsequent competitions.[47]

There is a further feature of positional goods that importantly contributes to the perpetuation, and indeed accumulation, of advantage. That is the fact that when positional goods are used, they typically are not used up. That is to say, they do not necessarily diminish with use. If anything, the more they are used the stronger they often become.[48]

Consider the various sorts of positional advantage outlined above. Status is reinforced by being invoked. The same may be true of institutional advantage: the more you assert your authority, the more authority you have—or are seen to have, which is what really matters. The same may be true of competitive advantage, through the workings of the 'law of anticipated reactions': the more you successfully deploy those resources that confer upon you competitive advantage, the less likely others are to enter into competitions against you in future. The same may be true of power, even in the physical brute force sense. Throwing your weight around is muscle-building. Even if you would have to burn something up to win, the other's knowing you have more means that you typically will not have to burn anything, given the law of anticipated reactions. Others with less brute-power will just roll over and spare themselves the costs of an almost certainly unsuccessful fight.[49]

---

[44] Frank and Cook 1995.
[45] Mill 1861/1977, ch. 6.
[46] Hacker and Pierson 2010.
[47] Haslanger (2015, p. 5), borrowing from Garfinkel (1981, p. 41), makes a similar point in relation to any competition in which outcomes are 'relationally constrained' (where 'relational' is understood in terms of a positional ranking of all competitors).
[48] I return to this theme in Section 9.2.
[49] See related discussions of this topic in Sections 2.1 and 7.1.

3.3 Separate Spheres

Those four types of positional advantage identified in Section 3.1 differ in many important respects. They differ, obviously, in their sources. They differ in their strengths. They also differ in their scopes.

Here I shall first discuss how there might be certain scope restrictions that are peculiar to each type of positional advantage (Section 3.3.1). That their scope restrictions can differ in those ways may lead us to suppose that each type of positional advantage might operate within its own 'separate sphere'.

Just how 'separate' those spheres really are—just how independent they genuinely are from one another—is an open question, however. Some hope that positional advantages might cancel one another out across spheres, with different people enjoying positional advantages in different spheres. I discuss that possibility, sceptically, in Section 3.3.2.

3.3.1 Differing Scope Restrictions

What you can do (and hence what you can gain) by leveraging each type of positional advantage is more-or-less tightly circumscribed. It is governed by a 'logic of appropriateness'—a set of rules, norms, customs, and practices, as well as of purely practical possibilities.[50] Furthermore, those scope restrictions are specific to each sphere.

Take the case of occupying a formal position in an institutional hierarchy, for example. What you can do in that position, and what advantages you can derive from what you can do, depend upon what that organization is itself authorized to do and what you are authorized by it to do in turn. Take the case of a political officeholder. What she can do is circumscribed by the official statement of duties and powers attached to her office. Any action she takes outside of that specification of her office's powers and duties would be *ultra vires*. Those actions would not be done with the authority of the state. Or take the case of an employment contract. An employment contract is by definition a 'relational contract', whereby the employee promises to do whatever the employer says—but only within the limits set down by law (labour law, tort law, criminal law, etc.) on the one hand and by the employment contract itself on the other.[51]

---

[50] March and Olsen 2006.
[51] Simon 1951. For other examples of 'relational contracts' see Williamson (1985); for a precursor, see Weber's (1968 vol. 2, ch. 8, sec ii, pp. 672-4) distinction between a 'status contract' a 'purposive contract'.

The same is true of your position in a formally organized competitive hierarchy. There are limits—some formal legal limits, others informal but nonetheless strong social constraints—on the ways in which competitive advantage can be mobilized in market dealings.[52] The richer you are the greater your positional advantage in market competition; but there are some things that money cannot buy.[53] Some competitive activities are literally constituted by the rules governing them, and you cannot violate the rules without cancelling the competition (as in 'That's not cricket!'). In other cases, if you violate the rules, norms, and understandings governing the competition, you will be subject to formal or informal sanctions, such as others refusing to engage with you in the future. Fear of the latter sort of sanction is what underwrites trust among traders in the Antwerp diamond exchange, for example.[54]

Likewise in status hierarchies there are behavioural expectations surrounding each of the various statuses. With rank comes duties: there are things that a person of a certain status must do and other things she must not do. If she does something that is 'beneath the dignity' of her status, she will lose not just respect but perhaps even her place in the status order itself.

Finally, there are even limits, if only of a pragmatic sort, to what can be achieved by brute force or naked power more generally. You cannot physically force someone to believe something (as opposed to pretending to do so).[55] That was John Locke's central insight in his argument for tolerating differing religious beliefs, for example.[56]

3.3.2 Do Different Positional Advantages Cancel One Another?

Each of the four types of positional advantage is thus subject to its own peculiar set of scope restrictions. Each might therefore be thought to constitute a 'separate sphere', giving rise to multiple hierarchies operating alongside one another at the same time in any given society. Often of course that is not at all the case—instead, there is a single hierarchy, or anyway a predominant one, that determines social outcomes across a wide range of applications; such cases will be in discussed Section 3.4 below. But in at least some places there might

---

[52] For an early example of legal regulation of the market, see the 1353 English Statute of the Staple, 27 Edw. 3, c. 2. On informal social sanctions participants in markets bring to bear on one another, see Macaulay (1963).

[53] Not only morally should not (Satz 2010; Sandel 2012) or socially cannot (Tobin 1970) but perhaps logically cannot (examples might include love, talent, respect).

[54] Bernstein 1992.

[55] That is arguably because people themselves do not have (direct, anyway) control over their own doxastic states (Alston 1989).

[56] Locke 1689/1946.

be a plurality of separate spheres, each operating within its own scope and according to its own rules.⁵⁷

Some writers, such as Michael Walzer, take comfort in the thought that 'separate spheres' (here, spheres of positional advantage) could yield 'complex equality'. That would be the case insofar as different people enjoy positional advantage in different spheres in such a way that, across all spheres taken together, everyone enjoys equal advantage. Different people are advantaged in different spheres, but looking across all spheres everyone is equally advantaged somewhere or another. Anyway, such is the hope.⁵⁸

Here is a vivid ethnographic illustration of how positional advantages across separate spheres might counterbalance one another. Among the Maori of Aotearoa New Zealand, women were traditionally disallowed from making speeches in formal debates. But it was also traditionally the duty of a speaker's older female kinfolk to sing the song that marks the end of their kinsman's contribution to the debate. Here is how one ethnographer describes those power dynamics playing out: 'if the speech is boring, they chatter among themselves, and when they decide it has gone on long enough, an old woman related to the speaker may start up his *waiata* [final song], bringing his oration to a forced conclusion.'⁵⁹ Maori men thus traditionally enjoyed a positional advantage in being empowered to speak; Maori women traditionally enjoyed a positional advantage in being empowered to end their kinsman's speech. Their positional advantages were equal and opposite, and hence they were (in the most literal of senses) mutually cancelling.

That might or might not be a common pattern, however. Spheres can be separate, yet the same people enjoying positional advantage in one sphere might enjoy similar positional advantage in other spheres as well. Positional advantage might be cumulative across spheres, for either of the reasons outlined in Section 2.2. Firstly, the same thing that lead to your being positionally advantaged in one sphere might also lead to your being positionally advantaged in another sphere. Secondly (alternatively or additionally), being positionally advantaged in one sphere might in itself *lead to* your being positionally advantaged in another sphere, however separate those spheres may be from one another in their source or their scope. So, for example, occupying a high position in a formal organization typically elevates you in the status hierarchy as

---

⁵⁷ Churchly and princely authority in the Middle Ages is often said to be a prime case in point (Berman 1983; Ermakoff 1997).
⁵⁸ Walzer 1983. Fishkin (2014) advocates 'opportunity pluralism' for similar reasons, although since he does not believe there is any way to render opportunity sets commensurable he resists any talk of 'equality' in this connection.
⁵⁹ Salmond 1975, p. 57.

well. Or, for another example, the riches that flow your way from occupying a positional advantage in competitive hierarchies often also elevate you in the status hierarchy as well.[60] Furthermore, through effects on nutrition, increased riches can improve your position in the brute-force hierarchy as well.[61]

The same may be all the more true in respect of disadvantages. Being disadvantaged in multiple separate spheres can not only mutually reinforce but also exacerbate the disadvantages experienced in each sphere.[62] Writers on intersectionality often make much of that point.

3.4 Nearly Universal Means

Let us now consider the opposite case. Suppose that, instead of positional advantage being distributed in different and mutually cancelling ways across a range of separate spheres, there is a single dominant dimension of positional advantage that determines distributive outcomes across virtually all aspects of social life. In terms of Section 1.3 above, positional advantage of that sort would amount to a 'resource for competition'[63]—but one of a very particular sort, one that serves as 'nearly universal means' to the attainment of end-use goods. The consolidation and accumulation of advantage, in respect of both end-use and positional goods, naturally ensues when a person's standing in one and the same positional good hierarchy determines virtually all distributions.

John Rawls devised his notion of 'primary goods' for more purely theoretical purposes. But that notion may have descriptive utility as well.[64] 'Primary goods' are, on Rawls's definition, goods that are necessary means to the attainment of any particular ends you might want to pursue.[65] His purpose in devising that notion, in connection with his theory of justice, was to allow him to remain agnostic as regards the theory of the good. No matter what ends

---

[60] For an anthropological account of the symbolic value of money see Codere (1968). Reflect upon the more prosaic account comment of oil baron H. L. Hunt that 'money is just a way of keeping score' (Applebome 1986; Peppard 2008).
[61] As discussed in Sections 1.3 and 1.4.1.
[62] For example, being not only a woman but also a woman of colour (Crenshaw 1991; Haslanger 2012, pp. 322–3). See also: Young 1980; Cho, Crenshaw, and McCall 2013; Chun, Lipsitz, and Shin 2013.
[63] Or in Hirsch's (1976) terms, a 'positional good'; or in Fishkin's (2014, p. 158), 'instrumental goods'.
[64] Sen (1980, p. 281) describes his 'basic capabilities' model as 'a natural extension of Rawls's concern with primary goods'—albeit a more limited one, extending just to the various specific 'functionings' which the 'capability' in question enables (rather than universally, to 'all possible functionings').
[65] Rawls 1971, sec. 15. Rawls (1971, pp. 93, 92) writes, 'whatever one's system of ends, primary goods are necessary means.... With more of these goods men can generally be assured of greater success in carrying out their intentions and in advancing their ends, whatever these ends may be.'

people might have,[66] they will necessarily want primary goods as a means to their ends.

But that is not merely a theoretical device. It has counterparts in the real world.[67] Money is the classic example.[68] Money is often said to be a 'universal solvent' in market societies.[69] Through the medium of money, everything that can be bought and sold is rendered commensurable. Money is thus, in the first instance, a 'value solvent'. But it is also a standard of value and a medium of exchange. In a barter economy, goods are exchanged for goods. In a monetarized economy, goods are bought for money.[70] Money can command anything that has a value denominated in terms of money.[71]

As I have observed in Section 3.3.1 above, there are some things that money cannot buy—or anyway is supposed not to be able to buy. But notice how few they are in number. Restrictions on what money can buy are interesting, precisely because they are so exceptional.[72] Furthermore, those restrictions are often easily circumvented. In societies where people are not supposed to exchange money for labour, they nonetheless can and do use money to buy grain that they turn into alcohol, which is then used to procure labour.[73] The equivalent in US politics might be the way in which, although money is not supposed to be able to buy elections, Political Action Committees officially unaligned with any candidate can collect vast sums of money and influence elections in their preferred ways.[74] Or again, bribery and other corrupt practices are prohibited in both business and politics, but there are various ways of obfuscating a bribe: you can pretend it is a 'gift', you can work through a third

---

[66] Or, more precisely, turn out to have, once they emerge from behind Rawls's 'veil of ignorance'—primary goods were a device enabling people to make choices in a setting where, *ex hypothesi*, they do not know what they want.

[67] Note well: this is my extrapolation from Rawls's theory, not his own.

[68] Blalock 1991, p. 33.

[69] As Marx (1844b/1959, p. 59) famously says, 'By possessing the property of buying everything, by possessing the property of appropriating all objects, money is thus the object of eminent possession. The universality of its property is the omnipotence of its being. It is therefore regarded as an omnipotent being.'

[70] As Adam Smith (1776, bk 1, ch. 5) writes in *The Wealth of Nations*, 'The butcher seldom carries his beef or his mutton to the baker or the brewer, in order to exchange them for bread or for beer; ... he carries them to the market, where he exchanges them for money, and afterwards exchanges that money for bread and for beer.'

[71] According to Jevons' (1875, ch. 3) famous taxonomy, money functions as a measure of value, a medium of exchange, a store of value, and a standard of value.

[72] Just notice how limited is the range of commodities discussed in classic works on the topic: Tobin (1970), Satz (2010), and Sandel (2012).

[73] One version of this story comes from Frederik Barth's (1967, p. 164) analysis of 'Economic spheres in Darfur'.

[74] Lead cases in which the Supreme Court facilitated that are *Buckley v. Valeo*, 424 US 1 (1976), and *Citizens United v. FEC*, 558 US 310 (2010).

party, you can weaken the temporal link between the bribe and the return favour, and so on.[75]

Money may be the most salient positional advantage that serves 'nearly universal means' in commercial societies like our own. In other sorts of societies caste, status, or educational attainment may serve (or anyway once have served) similarly as a 'nearly universal means'. More to the point of this chapter, any one of the positional advantages discussed in Section 3.1, or some mutually reinforcing set of them, might well serve (or anyway once have served) as a 'nearly universal means' of a similar sort. For example, position in the status hierarchy arguably did under feudalism. Position in the institutional hierarchy arguably did under communism, during the period that that amounted to 'rule by the *nomenklatura*'. Position in the naked-power hierarchy arguably did in primitive societies and arguably still does in authoritarian regimes that rule by pure force. And position in the formally organized competitive hierarchy of the economic market arguably does in neoliberal capitalist societies.

The focus of this book is on the accumulation and perpetuation of advantage. The reason that some positional advantage serving as a 'nearly universal means' to other goods matters, in that connection, is simply this. The same thing that determines the distribution of one good will, in that case, also determine the distribution of virtually all other goods. In consequence of that fact, people who get more of one good also get more of virtually all other goods. Insofar as those are what I called in Section 1.3 'resources for consumption', that makes them better off in consumption terms. But insofar as they are what I there called 'resources for competition', that increases the recipients' positional advantage in subsequent competitions for further resources as well.

3.5 Undoing Positional Advantage

How might the accumulation of advantage via positional goods get shut down? In Section 3.3.2 I discussed, sceptically, the suggestion that different types of positional advantage might be separately distributed in such a way as to be mutually cancelling. Here I shall consider more direct ways in which the effects of positional advantage on distributions might be circumscribed or even undone.

One way is through natural limits to accumulation. Those limits might be fixed for example by an individual's innate properties that must combine with

---

[75] Rose-Ackerman 1998. Schilke and Rossman 2018.

external resources to yield positional advantage. In the process of building a scientific reputation, for example, the Matthew Effect of the 'rich getting richer' might be circumscribed by the limits to the scientist's own innate skills. Or in the process of accumulating status or material resources for use in subsequent competitions, accumulation might be circumscribed by the limits of the individual's lifespan.[76] (Of course, if you can pass your positional advantage on to others, there might be a lineage effect even if any given individual stops accumulating positional advantages at some point.)

A second way that accumulation of positional advantage might be curtailed is through socially imposed limits to accumulation. Progressive taxes claw back some of the economic advantage that people could otherwise have deployed in subsequent rounds of economic competition, for example. Sumptuary laws, as in ancient Sparta and medieval Europe, prohibit the public display—and through that, further accumulation—of status and wealth.[77]

A third way that accumulation of positional advantage might be curtailed is by severing the link between the positional good and the outcome of the competition.[78] One interpretation of what democracy is all about is setting politics against markets, creating a separate currency (votes) which is distributed more equally than wealth and letting the allocation of certain things be determined by votes rather than money.[79] The aim—only imperfectly ever realized[80]—is to sever the link between the positional good of wealth and those particular allocations. There have been various other attempts to 'limit the domain of [economic] inequality' by allocating certain things by lottery (jury duty, military service).[81] And in China in the period of the central monarchy, status advantage defined in terms of one's ancestors was supplanted by success in passing examinations as a criterion of social standing.[82] Of course, changing the bases upon which a competition is conducted might not put an end to the competition being decided according to comparative positional advantage. It

---

[76] DiPrete and Eirich 2006, p. 285.

[77] Goodin 1990b, pp. 22-4. Richard the Lionheart, for example, tried to prohibit the extravagant wearing of fur by Crusaders under his command (Schoeck 1969, p. 261). Montesquieu (1748/1949, bk 7, sec. 6) recalls one Chinese emperor 'to whom some precious stones were brought that had been found in a mine ... order[ing] it to be shut up' for similar reasons. The English Acts of Apparel which had previously reserved the right to wear furs to the upper classes were relaxed in 1363, in the wake of the growing riches of the lower classes occasioned by the Black Death, to permit all but the lowest to wear furs (albeit only rabbit and cat); see A Statute Concerning Diet and Apparel, 37 Edw. III c.1, 3–19.

[78] This is an instance of the strategy discussed in Section 11.2.3 of reducing the differential benefits conferred.

[79] Esping-Anderson 1985.

[80] Lindblom 1977, chs 12–17.

[81] Tobin 1970.

[82] Weber 1946, pp. 422–3.

might (as it did in the Chinese case) simply change the positions to which advantage attaches, cumulatively so over time. That general pattern will prevail insofar as there is any general tendency for one or another positional advantage to become a nearly universal means at any given time in a society.

4
Network Confers Advantage

The previous chapter discussed competitive aspects of positional advantage. Central to that story were the ways in which one person's greater positional advantage privileges that person when competing for the same end-use goods with others who enjoy less positional advantage. In this chapter, I turn to more cooperative aspects of positional advantage which also confer competitive advantage on cooperators. Central to this story will be one's position in a network through which items of value (information, goods or services) are transmitted.[1]

The importance of such networks cannot be overemphasized. In the neoclassical economist's imaginary, the world may consist of isolated individuals competing with one another in a war of all against all. In the real world, however, 'most behavior is closely embedded in networks of interpersonal relations'.[2] Sociologists such as Georg Simmel and Mark Granovetter famously proclaim that fact.[3] But even the hard-bitten Chicago School economist Gary Becker has to make a lot of room for it in his models.[4]

Such networks of interpersonal connections—within families, friendship groups and firms, for just a few examples—facilitate cooperation and exchange internally and afford those within the network competitive advantage over others outside it.[5] Being well-placed within such a network is a considerable advantage not only in acquiring 'consumption resources' but also in acquiring 'competition resources'.[6]

---

[1] Since this book focuses on 'perpetuating advantage' I shall focus in this chapter on networks that transmit things of value. But notice that networks can also transmit things of disvalue (like infectious diseases), and it is to one's advantage either to be out of those networks altogether or to be as peripheral within them as possible.

[2] Granovetter 1985, p. 504. See further Burt (1982, ch. 2). For an early statement, see Pool and Kochen (1978/1979), which had been circulating in manuscript form for twenty years by the time it was eventually published.

[3] Simmel 1922/1955; Granovetter 1985.

[4] Especially, for example, in his models of racial discrimination, altruism, and the family (Becker 1976, chs 2, 11–13).

[5] Boissevain 1968, 1974; Ben-Porath 1980; Burt et al. 2013. This point is well-illustrated by studies of the economic effects of caste networks in India, for example (Munshi 2019). It has also been embraced by institutional economists such as Williamson (1985) and Simon (1991).

[6] In the terms introduced in Section 1.3.

Superior networks function as 'absorbing Markov chains'.[7] They incentivize people to get into them and, once in them, to stay in them. In that way, networks both create and perpetuate advantage.

4.1 The Nature of Networks

At its most general, a network is just a 'complex system ... of interrelated things'.[8] The key elements of a network, adapting the language of graph theory, are its 'nodes' (the things that are connected) and the 'arcs' connecting them.[9] What exact form those all take varies from one type of network to another.[10] So too does what is transmitted along the arcs.

The World Wide Web is one classic form of network. Its nodes are individual computers, and its arcs are electrical impulses carrying signals from one computer to another.[11] What is transmitted along those arcs is information. But the World Wide Web is just the latest instantiation of an information-transmitting network. In earlier decades information networks consisted of telephones (and earlier still, telegraph terminals) connected by copper wires. And since time immemorial information (or disinformation) has been transmitted through gossip networks consisting of people whispering into one another's ears.[12]

Although information is probably always at least part of what is carried on the arcs of a network, it is often accompanied by other more tangible things as well.[13] Consider the case of a trading network. What were carried along the trade routes of old were goods, with the arcs of the trade routes connecting nodes consisting of producers, consumers, and myriad traders in between.[14] Or consider supply networks in the production process, where the arcs of the

---

[7] Kemeny and Snell 1960, ch. 3.
[8] *Oxford English Dictionary*, qv. 'network (n.)', 4a. For overview, see Burt (1980) and especially the collection of classic papers in network theory edited by Newman, Barrabási, and Watts (2006).
[9] 'Adapting' rather than 'adopting', because terminology varies. What I here call 'arcs' are often called 'edges'. But I find that term non-intuitive and I fear that many may find it genuinely misleading. (Arcs connect nodes not only on the periphery of the network, which is what the language of 'edges' might most naturally seem to suggest, but also at its very core.)
[10] For a survey of the elements of social network structure see Jackson, Rogers, and Zenou (2017).
[11] Or, increasingly, light impulses that are converted to electrical ones in the telecommunications cabinet on the street.
[12] Gambetta 1994.
[13] Or less tangible things, such as religious beliefs (Collar 2013).
[14] Such trade routes connected even Bronze Age cities, judging from nineteenth century BCE Assyrian merchant records (Barjamovic et al. 2019) and the spread of the common house mouse in Phonecian times (Bakker et al. 2021). The 'Silk Roads' connecting China to the Middle East are perhaps the most famous (Blaydes and Paik 2021). Not only did goods travel along those routes: so too did traders bringing their goods to trade fairs (Milgrom, North, and Weingast 1990), market places, towns, or ports (Polanyi, Arensberg, and Pearson 1957). Being more closely connected via Roman trade routes significantly increases investment between two regions; 36 per cent of that effect is explained by the fact that modern transport networks overlap Roman ones, but 18 per cent of it is

supply network transmit the outputs of activities one node to other nodes that take them as inputs into theirs. Or consider the networks by which professionals pass clients and services back and forth among one another.[15] Or consider friendship networks in which people exchange favours with one another—the most notorious among them being the 'old boy's network' through which people who share school or university connections help one another get good jobs.[16] And of course there are clear analogies in the corporate and political worlds of corporatist intermediation and revolving-door lobbying.[17]

Sometimes the flow along an arc is in only one direction.[18] Indeed, sometimes all the arcs point in one and the same direction, making the overall flow through a network completely unidirectional. A supply network is largely like that, at least in respect of the production process where items proceed forward along the production line (although of course payment flows in the opposite direction). More often, flows along the arcs are bidirectional.[19] If all arcs in the network are like that, the flow will be evenly balanced across the entire network. Broadly speaking, information flows smoothly in all directions on the World Wide Web and on telephone and telegraph lines, for example. Yet other cases are mixed: the flow is unidirectional along some arcs but bidirectional along others. That is the aspiration at least the case of gossip networks, for example, where gossip is supposed not to get back to the person being gossiped about.[20]

Finally, networks can be more-or-less dense. A network is maximally dense if there is an arc connecting every node to every other node within it. A minimally dense network has one fewer arcs than it has nodes. Most networks lie between those extremes. Furthermore, some regions of a network might be denser than others: there might be clusters of nodes that are tightly interconnected with one another, but that are less well connected (i.e., by fewer arcs) with other regions of the network.

---

explained by the fact of similarities in values and preferences that have persisted across two millennia (Flückiger et al. 2022). Thus, cultural characteristics were also transmitted along trade routes, with effects that endure centuries and millennia later (Wang 2021).

[15] Heinz and Laumann 1982.

[16] The *Oxford English Dictionary* (qv. 'network (n.)', 5b) reports that one sense of 'network' is as 'a group of people having certain connections (frequently as a result of attending a particular school or university) which may be exploited to gain preferment, information, etc., esp. for professional advantage'. For examples see Michelman, Price, and Zimmerman (2022).

[17] On the former see Lehmbruch (1984). On the latter see: Hay and Richards 2000; OECD 2009; Brezis and Cariolle 2019; and Sections 2.4 and 8.3 infra. Subsequent employers are often quite frank about what they are buying when hiring an ex-public official. When Australian Treasurer Josh Frydenberg lost his seat in Parliament in 2022, Goldman Sachs hired him saying that he brings to the job 'connectivity' from which 'our Australian clients will greatly benefit' (Ikonomou 2022).

[18] In graph-theoretic terms, the graph is 'directed'.

[19] In graph-theoretic terms, the graph is 'undirected'.

[20] Gambetta 1994.

4.2 Network Power and Advantage

There are broadly three aspects to what is called in the network literature 'network power', and what I here call 'advantage conferred by one's position in networks'.[21]

First, you enjoy network advantage compared to others if you are connected to some network to which those others are not.[22] The reason is simply that you thereby have access to information and resources provided within that network that the others do not.[23] Other things being equal, that gives you an advantage over them in acquiring those resources. One study found, for example, that organizing the owner-managers of small, new Chinese firms into small groups that held monthly meetings for a year resulted in 8 per cent more revenue for those firms compared to other firms not networked in that way.[24] Other studies show how the spread of mobile phones in the developing world has rapidly increased access to 'mobile money' and 'branchless banking' in ways that have dramatically improved the prospects of those previously without access to such networks.[25] One Tanzanian study for example found that those with mobile money access were substantially more likely to receive remittances after heavy rainfall destroying their crops, and those remittances were sufficient to cover two-thirds of their loss from that economic shock.[26]

By the same token, it is more advantageous to be connected to some networks than others. One network as a whole can be said to be more advantageous than some other network if, for example, more of exactly the same resources are distributed through it (or at least as much of the same resources, plus some different resources, are distributed through it). Alternatively, one network as a whole can be said to be more advantageous than some other on account of 'network externalities' deriving from the fact that more people are connected to it. The value to you of being connected to a telephone or email network depends on how many others are connected to it, for example; if there are not many people with a phone, there are not many people you can ring

---

[21] Grewal 2008. This is sometimes what is meant by 'social capital'; see Burt (2000) for a network-based formulation of that term and for evidence as to the extent to which networks confer advantage on individuals well placed within them.
[22] A classic example in industry is 'vertically related firms [where] the suppliers of complementary goods ... try ... to encourage a generous supply of complements, while ... also trying to discourage the supply of complements to rivals' (Besen and Farrell 1994, p. 117).
[23] At least not in that way: of course, those others may have access to those same resources in various other ways, including (but not limited to) being connected to some other network.
[24] Cai and Szeidl 2018.
[25] Dermish et al. 2012.
[26] Riley 2018; see more generally Hamdan (2019).

with your phone.[27] Being connected to a more advantageous network than someone else makes you better able than that other person to acquire whatever resources those networks distribute, other things being equal.[28]

The second aspect of network power is your 'centrality' in a network.[29] There are myriad measures of 'centrality' discussed in the literature on networks.[30] But broadly speaking, one node is more central than another in any given network the more other nodes that are connected to it. A node's centrality is a (possibly complex) function of how many other nodes it receives from and transmits to directly. There is an indirect, second-order aspect of centrality as well: the centrality of any given node is also a function of how central are the other nodes to which that node is connected.[31]

A third aspect of network power, rather less discussed but in practice doubtless very important, might be called 'chokepoint power'.[32] That is to say, one node is powerful with respect to others the more nearly it is the exclusive path within the network structure by which something can be transmitted from one node to (some or all) others.[33] This was the source of Medici power in the Renaissance Florence, for example.[34] To say that the occupant of such

---

[27] In computing, Metcalfe's Law says that 'the systemic value V of a network is proportional to the square of the number of compatibly communicating devices: with N nodes each connecting to $N-1$ other nodes, V would be proportional to the total number of possible connections, $N \times (N-1)$, or approximately N^2' (Metcalfe 2013, p. 28). Metcalfe (2013) validates his law by reference to growth in Facebook users and its associated revenue. Economists refer to these as 'network externalities' (Allen 1983; Katz and Shapiro 1985; Besen and Farrell 1994; Liebowitz and Margolis 1994, 1998; Shapiro and Varian 1999, pp. 13–17 and ch. 7). Apparently the phenomenon was first noticed by Antonio de Viti de Marco in his 1890 analysis of the telephone industry (Mosca 2008, pp. 326–7). Network externalities will be discussed further in Sections 4.6, 6.1.2.1, 7.3 and 9.3.1 below.

[28] As Bourdieu (1986, p. 249) says, 'The volume of ... social capital possessed by a given agent ... depends on the size of the network of connections he can effectively mobilize and the volume of the capital (economic, cultural or symbolic) possessed in his own right by each of those to whom he is connected'.

[29] Consider, for example, Luther's central role in spreading Protestantism across the network of those connected to him during the early Reformation (Becker et al. 2020) and of rail and telegraph networks in spreading the Women's Temperance Crusade in the late nineteenth-century US (García-Jimeno, Iglesias, and Yildirim 2021).

[30] Borgatti 2005. These vary largely depending on the assumptions they make about the flow through the network: whether it must be through the most direct path; whether the same node may be revisited; etc. While those considerations matter greatly for specific measures of centrality, they do not matter much for the 'basic idea' of centrality which is what I am here discussing.

[31] And hence the more power-*cum*-advantage an occupant of the one node derives being connected to the others. For a survey of such models within sociology see Bonacich (1987) and within economics see Ballester, Calvó-Armengol, and Zenou (2006).

[32] This is the power that derives from providing 'brokerage' across what Burt (1992, 2000) calls 'structural holes'. In Fishkin's (2014) terms, this is the power associated with controlling 'bottlenecks'; in Tsebelis's (2002), it is 'veto power'; in Freeman's (1979) measure of network centrality, it is 'betweenness'.

[33] '[P]eople, groups and organizations have power to the extent that they have access to alternative sources of a valued resource, and the extent to which they control resources valued by others in the network' (Monge and Contractor 2003, p. 212, building on Emerson 1962).

[34] Padgett and Ansell 1993.

a node actually enjoys power by virtue of occupying that 'chokepoint node' presupposes, of course, that the occupant has a choice of whether or not actually to choke off further transmission of what has been received. People in a trading network or a gossip network clearly do enjoy such power (at least in ordinary circumstances). We generally think of telephone lines and electric circuits as transmitting signals and currents they receive further along down the line more automatically (although of course it is in principle possible for further transmission to be intentionally blocked there as well, as with the World Wide Web in China, for example).

Perhaps there are few literal 'chokepoints' in most network structures. There usually is a way of 'going roundabout', one node indirectly connecting to some other node through a series of other nodes even if the most direct pathway is blocked.[35] But that strategy typically comes with a cost. Typically, some portion of the resources being transmitted are lost (or information garbled) with each arc they pass through before reaching their final destination.[36] The upshot is that, even if there is some way of 'working around' a chokepoint that someone is blocking, more of the resources being transmitted will be lost or corrupted in the process of reaching their final destination than would have been the case if the chokepoint had not existed or not been blocked.

That fact of 'loss in transmission' also explains why 'centrality' is advantageous. Even if there is some pathway from peripheral nodes to all other nodes, the distance (in graph-theoretic terms, the number of other arcs and nodes that must be passed through along the way) is greater for occupants of those peripheral nodes than it is for occupants of more central nodes. In consequence, more of what they are trying to transmit will get lost or corrupted before reaching its final destination. That puts those at peripheral nodes at a disadvantage compared to those at more central nodes.

Furthermore, the fact of 'loss in transmission' incentivizes people to direct their transmissions through central rather than more roundabout pathways in order to minimize such losses. That in turn puts occupants of central nodes at an advantage vis-à-vis occupants of more nodes along more roundabout pathways within the network structure. Thinking of nodes as 'tollgates',[37] the occupant of the central node can charge a toll up to the sum of all of the tolls

---

[35] That is the 'strength of weak ties' in Granovetter's (1973) famous paper.

[36] In trading networks, each middleman takes his cut—as did the ruler of each polity through trade routes like the Silk Roads passed (Blaydes and Paik 2021, p. 118). In information networks, there is signal loss the more nodes the information passes through. In electric networks, resistance within the circuitry leads to power loss the further the current has to travel.

[37] That is to say, there is a charge to be paid for passing through each node-*cum*-gate, although that charge is not necessarily paid directly to the gatekeeper.

charged at all of the nodes along the best alternative roundabout pathway to the same destination.

4.3 Network Homogeneity and Homophily Advantages the Advantaged

One of the most robust findings in the study of social networks the tendency for people who are 'similar' in some relevant respect to cluster together.[38] Dimensions of similarity are many and varied. They include race, gender, ethnicity, social class, educational attainment, sporting interests, and so on.

The important thing to note, for present purposes, is that along each of those dimensions one subset of individuals—and hence one relatively self-contained cluster within the relatively homogeneous network—tends to be advantaged compared to the other(s) in whatever respects are most relevant to the network. And insofar as being well-networked with more advantaged others advantages you in turn, the tendency towards homogeneity in the formation and maintenance of social networks is another important mechanism that helps to perpetuate advantage. Those who are more advantaged cluster together, and in consequence of the benefits of closer network ties with others who are relatively advantaged, become more advantaged still.

There are multiple reasons for this tendency of people who are similar to cluster together in networks. To some extent, it is purely a matter of preference, 'homophily' pure and simple.[39] People simply prefer to be with 'their own kind'—or anyway not surrounded by too many of some 'other' kind. Thomas Schelling has shown how even a relatively weak preference of the latter sort can quickly lead to complete segregation of a dining hall or a residential neighbourhood.[40]

To some extent, however, there are more 'structural' forces at work in producing homogeneous networks.[41] Those relate to who is readily available to you with whom to form a new tie. Someone is 'readily available to you', in that way, if she is already directly connected to someone with whom you are already directly connected. In searching for new people to connect with, you could of course mount a completely new search. But searching is costly and people generally tend not to take on those costs gratuitously. When making

---

[38] McPherson, Smith-Lovin, and Cook 2001; Monge and Contractor 2003, ch. 8.
[39] The term was coined by Lazarsfeld and Merton 1954.
[40] Schelling 1971; 1978, ch. 4.
[41] There are also psychological pressures, other than homophilous preference, sometimes at work. In their study of 'friending' patterns on Facebook, Wimmer and Lewis (2010) also point to the social awkwardness of not reciprocating when someone befriends you there or not befriending a friend's friend ('triadic closure').

new connections, they tend to connect with 'friends of friends'.[42] And if your friends are similar to you, and their friends are similar to them, then this 'ready availability' dynamic will lead you to connect with new people who are similar to you in a less preference-based and more structure-induced way. If anything, this seems to be the more important of the two sources of homophily, although both forces are clearly at work.[43]

Furthermore, those two forces reinforce one another in ways that generate cumulative advantage and disadvantage. When a person chooses to form a new network link with someone else who is similar to him, he is bringing all the others who are already linked to him into closer proximity to all the others who are already linked to her. And by the structural 'ready availability' dynamic, that increases the chances of people already linked to him themselves forming a direct link with people already linked to her. Assuming most of those people are similar to one another in the relevant dimension, that increases the homophily the network.[44]

All those truisms about self-sorting and network dynamics have important implications for the perpetuation of advantage, insofar as people sort themselves within those networks along the dimensions of advantage. Those who are of the 'advantaged' type will increasingly cluster with others who are similarly advantaged, and those with who are of the 'disadvantaged' type will increasingly cluster (or be left clustered with) others who are similarly disadvantaged. Increasing cumulative advantage and disadvantage ensue as a result of that process.

4.4 Examples of Network Advantage in Action

In short, you derive an advantage *from* being embedded in a network, over others who are not, insofar your connections within it give you advantages over those others. You enjoy an advantage over others *within* the same network if you have more 'network power' than they do, typically either by having a more central position in the network yourself or else being relatively closely connected to someone who does.[45]

---

[42] Kossinets and Watts 2009, p. 434. See similarly Wimmer and Lewis (2010).
[43] Kossinets and Watts 2009.
[44] Kossinets and Watts 2009, p. 436.
[45] Bonacich 1987. You might still occupy a peripheral place in the overall network, despite one connection to someone who is central in it, if all your other connections are to people who are peripheral.

To show how network advantage plays out in these ways, let me now briefly sketch two slightly more extended examples. One concerns labour markets (Section 4.4.1), the other legal services (Section 4.4.2).

4.4.1 Labour Market Networks

Certain groups of people have conspicuously less success in labour markets than others. Blacks are less likely than whites to be employed in all sorts of positions, for example, and women are less likely than men to be employed in managerial positions. From simply observing those patterns, it is easy to leap to the conclusion that racial and gender discrimination, whether individual or institutional, is to blame.[46] Doubtless that is true, too. But to a surprising extent, those patterns might be explained by the networks to which each group has access, which differentially advantage some types of people over others.[47]

It is a well-established fact that about half of jobs in the US are obtained through informal contacts, such as family and friends.[48] Given that fact, it only stands to reason that the wider one's network of such informal contacts, the better one's access to the labour market—both in terms of finding a job at all, and in terms of finding a 'good', well-paying job.[49]

Now, it is also a well-established fact that black Americans have significantly smaller networks than do white Americans. The mean number of people with whom black Americans report discussing 'important matters' is 2.25, compared to whites' mean of 3.10.[50] And those 'disadvantages in the network of friends and relatives facing blacks' do indeed seem to affect their labour market outcomes. It is estimated that 'between 24% and 38% of the difference in employment rates between white and black youth is attributable to superior returns to the job referral networks of' young whites.[51]

---

[46] Carmichael [Ture] and Hamilton 1967. Cf. McIntosh 1988, 1998; Reskin 2003.

[47] Loury 1998, pp. 119–20. Of course the differential access that whites enjoy to such networks, compared to blacks, might itself reflect racial discrimination; if so, 'differential network effects' just constitute the intervening 'mechanism' variable that stands between 'attitude' (bias) and 'outcome' (getting a job) (Reskin 2003, p. 8).

[48] Montgomery 1991, p. 1408. See similarly: Granovetter 1974/1985; Reskin 2003, p. 8; Arrow and Borzekowski 2004, p. 3.

[49] For a fine-grained ethnographic study illustrating these processes see Royster (2003).

[50] Marsden 1987, p. 129, reporting data from the 1985 General Social Survey; in the 2004 version of that survey the numbers were proportionately lower for both groups (McPherson, Smith-Lovin, and Brashears 2006).

[51] DiMaggio and Garip 2012, p. 100, referring to findings by Holzer (1987) and Bortnick and Ports (1992).

The probability of a young black American finding a job through family and friends is 10.2 per cent, compared to 12.8 per cent for a young white American.[52] It is not that blacks are any less assiduous than whites in using their personal networks to find a job; if anything, blacks rely on their personal networks more heavily for those purposes.[53] The point is just this. If networks are relatively homogeneous (and they are),[54] then young black men have predominantly other young black men in their network; and if young black men are much less likely to be employed, then young black men are less likely to have others in their network who are themselves employed and hence are well-positioned to help them find work.

Similar network effects are arguably at work in disadvantaging blacks compared to whites in finding a good, well-paying job. That is once again partly because of the quality of those networks. Insofar as blacks network predominantly with other blacks, and the latter tend to have low-paying jobs, the former are less likely to find high-paying jobs through those networks.[55]

To some possibly large extent, the disadvantage that blacks experience in finding good, well-paying jobs may also be a function of the sheer size of their network.[56] Arrow and Borzekowski report the 'startling' finding, based on their modelling, that 'roughly 13%–15% of the variation in ... wages [across the workforce as a whole] is ... attributable to differences in the number of ties among individuals' in their networks.[57] And they go on to show that 'that reasonable differences in the average number of links between blacks and whites'—differences on the order of magnitude that are actually observed—'can explain the disparity in black and white income distributions' (a difference, in the period and groups that they studied, between average annual earnings of $25,322 for blacks and $31,802 for whites).[58]

---

[52] Holzer 1987, pp. 452, 447.
[53] Elliott 2001, p. 412.
[54] The racial/ethnic heterogeneity of blacks' networks, while slightly higher than that of whites', is still only 0.13 (Marsden 1987, p. 129). Given that blacks account for only 10 per cent of the general population, that means that blacks very predominantly still network with other blacks, who may not be the most useful interlocutors for helping them a good job (particularly young black males, among whom unemployment rates are particularly high). On heterogeneity in social networks more generally see: McPherson, Smith-Lovin, and Cook 2001; and Kossinets and Watts 2009.
[55] Braddock and McPartland (1987) report that atypical blacks who have networks that are less racially segregated tend to get jobs with higher wage rates than blacks whose networks are more racially segregated, suggesting that the composition of their networks is indeed responsible for producing this effect.
[56] Korenman and Turner 1996.
[57] Arrow and Borzekowski 2004, p. 9.
[58] Arrow and Borzekowski 2004, pp. 4, 11. Explaining the differential in that way requires that the mean network size of a black worker be 3.2 compared to 5.7 for a white worker. As they say, 'these values are not far from' Marsden's estimate of 2.25 ties for blacks and 3.10 for whites (Arrow and Borzekowski

Shifting now from race to gender, there are similarly notorious gender differences in who gets appointed to managerial positions in firms. There, too, differential access to the relevant networks is an important part of the story. The logic is simple: 'recruitment through workers' social ties tends to replicate an establishment's demographic composition'; and 'given men's predominance in managerial positions, using informal referrals should [be expected to] be associated with selecting male managers'.[59] That is of course just the familiar story of the 'old boys' network'—which the feminist movement advises female workers to overcome through 'networking' among themselves.[60]

To calibrate the importance of such network effects in helping males (and hindering females) to secure managerial positions, consider the findings of Reskin and McBrier's study of 516 firms. That study found that if a firm recruited managerial staff through informal networks, that produced a 14.8 per cent increase in the odds ratio of managers in that firm being male.[61]

4.4.2 Legal Services Networks

Marc Galanter points to similar network effects in explaining 'why the haves come out ahead' in the legal system. His crucial distinction is between 'one-shot' and 'repeat' players. The former 'have only occasional recourse to the courts', whereas the latter 'are engaged in many similar litigations over time'. Examples of one-shot players would include 'the spouse in a divorce case, the auto-injury claimant, [and] the criminal accused'. Examples of repeat players are 'the insurance company, the prosecutor, [and] the finance company'.[62] As those examples suggest, the 'haves' tend more often to be repeat players and the 'have-nots' tend more often to be one-shot players.[63]

Repeat players have several advantages over one-shot players. They are more well-informed about the rules and procedures, having litigated many similar

---

2004, p. 12; Marsden 1987, p. 129). The black/white ratio is similar (0.6 compared to 0.7 in Marsden's data). In absolute terms, Arrow and Borzekowski's estimates are somewhat higher for each group than in Marsden's, but that is due to the fact that the survey Marsden was discussing asked specifically about people with whom one 'discusses important matters'; that probably primes people to think in terms of more intimate, personal matters rather than the occupational ones of interest to Arrow and Borzekowski (Marsden 1987, p. 123; Arrow and Borzekowski 2004, p. 12).

[59] Reskin and McBrier 2000, p. 214.
[60] Welch 1980; Healy 2015.
[61] Reskin and McBrier 2000, p. 221.
[62] Galanter 1974, p. 97.
[63] Although not invariably: alcoholic derelicts are repeat players who come before the courts regularly, for one counter example to that generalization; wealthy criminal defendants who are only ever charged with one crime are another (Galanter 1974, p. 103).

cases before. They can afford to play the odds, adopting strategies that are likely to prove maximally advantageous over a long series of cases, whereas one-shot players can often ill-afford to take the risk of losing badly in the single case in which they will be involved.[64] But most especially, repeat players can establish relationships with other repeat players in the system, from which they derive not only superior insight into the workings of the system but also leverage over other repeat players, being able to reciprocate favourable or unfavourable treatment in subsequent encounters.[65]

Those 'facilitative informal relations with institutional incumbents' that Galanter identifies among repeat players are, of course, networks of precisely the sort I have been discussing in this chapter. They constitute, on his account, 'a position of advantage' for repeat players 'in the configuration of contending parties'. And as 'those with other advantages tend to occupy this position of advantage', they 'have their other advantages reinforced and augmented thereby'.[66] Availing themselves of that sort of network advantage is, for Galanter, an important part of the explanation of 'why the haves come out ahead' in the legal system.

4.4.3 A Dramatic Historical Speculation

The importance of networks in conferring and perpetuating advantage is dramatic enough in the contemporary examples just discussed. We can turn to history for an even more dramatic example, albeit inevitably one which is somewhat more speculative in nature.

The example concerns the economic fortunes of families in the American South whose slaves were emancipated without compensation after the Civil War. Surprisingly enough, they regained their former economic standing within a generation, at least arguably on the basis of their social networks.

In a world of chattel slavery, of course, the slaves that one owns constitute a significant part of one's wealth. When slavery was abolished without compensation in the wake of the US Civil War, that wealth evaporated. Since that wealth was no longer available to pass on to one's children, the children of former slave-owners would naturally be expected to be less wealthy, down the track, than the offspring of other families with equally large fortunes that had not been invested in slaves.

Yet over time the opposite was actually the case. In the short term, of course, slave-owning families certainly suffered substantial reductions in their wealth

---

[64] Galanter 1974, pp. 99–100.
[65] Luce and Raiffa 1957, pp. 97–102. Axelrod 1984; Kreps 1990, pp. 100–11.
[66] Galanter 1974, p. 103.

as a result of emancipation. But evidence from linked decennial censuses conclusively demonstrates that the sons of ex-slave-owners were on average nearly as wealthy as the sons of equally wealthy Southern parents who had held no slaves (and within another generation completely so).[67]

How so? The seminal paper establishing that finding tests, and conclusively rejects, a wide range of alternative explanations.[68] The most plausible explanation, the authors conclude, is that the Antebellum slave-owning elite had established social networks that enabled their sons to prosper by transitioning into lucrative white-collar careers, once the family's slave wealth had been destroyed.[69] But that is a speculation backed only rather indirect evidence.[70]

In the absence of firmer direct evidence, that example must be treated as speculative. Still, the speculation is more credible than any of the other plausible explanations on offer. And social networks must be very powerful indeed in perpetuating advantage, if they did in fact enable ex-slave-owning families so largely to recoup their financial position within such a modest period of time after such a severe financial shock as the unreimbursed emancipation of their slaves.

4.5 Sources of Network Effects: Information and Trust

Those examples illustrate two separate, but connected, ways in which networks confer advantages upon those who are well-placed within them.[71]

Being in a privileged position in a network, firstly, confers an advantage in terms of information. People in such a position are better able to receive information from, and to transmit information to, others in the network. Other things being equal, having more information better enables you to secure your

---

[67] Ager, Boustan, and Eriksson 2021. Moreover, an earlier Working Paper version of that article suggested that, for sons of the very wealthiest slave-owners, that happened more quickly and more dramatically: just fifteen years after the unreimbursed emancipation of their slaves, their wealth was fully 19 per cent greater than that of sons of Southern families that had been equally wealthy before the Civil War but had not owned slaves (Ager, Boustan, and Eriksson 2019, p. 18).

[68] Among the alternative explanations that they decisively reject is the hypothesis that ex-slave-owners' recovery was due to the substitution of exploitative share-cropping practices that served as the functional equivalent of slavery (Ager, Boustan, and Eriksson 2021, pp. 3783–5).

[69] Ager, Boustan, and Eriksson 2019, 2021. This is as Acemoglu and Robinson (2008) predicted, more generally. Of course, the sons of ex-slaveowners were also trading on their high social status that persisted even after the loss of their families' slaves; so 'position in the social status hierarchy' (as discussed in Section 3.1.1) is also an important part of this story. Still, without networks to enable them to capitalize on their social status in these ways, the ex-slaveowners' sons would not have been able to recover financially nearly so well or so quickly.

[70] Such as the fact that sons of ex-slave-owners tended to marry daughters of people who had themselves been wealthier before the Civil War (albeit not by much, only between 4 and 5 per cent) (Ager, Boustan, and Eriksson 2019, p. 19).

[71] For another example, recall Adam Smith's view that the sheer facts of communication and association via what I have here been analysing as networks were the keys to formation of economic cartels (Tuck 2016).

own ends; and having more control over the information that others receive better enables you to shape the choices of others in ways that suit you. In the labour-market example, people who are better networked to others who are already employed gives them better access to information about job openings for which they might themselves apply. In the legal-services example, repeat-players are better known to others with whom they recurringly interact and know more about them in turn, which works powerfully to their advantage.

Being in a privileged position in a network potentially confers a second advantage, in terms of trustworthiness.[72] Networks by their nature partition the world into 'insiders' and 'outsiders'. Sometimes networks are built around pre-existing trusting relations. But sometimes simply being in the same network, in and of itself, can generate trust among those who are within the same network and distrust of those who are outside of their network.[73]

Those explanations of the relationship between 'trust' and sharing the same network with one another are more psychological in form. There is another explanation of a more quasi-rationalist form, however, which is just this.[74] The more frequent and more direct interactions you have had with someone, the more you know about them and what you can expect of them. Most particularly, you better know whether you can trust them to do what they say they will do, or what you want them to do.[75] And you are more likely to play more cooperatively with others whom you have more reason for thinking that you can trust, which advantages those who can be more trusted by others in turn. That was key to the legal-services example. But it also figures in the labour-market example. There, people who were well networked with existing employees, who could vouch for them when they applied for positions at their firms, enjoyed a trust-based reputational advantage by virtue of that fact when seeking employment.[76]

My discussion in this chapter has mostly dealt with *informal* networks of one sort or another. But notice, now, that just as those two advantages arise

---

[72] I say more about trust in Section 7.4.

[73] Homans 1950; Teubner 2002. Gambetta (1994, p. 216) observes the same of gossip networks, saying 'gossip ultimately should generate *positional* trust: it increases mutual trust among gossiping agents at the cost of breaching trust with those who are the object of gossip'. Distrust of outsiders manifests itself in what Banfield (1967) calls the 'amoral familism' of peasant societies. Note however that that same distrust can have the advantage of helping to prevent them from being exploited by outsiders. If whipped up by group leaders, however, such distrust of outsiders can have serious consequences for inter-group conflict (Hardin 1995).

[74] Building on Coleman (1990, ch. 5), Hardin (1993, p. 507) calls this 'instinctive Bayesianism'.

[75] Where interactions are anonymous or pseudonymous, as in illicit on-line drug markets, 'trust in the market' can substitute for 'trust in known individuals' within it (Duxbury and Haynie 2021). The same is true of trust in 'hybrid networks' more generally (Teubner 2002).

[76] Montgomery 1991. See further Section 7.4 below.

naturally for people linked in informal networks, so too are they intentionally constructed by organizing people into *formal* networks.[77] Indeed, Section 3.3.1 has shown how formal organizations are constructed out of 'relational contracts' linking people to them and to one another within them.[78] Doing so reduces information and other costs associated with monitoring each other's behaviour, at the same time as it makes parties with the same relational contracts repeat-players vis-à-vis one another who can be expected to be more trustworthy because there will always be future opportunities to sanction and reward past behaviour in future interactions.[79]

4.6 Distributional Consequences of Network Externalities

Where network externalities are present, a network is more advantageous the more people there are in the network. Those advantages are the same for both old members and new. When someone new joins a network, existing members of the network are made better off by her joining—but upon joining, she too immediately comes to share exactly those same advantages. In that respect, at least, the effects of network externalities are equally distributed.

In two other respects, the distributional effects of network externalities are inegalitarian. First, and most obviously, those who are in the network are advantaged relative to those who are not. Network externalities magnify that difference between them by making it more advantageous to be in the network, as the network expands. Those within the expanded network are thereby further advantaged, both absolutely and relatively to those still not included in the network.

Second, even within the expanded network, the pre-existing members are likely to be advantaged vis-à-vis the new members. That would be the case insofar as new members are added at the periphery of the network, as commonly occurs. Where that is the case, the earlier a person joined the network the more central she would be within it—which as Section 4.2 argued is in itself a source of network power and advantage.

---

[77] Informal networks are often 'institutionalized', with sets of expectations growing up around them, with much the same effects. As Bourdieu (1986, p. 249) says, 'the network of relationships is the product of investment strategies, individual or collective, consciously or unconsciously aimed at establishing or reproducing social relationships that are directly usable in the short or long term, i.e., at transforming contingent relations, such as those of neighborhood, the workplace or even kinship, into relationships that are at once necessary and elective, implying durable obligations subjectively felt (feelings of gratitude, respect, friendship, etc.) or institutionally guaranteee (rights)'.
[78] Williamson (1985) and, before him, Simon (1951). See further Section 8.3 below.
[79] Kreps 1990; Powell 1990; Simon 1991; Nee 1998.

5
Language, Coding Categories, and Interpretive Schema Confer Advantage

In the last chapter, I discussed the ways in which social networks convey information and the advantages that accrue to people from being well-positioned in such networks. In this chapter, I focus on the ways in which the information thus conveyed is encoded and decoded—and how some people may be advantaged and others disadvantaged as a result of those processes.

More specifically, I shall discuss distributional biases that might be embedded in language (Section 5.1), in coding categories (Section 5.2) and in interpretive schema (Section 5.3). In conventional discussions of structural injustice, these might all be lumped together under the heading of 'ideological biases'. But analytically I think it is better to examine each of those sources of bias separately and in its own right. And even as regards 'interpretive schema', which come closest to what is ordinarily meant by 'ideology', adopting less loaded terminology will help us see more clearly how the mechanism actually works.[1]

5.1 Language as a Source of Advantage

In the most general terms, information is conveyed through language (a natural one or an artificial one such as computer code). Languages in turn embed biases of various sorts, which are broadly the subject of this chapter.

Any given language might advantage some users, some propositions or some positions over others—if only by making it easier for some people rather than others to express themselves, their propositions, and their positions more clearly, succinctly and persuasively. Language can also serve as a marker of social status, and hence a carrier of positional advantage of the sort discussed in Section 3.1.1. Finally, language can also be manipulated (again, more successfully by some people than others, perhaps) in such a way as to advantage

[1] Haslanger 2017.

persons, propositions, or positions. I shall discuss each of those sources of linguistic advantage in turn, after first discussing how the conventions of language can asymmetrically advantage some people over others.

5.1.1 Language Conventions Can Be Asymmetrically Beneficial

A language is, by its nature, a set of conventions shared among speakers of the language. It is only by sharing those conventions that they can understand what others mean by their utterances.

Conventions, in turn, are solutions to coordination problems. A coordination problem arises when (1) it would be mutually advantageous for us to coordinate our behaviour with one another's but (2) there are many possible ways in which to do so, and (3) coordinating with one another in any of those ways is better for each of us than not coordinating with one another at all. Conventions strive to solve coordination problems by identifying one of those many eligible ways of coordinating as that which one is to be pursued. And a convention succeeds in solving the coordination problem insofar as all (or enough) of those for whom coordination is a problem actually do abide by its dictates and reliably expect all others to do likewise.[2]

The classic form of a Coordination Game is as shown in Figure 5.1.[3] That figure represents the simple case of two speakers choosing between two languages, and making their choices independently of one another. If both of them choose the same language, they succeed in communicating and each gets a payoff of 10. If one speaker chooses one language and the other another, communication fails and each speaker gets nothing (a payoff of zero). In the cells of Figure 5.1 and all of the figures that follow, payoffs are written in the form: (Speaker 1's payoff, Speaker 2's payoff).

		Speaker 2	
		Language $L1$	Language $L2$
Speaker 1	Language $L1$	(10,10)	(0,0)
	Language $L2$	(0,0)	(10,10)

Figure 5.1 Language as an Equal Coordination Game

---

[2] Lewis 1969, chs 1–2.
[3] Figure 5.1 is adapted from Lewis (1969, p. 9).

In all the linguistic Coordination Games that I shall be discussing, the speakers want to coordinate on the same language. The reason is simple: if they do not, communication fails and neither speaker gets any payoff at all. But the distinctive feature of the Figure 5.1 scenario is that both speakers are indifferent between the two possible languages. The payoff each gets is the same, whichever language they coordinate upon. The game is, in that sense, an 'Equal Coordination Game'.[4]

Confronted with an Equal Coordination Game, players seek a convention—any convention—to dictate which language they will all speak. No one cares which language the convention picks out.[5] They merely want the convention to identify one of the languages clearly, so they all end up speaking the same language.

Not all Coordination Games are like that, however. Sometimes one option is better than the other, and that is the same option for all players. In Figure 5.2, each speaker gets a payoff of 20 if they coordinate on Language $L1$, and a payoff of 10 if they coordinate on Language $L2$ (and, as before, nothing at all if they fail to coordinate on the same language).[6] Imagine, for example, that Language $L1$ uses the Arabic numeral system, with its great advantage of having zero and the decimal, and Language $L2$ uses Roman numerals instead.

		Speaker 2	
		Language $L1$	Language $L2$
Speaker 1	Language $L1$	(20,20)	(0,0)
	Language $L2$	(0,0)	(10,10)

Figure 5.2 Language as a Cooperative Coordination Game

Clearly, in the Figure 5.2 scenario both speakers prefer to coordinate on the same language and for that to be Language $L1$. Hence, the Figure 5.2 scenario might be dubbed a 'Cooperative Coordination Game'. In such a scenario, all players prefer for the convention to pick out one and the same language.[7]

---

[4] This model is sometimes called 'two men rowing a boat' in deference to Hume's (1777, appendix 3, para. 8) early example.
[5] In an Equal Coordination Game it really is a matter of just 'picking' rather than 'choosing', in the terms of Ullmann-Margalit and Morgenbesser (1977).
[6] Figure 5.2 is adapted from Lewis (1969, p. 10).
[7] Schelling (1958) plausibly argues that they do so because the fact that both get more by choosing $L1$ constitutes a 'signal' to the players as to which strategy to choose because that is the one the other is most likely to choose.

Finally, consider a third sort of Coordination Game. There, once again, each player thinks one option is better than the other, but on this scenario different options are better for different players. In Figure 5.3, Speaker 1 prefers Language $L1$ to Language $L2$: if they coordinate on the former, his payoff is 20, compared to 10 if they coordinate instead on the latter (and zero if they fail to coordinate at all). Speaker 2, conversely, prefers Language $L2$ to $L1$: if they coordinate on $L2$, Speaker 2's payoff is 20, compared to 10 if they coordinate on $L1$ instead (and zero if they fail to coordinate at all).[8] Perhaps that difference arises because one of the speakers is more fluent in one language and the other is more fluent in the other; or it may arise because different languages are better suited to the sorts of discourse in which each speaker wants to engage (poetry versus engineering, say).

		Speaker 2	
		Language $L1$	Language $L2$
Speaker 1	Language $L1$	(20,10)	(0,0)
	Language $L2$	(0,0)	(10,20)

Figure 5.3 Language as an Unequal Coordination Game

Figure 5.3 depicts an 'Unequal Coordination Game'. It is still a *Coordination Game*, in the sense that both players would prefer to coordinate on one or other of the options rather than each choosing a different option. But it is an *Unequal* Coordination Game, in the sense that different options are differentially rewarding for different players. Choosing a convention in such circumstances therefore involves a distributional struggle in a way that choosing a convention to resolve an Equal or Cooperative Coordination Game does not. But however great the conflict of interest there may be among players over which convention is chosen, Unequal Coordination Games are still Coordination Games in which every player still prefers any of the possible conventions and associated coordinated solutions to not coordinating at all.[9]

The larger point is simply this. To say that 'language is a set of conventions to resolve coordination problems' is not to deny that the conventions of language may differentially advantage some speakers over others. True, insofar as language is a solution to a coordination problem, all speakers are better

---

[8] Figure 5.3 is adapted from Lewis (1969, p. 11). Luce and Raiffa (1957, pp. 90–3) dub it the 'Battle of the Sexes'. Hardin (1983) uses it to model the Pax Romana.

[9] And as Schelling (1958) argues, again, if there is something (perhaps in the labelling of the options, for example) to suggest to both players which of the coordinated solutions to pursue, even the player for whom that solution is second-best will opt to pursue it instead of risking a much more costly failure to coordinate at all.

off following the convention than not. But they are not necessarily all *equally* better off.[10]

5.1.2 The Choice of Language Confers Advantage and Disadvantage

It is, many say, a 'linguistic injustice' that some people enjoy advantages from their native tongue being the 'global language' while others suffer disadvantages from theirs not being.[11]

In part, that is a matter of the costs that the latter must bear, and the former need not, in learning the global language in addition to their own native tongue.[12] In part, that is a matter of native speakers of the global language typically being more proficient and hence more effective at communicating in their native tongue than those who acquired it as a second language.[13] In part, that is a matter of native speakers of the global language clustering in communities with other native speakers of it, and those communities being for that reason preferred sites for basing activities conducted in the global language.[14]

As has been widely observed, the ecology of languages worldwide is radically hierarchical:

> There are thousands of ['peripheral languages' which,] all together, ... are used by less than 10 percent of humankind .... [M]embers of the various peripheral [language] groups are ... likely to acquire one and the same second language, one that is therefore 'central' to these groups. All or most communication between the peripheral groups occurs through this central language.... At th[e] next level, a number of central languages are connected through their multilingual speakers to one very large language group that

---

[10] The focus of this chapter is on conventions of language, in particular. But notice that the same issues arise whenever everyone following the same convention is required to solve some social problem. In global trade and financial markets, there is for example a strong incentive for all participants to employ the same currency as the 'unit of account for invoicing' and as a 'safe store of value' (Gopinath and Stein 2021). The result is that all parties converge on the same currency—currently the US dollar, in previous eras the British pound sterling—which enjoys 'exorbitant privilege' in consequence (Eichengreen 2011). It has been estimated that the US economy gains US$100 billion per year from the US dollar being the global reserve currency (Herzog 2021b, p. 935).

[11] Kymlicka and Patten 2003. Van Parijs 2010, 2011. Arguably 'linguistic injustice' is *ipso facto* a 'structural injustice', since languages are after all themselves structures. But it is clearly so when, as 'in most situations', it is 'caused by social processes that reproduce the effects of past injustices', particularly in 'postcolonial contexts' (Song 2022, p. 350).

[12] Van Parijs (2011, sec. 2.1) thus describes 'Anglophones as free riders'.

[13] Van Parijs (2004, pp. 124–5) thus refers to 'undeserved linguistic rents'. See more generally Van Parijs 2011, chs 2–3.

[14] And, in consequence, attracting skilled migrants who are proficient in the global language away from their countries of origin where some other language is the native tongue (Van Parijs 2000).

occupies a 'super-central' position within the system. It serves purposes of long-distance and international communication. Quite often this is a language that was once imposed by a colonial power and after independence continued to be used in politics, administration, law, big business, technology and higher education. There are about a dozen of these super-central languages.... Th[e] 'hyper-central' language that holds the entire constellation together is, of course, English. In the present world English is the language of global communication.[15]

Those patterns can be easily explained in terms of 'network externalities' of the sort already discussed.[16] Just as with a telephone system, so too with a language: the point of language is to communicate with others; and the more people there are who speak any given language, the more valuable it is in those terms for you to speak it yourself. That explains how, once some language acquires a bit of an advantage over other languages, it quickly becomes dominant—central or super-central or hyper-central, in the above terms.[17]

Of course, that is not the whole story. The sheer *number* of speakers with whom you can communicate in any given language is one thing; the *value* of communicating with them is often quite another. If you want to talk to the powerful and important, you had better speak in their language.[18] That explains why English is the global *lingua franca*, despite the fact it has only half the total number of speakers (combining native and second speakers) as Mandarin.[19]

These processes of language acquisition and change currently being observed cross-nationally had of course previously occurred within countries. In most countries it was historically the case that 'the majority of the population had a mother tongue, typically labelled a "dialect", that differed notably from the national language, as used in the media and the educational system, in high culture and political life, and in business transactions beyond the local level.'[20] Those dialects were sometimes more-or-less mutually intelligible,

---

[15] De Swaan 2001, sec. 1.1. On language in colonial relations, see Gal (1989, pp. 355–8).

[16] In Sections 4.2 and 4.6 above; see also Sections 6.1.2.1, 7.3, and 9.3.1 below.

[17] Grewal 2008, pp. 71–88. When De Swaan (2001, ch. 2) describes languages as 'hyper-collective goods', it is that aspect of them to which he refers.

[18] For an example of these dynamics at the micro-level, 'Suppose that I am particularly anxious to be understood by you, because my interests can be seriously affected by your grasping or believing what I am saying, whereas for you nothing of any importance is at stake in our conversation. Both you and I are then more likely to use your better language, even if you are more fluent in my better language than I am in yours.... Consequently the wealthy will tend to be more often on the comfortable side than the poor, the bosses more often than the workers, the powerful more often than the powerless....' (Van Parijs 2011, pp. 19–20).

[19] Just over 500 million, compared to just over 1 billion, on most estimates; see e.g. <https://www.nationsonline.org/oneworld/most_spoken_languages.htm>.

[20] Van Parijs 2004, pp. 135–6.

sometimes barely so, sometimes not at all.[21] One or another of those dialects eventually became established as the national language (or one of a few officially recognized).[22] Sometimes that happened through deliberate top-down interventions, typically through the educational system.[23] Often it happened, at least in large part, through bottom-up processes of the sort just described.[24]

Within countries, as between them, those whose dialect became established as the dominant language enjoyed clear advantages vis-à-vis those whose dialects remained mere dialects.[25] There are of course sheer status advantages which flow simply from the prestige enjoyed by speakers by virtue of the sheer fact that their dialect has become the dominant one; I will say more on that score in Section 5.1.3. For the moment, let us concentrate purely on the pragmatics of the matter. Native speakers of what has become the dominant language are able to communicate more comfortably and effectively in the language in which matters of widespread general interest are discussed. Those who do not speak the dominant language or speak it only as a second language are at a linguistic handicap in those discussions.[26]

That in turn leads 'persons without adequate command of the ... prevailing language [to] exclude themselves from the pursuit of economic, political and social opportunities that require competence in that language and develop linguistically differentiated networks, institutions and economic niches.... Different language repertoires are [thus] implicated in the production and reproduction of inequality ... by virtue of their differential values as languages of participation and social connectedness'. This, Brubaker emphasizes, is importantly different from people being discriminated against on the basis of their linguistic skills.[27] Instead, it is a *self-organized processes of social separation.... It is a kind of agentless exclusion, an exclusion without excluders, but it is no less efficacious for that.*'[28]

Let us be clear as to how very consequential it can be to be on the wrong side of a linguistic divide. Laitin and Ramachandran offer robust evidence of various sorts that the official language of the country being distant from

---

[21] As I know well from having moved from Oxford to Glasgow for my first job. For a more formal discussion, see Haugen (1966, pp. 926–7).
[22] Haugen 1966. Even where multiple languages are officially recognized—in Belgium, Canada, and Switzerland, for example—'single languages are privileged within almost all territorial subunits, and the regime of strict parity holds, with a few exceptions, only at the federal level' (Brubaker 2015, p. 11).
[23] Gellner 1983, ch 3; Brubaker 2015. On the French case, see Weber's (1976) classic analysis *Peasants into Frenchmen*. On more recent African cases, see Mazrui (1972, esp. chs 6–7) and Laitin (2007).
[24] Van Parijs 2010, pp. 186–7.
[25] 'The elevation by authoritative fiat of a dialect to the status of an official language of a political entity' is the very first example Weber (1968, p. 941) offers in his discussion of 'domination'.
[26] Van Parijs 2011, pp. 97–102.
[27] And all the more so from Bourdieu's (1977a) 'symbolic domination'.
[28] Brubaker 2015, pp. 17, 19, 23.

local indigenous languages negatively impacts the health and human capital of people in that country. '[T]he magnitude of the estimates is large'—so large that, 'if a country like Zambia were to adopt Mambwe instead of English as its official language', the social and economic consequences of its doing so would cause it to 'move up 44 positions in the [Human Development Index] ranking and become similar to a country like Paraguay in human development levels'.[29] Those effects are not only strongly significant statistically in macro-level cross-national comparisons. They are likewise in individual-level data from India and 11 African countries, where it has been found that having a mother tongue distant from the official language significantly negatively impacts a person's educational, occupational, health, and wealth outcomes.

5.1.3 Languages as Status Markers

Language is often a marker of social status, and hence serves to confer (or confirm or reinforce) positional advantage of the sort discussed in Section 3.1.1. I shall turn to contemporary examples shortly. But let me begin by recalling some examples that are much older.

Consider the status of Latin—not just in the Roman Empire and not just in the Middle Ages, but well beyond. The Roman Catholic Church declared the Latin Vulgate its authorized version of the Bible at the Council of Trent in the sixteenth century.[30] The Roman Catholic Mass continued to be celebrated in Latin (a language most parishioners did not understand) until 1964 when the Second Vatican Council at long last permitted it to be celebrated in the local vernacular. Latin was also the language of learning down to the Enlightenment and beyond. While Hobbes published his *Leviathan* in English in 1651, the more authoritative version is the revised Latin edition he published in 1668.[31] Kant claimed a famous Latin phrase—'*sapere aude*' 'dare to know'—as the slogan of the Enlightenment, even if he himself often wrote in German.[32] In short, Latin was for very long the language of the elite, while the *hoi poloi* conversed in the vernacular.

In more recent eras, there were characteristically 'courtly languages' that differed from those spoken by the wider community. 'Whenever ... an elite is familiar with the language of another nation, it is tempting to make use of

---

[29] Laitin and Ramachandran 2016, p. 458.
[30] In contrast, English became the official language of the Church of England in 1559, shortly after its separation from the Church of Rome (Shagan 2017, p. 41).
[31] The English and Latin texts are presented in parallel to one another in Noel Malcolm's authoritative Clarendon Edition (Hobbes 1651/2012).
[32] In his 1784 essay, 'What is Enlightenment?' The phrase originates in Horace's *First Book of Letters* in 20 BCE.

this as the medium of government....'—not just 'as a matter of convenience' but, more nefariously, to insulate elite decision-making from popular inputs.[33] French was the *de facto* official language of the Russian royal court throughout the eighteenth and nineteenth centuries.[34] Frederick the Great of Prussia likewise preferred French to German, and enlisted the services of Voltaire himself to correct his own fractured French. And as Strachey remarks,

> Frederick was merely an extreme instance of a universal fact. Like all Germans of any education, he habitually wrote and spoke in French; like every lady and gentleman from Naples to Edinburgh, his life was regulated by the social conventions of France; like every amateur of letters from Madrid to St. Petersburg, his whole conception of literary taste, his whole standard of literary values, was French.[35]

Or, for one last example: part of Ataturk's project to modernize Turkey was to abolish the courtly language of 'Ottoman Turkish', which 'was an ornate, baroque language, used only by the elites of the decadent Ottoman court and its detached intellectuals'.[36]

Nowadays it is rare, in the developed world at least, for elites to speak a wholly different language from the masses over whom they rule and otherwise exercise power. But even if they 'speak the same language', they speak it in distinctly different ways.

Satirists ranging from playwright George Bernard Shaw to socialite Nancy Mitford have great fun with the fact that 'high' (or 'upper-class') forms of language differ markedly from 'low' (or 'non-upper-class') usage.[37] Sociolinguists have gone to great lengths mapping those differences across a wide range of languages.[38] Generalizing from his comparative study of Arabic, Swiss German, Haitian creole, and Greek, Ferguson concludes that high and low linguistic codes systematically differ in various ways: their function (the settings in which and purposes for which they are used); their prestige, their connection to the literary heritage in that language; their mode of acquisition (formal or informal); their standardization; their stability; their grammatical structure; their lexicon; and their phonology.[39]

---

[33] Haugen 1966, p. 928.
[34] Offord and Ryazanova-Clarke 2015.
[35] Strachey 1915/1922, p. 177.
[36] Tharoor 2014.
[37] Shaw 1913/1934; Mitford 1956.
[38] Ross (1956) described it as a difference between U (upper-class) and non-U (non-upper-class) linguistic codes. Ferguson (1959) described it as a difference between H (high) and L (low) varieties of the language. Bernstein (1971; cf. 1959) eventually came to describe it as a difference between a 'restricted' and 'elaborate code'.
[39] Ferguson 1959, pp. 328–36.

'The language of the upper classes is', of course, 'automatically established as the correct form of expression'.[40] Anyway, it is certainly the more prestigious. Time and again it has been shown that 'linguistic differences—in accent, variety, diction, stance, range of repertoires and so on—both express extra-linguistic inequalities and contribute to producing them'.[41] Indeed, in the nineteenth-century UK, 'Parliament successfully rejected petitions for universal suffrage on the basis of their "rough" linguistic style.'[42]

In his classic work on *Class, Codes and Control*, Basil Bernstein shows how the British class structure is perpetuated through educational institutions privileging more 'elaborate' linguistic codes over the more 'restricted' codes that working-class students employ in their interactions with their families, friends, and workmates.[43] In the US there are racially distinct linguistic codes and cultural codes more generally.[44] The necessity for minority group members to engage in code-switching when engaging with majority groups, particularly educationally and vocationally, constitutes a yet further burden that those already disadvantaged groups must bear.[45]

Now, the whole point of language is to communicate, and to communicate with one another you need to speak the same language. So insofar as already disadvantaged groups speak very differently, they will be dispreferred conversational partners for those who are among the advantaged. That constitutes a disadvantage in itself, and it can lead to further disadvantages of a more material sort as well. As Brubaker remarks,

> Homophily may become statistically visible as differential frequency of association with specific categories of others [which] ... may be generated by a vague and tacit sense of comfort, style, pleasure or compatibility, without any

---

[40] Haugen 1966, p. 925; Bourdieu 1977a, 1991.

[41] Brubaker 2015, p. 4. Of course, even in the absence of linguistic differences 'a speaker's membership in an already disadvantaged social group [can] make ... it difficult or impossible for her to deploy discursive conventions in the normal way, with the result that the performative force of her utterances is distorted in ways that enhance disadvantage'. Kukla (2014, p. 441) argues that 'discursive injustice' of that sort is encountered by people disadvantaged in terms of gender, race, class, home region, and disability. On such 'silencing' more generally, see Hornsby and Langton (1998).

[42] Gal 1989, p. 355, citing Smith 1984. As Fraser (1992, p. 119) observes, in the deliberative spaces that Habermas (1962/1989) reports opening up in the eighteenth century, 'discursive interaction within the bourgeois public sphere was governed by protocols of style and decorum that were themselves correlates and markers of status inequality. These functioned informally to marginalize women and members of the plebeian classes and to prevent them from participating as peers.'

[43] Bernstein 1971. The formal properties of these 'restricted codes' is subject to dispute within linguistics (Gal 1989, pp. 350–2), but the sociological effect of people being sorted by manner of speech is not.

[44] Baugh 2000.

[45] Fryer and Torelli 2005; Morton 2014; Brennan 2018. On code-switching more generally see Gumperz (1982) and Gal (1987).

identification of or orientation to specific categories of self or other. Linguistic repertoires and styles ... may be an important part of what generates this tacit sense of compatibility.[46]

Differences in cultural codes can have the same effects as differences in linguistic ones. According to Rosabeth Kanter, the best explanation for the absence of women in managerial ranks of US corporations before the 1980s was that, when hiring, male executives preferred 'ease of communication and hence social certainty over the strains of dealing with persons who are "different"'.[47]

5.1.4 Manipulating Language: The Implicit and Unspoken

Finally, note how differential facility with language can differentially enable people to manipulate language to their advantage. Not only is it a matter of some people being able to speak more smoothly, clearly, precisely, elegantly, or persuasively than others. Nor is it only a matter of some people being better schooled in the rhetorical arts than others. The capacity for language to be manipulated goes more deeply to the nature of language use itself.[48]

Language is used to communicate among people who, inevitably, have limited time and attention.[49] In consequence, most communication is to some greater or lesser extent gestural.[50] The full proposition being asserted and the reasons for believing it are not set out in tedious detail, certainly at least not in the first instance.[51] People say only as much as they think they need to say for

---

[46] Brubaker 2015, p. 18. He pointedly adds: 'When patterns of differential association arise in this way, ... they do not fit the discrimination ... paradigm.... [P]atterns of differential association can ... arise from the ubiquitous phenomenon of homophily. Discrimination presupposes an orientation, conscious or unconscious, to specific categories of insiders or outsiders; homophily does not.'

[47] Kanter 1977, pp. 49, 58, and ch. 3 passim; see similarly Reskin 2003, p. 3. This is a special case of 'cultural-matching' in hiring decisions more generally (Rivera 2012). On homophily in social networks more generally, see Section 4.3.

[48] Here I shall focus on the role of hidden presuppositions (and implications). But language can be manipulated to advantage in other ways as well; 'systematically misleading expressions' (Ryle 1931–1932) might be more successfully deployed by some than others, for example.

[49] On this, see further Chapter 10 below.

[50] As Lewis (1979, p. 339) puts it, 'At any state in a well-run conversation, a certain amount is presupposed.' See similarly Stalnaker 1973, 1999.

[51] Particularly among people who know each other well and hence have a pretty clear idea of what they can take as common background information when conversing with one another. This is what Gazdar (1979, cf. Bernstein 1971) argues is really going on when a 'restricted code' is seemingly being employed; this interpretation is supported by Ferguson's (1959, p. 329) finding that restricted codes are typically employed in 'conversation with family, friends and colleagues', whatever one's class position.

the other person to 'get it'.⁵² And only if the other obviously does not 'get it' do they bother elaborating.

Now, in this conversational shorthand much is left implicit and much is elided.⁵³ Furthermore—and this is where the possibility for deliberate manipulation enters the picture—much is implied without being said. 'Donald has not once gone to jail' implies that Donald has committed crimes (indeed, more than once).⁵⁴ 'Have you stopped beating your wife?' implies that you ever started. 'The king of France is bald' presupposes that there is a (singular) king of France.⁵⁵

Of course, other parties to the conversation can always call out the speaker and challenge the presupposition. Your interlocutor can cancel the presupposition by replying, 'But Donald has committed no crimes', 'I have never beaten my wife', or 'France has no king.' But the conversational implicature stands until and unless it is cancelled in that way.⁵⁶

Taking advantage of that fact, someone who is facile in manipulating language might in that way 'smuggle in' a presupposition that others would never accept had it been forthrightly asserted.⁵⁷ That is a way of 'laying linguistic traps' for others who are less linguistically adept. Calling the department of state responsible for the military the Department of Defense implies that the country is under threat, and so on—as any reader of Orwell's *Nineteen Eighty-four* will know.⁵⁸ Much propaganda works in a similar way, not by advancing the propositions it is trying to get accepted directly but rather by treating them as background assumptions from a stock of common knowledge that is 'not at issue'.⁵⁹

Implicit messaging like that is also crucial for communicating things that cannot be said explicitly. In her book *The Race Card*, Tali Mendelberg points to 'two contradictory elements in American politics: powerful egalitarian norms about race, and a party system based on the cleavage of race'. As she goes

---

⁵² That is to say, they follow the conversational maxims: 'be brief'; 'make your contribution as is required' but 'do not make your contribution more informative than is required' (Grice 1975, p. 67). As Lewis (1979, p. 339) remarks, 'it is peculiar to say, ... "All Fred's children are asleep, and Fred has children." The first part requires and thereby creates a presupposition that Fred has children; so the second part ... has no conversational point'.

⁵³ Stalnaker 1973; Lewis 1979.

⁵⁴ This is a variant on an example by Grice (1975, p. 65).

⁵⁵ Lewis 1979, p. 339.

⁵⁶ That is Lewis' (1979, p. 340) 'rule for accommodation of presupposition'. See similarly: Grice 1975; Stalnaker 2002.

⁵⁷ Whether it counts as 'lying' strictly speaking, or merely 'misleading', is an open question (cf. Stokke 2017, 2018; Viebahn 2020). But that issue need not be resolved for present purposes.

⁵⁸ Goodin 1980, pp. 96–101 and ch. 4 passim. Orwell 1949.

⁵⁹ Stanley 2015, pp. 134–5.

on to explain, 'The contradiction among these conditions can be resolved most effectively through implicit racial communications.'[60] This is the way that manipulative political dog-whistling works. George W. Bush could appeal to born-again Christians, without being seen to be doing so by other voters who would vote against him if they perceived him as being in the pockets of those religious fanatics, by employing a code-phrase ('wonder-working power') that sounded innocuous to non-fundamentalists but that was recognized by fundamentalists as their way of evoking the power of Christ.[61]

5.2 Coding Categories

The words of a language encode concepts, and concepts fundamentally constitute categories.[62] Those categorizations embedded in a language can, in themselves, also serve to create and perpetuate advantage.

According to one famous theory, how we perceive something is shaped in part by the concepts available to us for describing it.[63] Benjamin Lee Whorf states the theory most boldly:

> We dissect nature along lines laid down by our native language. The categories and types that we isolate from the world of phenomena we do not find there because they stare every observer in the face; on the contrary, the world is presented in a kaleidoscope flux of impressions which has to be organized by our minds—and this means largely by the linguistic systems of our minds. We cut nature up, organize it into concepts, and ascribe significances as we do, largely because we are parties to an agreement to organize it in this way—an agreement that holds throughout our speech community and is codified in the patterns of our language. The agreement is of course, an implicit and unstated one, but its terms are absolutely obligatory; we cannot talk at all except by subscribing to the organization and classification of data that the agreement decrees. We are thus introduced to a new principle of relativ-

---

[60] Mendelberg 2001, pp. 6–7.
[61] Saul 2018.
[62] The *Oxford English Dictionary* defines 'concept' (n., def. I.2) as 'a mental representation of the essential or typical properties of something, considered without regard to the peculiar properties of any specific instance or example'.
[63] Here I discuss categories that purport to 'describe' people and things. As a result of other forms of 'social categories ... individuals get conferred onto them a social status in contexts and this status consists in constraints and enablements on their behavior' (Ásta 2019, p. 392). See Section 3.1.1 for a discussion of that.

ity, which holds that all observers are not led by the same physical evidence to the same picture of the universe, unless their linguistic backgrounds are similar, or can in some way be calibrated.[64]

An extreme version of that hypothesis would say 'the limits of my language are the limits of my world', understood as 'you do not see what you cannot say'.[65]

There is reason to doubt that. For example, Bernstein reports that when a speaker of a lower-class restricted code is presented with a more sophisticated and elaborated way of expressing his thought, he will often say, 'That is precisely what I meant!'[66] If he is reporting accurately, he had the thought without having the words or the capacity to string them together in that more sophisticated way. So the limits of his language were not, as it turns out, the limits of his world.

Still, even if the bolder forms of that claim are not viable, a weaker version most certainly is correct. As Donald Davidson says, 'languages that have evolved in distant times or places may differ extensively in their resources for dealing with one or another range of phenomena. What comes easily in one language may come hard in another....'[67]

Others inspired by William James' psychology point out that 'reality is usually too complex to be perceived and apprehended without the help of categories', which 'are always to some extent simplifications of a more complex reality'.[68] Conceptual categories are akin to 'data containers'.[69] Novel phenomena tend to get assimilated, however inappropriately, to familiar coding categories—as for example when Tocqueville coded the birthright privilege of white Americans as akin to those of the European nobility.[70] And inappropriate or incomplete coding categories can profoundly distort our understanding

---

[64] Whorf 1940/1956. For one example, Greek has one word for a darker shade of blue (ble) and another for a lighter shade of blue (ghalazio). Thierry et al. (2009, p. 4567) say that this leads to 'faster perceptual discrimination of these colors in native speakers of Greek than in native speakers of English ... which establishes an implicit effect of language specific terminology on human color perception' (quoted in Ginsburgh and Weber 2020, p. 356).

[65] That is a widespread but inaccurate gloss on Wittgenstein's (1922, proposition 5.6) famous quotation. Given the 'picture theory of language' in the *Tractatus*, his meaning was surely the opposite: what is in the world to picture itself sets limits on how your language can talk about it.

[66] Bernstein 1959, p. 313.

[67] Davidson 1973-4, p. 6. Bernstein (1959, p. 312) similarly remarks, 'Language is ... one of the most important means of synthesising, and *reinforcing* ways of thinking, feeling and behaviour.... It does not, of itself, prevent the expression of specific ideas ..., but certain ideas and generalizations are facilitated rather than others.'

[68] Rydgren (2009, p. 75), building on James (1890).

[69] Hempel 1952; Sartori 1975, p. 20; Goodin 1980, p. 207 and ch. 3 more generally.

[70] Ikuta and Latimer 2021.

of one another and our social relations, as so powerfully shown in Charles Mills' famous work on 'white ignorance'.[71]

Data for which there is no container can easily get lost.[72] In that way, conceptual gaps cause people to overlook action opportunities.[73] For a macro-level illustration of that, consider how traditional economic data coding categories (focusing on 'factor share' of income accruing to labour versus capital, for example) obscured the disproportionate increases in the incomes of the richest 1 per cent of Americans. The absence of that coding category from traditional compilations of economic data made Piketty and Saez's findings about the rapid growth in those top incomes come as a huge surprise. That in turn led to 'the income share of the top 1 per cent' becoming a coding category of special interest in statistical collections going forward.[74]

Here is another dramatic micro-level illustration of how easily we might overlook things for which we have no ready conceptual category. It comes from psychological experiments on 'fault tree analysis'. Experimental subjects were presented with a hypothetical problem, 'The car won't start', and tasked with assigning probabilities to the various possible reasons for that. They were supplied with a 'fault tree' diagram listing various possible causes and, alongside those, a residual category of 'all other problems' to cover all causes not otherwise specified. Some of the experimental subjects were given a diagram with a more extensive itemization of possible causes, while others were given a 'pruned' fault tree that omitted several possible causes specifically itemized in the other subjects' fault trees.

Logically, those seeing the 'pruned' fault tree should attribute to the 'everything else' branch a probability that is the sum of the probabilities that the other group attributed to that branch plus all the branches omitted from the pruned fault tree. But by that standard, even expert auto mechanics substantially underestimate the probability of the cause being among the items not specifically itemized on a pruned fault tree. Those viewing the pruned version *should*, by that standard, have said that the probability of the fault lying along the 'other' branch was 44.1 per cent—whereas they *actually* estimated

---

[71] Mills 2007; but see also Martin (2021), who shows that there is more than merely Mills' cognitivist side to this story. See, more generally Dotson (2014).
[72] Or, alternatively, it goes unanalysed or misanalysed. Computer science teaches us that data must be pre-coded at least to some extent for it to admit of computer analysis: talk of '"raw data" is an oxymoron'; 'the more appropriate distinction for computer science is one between relatively less-structured and relatively more-structure data' (Koopman 2022, p. 347).
[73] Pocock 1971.
[74] Hirschman 2021; Piketty and Saez 2003.

it at under half that (21.5 per cent).⁷⁵ This constitutes dramatic evidence from the psychology laboratory of just how likely people are to overlook or underestimate that for which they have no proper coding category.

In the social world, many (Marxists and others) adopt a power-inflected interpretation of the biases built into cultural and linguistic codes.⁷⁶ They insist that

> authorized or hegemonic linguistic practices ... carry cultural definitions of social life that serve the interests of dominant classes.... The capacity of language ... to represent the world is not ... transparent and innocent ... but is fundamentally implicated in relations of domination. Whether the term is hegemony [Gramsci], symbolic domination [Bourdieu], oppositional culture [Williams], subjugated discourse [Foucault], or heteroglossia [Bakhtin], the central insight remains: control of the representations of reality is ... a source of social power....⁷⁷

Miranda Fricker similarly sees unequal power relations as underlying the 'asymmetrical cognitive disadvantage' that she associates with 'hermeneutic injustice':

> relations of unequal power can 'skew' the collection of hermeneutical resources. In other words, because those in power are able to determine the collection of hermeneutical resources that constitute a social imagination, they rarely find themselves without the words and phrases needed to communicate their experiences to others. The powerless, on the other hand, must make do with the social meanings available to them, many of which will be inadequate to the task of interpreting and communicating their own experiences.⁷⁸

I am myself inclined towards the less Manichean version of that story. It is not necessarily the case that linguistic and cultural codes were put into place with the intention of protecting existing advantage. Sometimes they might have

---

⁷⁵ Fischhoff, Slovic, and Lichtenstein 1978, p. 342. In psychological terms, they assign blame for this phenomenon to the 'availability' heuristic.
⁷⁶ As a variation on Marx and Engels' (1845/1972, I.A.2, pp. 136–7) declaration, 'The ideas of the ruling class are in every epoch the ruling ideas.... The class which has the means of material production at its disposal, has control at the same time over the means of mental production, so ... [they] rule as thinkers, as producers of ideas, and regulate the production and distribution of the ideas of their age: thus their ideas are the ruling ideas of the epoch'.
⁷⁷ Gal 1989, p. 348. To that list she might have added Fricker (1999).
⁷⁸ Fricker (2007, pp. 148, 161), as glossed by Dieleman (2015, p. 801).

been, of course. My argument is merely that that is not necessarily *always* the case.[79]

The version of all those claims that seems to me most credible rests on two planks. First, the facts of the world are simply too numerous for our limited minds to process completely.[80] We need some simplifying sorting categories into which to put them to limit the complexity.[81] Categories, in turn, make some things stand out as obvious, and submerge others.[82] Those categories, in addition, are not unbiased. They better serve the interests of some rather than others—sometimes deliberately, sometimes inadvertently.[83]

Second, for a great many purposes we need to coordinate socially on the categories we use.[84] The driver here is the same as underlies the imperative towards 'standardization' more generally. Standards can serve their purpose only if everyone (or enough others) within the relevant group employs the *same* standards.[85]

There is of course no denying that imposing standards is an exercise of power and an instrument of social control as well.[86] But bracket that. The

---

[79] Broadly, the alternative account that I offer below is in line with the 'social cognition processes' explanation of stereotyping and discrimination (Fiske 1998; Reskin 2000)—but with a twist at the end.

[80] 'The world provides us with more facts and distinctions than we could ever know what to do with', as Haslanger (1995, p. 101) puts it. I further discuss these issues in Chapter 10.

[81] Categories 'are fundamental to the ability to perceive, remember, plan and act' (Banaji 2002, p. 15102). '[O]ur brains seek to minimize cognitive effort in part through automatic categorization and association. According to considerable experimental evidence, we automatically categorize people.... We also automatically link certain traits to social categories. In other words, we stereotype people based on group membership' (Reskin 2003, p. 9; Tilcsik 2021). In his pathbreaking study of *The Nature of Prejudice*, Gordon Allport (1954/1979, p. 20) was firm on this point: 'The human mind must think with the aid of categories.... Once formed, categories are the basis for normal prejudgment. We cannot possibly avoid this process. Orderly living depends on it.'

[82] As Walter Lippman (1922/1997, pp. 54–5) said when introducing the concept of 'stereotypes' as applied to human groups: 'For the most part we do not first see, and then define, we define and then see. In the great blooming, buzzing confusion of the outer world we pick out what our culture has already defined for us and we tend to perceive that which we have picked out in the form stereotyped for us by our culture.' Lippman's point pertains to understanding and interpretation, but a similar point can be made about available action repertoires, which are similarly socially 'scripted' (Shiller 2019).

[83] Tilly (1998, pp. 10, 72, and ch. 3) speaks of 'exploitation' and 'opportunity hoarding' when discussing 'categories [that] support durable inequality'. That occurs, he argues, 'when they combine with hierarchies.... Each reinforces the other.... [A] relatively impermeable barrier reduces the likelihood that equal relations will form across it, while asymmetrical relations based on unequal resources justify the boundary and render it more visible.' See similarly Massey 2008.

[84] Wagner 1994; Thévenot 2016; Fourcade and Healy 2017a, pp. 288–9.

[85] That is to say, there are 'network externalities' in the sense described in Section 4.2 (Katz and Shapiro 1985). As Kindleberger (1983, p. 377) observes, 'Standards of measurement—whether linear, weight, bulk, temperature, time or value (i.e. the unit-of-account function of money)— ... have economies of scale. The more producers and consumers use a given standard, the more each gains from the use by others through gains in comparability and interchangeability.'

[86] Scott 1998; Timmermans and Epstein 2010. A prime example was the FHA's racial categorization of households for purposes making home loans: if there was a single non-white living in the household (other than servants), then that whole household was coded as non-white (Koopman 2022, p. 353; see further Section 8.2.1 below).

point remains that standardization is nonetheless an invaluable tool of social coordination. It renders the things that have been standardized comparable and compatible with one another. Once screw threads are standardized, you can use a screw from one manufacturer to replace one made by any other.[87] Once rail gauges are standardized, trains can travel without interruption across the entire network.[88] With the advent of standardized educational testing, universities can reliably compare applicants from different secondary schools.

Now put those two thoughts together. Coding things into categorical pigeonholes is essential to our understanding and acting in the world, and to a large extent it is essential that we (or a great many of us anyway) use the same categories for that purpose.[89] From that it follows that even those who would ideally prefer that some other set of categories will nonetheless often have a powerful interest in employing the same categories as others do. That is simply to say that the 'Unequal Coordination Game' model of language developed in Section 5.1.1 generalizes to a wide range of other coding categories as well.[90]

None of that is to deny that the coding categories thus adopted work to differentially advantage some over others—and by being reapplied time and again, persistently so. Consider for example the way schools apply categories to students, sorting them into more and less academic streams, graduates and dropouts, and so on.[91] Those coding decisions have powerful repercussions on those thus categorized throughout their lives.

Categories of race and gender, and the stereotypes associated with them, are much-discussed examples of category-based inequality.[92] They are so very familiar examples, however, that it is important to stand back and see what all might be at work in them.[93] One thing, obviously, is cognitive bias: the prejudicial attribution of characteristics to a group that are statistically inaccurate

---

[87] Whitworth 1841.
[88] Various of the original Australian colonies adopted different gauges, and the capitals of all the subsequent states were finally connected by the same gauge only in 1995.
[89] So too does implementing the idea of 'rule of law' require us to generalize in ways that inevitably involves 'profiles, probabilities and stereotypes' (Schauer 2003).
[90] For an analysis of the emergence of 'dominant currencies' along broadly these lines, see Gopinath and Stein (2021).
[91] Domina, Penner, and Penner 2017.
[92] Haslanger 1995, 2000, 2005, 2012; Ridgeway 2014.
[93] Another thing at work is that those subject to the stereotyping themselves 'internalize' it, after some fashion, in ways that compromise their performance thus making the stereotype a self-fulfilling prophecy (Steele and Aronson 1995; Inzlicht and Schmader 2011). This will be discussed more fully in Section 6.1.2.2.

descriptions of the true characteristics of that group.[94] That is obviously rife.[95] But notice that even if the stereotypes were perfectly accurate group-level characterizations, they would nonetheless engender greater between-group inequalities than would have otherwise existed.[96] They would do so even in the absence of any 'imputation of dishonorable meanings to stereotypes of group difference', which also quite commonly occurs.[97]

The reason that that occurs is simply that every member of the group is then treated as the average member of her categorically defined group, eliding variability within the group.[98] Take an example. It is presumably a statistically accurate stereotype that black Americans on average have fewer years of formal schooling than white Americans. But clearly there are many black Americans who are more educated than a great many white Americans, or even the average white American.[99] Stereotypes like that, which simply stand in for individualized facts that can easily be checked whenever it really matters (as in hiring decisions for example), may not matter so much.[100] But stereotypes that stand in for unobservable attributes are much more invidious.[101]

Take another example: the way in which actuaries assess a person's risk profile when deciding how much to charge that person for insurance against some untoward event. They do so by sorting people into categories according to their fixed characteristics (demographic, medical history, etc.) and assigning to

---

[94] Cognitive biases are often at work. But that can also occur because the descriptors are being employed as 'generics'. Those can be true without the descriptor being true of remotely all tokens of the type. For example, it is generically true that 'birds lay eggs' even though a large proportion of (male) birds do not; and it is generically true that 'mosquitos carry West Nile virus' even though less than one percent of mosquitos actually carry the disease (Haslanger 2012, p. 450).

[95] For just one example: comparing the actual rates of offending while released on bail among black and white defendants while on bail, it is clear that bail judges are biased against blacks based on exaggerated stereotypes (Arnold, Dobbie, and Yang 2018).

[96] I focus here on stereotyping, but similar problems arise with predictive statistical models such as those used by parole boards to predict recidivism: instruments that are racially fair (equally predictively accurate) for all races can have disparate racial impact in generating different rates of false positives and false negatives for different races, if the base rates of recidivism among them differ (Chouldechova 2017; Kleinberg, Mullainathan, and Raghavan 2017; see similarly Goodin 1985a). This case is further discussed in Section 10.2.

[97] Due to an array of cognitive biases summarized by Anderson (2010, ch. 3).

[98] Blackburn (1998, p. 35) talks about the same phenomenon under the description 'typecasting'. Here I am adopting a 'descriptive' view of 'stereotypes' (Beeghly 2015; Tilcsik 2021)—what Leslie (2007) would call 'majority generics'.

[99] Similar 'statistical theories of discrimination' are offered by Arrow (1971) and Phelps (1972) and further discussed by: Akerlof 1976; Bolinger 2020; and Rosola and Cella 2020.

[100] There are things that can be done, in the organization of the workplace for example, to bring those individualized facts to people's attention and thus weaken the power of stereotypes (Reskin 2000, pp. 324–6; Tilcsik 2021).

[101] Loury (2002, p. 23) thus focuses upon 'statistical generalization[s] about some class of persons regarding what is taken with reason to be true about them as a class, but cannot be readily determined as true or false for any given member of the class'.

each individual a probability corresponding the frequency with which individuals in that categorical group have, on average, actually experienced that event in the past.[102] Typically actuaries have no other way to make that probability-cum-risk assessment. But notice that the consequence, once again, is to assign the same value to every individual within the categorical group, regardless of however much variation there might actually be within that categorical group.[103]

Attributing properties of the group to each individual member of it, and engendering inter-group inequalities as a result, is a consequence of category-based thinking quite generally. The specific problems to which that gives rise are, of course, a function of our drawing particular categorical distinctions where we do. Had we differentiated people according to some alternative categorical criteria, the group averages would have been different.

Still, insofar as there is any appreciable difference both among people within each of those categorical groups and between the group averages, the same sorts of effects would come about. There would be injustice to individuals, insofar as the categorical average is wrongly attributed to them individually.[104]

5.3 Interpretative Schema

The previous sections have dealt with the ways in which the choice of language and conceptual coding categories within them can bias social outcomes, advantaging some and disadvantaging others. The same, I shall now argue, is true of schemes for interpreting the world built out of those linguistic and conceptual materials and acting back upon them.[105]

Schemas, at their most general, are packages of interrelated categories and concepts—often ostensibly interrelated in a logical or causal way—that are

---

[102] Landes 2015, p. 521. I am grateful to Emily Katzenstein for reminding me of this example.

[103] Typically, of course, insurance underwriters will use several of a person's characteristics to determine what premium to charge, blending together actuarial risk assessments associated with each of them. That makes the assessment a little more 'individualized' (in the sense it is responsive to the particular constellation of characteristics displayed by any given individual); but this 'individualization' is still at root based on categorical group averages.

[104] Blum 2004, pp. 272–3, 282.

[105] As I put it elsewhere, 'Language ... is responsive to demands made on it. Suppose a language were originally neutral between various scientific theories.... Now suppose one becomes installed as the dominant paradigm and preeminent topic of scientific conversation. New distinctions required by that theory will inevitably find their way into the language, and at that point the language will begin looking biased.... The tendency for scientific language to be slanted in favour of the dominant paradigm appears to be merely an aspect of a more general phenomenon. It seems likely that linguistic biases in general reflect reality, and the need for people to talk about that reality, rather than the other way around' (Goodin 1980, p. 69).

used for interpreting, explaining, and acting upon the world.[106] Schemas are the 'mental' component of structures.[107] Social structures, on the best account of them, are 'composed simultaneously of schemas ... and of resources [that] ... mutually imply and sustain each other over time'.[108]

'Although schemas are variable and evolve across time and context', Haslanger rightly remarks that 'their elements are sticky and resist updating'.[109] Of course it is possible for schemas to be challenged and changed, repudiated and replaced. Paradigm shifts and revolutions, scientific and otherwise, are particularly dramatic instances of that.[110] More mundane shifts in interpretive schemes occur as multiple structures intersect and interact with one another, requiring each to adjust to the interpretive schemes embedded in the other.[111]

In extraordinary moments interpretive schemas might be highly visible and sharply contested. In more ordinary circumstances, however, schemas operate much more in the background.[112] Acting relatively invisibly, they channel our thought and, through it, our actions.[113] By operating in the background rather than foreground, interpretive schemas furthermore serve as sources of bias that remains only 'implicit'.[114]

The way in which they do so is this. Our interpretive schemes highlight some features of the world for us, while eliding others. They highlight some connections and associations, while eliding others.[115] In social psychological terms,

---

[106] As Haslanger (2015, p. 4) puts it, 'schemas are clusters of culturally shared (public) concepts, propositions, and norms that enable us, collectively, to interpret and organize information and coordinate action, thought, and affect'. See similarly: Sewell 1992, 2005; Aragon and Jaggar 2018, p. 450; Sangiovani 2018, p. 461; Haslanger 2019.
[107] Bourdieu 1977b, 1985.
[108] Sewell 1992, p. 13 (internal parentheses added).
[109] Haslanger 2015, p. 4. This is in part due to the looping feedback structures involved (Haslanger 2012, pp. 465–7; 2019, pp. 245–6). It is also due in part to the very fact that they are solutions to coordination problems, and changing them risks failures to coordinate.
[110] Kuhn 1962; Haslanger 2012, pp. 467–75.
[111] Sewell 1992, p. 19; Haslanger 2019.
[112] Haslanger (2017, pp. 149–50) thus distinguishes two kinds of 'oppression'. One is 'repressive' and is 'forced upon individuals through coercive measures'. The other is 'ideological' and is 'enacted unthinkingly or even willingly by the subordinated or privileged', who 'hardly notice their participation in practices that sustain ... privilege and power....'
[113] Sewell (1992, p. 22) similarly observes that the interpretive schema associated with 'deep structures' in particular 'tend to be relatively unconscious, in the sense that they are taken-for-granted mental assumptions or modes of procedure that actors normally apply without being aware that they are applying them'. Haslanger (2015, p. 1) similarly observes that, 'Our cognitive systems are constructed in such a way that perception, thought, and action are substantially influenced by cognitive structures that are not normally evident to us.... [E]xplicit deliberation enters the process for deciding how to act quite late, or only in special circumstances, if at all.'
[114] Haslanger (2015) similarly emphasizes the importance of situating 'implicit bias' in a larger structural setting, involving interpretive schemes and systems of social meaning. On implicit bias specifically, see: Greenwald and Banaji 1995; Greenwald and Krieger 2006; and Gendler 2011.
[115] DiMaggio 1997; Strauss and Quinn 1997; Hunzaker and Valentino 2019. See related discussions of 'connectionism' within cognitive science (Churchland 1995).

they provide 'frames'—which are a famous psychological source of heuristics and biases.[116] Our interpretive schema make some things seem natural and obvious, and others obscure or odd. They make some things seem to be just plain 'common sense'.

Yet we must see common sense itself as a 'cultural system', as Clifford Geertz has taught us.[117] Interpretative schema are social constructs. Their social construction is not completely unconstrained; they have to fit the external world tolerably well to do the interpretative work that has been set for them.[118] Still, just as with the choice of language in Section 5.1.1, so too are there multiple possible schema that would fit the external facts of the world about as well as one another. And, as in Section 5.1.1, different people might well differentially gain or lose, depending upon which schema is employed.[119]

There is another feature that the choice of interpretive schema and the choice of language have in common. For language, it is analytically true that people have to speak the same language (or anyway mutually intelligible ones) if they are to communicate at all, which is of course the whole point of language. With interpretive schema as well, it is often the case (if only contingently, but nonetheless commonly) that people must employ the same schema as those with whom they are interacting in order to succeed in pursuing their goals in interacting at all.[120] It may be logically possible for each person to interpret the world according to his own unique schema. But insofar as people are engaged in joint projects, either to interpret the world or

---

[116] Haslanger (2017, p. 156) for example calls 'cultural technes' 'a frame for socially meaningful action'. For psychological work on framing effects, see: Kahneman, Slovic, and Tversky 1982; Kahneman and Tversky 2000.

[117] Geertz 1975. 'Culture', in turn, 'is a set of social meanings tat shapes and filters how we think and act' (Haslanger 2017, p. 149). Some sociologists say that 'common sense' being 'a cultural system' is most clearly evident among small and episodic groups, such as Little League teams (Fine 1979). But Haslanger (2012, pp. 3–4) offers an even more compelling example from her personal history: just try moving from Connecticut to Louisiana in 1963, and you'll see how much 'common sense' you will have to 'relearn'.

[118] Of course those constraints are loosened to the extent that certain aspects of the world they are charged with interpreting are shaped, or even created, by those very schema themselves.

[119] For a prime example, consider the case of 'cognitive capture' of California regulators by the electricity industry there, which served to blind the regulators to the emergence of market power in that market. That resulted, on Rilinger's (2021) analysis, from a 'worldview problem' rather than an 'information problem'.

[120] Haslanger (2017, p. 156) writes that 'cultural technes have a function: they enable us to coordinate by providing the paths and signals that structure our [social] practices'; see similarly Haslanger (2012, pp. 455–65; 2018, pp. 237–40, 245; 2019). Sharing broadly the same understanding of the world (the same 'interpretive schema', as I have been calling it) is as necessary as sharing the same language in 'making ourselves understandable to one another' (McGeer 2007, p. 148). Enjoying a 'shared reality'—Hardin and Conley's [2000] term for my 'interpretive schema'—'helps people coordinate their expectations and behavior with respect to each other.... It is epistemically useful for individuals engaged in joint inquiry, as it keeps them "on the same page"' (Anderson 2012, p. 170).

to act in it, those projects are clearly facilitated by their seeing the world in broadly the same ways.[121] Insofar as it is necessary (or anyway very advantageous) for people to coordinate on the same interpretive scheme, each would once again prefer to accede even to a coordination scheme that is relatively disadvantageous for them rather than to fail to coordinate at all (just as in Section 5.1.1).

So far I have been discussing what follows from everyone wanting to use broadly the same interpretive schema as everyone else, to facilitate social coordination quite generally.[122] Next, suppose that people want more specifically to coordinate with one another on the same course of action, and notice how their shared interpretive schema shapes their choice of that.

Interpretive schema, as I have said, make certain things seem 'obvious'.[123] Suppose you want to coordinate on the same course of action (or whatever) as others around you do, and you know that those others want to do the same. Furthermore, you know that, given the interpretive scheme you know you share with the others, one of the alternative coordinated solutions will stand out as 'obvious' to all concerned. Then you can be confident that that is the one that will naturally be chosen by each of them. You might yourself actually prefer some other solution, and you might suspect that that is true of many others as well. But each of us can only benefit at all if every one of us chooses the same solution. The solution that everyone finds 'obvious' is the solution that others are most likely to choose, so that is the one you will (perhaps reluctantly) opt for yourself.

This is just an application of Thomas Schelling's famous theory of 'focal points' as solutions to coordination problems. Here is his example:

> Two people parachute unexpectedly into [an area], each with a map and knowing the other has [the same] one, but neither knowing where the other has dropped nor able to communicate directly. They must get together quickly to be rescued.[124]

---

[121] Goodin and Brennan 2001. As Sewell (1992, p. 21) says, 'The transpositions of schemas and remobilizations of resources that constitute agency are always acts of communication with others. Agency entails an ability to coordinate one's actions with others and against others, to form collective projects, to persuade, to coerce, and to monitor the simultaneous effects of one's own and others' activities.'

[122] I say more about coordination imperatives in Chapter 8.

[123] 'Nothing is so treacherous as the obvious', Schumpeter (1950, ch. 20) observes. Mary Douglas (1975) has similar things to say about 'self-evident' truths.

[124] Schelling 1960, p. 54; this is just an extension, with a homely story attached, of Schelling's (1958) earlier work on coordination games. See further Goodin (1980, pp. 212–13). For experimental evidence on the usefulness of salience in coordination see Mehta, Starmer, and Sugden (1994).

Where will they head to rendezvous? To whatever place is most salient on the map that they know they both share—the only bridge that is marked on the map, for example, if there are multiples of everything else.

Importantly, they will keep walking towards the one bridge that is marked on their shared map even if, along the way, they pass several other bridges unmarked on their shared map. What matters is not that it is *really* the only bridge, or even that each thinks that the other believes it to be. What matters is that, because it is the only bridge marked on the map, each believes that the other will regard it as the salient point in terms of their shared map at which they should rendezvous.[125]

Shared interpretive schema operate the same way as the parachutists' map in picking out certain solutions as 'obvious' ones upon which people who want to coordinate with one another can do so. They will play that role, even though the solution thus picked out is more advantageous for some than others, because even the latter prefer to coordinate on that solution rather than not coordinating at all. The relatively disadvantaged thus accede in coordination arrangements that leave them relatively disadvantaged, once the interpretive schema has 'rigged' perceptions of obviousness in this way.[126]

5.4 What Is to Be Done?

The standard solution proffered to structural injustice that is perpetuated by the mechanisms of language, coding categories, and interpretive schema is explicitly 'ameliorative'.[127] The suggestion is to alter them so as to cease perpetuating unfair disadvantage. Adopt gender-neutral language, for example. And more generally, ask ourselves,

> What is the point of having these concepts? What cognitive or practical task do they (or should they) enable us to accomplish? Are they effective tools to accomplish our (legitimate) purposes; if not, what concepts would serve these purposes better?[128]

---

[125] Goodin 1980, pp. 212–13.

[126] Worse still, they might be excluded from mutually beneficial joint action because their interpretive schema is 'simply incomprehensible' to those who are more advantaged: from the perspective of the advantaged, what the disadvantaged are saying may make no sense, because the interpretive resources they have developed to make sense of the experiences the advantaged share with one another are inadequate for comprehending the experiences of those from whom they are isolated' (Anderson 2012, p. 170).

[127] Many of those proposals go under the name of 'conceptual (re)engineering' (Burgess, Cappelen, and Plunkett 2020; Haslanger 2020; Podosky 2021, 2022).

[128] Haslanger 2000, p. 33; 2012, p. 367.

Of course 'our legitimate purposes' are multiple. The primary purpose of languages, coding categories and interpretive schema is presumably to understand, to explain and to communicate. I will call those collectively 'explanatory purposes'; and I presume that they are perfectly legitimate so far as they go.[129] But there are potentially competing 'political' purposes—eradicating oppression or social injustice, for example—for which some different languages, coding categories and interpretive schema might be better suited.[130] In her book *The Minority Body*, for example, Elizabeth Barnes embraces 'disability' as a 'social category people have found useful when organizing themselves in a civil rights struggle'—and she suggests that at least for those purposes 'disability *just is* whatever the disability rights movement is promoting justice for.'[131]

Explanatory and political purposes can work hand-in-glove, insofar as 'explaining social injustice is part of what will help us to address it'.[132] But they can also be in tension. A language, coding category, or interpretive schema that serves as a useful rallying cry for movement activists may be unhelpful, or worse, for understanding and explaining the phenomenon they are rallying against. Allowing anyone who so desires to claim (without further evidence or explanation) to be a victim of a certain sort of abuse and to claim compensation on that basis might be useful in expanding the support base for the movement against such abuse, for example, but it does so at the risk of emptying the concept of that abuse of any empirical meaning.

In a more dynamic sense, however, those explanatorily unhelpful self-descriptions around which people initially organize can sometimes be improved upon as a direct result of their self-organizing around them.[133] In that case, explanatory purposes may be well served by people who are similarly oppressed coming together and developing language, coding categories and interpretive scheme that help them, and others, better understand the conditions that oppress them. Of course, there is no guarantee that things will actually work out that way. Outsiders may be sceptical of the prospects. Still,

---

[129] Dougherty 2020.
[130] Haslanger 2000, p. 34,
[131] Barnes 2016, pp. 41, 43.
[132] Barnes 2016, p. 14.
[133] As Young (2000, pp. 165–6) writes, 'When a group's suffering or grievance cannot be expressed, or cannot be fully expressed, in hegemonic discourses, associational activity can support the development among those silenced new ways of seeing social relationships or labelling situations as wrong. In these self-organizing activities disadvantaged or marginalized sectors and groups sometimes articulate alternative self-conceptions in response to denigrating or devaluing positionings from the wider society.' Barnes (2016, pp. 41–2) sees 'disability' as 'a social category that people have used to explain what their experiences of social oppression have in common'—'a social category people have used to group themselves to work for progress and change'.

part and parcel of what it is to act in 'solidarity' with oppressed groups is to defer to their own strategic choices, of languages, coding categories, and interpretive schema among many other things.[134]

The worry with this strategy is of course ghettoization. The risk is that the new language, coding categories, and interpretive schema that the oppressed group develop among themselves will not catch on among the wider community, and it will remain something of a 'private language' among the oppressed. Private languages can have their uses, to be sure. In the Antebellum South of the US, plantation slaves used them to communicate subversive thoughts in ways that overseers would not detect; and 'hidden transcripts' more generally can be powerful 'weapons of the weak'.[135] If however the aim is not merely to facilitate private communication among the oppresses themselves, but instead (or in addition) to help others better understand the conditions that oppress them, then languages, coding categories and interpretive schema that remain confined to the oppressed group itself will fail in that further task.

---

[134] Kolers 2016. This is what Taylor (2015) calls 'expressional solidarity'.
[135] Genovese 1974, p. 436. Halliday 1976; Scott 1986.

6
Social Expectations and Norms Confer Advantage

Social expectations and norms underlie all of the linguistic codes, categories and interpretive schema discussed in the last chapter. Whenever people need to adopt the same of those as one another, each will opt for whichever she *expects* the others to adopt. And once (enough) others do so, that will become the *norm,* both a descriptively and prescriptively, among them.

Social norms and expectations also underlie all manner of other social practices and behaviours, as this chapter will show.[1] In those cases, as in the last chapter, the specific social norms and expectations that are in place benefit some more than others—and persistently so, since norms and expectations, once established, tend to be 'sticky 'and' self-perpetuating', applying the same way time and again.[2]

Norms and expectations serve as social stabilizers.[3] We naturally expect the future to be much like the past. I expect the sun to rise in the east tomorrow, just as it has done every previous morning.[4] Socially, too, our most realistic expectation about what other people will do or be in the future is what they have done or been in the past. The same is true of social norms. A few norms may be genuinely disruptive (think of Carnival, for example, and the norms surrounding it).[5] By and large, however, norms serve to facilitate social

---

[1] Furthermore, they are 'structural effects' (in the title of Blau's [1960] paper), in the sense that they are group-level rather than individual-level effects.

[2] The focus of this book is on the perpetuation of advantage, so this chapter will focus on the way in which the stickiness of norms helps to produce that result. But notice that when norms change (as sometimes they obviously do, sometimes precipitously), the distribution of benefits and burdens changes with them, sometimes dramatically. A prime example of 'norm substitution' with far-reaching consequences is when the IMF was suddenly converted to neo-liberalism (Kentikelenis and Babb 2019).

[3] As Mary Astell long ago said of 'custom': 'it is the most difficult thing imaginable to recall [i.e., retract, withdraw] our thoughts and withdraw the stream of our affections from that channel in which they were used to flow' (Astell and Norris 1695/2005, p. 117). See similarly Ross (1901, chs. 13, 15).

[4] This natural tendency carries over to circumstances in which it is almost certainly objectively not warranted. For example, warnings of the risk of earthquake after-shocks are discounted by people who escaped damage during the initial earthquake on the grounds that 'the first impact did not effect [sic.] me negatively, therefore, subsequent impacts will also avoid me' (Mileti and O'Brien 1992, p. 53).

[5] '[C]arnival celebrated temporary liberation from the prevailing truth and from the established order; it marked the suspension of all hierarchical rank, privileges, norms and prohibitions' (Bakhtin 1984, p. 10).

Perpetuating Advantage. Robert E. Goodin, Oxford University Press. © Robert E. Goodin (2023).
DOI: 10.1093/oso/9780192888204.003.0006

interactions along familiar lines and in that way ensure the smooth functioning of the existing social order. In so doing, of course, they help to reproduce the existing social order.[6]

In helping to perpetuate both themselves and the existing social order, social norms and expectations also tend to help perpetuate existing patterns of advantage and disadvantage. The patterns of normative expectations that in the past sustained certain people in privileged positions, and others in underprivileged positions, will most likely continue to do so into the future.

The first half of this chapter is organized around a distinction between 'descriptive' and 'prescriptive' norms and expectations.[7] Something is descriptively the norm if it is what most commonly actually occurs.[8] Something is prescriptively the norm if it is what ought to occur—however frequently or infrequently it might actually occur. Descriptive expectations pertain to what people think *will* happen; prescriptive expectations pertain to what people think *should* occur.[9] When someone says, 'I expected better of you', it is typically the latter sense that they are invoking. Both descriptive and prescriptive norms and expectations can serve to perpetuate advantage and disadvantage, as I shall proceed to demonstrate.

6.1 Descriptive Norms and Expectations

We have already seen in section 5.2 how judgments relying on a descriptive statistical norm can serve to cement in social disadvantage. Suppose you have no reliable information about the particular individuals before you, but you do have reliable statistical evidence that on average people with some trait (racial, for example) perform less well in some relevant respect than people with some other trait. Then you naturally will tend to hire someone with the latter trait

---

[6] In his classic analysis of the race problem in the mid-twentieth-century US, Myrdal (1944, pp. 1031–2) notes this implication of Sumner's (1934) discussion of 'mores' and dissents vigorously from it, saying it is 'crude and misleading when applied to a... society characterized by ... unceasing changes and differentiations of all valuations and institutions....' The subsequent history of race relations in the US more nearly bears out Sumner's characterization than Myrdal's on this point.

[7] For some purposes, we may be interested in the disjunct of 'what "is" *or* what "ought to be"'. For example, Nozick (1972, p. 112) distinguishes coercive 'threats' from non-coercive 'offers' by reference to what would have happened 'in the normal and expected course of events', where 'the term "expected" is meant to ... straddle *predicted* and *morally required*'. While that may be true to the colloquial understanding of 'coercion', analytically it is nonetheless important to draw a sharp distinction between descriptive and prescriptive.

[8] I thus use 'descriptive norm' to mean 'statistical norm', without regard to *why* that is the most common occurrence. This is in contrast to Muldoon et al. (2014, p. 8) who use the term to refer exclusively to cases that arise from 'the desire to conform to the behavior of others'.

[9] Both norms and expectations, in both their descriptive and prescriptive forms, admit of degrees. I can more or less strongly expect that something will or should occur; and the descriptive and prescriptive norms associated with those expectations can likewise be more or less strong. Shackle (1943) cashes out the descriptive aspects in terms of how 'surprised' you would be were that to occur.

rather than the former.[10] Statistically descriptive norms thereby form the basis for expectations, which in turn drive hiring decisions in ways that disadvantage members of the group that is expected to perform less well, who end up not being employed.

There are two ways in which acting on descriptive expectations can perpetuate existing advantage and disadvantage. First, as in the hiring case just described, acting on your *own* expectations makes those expectations (or something closely akin to them[11]) come true. And insofar as your expectations about what will occur in the future are based on what has occurred in the past, that process will serve to perpetuate the advantages and disadvantages that people have experienced in the past.

Whereas the first class of cases involves acting on your *own* expectation, the second class of cases involves acting on the basis of what *others* expect to occur. You may have various sorts of incentives to do that.[12] Once again, acting on the basis of what others expect to occur tends to make those expectations (or something closely akin to them) come true. In this second class of cases, however, it does so in ways that reinforce more widespread social understandings—and not just your own (possibly idiosyncratic) personal views—about what is to be expected to occur.

6.1.1 Acting on What *You* Expect to Happen

Here is a classic example of how expectations, when acted upon, become self-fulfilling prophecies.[13] A teacher expects a certain student (or type of student) not to perform well academically and, accordingly, does not invest much

---

[10] Arrow 1971. Phelps 1972. Rosola and Cella 2020. Tilcsik 2021. Another, probably more important, source of discrimination in hiring decisions is not informational but rather cognitive bias (prejudice, etc.) (Correll and Benard 2006). That, too, serves to ground expectations, and acting on those expectations leads to discrimination in hiring. 'Expectation states theory' predicts that people will create a status hierarchy based on expectations about people with certain attributes being better at accomplishing the task in view (Berger, Cohen and Zeldich 1972; Correll and Ridgeway 2003; Ridgeway 2014).

[11] In the hiring case, for example, the expectation in question was 'people with trait X are less employable' and the outcome was 'people with trait X are less likely to be employed'.

[12] The 'incentive' in question might just be your own desire, either simply to 'conform' to what others are doing (Muldoon et al. 2014) or to 'emulate' others whom you esteem (Goodin 2018b). But the more interesting cases, for purposes of this book, are those in which there is some compelling instrumental reason for doing so, rather than just the brute fact that you want to do so. One such instrumental reason might be that you think the others know something you do not (Bikhchandani et al. 1992; 1998; Hedström 1998, p. 307). Another might be that the value of a good to you is an increasing function of the number of others using the same good, as in the case of network externalities (introduced in chapter 4, and about which I shall more in sections 6.1.2.1, 7.3 and 9.3.1 below).

[13] Merton 1948; Biggs 2009; Schelling 1978, pp. 115–9; Blank 2005. As Schelling (1998, p. 38) says, 'a somewhat better term would probably be "self-realizing expectations"', with prophecies being only one source of the expectations'. Hedström and Swedberg (1998b, p. 18) define 'self-fulfilling prophecies' as cases where 'an initially false belief of a situation evokes behaviour that eventually makes the false

effort in that (or that type of) student. Being undertaught, and demotivated in consequence, those students underachieve academically—just as the teacher expected. That might have happened anyway, of course; the teacher might have assessed the students' academic aptitude perfectly correctly.[14] But even if the teacher had been wrong in that assessment, acting upon the expectation that those students would fail ensured that they failed. Conversely, students whom a teacher 'expects to go far' will be showered with opportunities and assistance, greatly facilitating their subsequent academic success and thus fulfilling he teacher's expectations.[15] One particularly well-designed study found, for example, that having a tenth-grade teacher who expects you will go on to complete university increases your chances of actually doing so by about as much as does your having enjoyed the benefits of being taught in small classes in primary school.[16]

Something similar happens with insurance. Actuarially fair insurance transforms statistically expected losses into sure-thing equivalents.[17] By definition, the price for 'actuarially fair' insurance against a loss (of your house in a flood, for example) *just is* the probability of the loss's occurring times the cost if it does occur.[18] Buying insurance at that price removes the risk, to be sure.[19] In so doing, however, it entrenches the disadvantage of those who were more at risk, baking that disadvantage into the cost of insurance to them.[20]

Something similar also happens on the stock market. When a firm reports poor quarterly earnings, its share price often does not decline much at all. Why? Because that result had been expected, and the market had already

---

conception come true': but the initial belief need not necessarily be false; acting on a true belief can sometimes contribute to (even if simply by overdetermining) its being or becoming true.

[14] Jussm and Harber 2005. Papageorge, Gershenson and Kang's (2020) cleverly designed studies clearly show that is not the whole story, however.

[15] Becker 1952. Rosenthal and Jacobson 1968. This occurs at all levels, from first learning to read (Stanovich 1986) to advanced education in science. Zuckerman (1977, pp. 248, 250, similarly pp. 61–2) finds that 'the accumulation of advantage in science' is driven by the fact that 'scientists who show promise early in their careers [are] given greater opportunities in the way of research and training.... This facilitates research performance, which in turn confirms the prediction.'

[16] Papageorge, Gershenson and Kang 2020, p. 242.

[17] Heath 2018.

[18] That fact gives rise to fairness-based arguments against actuarially-fair insurance, of course (O'Neill and O'Neill 2012). As Stone (1993, pp. 293–4) says, 'If the actuarial fairness principle could be perfectly implemented, if we had perfect predictive information and precise rating, each person would pay for her- or himself. This, of course, would be the antithesis of insurance.'

[19] As Hume (1739, bk. 3, pt. 2, sec. 2) puts it, 'by mutual succor we are less expos'd to fortune and accidents', thus providing 'security'.

[20] That is one reason so many homes flooded by Hurricane Katrina were uninsured in poor, low-lying areas of New Orleans (Stamberg 2005; see more generally Young 2006a; Johnson and Rainey 2007). For another striking example, actuarially fairness dictates that victims of domestic abuse should pay more for health insurance or denied coverage altogether because they are more likely to suffer further domestic abuse—a practice several US states have outlawed (Hellman 1997).

factored the expected result into the price of shares in the firm.[21] Conversely, when people expect a company's shares to increase in value, they buy more of its shares and the shares increase in value, thus confirming those investors' expectations and inducing more and more people to invest. The self-reinforcing cycle persists, until something happens to burst the 'bubble' and bring the company's shares back into line with the company's 'real value'.[22]

Something similar happens, finally, in credit and debt markets. People lend money to others only if they expect it to be repaid.[23] Those expectations, in turn, are based on prospective borrowers' past records of repaying previous loans, which form the basis of a person's 'credit ratings'.[24] Vicious cycles emerge as those who have not previously secured a loan have no credit history and hence less chance of being lent money in the future, and those who have previously had difficulty servicing their loans will be lent more money only at high interest rates that make it more difficult for them to service their new loan.[25] In Marx's pithy aphorism, 'credit is given only to him who already has'.[26]

In all of those cases, people have descriptive expectations about what they expect is most likely to occur, and in acting on those descriptive expectations they make what they expect (or something closely akin to it[27]) actually occur. Sometimes of course those expectations are unwarranted or, worse, rooted in blind prejudice. But even when people's descriptive expectations are statistically well-founded, people's acting on those expectations transforms statistically-expected disadvantage into actually-experienced disadvantage—and of course statistically-expected advantage into actually-experienced advantage, likewise.

---

[21] The Rational Expectations model within economics elaborates on that phenomenon (Muth 1961; Lucas and Prescott 1971; Kantor 1979).
[22] Basu's (2018, p. 201) example is of the housing market, but the same is obviously true of the stock market.
[23] And on terms that reflect the probability they attach to being repaid: the 'democratization of credit' made it possible for people with poor credit ratings to receive credit, but only at much higher interest rates (Fourcade and Healy 2013).
[24] Or, for larger loans, if they put up good collateral sufficient to secure the loan (Heath 2018). But of course that just creates an analogous vicious cycle, as who lack access to good collateral cannot get credit to help them acquire things that could subsequently serve as good collateral (Meyer 2018a, b; Dietsch 2021).
[25] Rona-Tas 2017. Dwyer (2018) argues that, under current conditions of 'financialized capitalism', inclusion in and exclusion from credit markets is a major source of social inequality. See similarly Fourcade and Healy (2013). On the ethical issues involved in decisions to extend credit, see: Fourcade and Healy 2007; Meyer 2018a, b; Kiviat 2019.
[26] Marx 1844a/1975.
[27] In the insurance case, correspondingly higher insurance premiums for those at greater risk of suffering the insured-against eventuality.

6.1.2 Acting on the Basis of What *Others* Expect to Happen

In the previous cases, people are acting upon their *own* expectations, completely independently of the expectations of others.[28] Of course, the others may well also have had expectations—indeed, they may have had exactly the same expectations. But in the previous cases, one's own choice of actions is not in any way *based* on what (or what one thought) others expected to occur. Take the stock market example. If an investor expects that a firm's upcoming earnings statement will be much better than other people are expecting it to be, he can profit from investing in that firm all by himself. If his expectations are borne out, his investment will be all the more profitable precisely because others' had the opposite expectation, depressing the price of the firm's shares when he bought them.

Let us turn now to the second class of cases, where people act on the basis of the expectations of others. They may do that either as a rational response to certain aspects of the situation (section 6.1.2.1) or out of more purely psychological motivations (section 6.1.2.2).

6.1.2.1 As a Rational Response

Sometimes each person needs literally to *align* his expectations with those of others. Take the case of deciding whether to adopt a technology with network externalities, which make the technology more valuable to you the more other people who also adopt it.[29] My running example will be VHS versus Betamax, two competing and mutually incompatible forms of video recording technology in the days before DVDs. You wanted to buy a VHS recorder only if you expected most others to do likewise, which would lead to more videos being available in that format.[30] But what others do depends on their own expectations, in turn, concerning what others will do. So in this case you needed to

---

[28] In the paradigm cases, anyway.
[29] This is further discussed in sections 4.2 and 4.6 above and sections 7.3 and 9.3.1 below.
[30] As Shapiro and Varian (1999, p. 14) say, 'In competing to become the standard or at least to achieve critical mass, consumer expectations are critical. In a very real sense, the product that is expected to become the standard will become the standard. Self-fulfilling expectations are one manifestation of positive-feedback economics and bandwagon effects. As a result, companies participating in markets with strong network effects seek to convince customers that their products will ultimately become the standard while rival, incompatible products will soon be orphaned' (see similarly Allen 1983). Strictly speaking, however, 'cascade' or 'bandwagon' models pertain to *sequential choice*, where the question is whether you want to adopt the technology *given* that a certain number of others have *already* done so (Bikhchandani, et al. 1992; 1998). That is different from the case here under discussion, which is a *simultaneous choice* situation in which you adopt a technology or not depending on what you *expect* others *will* do in the future.

positively align your own expectations with theirs. You needed to expect what you expected (most) other people to expect.

In other cases you merely need to choose your own action on the basis of your perception of others 'expectations *rather than* your own. Here, you do not yourself need actually to 'expect what others expect', as in the VHS-Betamax example; you do not need literally to align your expectations with theirs. You need only align your *actions* with their expectations about what is likely to occur. Consider, for example, the choice of a new mainframe computer for your firm. You yourself might expect a Burroughs mainframe to perform better than an IBM. But if everyone else in your firm expects an IBM to perform better, then you had better go with IBM. As the saying goes, 'No one ever got fired for buying IBM'.[31] Or as Keynes put it more prosaically, 'Worldly wisdom teaches us that it is better ... to fail conventionally than succeed unconventionally.'[32]

Suppose you need to hire someone for a particular job, in circumstances in which there are no good direct indicators of the quality of people's likely performance in that role. Then how well one will perform the task is often inferred on the basis of one's status attributes. Sometimes those status markers are impersonal attributes such as gender, race or class: certain ones of those are regarded as more competent at the task at hand than are others, as in the hiring case discussed in section 6.1.1. Sometimes, however, those ascriptions of status are based on one's own past accomplishments (scientific discoveries, for example, in the case of the status pecking order among scientific researchers)— the expectation being that those who have done well at the task in the past are more likely to do well at it in the future.[33]

Now, the choices that are guided by such status ascriptions (of who we should hire for this task, or whatever) often have to be *agreed* among many people.[34] Where they do, the ranking of status attributes made by each of those people needs to track the status ranking of (most) others if they are to make that choice successfully. And that fact in turn leads each to choose the ranking

---

[31] Correll et al. 2017, p. 300.
[32] Keynes 1936/1964, p. 158. 'Doing as others do' insulates you from criticism for untoward outcomes, both in the case of physicians prescribing new drugs (Coleman, Katz and Menzel 1957, pp. 268–9) and of financial analysts forecasting company earnings (Hong, Kubik and Solomon 2000).
[33] Zuckerman and Merton (1971, p. 81) describe 'the stratification system of science as a distinctive compound of egalitarian values governing access to opportunity to publish and a hierarchical structure in which power and authority are largely vested in those who have acquired rank through cumulative scientific accomplishment. It is a status-hierarchy, in Max Weber's sense, based on honour and esteem. Although rank and authority in science are acquired through past performance, once acquired, they then tend to be ascribed (for an indefinite duration).'
[34] Goodin and Brennan 2001.

of status attributes that she expects others are most likely to employ, even if she herself expects that is not the best indicator of the likely quality of the performance of alternative candidates. If it is crucial that all converge on the same choice, then each submerges her own judgment and chooses on the same status basis upon which she expects others to choose.[35]

Here is a more concrete example. Suppose you are a member of a committee charged with nominating someone for some important task (leading the country, for example), and your committee's nominee will then be voted upon in competition with candidates nominated by other committees. Finally, suppose that your committee's nominee will be much more likely to win that competition if your committee's recommendation is unanimous than if it is not.[36] Various different attributes are arguably relevant to the performance of the task for which the person is being nominated. You yourself expect one of those attributes (past performance) to be more relevant, but you expect most of the others on the committee expect some other attribute (personal charisma) to count as more relevant. Given the importance of you all agreeing on the same ranking of attributes in order to agree on the same candidate, you will cast your vote within the committee on the basis of the attribute that you expect most other committee members expect to be most relevant and for the candidate that you expect others to expect to best embody it.[37]

In that case, as in a range of cases already discussed in chapter 5, each person wants to do what she expects the others to do—even if that is not what she herself thinks best. Here, each makes her choice not on the basis of what she herself expects, but on the basis of what she expects that the others expect. Unsurprisingly, that has a tendency to reinforce the existing order, with everyone doing what is 'conventional' not because anyone necessarily thinks it best but rather because (its being conventional) that is what everyone expects the others to do.[38]

---

[35] As Roger Gould (2002, p. 1148) puts it, 'collective adherence to socially provided assessments reproduces and thereby validates those very assessments. The status rankings of individuals, groups, or other social entities that result are consequently stable, not because of stable intrinsic differences among actors but because of the self-validating character of social judgments'.

[36] Hence the practice of US national party conventions nominating candidates for president: once the winning candidate has securing a winning majority of convention votes, the convention invariably proceeds to 'make it unanimous'. At the end of the 1968 Republican National Convention, for example, defeated candidate Ronald Reagan stepped up to the podium and moved that the convention to make its nomination of Richard Nixon unanimous (Mailer 1968, p. 70).

[37] Thus is Urfalino's (2014) 'rule of no-opposition'.

[38] A good body of empirical research shows that this does indeed happen, both in experimental settings (Correll et al. 2017) and in the world at large. White and Laird (2020) offer an array of evidence explaining near universal support for the US Democratic Party among Afro-Americans in terms of a felt need for group solidarity in the face of continuing injustice, combined with the expectation among

6.1.2.2 As a Psychological Tendency

So far I have been discussing cases in which people have some instrumentally rational reason to act on the basis of what others expect. But there is an important psychological story to be told about the various ways in which people end up acting in line with others' expectations, even when they have no instrumentally rational reason to do so.

One version of that story might be dubbed 'sheer conformism'. People want to 'fit in', and as part of that they strive to bring both their beliefs and their actions into line with what they perceive to be the ones that are conventional among those around them.[39] That applies most conspicuously to people's actions. Consider the case of a standing ovation: people want to stand to applaud a performance if, but only if, (enough) others in the audience are also going to stand to applaud.[40] But it applies to people's beliefs as well. In Solomon Asch's famous 'group conformism' studies, experimental subjects denied the clear evidence of their own eyes to report a longer line as the shorter when all the others in the experiments (who were in truth confederates rather than genuine subjects) reported believing that that was so.[41]

Sometimes people are psychologically driven to act on the basis of others' expectations without wanting to, perhaps without even realizing that they are doing so. What social psychologists refer to as 'stereotype threat' is a case in point. There, the people who are subject to a negative stereotype do not 'internalize' it themselves. Nevertheless, realizing that others expect the stereotypical things from them causes them to behave in ways that more closely resemble the stereotype. There are various ways that might work. One is that, knowing the others' low expectations of them, the stereotyped individuals fail even to *try* to do better than expected. Another way that might work is that knowing the others' law expectations of them *discourages* or *distracts* the stereotyped individuals in ways that prevent them from doing better.[42]

Afro-Americans that others among them will vote Democrat out of loyalties born of the Civil Rights movement. That of course is a case of solidarity among the downtrodden seeking social justice, but it nonetheless has the consequence of perpetuating the electoral advantage that the Democratic Party enjoys from being able to take the Afro-American vote for granted.

[39] Bernheim 1994.
[40] Schelling 1978, p. 93. Muldoon et al. 2014.
[41] Asch 1951; 1956. Strictly speaking it is unclear whether this is evidence of 'act-conformism' or 'belief-conformism', since stating your belief is itself an act.
[42] Steele and Aronson 1995. Steele 2010. Inzlicht and Schmader 2011. Ridgeway 2014. Carlana 2019. Jones (2012a) discusses a related phenomenon under the heading of 'intellectual self-trust'.

6.2 Prescriptive Norms and Expectations

Whereas descriptive norms and expectations pertain to people's views about what *actually is* the case, prescriptive norms and expectations pertain to their views about what *should be* the case.[43]

Our interest in prescriptive norms and expectations, here, lies in how those shape people's behaviour. Accordingly, our interest lies not in what *objectively* should be the case (if there is such any such thing). Our interest is, instead, in what people *think* should be the case, for whatever reason[44]—because it is morally required (section 6.2.1), because it is the social norm in their community (section 6.2.2), because it is a requirement of some particular role that they occupy (section 6.2.3), or whatever.

Prescriptive norms, once established (or perceived to be established) within a community, are sticky in ways akin to evolutionary biologists' models of 'replicator dynamics'. Those models assume that players are locked into strategies, and they do not change the strategy that they play from one round of the game to the next.[45] In just that way prescriptive norms, being sticky, lock you in into acting the same in the future as in the past. And insofar as they do, they can help to perpetuate existing advantage.[46]

6.2.1 Moral Norms

One source of prescriptive norms is of course morality itself. Morality prescribes that people should do what is right and pursue what is good. What is morally required is socially expected, at least among the community of people who internalize that moral code.[47]

Here, I reiterate, we are talking about what might be called the 'positive morality' of a society. Those are principles that are accepted by people within that society *as* being requirements of morality; they are principles that people in that society *think* are moral ones.[48] Whether those are the true principles of

---

[43] This is what Ross (1901, p. 153, see also ch. 24) refers to as 'the force of expectations'.

[44] That is a special case of the famous Thomas Theorem: 'if men define situations as real, they are real in their consequences' (Thomas and Thomas 1928, p. 572).

[45] Cressman and Tao 2014.

[46] That is particularly so, insofar as the upper classes benefit from others being bound by them while themselves being more exempt from them (Phillips and Zuckerman 2001).

[47] That is only contingently (but quite commonly) true. Logically, it is perfectly possible for people to internalize the code, and indeed employ it as a basis for criticizing others, without acting on it themselves. They would of course be hypocritical in doing so; but 'hypocrisy is vice's homage to virtue' (La Rochefoucauld 1664/2007, p. 341).

[48] Brennan et al. 2013, pp. 5–6, 57.

critical morality (if there are any such principles) is a separate question. What matters for the present project is simply that people in that society suppose that what they regard as 'moral norms' are grounded in external moral principles rather than being grounded merely in facts internal to their society's practices (as with purely 'social norms', to be discussed next).[49]

There may be some occasions when what is required by a moral norm is of little importance to anyone. Think of keeping an inconsequential promise, for example. More typically, however, people are acutely anxious that (what they take to be) the demands of morality be satisfied. Hence, the requirements of morality are ordinarily regarded as particularly stringent, compared to other sorts of social demands. The prescriptive expectation that they will be met, and the social opprobrium that when they are not, are correspondingly stronger.

It is for that reason, perhaps, that people so often treat whatever is particularly important to them as if it were *ipso facto* a matter of moral concern. This is an odd sociological inversion of the ordinary moral logic, to be sure. The latter holds, 'if it is a matter of moral concern, then it is likely to be very important'; the former holds, 'if it is very important, then it is likely to be a matter of moral concern'. Fallacious though that inversion may be it is nevertheless sociologically common.

Beneficiaries of the traditional racial and gender orders have in this way long treated their privileges as high moral entitlements, often claiming them to have been ordained by God. Baptist minister Jerry Falwell founded an organization explicitly entitled the 'Moral Majority' in 1979 to stop what he (and viewers of his television programme 'The Old Time Gospel Hour') regarded as a deterioration of America's moral fabric. Among the targeted sources of ostensible moral rot were feminism, abortion and homosexuality. A few years earlier, the rise of youth culture had given rise to what was aptly described as a 'moral panic'.[50] As John Stuart Mill says, in a passage reminiscent of Marx and Engels, 'Wherever there is an ascendant class, a large portion of the morality of the country emanates from its class interests, and its feelings of class superiority.'[51]

---

[49] Brennan et al. 2013, ch. 4. This is the collective analogue of Williams' (1981, ch. 8) individual-level distinction between 'internal' and 'external' reasons.
[50] Cohen 1980. Roszak 1970.
[51] Mill (1959/1977, ch. 1, p. 221) here echoes Marx and Engels (1845/1972, p. 136): 'The ideas of the ruling class are in every epoch the ruling ideas, i.e., the class which is the ruling material force of society, is at the same time its ruling intellectual force.'

6.2.2 Social Norms

Whereas moral norms are (or, rather, are seen to be) externally given, social norms are and are seen to be purely internal to the society in question.[52] Occasionally the norms were brought into being at some specific time and place by some specific set of actors.[53] More typically, norms evolve through the repeated interactions of individuals within the society, often in relation to problems in organizing cooperation or coordination.[54] Social norms that arise in that way tend to be particularly 'sticky', because there is no formal mechanism for changing them, which can only be done through the same slow process of social evolution.[55]

However a social norm came about, once it has become established there is serious social pressure to abide by it. Formal and informal social sanctions of one sort or another are brought to bear for non-compliance, of course.[56] But perhaps more important than all that is the fact that people themselves typically internalize the social norms, and they take a critical reflective attitude toward their own conduct assessed in light of the norms.[57] And after some point, abiding by the social norms becomes 'second nature' and people do so without thinking much about it at all.[58]

Social norms vary wildly in their content and in their impact. Some genuinely work to the advantage of all who are subject to them; some even do so equally for all concerned.[59] Other social norms support grossly unequal social arrangements, reinforcing the power and advantage of some groups over others. Racial discrimination in the American South in the century following the Civil War was rooted not only in state legislation but also in an

---

[52] That is the analytic distinction between them, anyway. Historically, what we now regard as purely 'social norms' might have originally been invested with moral (or even divine) force. As Schlesinger (1946/1968, p. 64) writes of social manners: 'At first, politeness was so closely identified with morality as to be scarcely distinguishable. It was then usual', Schlesinger says referring to Emerson (1882, vol. 3, pp. 135–6), 'to define manners as "minor morals."'

[53] The *Code Duelo*, governing the fighting of duels, was like that (Brennan et al. 2013, pp. 123–4).

[54] Bicchieri 2006; Brennan et al. 2013, ch. 5. It is for this reason that they are sometimes called 'customs' (Bikhchandani, Hirshleifer and Welch 1992), 'conventions' (Lewis 1969; Young 1993) or 'folkways' (Sumner 1934).

[55] Brennan et al. 2013, pp. 240–4.

[56] These are nicely taxonomized by Dahrendorf (1968, p. 41).

[57] Ross 1897; Brennan et al. 2013, ch. 2. Such internalization is how Hart (1961, pp. 55–6) distinguishes a norm from a mere 'habit': it may have been the statistical norm that most Englishmen of his generation went to the cinema on Saturday, but no one would have felt any personal discomfort or experienced any social scorn for failing to do so.

[58] As Mill (1859, ch. 1, p. 220) says, 'The rules which obtain among themselves appear to them self-evident and self-justifying. This all but universal illusion is one of the examples of the magical influence of custom, which is not only, as the proverb says, a second nature, but is continually mistaken for the first.'

[59] See the discussion of coordination games in sections 5.1.1 above and 8.1 below.

overbearing code of social etiquette involving strong social norms requiring ritualized deference of blacks to whites.[60] Even today, psychological experiments show that people are more inclined to make racial slurs the more people in their community who do so.[61]

Even when the social norms do not directly and deliberately advantage one group over others in that way, they can often tend to reinforce and perpetuate the advantage of those who already are most advantaged. The reason is simply that the already advantaged are the ones who tend to be best schooled in the norms; and insofar as everyone valorizes the norms, people who are seen as best reflecting them enjoy correspondingly high social status and social benefits accruing from that. The norms of etiquette are the prime examples here. But all manner of other norms also serve as social status markers and hence social sorting mechanisms.[62]

6.2.3 Role Norms

A special case of social norms are those norms that are imposed upon people in respect of some specific social role that they occupy. There are certain things that one is prescriptively expected to do, or to refrain from doing, in one's capacity as occupant of that social role; and those prescriptive expectations essentially are the same for everyone occupying the same social role.[63] Some philosophers, following sociologists a couple of generations earlier, literally define the 'social structure' as 'an abstract representation of the patterned social relations possible for a given set of roles'.[64]

Some roles derive from formal social positions, such as public officials and professionals such as doctors and lawyers. What is expected, prescriptively and hence descriptively, from people in those formal roles tends to be set out (often in some detail) in codified standards of conduct.[65] Other social roles are

---

[60] Woodward 1955. Myrdal 1944, pp. 60–7.
[61] Ford and Ferguson 2005. Paluck, Shepherd and Aronow 2016. Paluck and Chwe 2017.
[62] See section 3.1.1.
[63] In terms of the underlying 'theatrical metaphor', role occupants are playing '"parts" for which "scripts" were written' (Biddle 1986, p. 68); so everyone playing the same 'part' must speak to the same script. See similarly Dahrendorf 1968, pp. 29–32. There may be various different ways of playing any given role, to be sure, but those too often fall into a handful of stylized modes: Thomas (1921/1966) distinguishes among several ways of playing 'the immigrant role' for example.
[64] Sangiovanni 2018, p. 461.
[65] As Petersen (2009, p. 127) says, 'Professions... engage in both opportunity hoarding through restricting the opportunities of competing professional groups and exclusion of unlicensed practitioners, and at the same time restricting own choices and opportunities, in the sense of self-binding through professional codes. It may be that the very practice of restricting the choice and opportunities of others also compels the professions to put restrictions on own choices and opportunities.'

not formalized to that extent. But there are nonetheless strong (albeit typically uncodified) social understandings of what can be expected of the occupants of roles such as parent, partner, teacher or trade unionist.[66]

Role occupancy empowers, at the same time as role expectations constrain. As the reference to the role of 'professionals' (doctors, lawyers and so on) clearly indicates, roles quite often constitute positions of privilege to which many benefits accrue. The fact that those roles come circumscribed by expectations that constrain what role occupants may and must do moderates that privilege only very much at the margins.[67]

Regularizing recurring social interactions into established roles, with associated privileges and expectations, both creates and perpetuates those islands of constrained privilege.[68] Role occupants change over time, to be sure, but over long stretches the same persons occupy the same role and enjoy the same (constrained) privileges accruing to them. In any case, roles constitute positions of social power and advantage that persist over time, even as their occupants change. For a historically conspicuous example of each, consider the case of established religions and their authorized celebrants. But 'the professions' more generally—and the specific lawyers and doctors filling those roles—are the modern equivalents of the priestly classes of old.[69]

Roles and role expectations typically serve to perpetuate advantages, but there are some examples of them doing the opposite. Sometimes role occupants have obligations to do things that reduce existing social advantages and disadvantages. Sometimes those are internal obligations of the role, as in the case of the 'public defender' whose role is to assist low-status indigent clients by defending them in court. Other times, such moral or social obligations arise as an external consequence of one's occupying a role and enjoying the privileges accruing to it. The social (and perhaps moral) expectation that a rich businessman should contribute to the building of a new community hospital

---

[66] Dahrendorf 1968, pp. 34–8.

[67] Sangiovanni (2018, p. 461) offers a more historical example: 'Courtly life in the Renaissance... had an abstract structure composed of not only the formally stated roles, prohibitions, and permissions defining courtly life but also... "not always conscious" informal "conventions, recipes, scenarios, principles of action, and habits of speech"—including the shared concepts, beliefs, assumptions, and other attitudes with which individuals make sense of the social world and their place in it. These rules, concepts, beliefs, assumption, conventions, recipes, scenarios, principles of action, and habits of speech are the stuff of cultural and social anthropology. Sewell aptly calls them schemas. They define the positions at court; the rules, conventions, scenarios, that govern possible moves within courtly life (including what is "out of bounds"); and the character of the social relations which can be constituted by particular applications of the schemas.'

[68] Gambetta (1998, pp. 105–9) offers the striking example of the Italian academic system, in which the role of junior academics is to serve as sycophants to 'il patrono', whom they succeed in turn.

[69] Laumann and Heinz 1982; Laumann et al. 2005.

arises not in consequence of his being in the role of 'businessman' but, rather, in consequence of the riches that he has amassed in that role. In yet other cases, people who occupy some role (a 'shareholder' for example) may have a moral or social duty to use the power that accompanies the role for good purposes.[70] Another example along those lines would be that of the mayor who is expected to set a good example by conspicuously giving blood to the Red Cross collection.[71]

6.2.4 Legal Norms

Some role requirements, social norms and principles of positive morality are actually enacted into law. When they are, they acquire yet another source of prescriptive power and another set of incentives for compliance with them.

Note, however, that the prescriptive force of legal norms is logically independent from other non-legal sources of prescriptive force. Some of the things prohibited by the law are *malum in se,* morally bad in themselves; but some are *malum prohibitum*, bad only because they are legally prohibited. Some of the things required by law reflect pre-existing social norms and conventions; in other cases, the law is what creates the convention. The duty-imposing branch of the law is typically of the former sort; the power-conferring branch is characteristically of the second sort.[72] Not only is there no morally right way to make out a will; there is not even very much by way of social convention surrounding the practice, until it is given legal form.[73]

It goes without saying that the way in which any given legal norm is crafted typically advantages some people and disadvantages others. And it goes without saying that the way the law is written typically works to the advantage of those who are already advantaged. As Rousseau says, lawmaking characteristically serves to 'transform … power into right'.[74] Jim Crow laws oppressing blacks in the post-Civil War American South have already been mentioned; two centuries earlier, King Louis XIV had promulgated the *Code Noir*, a detailed set

---

[70] Zheng (2018b) seems to have this third sort of case in mind.
[71] 'Behold our deeds transcending our commands', as Homer (1909, bk. xii, p. 232) has his hero Sarpeon say in trying to persuade Glaucus to join him leading their forces into battle.
[72] Hart 1961. Goodin 2010a.
[73] As Maine (1901, ch. 6, pp. 172–3) says, 'The barbarians were confessedly strangers to any such conception as that of a Will. The best authorities agree that there is no trace of it in those parts of their written codes which comprise the customs practised by them in their original seats, and in their subsequent settlements on the edge of the Roman Empire. But soon after they became mixed with the population of Roman provinces they appropriated from the Imperial jurisprudence the conception of a Will, at first in part, and afterwards in all its integrity.'
[74] Rousseau 1762/1973, bk. 1, ch. 3.

of regulations governing slavery throughout France's Caribbean colonies.[75] Until the 1870 passage of the Married Women's Property Act, all wealth that an English woman brought into a marriage was automatically the property of her husband.[76] Trade and labour laws across several centuries systematically advantages capital over labour.[77]

Of course we are well accustomed to thinking of the law as a site of structural injustice in precisely those ways. But the focus of this book, as announced in chapter 1, is on *mechanisms* rather than sites of social injustice. The claim of this chapter is that what makes legal norms effective instruments for perpetuating unjust social advantage is the way in which they shape the prescriptive (and hence descriptive) expectations of people.

6.3 The Relations Between Descriptive and Prescriptive Norms

There are three ways in which descriptive and prescriptive norms might be related to one another. I hasten to emphasize that these are sociological (or perhaps psychological) relationships, not logical ones. Indeed, one of them is actually logically fallacious.

One way in which people's descriptive and prescriptive norms might be related is that people think that what *is* the case *should be* the case. In its boldest form, this is what philosophers dub the 'naturalistic fallacy', the attempt to derive 'ought' from 'is'.[78] Logically fallacious though that may be, sociologically the practice is common enough. People often enough think that something ought prescriptively to be the norm, merely because it is (and, they often add, 'has long been'[79]) descriptively the case.[80] Such a sentiment has long lain at the heart of 'conservatism', analytically conceived.[81] Insofar as that sentiment holds sway socially, it will have the clear consequence of perpetuating existing advantages and existing disadvantages.

---

[75] Louis XIV 1685.
[76] Mill 1869/1984.
[77] Goodin 2017.
[78] So termed by Moore (1903), but the observation is much older (Hume 1739, bk. 3, pt. 1, sec. 1).
[79] Pocock 1957.
[80] Tax compliance might be one such example: people think they should pay their taxes because people generally do pay their taxes, and people think ill of people who do not do so. But when a manifestly unfair tax is imposed people's intrinsic motivation to comply and social pressure to comply both go down. Besley, Jensen and Persson (2022) find, for example, that whereas UK tax evasion was historically under 3% it jumped to between 10 and 15% in response to Thatcher's grossly regressive Poll Tax.
[81] Brennan and Hamlin 2004. Cohen 2013.

Notice that there is another non-fallacious variation on that thought which can have much the same consequences. Often, what is descriptively expected is thought to be prescriptively required, simply on the grounds that one should not disappoint other people's expectations.[82] I shall discuss that sort of reasoning more fully in section 6.4 below. Clearly, there is something to be said on behalf of that reasoning. But whatever its other merits, implementing that reasoning has an unfortunate tendency to perpetuate existing advantage and disadvantage around which those expectations are built.

A second way in which descriptive norms might relate to prescriptive ones is logically appropriate but only contingently true. Insofar as people embrace and act upon the same prescriptive norms, then the pattern of behaviour that those norms prescribe will descriptively be the statistical norm among those people as well. Logically, that is as it should be. The direction-of-fit is correct: what 'is' is being brought into line with 'what ought to be' (rather than the other way around, with the 'naturalistic fallacy'). But of course it is an empirically contingent matter whether people actually embrace and successfully act on the prescriptive norms. Insofar as people embrace but fail to act (or to act successfully) on the prescriptive norms that they all embrace, there will be a disjuncture between prescriptive and descriptive norms among that group.

Finally, descriptive norms might relate to prescriptive ones as part of a complex power play associated with the process of 'normalization'. Here is how Iris Young describes the process:

> Normalization consists in a set of social processes that elevate the experience and capacities of some social segments into standards used to judge everyone. In this process the attributes, comportments, or ways of life that are 'normal', in the sense of exhibited by a majority or by dominant social segments, come also to have the connotation of being 'best'. To the extent that other people do not fit or fail to measure up to these standards because of their bodily capacities, group-specific socialized habits and comportments, or cultural membership or way of life, they tend to suffer stigmatization and disadvantage. The assumptions carried by many institutional rules and practices often operate to enforce and reinforce these norms that stigmatize and disadvantage. These norms often make a large class of people deviant, and the disadvantages they suffer as a result usually affect central aspects of their lives.[83]

---

[82] So long as those expectations are 'reasonable' ones, anyway.
[83] Young 2006b, p. 95. See further Young 1990, pp. 136–41.

This phenomenon is much discussed among theorists of gender and of disability. It is something that also happens well beyond those realms as well, of course.[84] But let us take as our working example the 'normalization of heterosexuality'. Normalization involves a complex mixture of the descriptive and prescriptive. First there is the descriptive claim that heterosexuality is statistically the norm; then there is the prescriptive claim that (if only just prudentially, in order to fit in) one ought to present as heterosexual.[85]

That can be a powerful strategic ploy, and advantages and disadvantages predicated upon it can persist for long periods of time. But it is obviously highly vulnerable to being undermined by evidence that its descriptive component is actually untrue. The Kinsey reports did that with respect to sexual behaviour and orientation, early on.[86] And as more homosexuals 'come out of the closet', more are emboldened to do so. Once that starts happening in earnest, 'normalization' takes on a wholly different meaning: instead of treating the previously outcast group as abnormal, accept them as among the statistically normal. As that process unfolds, 'normalization' can thus become a battle-cry for those advocating for that change. In South Africa at the end of the apartheid era, for example, to 'normalize' sport meant to desegregate it, thus making South African sport conform to what was globally statistically 'normal'.[87]

Cases of so-called 'pluralistic ignorance' have much the same structure. There the false beliefs surround what is descriptively true about the prescriptive norms to which people suppose that others around them subscribe. The classic study found that university undergraduates drank far more than they personally thought that they should, simply because that is what they thought *others* thought that they should do; and once that illusion was dispelled, the 'hard drinking norm' simply evaporated.[88] There have been similarly precipitous declines in foot-binding, female genital mutilation and East European communist rule as a result of people's beliefs about others' beliefs being exposed as incorrect.[89]

---

[84] Importantly, people 'normalize' social and natural phenomenon in much the same way—by treating it as if it were some naturally-occurring phenomenon. Thus, people living in earthquake-prone areas 'normalize' the risks to which they are exposed (Mileti and O'Brien 1992) in much the same way as people employed in 'dirty work' 'normalize' the taint associated with their occupations (Ashforth et al. 2007).
[85] Martin 2009.
[86] Kinsey et al. 1948; 1953.
[87] *Oxford English Dictionary*, q.v. 'normalize, v.', definition 5. Note similarly the long campaign to 'normalize' post-Nazi Germany (Olick 1998) and processes for establishing a 'new normal' after severe disruptions more generally (Mohr, Contini and Branco 2022).
[88] Prentice and Miller 1993.
[89] Mackie 1996. Kuran 1991; 1995.

6.4 The Value of Knowing What to Expect

Norms and expectations have the power that they do simply because it is so very valuable for a person to know what descriptively to expect to occur. While the expectations in question are descriptive ones in the final analysis, they may of course have their roots in prescriptive ones which are characteristically acted upon.

6.4.1 Successfully Exercising Temporally Extended Agency

Human lives are not just moment-in-time affairs. Instead, they are temporally extended.[90] What you do now has consequences for what happens to you in the future, for better or worse. People who are prudent planners avail themselves of that fact to formulate and act upon plans that, when and if they come to fruition, will (they anticipate) benefit them in some way. That is to say, they exercise 'temporally extended agency'.[91]

The possibility of exercising 'temporally extended agency' enables people to orient their lives around ongoing 'projects' that give continuity and shape ('coherence', 'unity' or even 'meaning') to their lives in ways that they find not only personally satisfying[92] but also objectively more rewarding.[93] The exercise of temporally extended agency is what is required if we are to be able to make commitments both to ourselves (that we will subsequently carry out plans that we make today) and to others (that we will subsequently keep the promises that we make today).

To exercise temporally extended agency successfully, we need to be able reliably to anticipate the future. Where the future is radically uncertain,

---

[90] Of the jurists who preceded him, Bentham (1838, p. 308) complained that 'the word expectation is scarcely to be found in their vocabulary'. He deemed this a grievous omission, saying 'man is not like the brutes limited to the present time, either in enjoyment or suffering.... The idea of his security must be prolonged to him throughout the whole vista that is imagination can measure. This disposition to look forward ... may be called expectation – expectation of the future. It is by means of this that we are enabled to form a general plan of conduct; it is by means of this, that the successive moments which compose the duration of life are not like insulated and independent points, but become parts of a continuous whole. Expectation is a chain that unites our present and future existence, and passes beyond ourselves to the generations which follow us.... Every injury which happens to this sentiment produces a distinct, a peculiar evil, which may be called pain of disappointed expectation.'
[91] Bratman 2007, esp. pp. 21–46.
[92] Williams 1973, pp. 108–18; 1981, ch. 1. Nozick 1981, pp. 403–51. Wollheim 1984.
[93] Harsanyi 1977. Goodin 1990c, pp. 547–50; 1991, pp. 151–4.

attempting to exercise temporally extended agency is futile.[94] Being unable to plan for the future, you have no recourse but to live in the moment.[95] And that is unsatisfactory, insofar as it deprives you of all of the benefits just described that come from exercising temporally extended agency.

Strictly speaking, all that is required for the successful exercise of temporally extended agency is that you have relatively confident, settled expectations about the future.[96] Successful planning for the future does not require that the future be exactly like the present. It requires only that you can tolerably well anticipate how it will differ, at the point of planning.

Your capacity to plan for the future is enhanced, of course, if you can reasonably assume broad continuity across time. Continuity in your holdings—and more generally what you are able to do, permitted to do and required to do—is generally thought to be a very important part of that. David Hume famously argues on that basis for the stability of property: no one would invest in improvements that he cannot be relatively confident of being able himself to enjoy.[97] Bentham, following him, declared that 'security' is 'the principal object of the laws', adding 'without law there is no security; consequently no abundance, nor even subsistence .... Law alone has been able to create a fixed and durable possession which deserves the name of property.'[98]

So too, and for the same reason, is it good for you know what you can expect of others—and, by the same token, they of you. That is an important part of knowing what you can expect to occur in the future, so you can plan your life around it.

Therein lies the value of being able to make, and receive, binding commitments. Therein lies the value of there being a body of rules (legal, social or moral), known to all and relatively reliably adhered to.[99] What you lose by being thereby constrained in what you can do is more than compensated by your being able to confidently expect, and plan around, what you can expect others to do.

---

[94] It represents a triumph of hope over reason, a manifestation of what Keynes (1936/1964, p. 162) dubs 'animal spirits'. Insofar as agents still talk in terms of 'expectations' in those circumstances, they are 'fictional expectations' (Beckert 2016).
[95] Western et al. 2012.
[96] Goodin 2012b.
[97] Hume 1739, bk. 3, pt. 2, secs. 2–3; 1777, sec. 3, pt. 2. See similarly: Say 1821, bk. 1, ch. 14; Bentham 1838, chs. 7–10; Mill 1848/1965, bk. 2, chs. 1–2; Furubotn and Pejovich 1972.
[98] Bentham 1838, p. 307.
[99] Harsanyi (1977, p. 25) decisively proves the superiority of rule utilitarianism over act utilitarianism based on that 'expectation effect' which he remarks has 'surprisingly enough ... been almost completely neglected in the philosophical literature'. A partial exception is Hodgson (1967).

6.4.2 Stabilizing Expectations and Its Distributional Consequences

Thus there are considerable advantages, to each and hence to all, of being able to craft one's plans and ongoing projects around relatively confident expectations about future circumstances—what you will have, and what others will do. Let us call those 'reasonable expectations' if they are descriptively well grounded—which is to say, you had good grounds to expect that those circumstances would obtain, at the time of formulating and locking in your plans.

Sometimes, reasonable expectations are thwarted by untoward events that one could not reasonably have anticipated. In consideration of the value of stable expectations and making plans and commitments predicated on them, we often offer compensation to rectify the threat that those untoward interventions pose to people's plans and commitments.[100] At law, we require that people be compensated for tortious wrongs committed against them and for 'takings' of private property for public purposes.[101] When people have reasonably relied upon existing laws and regulations in making costly-to-change plans for the future, we often as a matter of policy either exempt them from or compensate them for changes to those laws and regulations.[102]

When there are anticipatable risks of such interruptions, we can and often do insure against them, either privately or publicly. A great many social insurance schemes have as their principal purpose the underwriting of stable expectations in this way. Public unemployment and sickness benefits are prime examples: they pay (at least for an extended period of time) benefits that are a typically large fraction of what the beneficiary had been earning before unemployment or sickness befell him.[103]

Notice, however, the distributional consequence of these policies of stabilizing expectations by paying compensation or earnings-related benefits. The effect is to lock in the distributional *status quo*.[104] The explicit aim of policies of 'compensation' is (as expressed in tort law) to 'restore the *status quo ante*'.[105] The clear aim of earnings-related benefits is to restore the beneficiary's income

---

[100] Goodin 1989; 1990c; 1991.
[101] On torts see: Prosser and Wade 1979, secs. 903 ff.; Atiyah 1980. On takings see: Michelman 1967; Epstein 1985.
[102] Feldstein 1976. Cordes and Goldfarb 1983.
[103] Goodin 1990, pp. 544–7.
[104] As noticed by Bentham (1838, ch. 11) in a chapter entitled 'security and equality – their opposition'.
[105] Insofar as the payment of monetary compensation can accomplish that: sometimes it cannot (Goodin 1989).

stream to, typically, some large fraction of what it had previously been, during this temporary interruption.

There may be good reasons for having such policies, in their own right. And there may be good reasons for insisting that redistribution should be done in a different and more systematic way, rather than letting it happen through random chance events. Be all that as it may, the effect of social policies to underwrite stable expectations in these ways is to perpetuate previously existing advantage. Restoring holdings and income streams that people previously enjoyed is the very antithesis of redistributing them. Policies stabilizing people's expectations fundamentally preserve existing patterns of distribution and the advantages to some people and disadvantages to others that are embodied in that existing distribution.[106]

---

[106] Goodin 1991.

7
Reputation Confers Advantage

Reputation is a special sort of expectation, based on what the person harbouring the expectation takes to be 'common knowledge' about some other person or thing.[1] Note that, unlike a stereotype, a reputation is specific to a particular person or thing.

The *Oxford English Dictionary* defines 'reputation' as 'the fame, credit, or notoriety of being, doing, or possessing something'.[2] As that definition makes clear, reputations can attach to multiple different attributes. Here I shall distinguish four:

- reputation for power (Section 7.1),
- reputation for status position (Section 7.2),
- reputation for network position and influence (Section 7.3), and
- reputation for reliability and trustworthiness (Section 7.4).

In each of these cases, possessing such a reputation tends to cause one to come to have what one is reputed to have. Whether or not the reputation was warranted *ex ante*, it will tend to be *ex post*. Having a reputation for having advantages is advantageous, because it tends to confer upon its possessor those very advantages that he is reputed already to have.

That is the general pattern that will be running across this chapter. It plays out somewhat differently depending on the particular kind of reputation under discussion, as I shall proceed to show.

7.1 Reputation for Power

Thomas Hobbes famously declared that a 'reputation for power is power'.[3] But why should that be so? By what mechanisms, precisely, does the reputation for power convert itself into power as such?

---

[1] Origgi 2018. For the 'common knowledge' standard, as applied in a somewhat different setting, see Lewis (1969, pp. 52–60). In Dasgupta's (1988, p. 62, emphasis added) more economistic formulation, 'a person's reputation is the "*public's*" imputation of a probability distribution over the various types of person that the person in question can be in principle'.
[2] OED, qv. 'reputation (n.)', definition 4.
[3] Hobbes 1651, ch. 10.

Hobbes' own gloss on his aphorism is that 'reputation of power is power, because it draweth with it the adherence of those that need protection'. An implicit premise in that analysis is that having adherents attached to you is a source of power, even if those adherents are not themselves particularly powerful—even if, indeed, they are themselves so powerless as to need protection, which is why they adhere to you. That premise might be plausible in some circumstances (if for example you can collect rents from your adherents in exchange from protection)[4] but not in others (if for example having more adherents to protect stretches your resources too thinly).

Insofar as that premise is true, and having more adherents makes you more powerful, Hobbes' model becomes a case of more general 'preferential attachment' models. I shall discuss those models more fully in Section 7.3 in relation to network power, where such models are most commonly discussed. But the basic idea of a preferential attachment model is that people prefer to attach themselves to someone to whom many others are already attached (and who is, on this premise, therefore stronger); and as they do so that person attracts yet more adherents and thus becomes yet stronger.[5]

There is another way of unpacking the Hobbesian aphorism that 'reputation for power is power', however. That alternative unpacking points to what is nowadays called the 'law of anticipated reactions', mentioned already in Section 2.1.[6]

This explanation takes its starting point from another Hobbesian aphorism, according to which 'the "power of a man"... is his present means, to obtain some future apparent good....'[7] In the terms introduced in Section 1.3, power is a 'resource for competition' rather than a 'resource for consumption'. That is to say, power resources are purely instrumental goods. They are of no end-use value to you in themselves; their value to you is purely their usefulness to you instrumentally, in obtaining other goods that are of end-use value to you.

To that, add the observation that 'power' is a quintessentially 'positional good', in the terms introduced in Section 3.2. That is to say, how much of an end-use good your power buys you depends purely on how much power you have and care to devote to that cause, compared to how much power others in competition with you for that end-use good have and care to devote to that cause.[8]

---

[4] As in Weber's (1968, pp. 1070–1110) discussion of feudalism or Olson's (1993) of 'stationary bandits'.
[5] Feld 1991; Barabási and Albert 1999.
[6] Friedrich 1941, p. 592.
[7] Hobbes 1651, ch. 10.
[8] Goodin and Dryzek 1980. Thus, predatory price-cutting to drive early entrants out of the market, though itself costly in the short run, may benefit a firm in the long-term by creating a reputation that deters other firms from trying to enter the market (Milgrom and Roberts 1982).

That is where the 'law of anticipated reactions' kicks in. Here is how the standard version of that story goes.[9] If others think you have more power than they do (or, more precisely, will devote more power resources than they will to the competition),[10] then they will not enter into competition with you at all for that end-use good.[11] To do so would waste their power resources, without any realistic prospect of success. Their standing aside, of course, means that you get the end-use good without using any of your own power resources in a struggle against them to acquire it. You keep all your power resources, and you get the end-use good for free, as it were.

The same dynamic would work, of course, if what you were trying to acquire is some other instrumental good that would serve to enhance your power in subsequent rounds of competition. If others think that you have (and will commit) more power resources than they have (or will commit to that competition), then they will stand aside and let you take those additional instrumental goods that will enhance your power in subsequent rounds of competition.

Now, the pragmatics of all of this would be unexceptionable, if in other ways unfortunate, were people's assessments of everyone's relative power wholly accurate. They may not be, however. Some people may have a reputation for more power than they actually possess. In that case, their reputation for power can over the course of interactions as just described serve to confer upon them precisely the power that they were reputed to have had.

Knowing all this, people may expend more than they can actually afford in trying to secure a reputation for power. Think of it as an investment, pure and simple (or anyway a not-unreasonable gamble). They may go into debt initially in the process. But if the gambit pays off, they will profit many times over as they win without contest in subsequent rounds. Conspicuous consumption is like that, designed to persuade people that you have far more resources than you actually have.[12] Diego Gambetta recalls Ovid's tale about how, in 387 BCE, Romans under siege by the Gauls threw down loaves of bread

---

[9] As described in Section 2.1. This version is couched in terms of physical power resources, but the same may well apply to less material forms of power resources. Notice, however, that both versions of the account are subject to the modification introduced at the end of Section 3.2.

[10] As Hirshleifer (2001, chs 3–4) rightly observes, the less powerful might sometimes be prepared to devote a larger proportion of their smaller stock of power resources to the fight.

[11] This is one important source of 'non-decisions'—matters that should in principle be of general concern within a community never arising for political decision (Bachrach and Baratz 1963). Crenson (1971, p. 177) for example traces the failure of the polluted air in Gary and East Chicago to become a political issue for so long to this source: 'power need not be exercised in order to be effective', he concludes; '[t]he mere reputation for power, unsupported by acts of power, can be sufficient to restrict the scope of local decisionmaking'.

[12] Veblen 1899; Moav and Neeman 2012.

upon their shields: with that, 'the expectation that they could be starved out vanished' and Gauls withdrew.[13]

An objectively unwarranted reputation for power is itself a source of power, of course, only so long as it goes unchallenged. Once someone challenges the person with the unwarranted reputation, who fails to produce the objective power resources he is reputed to possess, his reputation immediately evaporates.[14] But having the reputation discourages challenges that would-be challengers can only expect to fail. Hence a reputation for power, once established, tends to be self-sustaining—and perhaps even self-enhancing, insofar as having a reputation for having a reputation further feeds one's reputation.

7.2 Reputation for Status Position

As discussed in Section 3.1.1, enjoying an elevated position in a status hierarchy is both satisfying in itself and can be instrumentally beneficial in securing other social outcomes. As Pierre Bourdieu observes, 'possessors of an inherited social capital, symbolized by a great name, ... are known to more people than they know, and their work of sociability, when it is exerted, is highly productive'.[15]

Having a *reputation* for high status can successfully serve that instrumental purpose, even if that reputation is false.[16] The dynamic at work here is much the same as with a reputation for power, just discussed. Insofar as people's relative status positions determine who wins and who loses competitions for end-use goods, people in lower status positions will not enter into competition with others whom they believe (rightly or wrongly) occupy higher status positions than they do themselves. Those reputed to occupy the higher status position will thus win by default.[17]

In the case of status-based competitions, that will presumably play out in terms of the social deference typically paid to people with higher status positions.[18] If people *believe* that you are in such a position, because you have a

---

[13] Gambetta (2009, p. 179), referring to Ovid (8, bk 6, June 9 The Vestalia).
[14] Wrong 1968, pp. 678–9. That is simply to say that reputations are hard to build and easy to lose.
[15] Bourdieu 1986, pp. 250–1.
[16] Here I am obviously employing an objectivist account of 'status', such that there is an external fact-of-the-matter about whether or not one truly has that status. That might be a sociological fact, however, as I go on to discuss. Some might suppose that, insofar as one's status consists wholly in other people's beliefs about one's having a status, one's having that status just is equivalent to having a reputation for having that status. But a reputation is based on your beliefs about what others in general believe, about which you might of course be incorrect—in which case you can have a reputation for status without truly having that status.
[17] Ridgeway 2014.
[18] Indeed, sociologists typically define status in that way: 'Status ... is broadly understood as the position in a social hierarchy that results from accumulated acts of deference', say Sauder, Lynn, and

reputation for being so, then they will defer to you in that way. If your reputation is undeserved, and you do not actually occupy that high-status position, then their deference will of course be in error. But they will defer nonetheless, as long as they believe what is reputed to be true.[19]

Many, if not all, of the intrinsic satisfactions that accrue from a position of high status can also accrue from the sheer reputation for (rather than the reality of) occupying that high status. Consider 'social esteem' for example.[20] People will esteem you on the basis of your high-status position just so long as they believe you to occupy such a position; and they can believe that to be the case on the basis of your reputation for occupying such a position, even if you do not actually do so. Of course, some of the more purely internal, intrinsic satisfactions (such as pride, self-esteem, etc.) do not arise, insofar as you know your reputation for high status is not actually deserved.

All status orders, of course, are socially constructed. But with some of them, the construct involves some objective factors that are socially construed as conferring high status upon someone. Thus, hereditary monarchy is obviously a social construct.[21] But once its socially constructed rules are in place, there is some objective fact of the matter as to who should succeed to the throne—'the eldest legitimate offspring of the deceased monarch', for example. People in general might harbour false beliefs about who fits that description (believing the first child of the deceased king's wife to be his, when in fact the old king had been cuckolded, for example). In such cases a person's reputation, and social status based on it, can be unwarranted.

In other cases, social statuses are socially constructed in a more thorough going way. There, the general belief literally constitutes the status in question. Take the status of being 'a respected elder' of the community, for example. That status is arguably completely constituted by what everyone thinks everyone

---

Podolny (2012, p. 258), pointing to Whyte (1943), Goode (1978), and others. That deference extends to their opinions as well of course. As Gould (2002, p. 1147) writes, 'The opinions of a respected public figure, for example, receive more attention and credence than those of ordinary folk, even when the opinions themselves are quite mundane. The difference is no doubt due in part to the past achievements that made the public figure's reputations in the first place; but it is also, according to my argument, due to the recognition by observers that all other observers are prepared to give the opinion in question a great deal of attention. The status of public figures, then, is the respect accorded to them by each observer just because they are accorded respect by everyone else....'

[19] Note too that 'the status of those with whom an actor associates affects that actor's own status' (Ridgeway 2014, p. 6). In consequence of that fact, status-seekers will seek to associate with people who already have more associates—leading to a 'preferential attachment' dynamic akin to those to be discussed in Section 7.3 below. The same applies within a status hierarchy of firms (Sauder, Lynn, and Podolny 2012, pp. 268–9).

[20] Ross 1901, ch. 24; Brennan and Pettit 2004.

[21] And a pretty arbitrary one at that. Pascal (1670/1958, no. 320) asks, 'What is less reasonable than to those the eldest son of a queen to rule a State? We do not choose as captain of a ship the passenger who is of the best family.... [But] whom will men choose as the most virtuous and able? We at once come to blows, as each claims to be the most virtuous and able. Let us then attach this quality to something indisputable' (quoted in Elster 2009, p. 211).

else thinks about the person in question.[22] If the person is generally thought to be a 'respected elder', then his reputation as such suffices to make that proposition true. And of course it is perfectly possible for everyone to think everyone *else* thinks about the person in that way (i) even if each herself knows the person not to be particularly 'elderly' and (ii) even if each herself does not particularly 'respect' that person (so long as each thinks everyone or virtually everyone else does).[23] The latter possibility enables a person to have a status reputation that is 'false', even in cases where status consists purely in what others believe (others to believe) a person's status to be.

Not all reputations for status are self-validating in that way. But some are, or can be. When they are, they also tend to be self-reinforcing.[24] Having the reputation—everyone believing that the vast majority of others believe that it is so—tends not just to make it the case but to keep it the case that one actually has the reputed status. Or anyway, believing that the vast majority of others believe that it is so insulates the reputation from being eroded by the realization that you and the handful of others you know well do not share that belief.

7.3 Reputation for Network Influence and Preferential Attachment

The notion of 'preferential attachment' has already been introduced briefly in Section 7.1 above.[25] The general idea of 'preferential attachment' is that people prefer to attach themselves to others who already have more people attached to them.[26]

---

[22] That is a report that can be made 'from the outside', as it were, by someone who is not a member of the community in question or hence party to the assessment. For example, Aboriginal leader Noel Pearson (2014) eulogized former Prime Minister Gough Whitlam saying, 'when he breathed he truly was Australia's greatest white elder'.

[23] The phenomenon of everyone thinking everyone else thinks something that they do not is just a classic case of 'pluralistic ignorance', as discussed in Section 6.3; see Prentice and Miller (1993) and Kuran (1995).

[24] Reputations of institutions as well as individuals can be self-reinforcing in various ways as well of course. Stinchcombe (1998, p. 276) describes the 'self-reinforcing causal circle' sustaining the reputations of elite universities, for example.

[25] 'Preferential attachment' is similar to, but importantly different from, the 'network externalities (discussed in Sections 4.2, 4.6, 6.1.2.1m and 9.3.1). With 'network externalities', people's willingness to join a network is a function of the number of people already in that network (i.e., already connected to *that network*). With 'preferential attachment', people's willingness to connect with some particular person in a network is a function of the number of people already in that person's network (i.e., already connected to *that person*).

[26] I shall here concentrate on preference-based versions of the 'power law' phenomenon. In other versions, the phenomenon is more of a statistical artefact: the more populous a city is, the more populous it becomes, purely because there are more people there to procreate; or the more distinct species

My earlier example drawn from Hobbes involved vulnerable people attaching themselves to stronger people for protection, with people being better able to provide that protection the more people they have attached to them. But the same basic dynamic works in various other contexts as well. Consider the quest for popularity, for example. Insofar as your own popularity is a function of being friends with popular people, you prefer to make friends with someone who herself has more rather than fewer friends.[27] Both are cases of 'preferential attachment', people preferring to attach themselves to people who already have more people attached to them—and the 'rich' get 'richer' in that respect as well.[28]

Here I am going to focus in particular on that more general phenomenon as it relates to the growth of attachments within social networks. Section 4.2 detailed several aspects of what it might mean to be in a position of 'power' in a network. One of the more crucial elements in that is the number of people to whom you are connected. Other things being equal, your being connected to more people within the network makes you a more effective disseminator of information and other valued resources within that network. And anyone who wants to receive or transmit information or other resources within that network will prefer to be connected to people who are better connected within it than those who are not. As they act on those preferences, and form differentially more connections to the already better-connected, the better-connected become still better connected.

In terms of network connectivity as so much else, therefore, the 'rich get richer' purely as a result of preferential attachment, as people differentially attach themselves to already well-connected nodes in the network. Furthermore, the process snowballs: the rich get richer at a progressively increasing

---

there are within a particular genus of flowering plant, the more the number of different species within that genus will grow, simply because the more species there are the more opportunities there are for some species to mutate (Yule 1925; Simon 1955).

[27] Hence the apparent paradox first noted by Feld (1991) that 'your friends have more friends than you do'—or anyway, you definitely want that to be the case. The pattern Feld discovered in a US high school is greatly magnified nowadays by social media. Hodas, Kooti, and Lerman (2013) report that 98 per cent of the Twitter users they studied had fewer followers than do the people whom they follow (typically far fewer: on average, one-thousandth as many). Again, I focus on the preference-based version of the story here. But note that even in a random network something similar would emerge: if a small portion of the group are randomly assigned twice as many friends as the rest of the group, then the average person (who will be in the latter subset) will have fewer friends on average than her friends (some of whom will be in the former subset).

[28] The 'poor' (in terms of power, popularity, status, etc.) may or may not get correspondingly 'poorer' however. 'When actors' status levels are strongly influenced by the status levels of those dispensing recognition to them, then eventually the top-ranked actor is nearly matched in status by the lower-ranked actor she endorses [and] elites may unwittingly and paradoxically destroy their cumulative advantage beneath the weight of their endorsements of others' (Bothner et al. 2010, p. 80; see similarly Schelling 1978, pp. 189–90).

rate, since the more people to whom they are already connected the more anxious others will be to become connected to them.[29] Some such 'multiplier effect' is built centrally into the feedback loop of preferential attachment.[30]

Consider now the ensuing network dynamics. There are of course many ways of modelling this. Some models ask what happens when new people enter the network, preferentially attaching themselves to those who are already the most connected within it.[31] But for our purposes, a more interesting model would involve a network consisting of a fixed set of people who are rearranging their connections with one another within that network.

For purposes of this modelling, assume that servicing each network connection is costly and, having limited resources,[32] any individual can therefore have only a fixed number of connections. (That number is not the same for every individual, it merely is fixed for any given individual.) Assume further that individuals can sever old connections and make a corresponding number of new connections in each round of the game.[33] Finally, assume preferential attachment, so people sever ties with people with fewer connections and replace them with ties to people with more connections. Over multiple rounds of the game, this will result in ever-intensifying clustering of people around a few particularly well-connected people, and an emptying-out of the space in between them.

A political manifestation of that phenomenon is a clientelist form of 'polarization', with clusters of people increasingly tightly connected to one another and decreasingly connected to those outside their cluster.[34] The sociological interpretation of that phenomenon is growing inequality in connectivity, with those already well connected becoming ever more so, and indeed at increasing rates. Even if those people initially started with only slightly more connectivity than others, preferential attachment increases their advantage exponentially over multiple rounds of the game. And there is no way, within the model of preferential attachment itself, to undo that effect.[35]

---

[29] In the words of the classic paper that coined the term, 'Because of the preferential attachment, a vertex that acquires more connections than another one will increase its connectivity as a higher rate; thus, an initial difference in the connectivity between two vertices will increase further as the network grows' (Barabási and Albert 1999, p. 511).
[30] Typically taking the form of a 'power law' distribution (Yule 1925; Zipf 1949; Simon 1955).
[31] Perc (2014, p. 5) presents a visualization based on such models.
[32] Especially but not exclusively of time and attention, as will be discussed further in Chapter 10.
[33] This is actually a continuous process, but for purposes of modelling (and description) it helps to think in terms a series of discrete 'rounds'.
[34] We can get opinion-based polarization by adding the further assumptions that (1) different people have different opinions and (2) people prefer to connect to well-connected people of the same opinion as themselves. Miller (2011, p. 1815) presents graphic evidence of clustering of liberals and conservatives on Twitter. See more generally Pew Research Centre (2014).
[35] There may be ways to slow it within the model, but literally to reverse it we have to look outside the model to find ways of overriding the effects of preferential attachment.

7.4 Reputation for Reliability and Trustworthiness

Finally, one can possess a reputation for reliability and trustworthiness.[36] That can be regarded either as a general character trait or else as a directed disposition. In the first case, the person is presumed (and hence reputed) to be reliable and trustworthy in her dealings with anyone and everyone.[37] In the second case, the person is presumed (and hence reputed) to be reliable and trustworthy exclusively or particularly vis-à-vis specific others (or some specific, independently identifiable type of other person).[38]

Furthermore, one can be deemed trustworthy and reliable with respect to some performances but not others. For example, you might be able to trust a person 'to keep his word' without being able to trust that person 'with your money or your daughter' (unless of course he has given some specific undertaking with respect to them, in which case the latter becomes an instance of the former).[39]

Finally, one can be deemed trustworthy and reliable in respect either of the specific actions to be performed or the more general objectives to be pursued. You trust your lodger to lock the door when he leaves, whereas you trust a legal guardian to serve the best interests of her ward across the board.

7.4.1 Why Trust Matters

Being able to trust or rely upon someone in any of those ways is not only intrinsically satisfying, a source of comfort and peace of mind. It is also instrumentally valuable to you in all the same ways that reliable expectations are valuable to you (as discussed in Section 6.4 above). Indeed, when you trust someone to act in a certain way, that just *is* to have a 'confident expectation' that she will act in that way.[40] And being able to form a confident expectation about what others will do allows you to frame your own actions and reactions accordingly.

---

[36] I shall here use those terms interchangeably. The *Oxford English Dictionary* defines each in terms of the other. As applied to 'a person or information', 'reliable (adj.)' (qv. 1a) is defined as 'able to be trusted; in which reliance or confidence may be placed; trustworthy, safe, sure'. 'Trustworthy (adj.)' is defined as 'worthy of trust or confidence; reliable, dependable'. Blackburn (1998, p. 34) proclaims more baldly, 'The austere basis of trust ... is just reliance'.

[37] This is 'generalized trust' (Uslaner 2002). In this chapter I am speaking primarily of individual reputations and interpersonal trust, but many of the same this can be said of the reputations of corporations and trust in them that is predicated of that (Chen and Wu 2021).

[38] Blackburn (1998, pp. 30–1) points to some such distinction as this and those in the next two paragraphs.

[39] Hardin 1993, p. 506.

[40] *Oxford English Dictionary*, 'trust (n.)', qv. 3. Knez and Camerer (1994, pp. 102, 105 n. 7) dub 'trust' an 'expectational asset'.

Engaging with people whom you can[41] trust is more rewarding, for at least two reasons.[42] One reason is that that reduces the risk that others will double-cross you, and bearing a risk of suffering high costs is in itself costly.[43] In the language of game theory, it permits you to play the 'cooperate' move in an Assurance Game, in confidence that the other(s) will do likewise.[44] The other reason, connected to that, is that you can dispense with costly monitoring and sanctioning of one another's behaviour. If you know you can trust them to do the right thing, you do not need to waste resources checking to see if they have done so or preparing to punish them if they do not.[45]

Many markets work on the basis of trust in just that way. Consider the case of traders on the floor of an old-fashioned open-outcry bourse. Trades are concluded on the basis of a handshake (or, rather, a hand signal) instead of a contract. Anyone who fails to deliver on the agreement thus concluded will be sanctioned under the extra-legal rules of the exchange and also, more importantly, never be trusted by other traders again.[46] Similarly in diamond exchanges, sellers often give buyers up to sixty days to pay for the rough stones they purchased (to give them time to cut, polish and sell on the diamond). If both buyer and seller are members of the bourse, default is once again subject to sanctioning through the extra-legal rules of the exchange. Buyers who are not members of the bourse secure their loans purely (and those who are, largely) through the 'reputational bonds': if they default, no vendor of rough diamonds will lend to them again.[47]

Although those may seem to be very special cases, most business actually proceeds on the basis of trust and a careful eye to one's reputation in on-going business relationships.[48] Even when legal contracts have been signed, litigating them is always a last resort rather than a first recourse. Stuart Macaulay's classic

---

[41] Objectively can, and not just subjectively do.

[42] Zucker (1986) traces how trust broke down, and was reestablished, over the course of American economic history from 1840 to 1920.

[43] It does not eliminate the risk fully, because in practice of course some uncertainty inevitably surrounds one's reputation for trustworthiness (Origgi 2018, ch. 4).

[44] Sen 1966. See Section 8.1 below for a fuller discussion of the Assurance Game itself.

[45] It may well be essential that enforcement mechanisms and sanctions exist in the background, of course (Hardin 1991; 2004, ch. 1; cf. Goodin 2000b). My point here is that there are benefits, on any given occasion, from not having to resort to them.

[46] Abolafia 1984. See, for example, the rules of the Chicago Mercantile Exchange (CME 2019b) and the hand signals used there (CME 2019a). The same is true among merchant bankers in the City of London: 'The visitor in the City is impressed by the absolute confidence placed in the spoken word. A press photograph of the floor of the stock exchange was titled "Where a word is as good as a contract." A lot of business is done with very little paperwork. Every day countless verbal promises, involving millions of pounds, are made over the telephone.... The merchant banker's business is based on this anatomy of trust' (Wechsberg 1966, pp. 40–1, quoted in Coleman 1990, p. 109).

[47] Bernstein 1992, pp. 138 ff; Richman 2006; cf. Richman 2017. This is Coleman's (1988, pp. S98–9) prime example of trust (see also Coleman 1990, p. 109).

[48] Macaulay (2000) refers to 'relational contracting' in this connection; I shall return to discuss a slightly different variant on that in Section 8.3.

paper on 'Non-contractual Relations in Business' quotes one businessman as saying, 'If something comes up, you get the other man on the telephone and deal with the problem. You don't read legalistic contract clauses at each other if you ever want to do business again.' Macaulay quotes another as saying, 'You can settle any dispute if you keep the lawyers and accountants out of it. They just do not understand the give and take needed in business.'[49]

Macaulay illustrates the point with an extended analysis of the archived correspondence between Frank Lloyd Wright and the General Manager of S. C. Johnson & Son, for whom the notoriously difficult architect was building a fabulous new corporate headquarters in Racine, Wisconsin. They certainly had their spats. At one point, the General Manager told Wright that if he did not 'give me something soon' to solve a leaky skylight he would 'ruin your building' by 'buying a few sheets of ... [ugly] ordinary wire glass that they put in factory windows and slapping it on top of the skylights'.[50] But through all their spats, they never once quoted contract terms to one another, apparently.

Cooperative enterprises thus work most successfully on the basis of parties trusting one another. If others deem you trustworthy, they will be more likely to offer to cooperate with you and to do so on more favourable terms. That, in turn, gives you an incentive to cultivate a reputation for trustworthiness.

Your reputation for trustworthiness is based on 'observables'—what you are known, or reputed, to have done in relevantly similar situations in the past. That, in turn gives you an incentive to invest in 'building a reputation' for trustworthiness, by behaving in each round in ways that you think likely to make you appeal to prospective future partners in trusting relationships. Thus, even people who are not 'really' trustworthy, in terms of their natural disposition or deeper character traits, have an incentive to behave in a trustworthy fashion.[51] And that is fine, insofar as their behaviour—whether or not they betray the trust—is all that matters to others with whom they are dealing.[52]

As David Kreps says, a reputation for trustworthiness is 'circular': 'it works because it works'.[53] You do what others trust you to do, not because you want to do that independently, but rather because you want them (and others like them) to trust you in the future. Acting in line with, and for the sake of, your

---

[49] Macaulay 1963, p. 61.
[50] Macaulay 1996, p. 95.
[51] In all but the last round of an iterated game, anyway. There may be a sense of 'real trustworthiness' that requires proper dispositions and character traits (Jones 2012b); and strategic situations that mask whether or not a person actually has them may well undermine others' trust in them in other situations where such strategic incentives are missing. Something like that seems to underlie Spinoza's arguments against compelling (possibly false) professions of faith and allegiance (Gais 2020).
[52] Dasgupta 1988, p. 70; Coleman 1990, p. 77; Kreps 1990, pp. 100–11, esp. pp. 106–8; Hardin 2004, pp. 17–20.
[53] Kreps 1990, p. 107.

reputation solidifies and confirms your reputation.[54] It is not quite the same 'bootstrapping' dynamic as made expectations self-fulfilling in Chapter 6. But it is a powerfully reinforcing dynamic, nonetheless.

The same thing that is true of individuals is true of firms, in this respect. Product differentiation and branding are crucial to commercial success. New buyers will gravitate to products with a good reputation, and return buyers will loyally stick with products that they have found to be good in the past.[55]

Here is one quaint example. In the early days of the automobile industry, highly publicized racing competitions were held to demonstrate speed and endurance of different manufacturers' vehicles. Those competitions served to establish the reputation of motorcar manufacturers for producing quality products: those who won multiple competitions persisted while those that did not soon exited the market.[56] For another example, consider how investment bankers slightly under price the initial public offering of shares in a company, in order to avoid getting a reputation with buyers for price gouging.[57]

But of course having a good reputation is essential for the success of a business of any sort.[58] That is equally true whether it is selling a product or a service. It is equally true whether it is a multinational corporation or a small corner shop. 'Moody's ranking of insurance companies, Michelin's and AAA's rankings of restaurants, and J.D. Power's ranking of automobiles create perceptions of the status of organizations that ultimately influence their survival chances.'[59] Favourable reputations and rankings help to sustain those possessing them in positions of comparative advantage, unfairly so vis-à-vis others who have not had a chance to acquire such favourable reputations or rankings even objectively they merit them.

7.4.2 Assortation by Reputation: Trust-based Network Construction

The advantages that come to you from being able to trust, and being trusted by, those with whom you deal provide an incentive in turn for you to shape the circle of people with whom you deal accordingly. People who can trust

---

[54] The same is true of your reputation for status as for trustworthiness, as Bernheim (1994) shows.
[55] Hirschmann (1970) bases his political model of *Exit, Voice and Loyalty* on the 'brand loyalty' analogy.
[56] Rao 1994.
[57] Beatty and Ritter 1986.
[58] Fombrun and Shanley 1990; Podolny 1993; Fombrun 1994.
[59] Sauder, Lynn and Podolny 2012, p. 269.

one another prefer to deal with one another, rather than those in whom they cannot be confident.

This is the process of 'assortation', or people sorting themselves into groups of people with whom they will interact in an on-going way for certain specific purposes.[60] The formal models of this process are much as the one described at the end of Section 7.3, except here people choose whom to include and whom to exclude on the basis not of how many people are connected to the person in question but instead on the basis of whether the person in question can be trusted in the domain in question.[61] The result of this assortation is once again a clustering, here of people who are prepared to deal with one another on beneficial terms because they are able to trust one another.

Sometimes people are selected in or out of these circles on the basis of their own past performances. Sometimes they are selected in or out—in the first instance, anyway—on the basis of ascriptive characteristics and behavioural traits associated with them.[62] The diamond merchants described in Section 7.4.1 trusted one another, for example, because they were all orthodox Jews who were prohibited by religious strictures from cheating other Jews—and the old norms of trusting relations broke down in the diamond exchange when other ethnic groups got involved in the trade.[63]

Some say these are like a form of 'private government'.[64] Those groups of people bound by trust in one another are self-policing entities.[65] They set their own standards for inclusion and exclusion. They set their own rules of conduct, and they reward and punish members for compliance or non-compliance. These are sometimes formally organized entities with formal rules

---

[60] Borrowing from Geertz (1962), Coleman (1984, pp. 84–5; 1988, p. S102–3) offers the example of 'rotating credit associations' in Southeast Asia. Bowles and Gintis (1998) similarly build their model of the 'evolution of pro-social norms' on the basis of 'reputation, retaliation, segmentation and parochialism'.

[61] Spiekermann 2007, 2009; Rivera, Sonderstrom, and Uzzi 2010.

[62] Akerlof (1976, pp. 609–16) describes and models the case of caste in India, where people are 'selected in' on the basis of an ascriptive characteristic but then 'selected out' (or anyway singled out for less advantageous treatment) on account of their failure display the behavioural traits appropriate to their caste.

[63] Coleman 1988, p. S99; Richman 2006, 2017. As discussed in Section 4.3, there is a large literature on 'homophily'—the tendency of people to form connections with others who are 'similar' to them in some respect or another (McPherson, Smith-Lovin, and Cook 2001; Kossinets and Watts 2009). That people think they can trust (or anyway 'know what to expect from') people like themselves might be one partial explanation of that larger pattern (Melamed et al. 2020).

[64] Galanter 1981.

[65] As Burt, Kilduff, and Tasselli (2013, p. 541) say, 'dense clusters produce trust and reputation, which constitute the governance mechanism in social networks.... The more embedded a relationship, the more likely bad behavior by either party will become known, thereby creating a reputation cost for bad behavior, which facilitates trust and collaboration. With bad behavior likely to be detected, people are expected to be more careful about their behavior. Thus, trust is facilitated between people in a closed network, making collaborations possible that would otherwise be difficult or unwise.'

and procedures, such as the bourses discussed in Section 7.4.1. As often, they are informal associations having tacit but pretty fully mutual understandings of what constitutes proper conduct on the part of members, and whose principal form of sanction is simply to shun miscreants.

Notice the distributional consequences of people sorting themselves into such cabals of mutually trusting cooperators. Those who are included in the cabal are indeed advantaged by trusting and being trusted by one another, in just the ways described in Section 7.4.1. They are clearly made better off by the formation of the cabal. But notice, too, that those who are excluded from them because others could not be as confident that they could be trusted are correspondingly disadvantaged by their exclusion. They are not equally able to enter into beneficial arrangements on equally advantageous terms, because they stand outside the circle of trust. And since gains in one round serve as the basis for investments in the next, the relative advantage of the two groups pulls increasingly apart over time.

In effect, those who deem one another trustworthy form a 'club'. Within the club, the same public goods are equally available to anyone—pre-eminently interacting on the basis of the favourable, trust-based rules of the club. For anyone outside the club, however, those public goods are unavailable. It is a clear form of 'clubbish justice'—or certainly, anyway, clubbish mutual advantage.[66]

---

[66] Goodin 2008. For background, see Buchanan's (1965) proposal for a 'club goods' alternative to Samuelson's (1954) 'public goods'.

8
Coordination and Organization Confer Advantage

George Bernard Shaw's play *The Apple Cart* depicts a wily king running rings around his fractious cabinet. Prime Minister Proteus admonishes his cabinet colleagues, 'If you all start quarrelling and scolding and bawling ... it will end with his having his own way as usual, because one man that has a mind and knows it can always beat ten men who haven't and don't.'[1] True though that may be, the converse is also true. Ten men, united and of one mind, can often prevail over someone much more powerful than any of them taken individually. That speaks to the advantage that is conferred by coordination and organization.[2]

In this chapter I will discuss various forms that such coordination and organization might take. Each has its advantages and disadvantages. But being coordinated or organized in any of these ways is ordinarily better than not being.[3] All of these are mechanisms by which those who are coordinated or organized obtain and retain significant advantages over those who are not.[4] Furthermore, coordinating in one way rather than another differentially advantages some over others among those who are thus coordinated. Finally, because coordinated solutions and organizational structures are sticky and hard to change, the differential advantages that they confer will persist and indeed grow over time.

We saw that, for example, in Chapter 5's discussion of languages, coding categories, and interpretive schema. There are great advantages, perhaps

---

[1] Shaw 1928/1934, Act I, p. 1016.
[2] As Benjamin Franklin is reputed to have said upon the signing of the Declaration of Independence, 'We must all hang together, or most assuredly, we will all hang separately.'
[3] For example, in their analysis of data from 186 countries Chilton and Versteeg (2016) find that constitutional rights to organize (to form unions and political parties) make more difference to government behaviour than individual constitutional rights, precisely because they give rise to powerful organizations (unions, political parties) with an interest in protecting those rights.
[4] Alkire (2006) argues that coordination is implicated in both the cause and the cure for structural injustice: 'in the case of structural injustice, multiple agents coordinate joint action, the fruits of which are unjust' (p. 47); and overcoming structural injustice is an 'embedded collective action problem' (p. 58).

sometimes even urgent necessities, in employing the same ones of those as do others with whom we are interacting. But while coordinating in that way advantages us all compared to not coordinating at all, the choice of which particular languages, coding categories, or interpretive schema around which to coordinate advantages some of us more than others.

All that is true not only of languages but also of social structures more generally. They consist in a set of 'interdependent social practices' that are 'more or less coordinated'.[5] Even where everyone involved benefits from being coordinated in that way, some benefit more than others; and they benefit more than they would have benefited had we opted for structures and practices that coordinated us in some different way.[6]

8.1 Varieties of Coordination Problems

As Herbert Simon succinctly puts it, 'coordination simply means organizing activity in such a way as to handle the problems that arise because the behaviors of each participant depends in some ways on the behaviors of the others'.[7]

I have already begun discussing coordination in relation to language choice in Section 5.1.1. As I said there, coordination takes many forms. Indeed, it takes even more forms than canvassed in that previous discussion. as I shall now show.

One occasion for coordination can be described as a 'Pure Coordination Game' (the same as Section 5.1.1's 'Equal Coordination Game'). There, each actor is absolutely indifferent as among all the possible coordinated solutions. In Figure 8.1, there are two coordinated solutions: one in which both agents choose option O_1; the other in which both choose option O_2. Each agent prefers either of those outcomes to all others, but each agent is indifferent between both of them choosing O_1 or both choosing O_2. They simply need to coordinate on one or the other.

---

[5] Haslanger 2012, pp. 20–1.

[6] To be clear: I am not here claiming that *all* instances of structural injustice are necessarily solutions to coordination problems with these characteristics. Some might be exercises in pure oppression, making the oppressed worse off than they would have been without any such exercise. Young's (1990, ch. 2) early treatment suggests as much. My claim here is merely that solutions to genuine coordination problems involve creating structures that distribute benefits and burdens differentially, and persistently so, in ways that could often be regarded as morally without warrant and 'unjust' for that reason.

[7] Simon 2000, p. 750. Malone and Crowston (1994, p. 90) similarly define 'coordination' as 'managing dependencies between activities'. 'Coordination problems' arise if and only if there are such dependencies between the activities in question.

		Agent A_2	
		Option O_1	Option O_2
Agent A_1	Option O_1	(1,1)	(0,0)
	Option O_2	(0,0)	(1,1)

Figure 8.1 Pure Coordination Game

'Unequal coordination games'—ones in which different agents prefer different coordinated solutions—are also possible. Those genuinely count as coordination games, just so long as each actor prefers *any* of the alternative coordinated solutions to any of the non-coordinated solutions. Figure 8.2 depicts an 'Unequal Coordination Game' familiar from Section 5.1.1. That game has two coordinated solutions: one in which both agents choose option O_1, the other in which both choose option O_2, once again. Here, however, the agents are not indifferent between those two outcomes. Agent A_1 prefers that both choose option O_1; and agent A_2 prefers that both choose option O_2. Still, coordinating on either of those sets of choices, (O_1, O_1) or (O_2, O_2), is better for each agent than either of the other possible outcomes.

		Agent A_2	
		Option O_1	Option O_2
Agent A_1	Option O_1	(2,1)	(0,0)
	Option O_2	(0,0)	(1,2)

Figure 8.2 Unequal Coordination Game

There are other strategic constellations, not conventionally classed 'coordination games', in which it would be strategically advantageous for every agent to coordinate their choices with one another's. Consider, for example, the Assurance Game.[8] That depicts the situation where both agents actually prefer the same outcome, and each merely needs to be assured that the other will choose it as well. In Figure 8.3, the best outcome for both agents comes when both choose option O_1. But insofar an agent expects the other to choose option O_2, he will himself choose instead option O_2, which at least pays him

---

[8] Sen 1966. Sometimes, after Rousseau's (1755/1973, pt. 2, para. 9) famous example, it is called the 'Stag Hunt' (Skyrms 2001, 2004). On the limitations of this model, see Elliott (2011).

1 instead of 0.[9] If both do that, however, each receives a payoff of 1 rather than the 3 each would have received had they both chosen option O_1. As in the Pure Coordination Game, there is no conflict of interest between the actors. They merely need to coordinate on the solution in which each of them chooses option O_1, which is what each most prefers.

		Agent A_2	
		Option O_1	Option O_2
Agent $A1$	Option O_1	(3,3)	(0,2)
	Option O_2	(2,0)	(1,1)

Figure 8.3 Assurance Game

Finally, consider the classic Prisoner's Dilemma scenario.[10] In it, each agent has a strictly dominant strategy, that is, a move that is best for her regardless of what the other chooses to do. But both playing their strictly dominant strategies leads to an outcome that is worse for each than if each had chosen some other strategy. That is where the 'coordination' aspect of the game arises. In Figure 8.4, the strictly dominant strategy for each agent is option O_2; but when both choose that option each gets a payoff of 1, whereas had each chosen option O_1 they each would have received a payoff of 2. The task of coordination there is to overcome the temptation for each player to play her strictly dominant strategy and, instead, to ensure that both agents act in ways that taken together lead to a better outcome for each.

		Agent A_2	
		Option O_1	Option O_2
Agent A_1	Option O_1	(2,2)	(0,3)
	Option O_2	(3,0)	(1,1)

Figure 8.4 Prisoner's Dilemma

---

[9] A risk-averse agent who has no expectations either way might likewise choose O_2 simply because in that way the worst outcome for her (payoff of 0) can be avoided.

[10] Luce and Raiffa 1957, pp. 94–7.

8.2 Methods of Coordinating

Having seen the various circumstances in which coordination might be advantageous, let us now turn to consider ways in which it might be achieved.

8.2.1 Formal Coordination by Mutual Agreement

One way for people to coordinate their actions with one another's is for all of them to enter into a formal agreement to do so. This agreement must, at a minimum, specify what each is to do or specify some procedure for determining that.

In situations where there are strategic incentives for agents to do something other than what is thus specified, the agreement must do something more. It must also institute sanctions sufficient to deter those who might be tempted to defect from the agreement.[11] In terms of the game matrices in Section 8.1, the effect of those sanctions is to change the structure of the game. For example, in the Prisoner's Dilemma (Figure 8.4) the coordination agreement would dictate that each agent opt for O_1, and it would impose a sanction for not doing so that is sufficient to make O_2 pay each less than O_1. Once the cost of that sanction is taken into account, O_2 ceases to be each actor's strictly dominant strategy, and O_1 becomes strictly dominant for each instead.

Writ large, this is Hobbes' solution to the problem of social order.[12] Writ small, it is the essence of private contracting. Crucial to the working of contract law is what Schelling calls 'the "right" to be sued'. The possibility of suing you for defaulting is what gives other parties to the contract sufficient confidence to rely upon and hence to comply with the contract themselves.[13]

Formal coordination agreements can be bilateral, involving just two parties, or they can be multilateral. They can be narrow or wide scope, covering just one type of coordination problem or many at once. They can be one-off or temporally extended, applying just on this occasion or to similar coordination problems that may arise over an extended period of time.

Sometimes formal coordination agreements give rise to formal organizations, with formal decision-making procedures, formal command structures and formal enforcement mechanisms. Such formal organizations will be the topic of Section 8.3. But there may be no need for any of that if the coordination

---

[11] 'Mutual coercion mutually agreed upon', in Garrett Hardin's (1968) famous phrase.
[12] Hobbes 1651.
[13] Schelling 1960, p. 43.

agreement is simple and self-enforcing. In Figure 8.1's Pure Coordination Game, for example, agreement on which solution to pursue is all that is required in order to secure the desired coordination. Similarly, in Figure 8.3's Assurance Game, agreement that all will pursue the coordinated solution is all that is required to ensure that all do so.

For a striking example of how formal coordination arrangements can create and perpetuate disadvantage, consider the practice of 'redlining' US real estate. The practice began in the wake of the Great Depression, as the federal government moved to stabilize the housing market. Stabilizing house prices involved, among other things, preventing radical shifts in the racial composition of a neighbourhood that would drive down house prices. Preventing that obviously required coordination among those selling houses there. A Federal Home Loan Bank Board was established to oversee the newly created federal savings and loan associations. An offshoot of that Board, the Home Owner's Loan Corporation, undertook

> to introduce a systematic appraisal process that included neighborhood-level characteristics when evaluating residential properties....[14] Using the new appraisal system, the HOLC drew residential [lending] 'security' maps for 239 cities between 1935 and 1940.... The maps and the appraisal process were seen as a mechanism for solving a coordination problem that would help ensure the continued stability of property values throughout the nation.[15]

Lines on those maps indicated how safe it was deemed to be to invest in, and make loans on, real estate in various neighbourhoods. Red lines on the map indicated the riskiest 'D' rating. That of course became a self-fulfilling prophecy, insofar as being redlined naturally caused a yet further decline in investment and property values in a neighbourhood.[16] The

---

[14] Among those 'neighborhood-level characteristics', 'there is clear evidence that the racial makeup of neighborhoods were explicit factors that were often pivotal in assigning grades to neighborhoods' (Aaronson et al. 2019, p. 7). See similarly Koopman (2022, pp. 345–6).

[15] Aaronson et al. 2019, p. 6. Explaining why this was seen as a coordination problem, they quote Hillier (2005. p. 210) citing an FHLBB document saying that HOLC 'experts believe that since its interest is duplicated by that of all home-financing and mortgage institutions, a program can be evolved which will reclaim large residential areas which are doomed unless some concerted action is taken. Those experts believe that a joint program of Government agencies and private capital can save millions of dollars in property values now being wasted each year.'

[16] Helper 1969; Lang and Nakamura 1993. In their econometric analysis, Aaronson et al. (2019, pp. 34–5) 'consistently find a significant and persistent causal effect of the HOLC maps on the racial composition and housing developments of urban neighborhoods. ... [T]he maps led to reduced credit access and higher borrowing costs which, in turn, contributed to disinvestment in poor urban American neighborhoods with long-run repercussions. We show that being on the lower graded side of D-C boundaries led to rising racial segregation from 1930 until about 1970....'

effect was to entrench decaying inner-city neighbourhoods as ghettos inhabited predominantly—and increasingly exclusively—by impoverished racial minorities.[17]

8.2.2 Shared Norms or Conventions

Coordination can also be achieved without formal agreement. If coordination is mutually advantageous, a norm or convention might arise among the agents involved which is sufficient to achieve that purpose.

In a Pure Coordination Game (Figure 8.1), a simple convention will suffice. There, all that is required is for everyone to know what everyone is expected to do, and everyone will do it.[18] David Lewis offers the example of re-establishing a telephone link after you have been cut off: if both parties try ringing the other back at the same time, each will get an engaged signal and the call will not go through; but if both parties know that the convention is for the party who originally initiated the call to ring back, and if both abide by that convention, the call will be successfully re-established. Since neither party cares which of them rings the other back, and they want only for the connection to be re-established, neither party has any motive for doing anything other than that convention prescribes.[19] The same is true in trumps in an Assurance Game (Figure 8.3). There, abiding by a convention that dictates each do what is required to achieve the coordinated solution yields the best possible outcome for each player. Not only does neither of them have any motive for deviating from the convention; each has a strong positive motive for abiding by it.

In the Prisoner's Dilemma (Figure 8.4), in contrast, each player has a strong temptation to defect from the coordinated solution (O_1, O_1). If the other plays O_1, your playing O_2 would pay you more than would your playing O_1, which is what the coordinated solution requires. So something more than a simple convention—something more than common knowledge about what the others will do—is there required in order for the coordinated solution to be achieved.

---

[17] These maps were used to guide the lending practices of the US Federal Housing Administration. The instructions in its 1938 *Underwriting Manual* were even more explicit in directing that loans not be made on properties in areas with 'inharmonious racial groups' (US FHA 1938, pt 2, sec. 9). See further: Jackson 1985, ch. 11; Rothstein 2017; Aaronson et al. 2019, pp. 9–10. What Hwang and McDaniel (2022) call residential neighbourhood 'hierarchy endurance' ensures that those patterns of housing segregation persist even after those formal mechanisms have long been abandoned.

[18] Artistic performances—an orchestra's playing a symphony, for example—rely on a huge array of conventions. In art worlds as elsewhere, 'conventions make collective action simpler and less costly in time, energy and other resources; but they do not make unconventional work impossible, only more costly and more difficult' (Becker 1974, p. 775).

[19] Lewis 1969, pp. 43–4.

Norms, backed by material and psychological incentives of one sort or another, are needed.

Sometimes such norms are formally agreed and imposed, as in Section 8.2.1. But norms can, and often do, arise without any formal agreement. Consider for example the norm that arose among whalers operating off Greenland in the early nineteenth century. According to that norm, if a whale carcass is fixed fast to your ship by a line or otherwise, it is your property; but if is loose and floating free any ship is entitled to put a line on it. What we know today of those norms by and large comes from court cases that invoked and deferred to them 'as binding on persons of all nations'. But, clearly, the pre-existence of those informal social norms is what provided the grounds for their legal recognition.[20]

Two defining features of such informal social norms are their 'normative authority' and their 'presumed practice dependence'. That is just to say that people in general think that others typically do, and think that they should, comply with the norms of their society.[21] That makes the selection of and adherence to social norms a coordination problem. People want to internalize and act upon the same norms as do others around them.

Perceptions of what others think about social norms are, thus, central. Yet those perceptions can often be wrong, as shown by various studies of 'pluralistic ignorance' surrounding norms of racial segregation in the mid-twentieth century American South.[22] One study asked parishioners of a segregated church (a) what *they* would think about its admitting blacks, and (b) what they think *other parishioners* would think about it. Although 47 per cent said that they themselves would be 'tolerant', only 8 per cent expected others would be.[23] Obviously, both cannot be correct. Another 1968 survey found that, while only 32 per cent of Southerners actually reported themselves being in favour of segregation, fully 61 per cent of them thought that a majority of people in their area were.[24] Again, both cannot be correct. Such studies suggest that segregationist norms persisted, and continued to shape public life in the South, less out of people's actual preferences and more out of the erroneous misperception of the extent to which others supported those norms. The persistence of norms of racial segregation in the American South in mid-twentieth century is thus powerful testimony to the way in which norms can

---

[20] Ellickson 1991, pp. 192–206. The quotation is from *Fennings v. Lord Grenville*, 1 Taunt. 241, 127 Eng. Rep. 825, 828 (Ct. Comm. Pleas 1808), quoted in Ellickson (1991, p. 193, n. 26). See further: Ullmann-Marglit 1977; Bicchieri 1990, 2006; Brennan et al. 2013, ch. 5.
[21] Brennan et al. 2013, pp. 35–9 and 76–81.
[22] The phenomenon of pluralistic ignorance is also discussed in Sections 6.3 and 7.2.
[23] Breed and Ktsanes 1961, p. 385.
[24] O'Gorman 1975, p. 318.

create and perpetuate advantage, even without anyone (or anyway, anything like a majority of people) wanting them to do so.

8.2.3 Mutual Adjustment

So far I have discussed ways of coordinating with one another through formal agreements and through informal social norms and conventions. In all those cases, there is something (an agreement, norm or convention) that is shared among those being coordinated, and coordination consists in their acting on the basis of that thing that they share. Next I shall discuss how people can coordinate with one another, after a fashion, without sharing any of those things.

The complete antithesis of coordination would be auturky. There, each agent makes her decisions impervious to the actions and choices of any other agents. Doing so makes no sense, however, in a world where the payoffs to each are a function of the actions and choices of all.[25] At the very least, in such circumstances, you should try to *anticipate* what the relevant others will do and select what you think would be your 'best response' to the anticipated actions and choices of the others. That is simply to say that you should choose 'strategically' in the ways prescribed by non-cooperative game theory.[26]

In so doing, you would certainly not be 'cooperating' with them, or even 'coordinating' with them. Still, insofar as your make your choices in response to your expectations about their choices, and they theirs in response to their expectations about yours, there is 'mutual responsiveness' of a sort. At least that is not a world of pure autarky.

Sometimes that mutual responsiveness takes a more robust form. In repeated interactions, agents can make their present choices in response to, or in anticipation of, one another's past or future choices. That opens up the possibility for tit-for-tat retaliation or reward over a sequence of repeated plays. That can make 'nice' moves attractive in a Prisoner's Dilemma situation, even though 'nasty' moves would have been strictly dominant in a one-shot game.[27] That can systematically evoke 'nice' moves in an Assurance Game, which might have otherwise been risky.

---

[25] That is to say, agents must form 'intersubjective beliefs' that 'each of us (players of game G) aims to maximize individual payoff'. They need to form those sorts of beliefs if only to make optimal strategic choices for themselves, even if those beliefs do not transform the strategic situation in the ways Brown (2020, p. 356) envisages.

[26] Luce and Raiffa 1957, ch. 5. This, of course, is what happens in markets (Simon 2000, pp. 750–1) and in political processes akin to them driven by 'partisan mutual adjustment' (Lindblom 1965).

[27] As already noticed by Luce and Raiffa (1957, pp. 97–102) and famously elaborated by Axelrod (1984).

There might even emerge some 'implicit bargaining' in such situations. Each might, by their play in one round, signal a very specific sort of intention: 'I will if you will'; and 'I will if (you will if I will).'[28] Insofar as both players believe that each other genuinely to have that constellation of intentions, coordinated action can emerge without anything more formal.[29]

In the literature on collective action, this is ordinarily taken to be very good news. In certain respects it clearly is. Mutual responsiveness in repeat-play situations aids in the management of exhaustible common pool resources, such as fisheries.[30] It enables cattlemen and ranchers to coordinate with one another when their cattle trespass on others' property on the high plains.[31] It was even used by opposing troops in the trenches to prevent pointless slaughter on the Western Front during World War I.[32]

In such ways, mutual responsiveness in repeat-play situations can be advantageous for the agents directly involved in them. But their securing advantages in those ways can of course have correspondingly negative consequences for others who are not party to those interactions. It can, as I argued in Section 7.4.2, lead to a form of 'clubbish justice', where good treatment is accorded to all but only those who are 'members of the cooperating club'.[33]

For an example of this phenomenon in action, consider how modern oligopolies fix prices to increase their profits at the expense of the larger public via 'mutual responsiveness' in the form of 'follow-the-leader' price setting.[34] In 1962, US Steel raised its prices and, within hours, literally all five other major American steel manufacturers did likewise. President Kennedy reacted angrily.[35] He directed the FBI to investigate. But it could find no evidence of

---

[28] Standard discussions of 'I will if you will' mechanisms such as Oppenheimer and Frohlich (1970) and Oppenheimer, Frohlich, and Young (1971) omit the second intention. But without the 'I will if (you will if I will)' clause, they lack a trigger for actually activating this conditional cooperation (Goodin 2012a).

[29] Axelrod 1981; Taylor 1987.

[30] Ostrom 1990.

[31] Ellickson's (1991, p. 227) interviews in Shasta County, California, revealed that for cases of non-negligible damage a rule is employed that is identical to 'tit-for-tat' reciprocity. 'Most rural residents are consciously committed to an overarching norm of cooperation among neighbors. In trespass situations, their ... norm, adhered to by all but a few deviants, is that an owner of livestock is responsible for the acts of his animals. Allegiance to this norm seems wholly independent of formal legal entitlements.... The neighborly response to an isolated infraction is an exchange of civilities. A trespass victim should notify the animal owner that the trespass has occurred and assist the owner in retrieving the stray stock.... [A] cattleman who is a good neighbor will quickly retrieve the animals ..., apologize for the occurrence, and thank the caller' (Ellickson 1991, pp. 52–3).

[32] Axelrod 1984, ch. 4. For other examples see Oye (1986).

[33] Goodin (2008), building on Buchanan (1965).

[34] Scitovsky 1971, pp. 426–7. Nicholson 1972.

[35] Kennedy fumed, 'Some time ago I asked each American to consider what he would do for his country and I asked the steel companies [the same]. In the last 24 hours we had their answer.... [T]he

direct collusion. Instead, it was simply a case of all other companies following the lead of US Steel. That is an example of how coordination achieved purely through mutual responsiveness can, in that way, serve to create and perpetuate advantage.

8.2.4 Mutual Alignment

In the cases of 'mutual responsiveness', each individual agent decides what is best for him to do in response to what others have done or are expected to do. Furthermore, each agent decides individually: 'what I should do' on the basis of 'what is best for me'.

Next I shall consider cases of 'mutual alignment'. Here, each individual is still deciding on his own, separately from others. But in these cases his *decision frame* is collective. That is to say, he asks himself, 'What should *we* do, and what should I do as *part* of that?' It is not yet a case of 'joint action', however. No group agent has yet been created and vested with a decision procedure all its own. This is still very much individual action, albeit individual action chosen on the basis of a joint perspective.[36]

This type of coordination, too, can create and perpetuate advantage and disadvantage. Among the most notorious examples of that are the infamous dinners hosted by Elbert Gary, chairman of the board of US Steel, at the beginning of the twentieth century.[37] Over those dinners, the leaders of all the major US steel manufacturers discussed 'frankly and freely what they were doing, how much business they were doing, what prices they were charging, how much wages they were paying their men, and ... all information concerning their business'.[38]

---

suddenness by which every company in the last few hours, one by one as the morning went by, came in with their almost ... identical price increases ... isn't really the way we expect the competitive private enterprise system to ... work' (quoted in Godden and Maidment 1980, pp. 329–20, 321).

[36] Collins (2019, ch. 5) identifies this distinct mode of action, building on materials from Bratman (1993, 2014), Sugden (2003), and Toumela (2007, 2013). Marschak and Radner (1972, p. 9) offer an 'economic theory of teams', where a 'team' is defined as an organization the members of which have only common interests and hence 'act as one' (indeed, they commence their analysis of 'teams' through the analysis of the degenerate case of a 'one-person team'). Even when are 'working for a common end which each man desired', as in Lindsay's (1924, p. 73) example of support companies in the British Army during World War I, coordination (there provided by a command structure) is required to tell each company what exactly it is to do in the service of that common end.

[37] As notorious is the story of coordination and cooperation among railroad companies in the nineteenth-century US, recounted in Chandler (1977, chs 3–5; cf. Roy 1997, ch. 4).

[38] As Elbert Gary testified at the subsequent trial where the practice was held to be illegal (Page 2009, p. 597).

Those dinners were convened with the intention of 'stabilizing' the steel industry during an economic panic, and to do so in a way that would not violate anti-trust law. According to the leading anti-trust case at the time, Gary thought, 'the law does not compel competition; it only prohibits an agreement not to compete'.[39] Hence, Gary arranged what he described as 'frequent meetings and the interchange of opinions ... without making any agreements of any kind'.[40] The discussions focused purely on what would be best for the industry overall. Judge Gary insisted that:

> We are independent [and] can go out of this room and do exactly as we please, without violating any agreement or understanding.... [A]ll must depend upon the belief that, as honorable men, we are desirous of conducting ourselves and our business in such a way as not to injure our neighbors....[41]

Even though no formal agreements had been made, the US Supreme Court nonetheless held that the sort of 'we-thinking' conjured up at the Gary dinners had a 'common object' and hence amounted to 'concerted action' of a sort that constitutes an unlawful combination in restraint of trade.[42] It is again an example of how coordination—here, achieved via mutual alignment—can perpetuate advantage.

8.3 Structures for Coordinating: Organizations, Formal and Informal

There are three distinct types of structures within which the various methods of coordinating just described can occur. One is a formal hierarchical organization based on command and control exercised from the top. A second structure is an informal network of approximate coequals in repeated, trusting interaction with one another. A third structure is a set of market-style institutions that simply set ground rules for isolated individuals to make one-off exchanges with one another.[43] In the real world, of course, admixtures among those classic 'ideal types' are far more common than their pure forms.

---

[39] Gary, quoted in Page 2009, p. 607.
[40] Gary, quoted in Page 2009, p. 600. As Mill (1848/1965, bk 1, ch. 9, § 24) had observed, 'Where competitors are so few, they always end by agreeing not to compete.'
[41] Gary, quoted in Page 2009, p. 609.
[42] *United States v. U.S. Steel Corp.*, 251 US 417, 442 (1920).
[43] These broadly correspond to the types of socio-political processes for coordination identified by Dahl and Lindblom (1953, chs 6–13): my 'hierarchy' is the same as theirs, my 'market' is their 'price system', and my 'networks' combines their 'polyarchy' and 'bargaining'.

Economics traditionally offers us a stark choice between 'markets' or 'hierarchy'. According to the received theory, a production process will be organized within a firm if and only if doing so is more cost-effective than buying the product of such a process on the open market.[44] Typically that will be the case because it is harder to externally assess (or specify contractually in advance) the quality of a required product than it is to internally monitor the quality of the process producing it.

Disputes rage over which pattern—market or hierarchy—is the more common. Some depict firms and other formal hierarchical organizations as 'islands of planned co-ordination in a sea of market relations'.[45] Others see 'business (and governmental) organizations' as the 'principal coordinators of economic activity'.[46] Both sides of that dispute, however, endorse the received view within traditional economics that those are the two principal mechanisms for achieving social coordination.

That account overlooks all manner of informal organizations, however. Prominently among them are the networks discussed in Chapter 4.[47] Also among them are loose alliances such as trade associations that lobby governments to promote the shared interests of their members.[48] Repeated interactions among firms also give rise to more-or-less dense patterns of semi-organized cooperation.[49] Some go so far as to call these sorts of relationships a form of 'private government', as I have already noted in Section 7.4.2.[50]

Indeed, it was from these dense networks of interconnected relationships that modern markets historically emerged.[51] Markets did not 'spring full blown with the Industrial Revolution'. Instead, 'the history of modern

---

[44] Coase 1937. Chandler (1977) shows that US economic history supports this proposition; cf. Roy 1997, chs 1–2. A whole school of 'transaction cost economics' grew up around this insight (Williamson 1975).

[45] Richardson (1972, p. 883) coined this delightful phrase but went on to dissociate itself from its claim.

[46] Simon 2000, p. 751; see further Simon 1991.

[47] Powell 1990.

[48] Berry and Wilcox 2018.

[49] Richardson 1972. '[W]e find companies involved in an intricate latticework of collaborative ventures with other firms, most of whom are ostensibly competitors. The dense ties that bind the auto and biotechnology industries' are most accurately characterized, Powell (1990, p. 301) thinks, 'as networks rather than as joint ventures among hierarchical firms'.

[50] Macaulay 1986.

[51] Likewise, arguably, bureaucracies. Martimort (1997, p. 555) argues that bureaucratic structures—what Dalton (1959) calls 'horizontal cliques'—emerge within an organization 'from a self-enforced norm of reciprocity between agents in an organization who exchange favors and promote subgoals which differ from the objective of the firm. Such collusive behavior becomes harder and harder to prevent over time', and the organization becomes less efficient in pursuing its larger goals in consequence. See further Tirole 1992.

commerce ... is a story of family businesses, guilds, cartels and extended trading companies—all enterprises with loose and highly permeable boundaries.'[52]

Just as the conventional view of markets elides these strong elements of collaboration and coordination within them, so too does the conventional view of hierarchy overstate the amount of command-and-control exercised within it. The employment relationship was traditionally treated as being virtually akin to a slavery contract, in which the employee promised to do whatever the employer directed (within the limits set by the terms of the contract and by labour and other law).[53] Indeed, the traditional term for 'employment law' was 'the law of master and servant'.[54]

Such is the mythology. In real world organizations, however, managers cannot simply issue orders and expect them to be obeyed. They need to negotiate, persuade, cajole.[55] Richard Neustadt famously tells the story of President Truman expressing sympathy for his soon-to-be successor, Dwight Eisenhower: 'He will sit there, and he will say, "Do this! Do that!" And nothing will happen. Poor Ike—it won't be a bit like the army.'[56] But it turned out to be just like the army, where Eisenhower had already mastered that lesson.

Not only is there 'control loss' within formal organizations, with people decreasingly able to exercise effective control over notional subordinates much further down the hierarchy.[57] The orders that they issue are also typically open-ended, as well: they specify outcomes to be achieved but leave the choice of means to the subordinates' discretion;[58] or they specify 'premises' for subordinates to take into account in making decisions, without mandating that those must necessarily play a determinative role in those decisions.[59]

Within a single organization, the density of interactions varies. Achieving coordination through formal organizational mechanisms 'is costly and imperfect', so we want to 'introduce no more of it than the structure and intricacy of our goals calls for'. How much coordination is needed, and where, is a question of how strong are the interdependencies among the particular activities involved. Optimal organizational design dictates that we collect together within the same subunit activities that have high interdependencies

---

[52] Powell 1990, p. 298.
[53] Simon 1957. Corporations have long been seen as 'little republics' unto themselves (Blackstone 1765, bk 1, ch. 18, p. 456). For recent critical examinations of that view see: Ciepley 2013; Landemore and Ferreras 2016; Anderson 2017; and González-Ricoy 2022.
[54] Blackstone 1765, bk 1, ch. 14.
[55] Moore 1985, p. 114.
[56] Neustadt 1960, p. 9.
[57] Blau and Scott 1963, ch. 7; Williamson 1971.
[58] Arrow 1964, p. 400.
[59] Simon 1991, pp. 31–2.

with one another. Within subunits thus constructed there is intense interaction, but between them there are fewer interdependencies and hence fewer interactions.[60]

While 'it is widely assumed that the hierarchy of authority is essential for coordination in complex organizations', empirical reality is otherwise. '[I]n the very organizations where interdependent specialization is most pronounced, and where, consequently, the problems of coordination ore most acute, coordination is most typically' horizontal rather than vertical. It is simply not the case that 'every problem that arises between departments is delayed until relevant information has been passed up the hierarchy and a decision has been made and sent down again'. Rather, coordination was most often achieved through 'direct contact between employees at the same level'.[61]

Networks are often regarded as the antitheses of formal organizations on account of their flat organizational structure.[62] The internet itself was initially conceived at RAND and implemented by the US Defense Department's Advanced Research Projects Agency as a decentralized communication system with no central node that could be knocked out by a first nuclear strike, should the Cold War turn hot.[63] Today the internet is celebrated as a 'new and important cooperative and coordinate action carried out through radically distributed, nonmarket mechanisms that do not depend on proprietary strategies'.[64]

Yet in reality networks are not nearly as flat as they might initially seem. As argued in Chapter 4, some people and organizations occupy central positions of power and advantage within them. Even internet enthusiasts have to face up to the challenge that, although they were hoping for it enable a shift 'from the mass-mediated public sphere to a networked public sphere, ... the emerging patterns of Internet use show that very few sites capture an exceedingly large amount of attention, and millions of sites go unnoticed'.[65]

---

[60] As Simon (2000, p. 752) says in explaining the logic of decomposable systems, 'The first step in designing an effective organization is to determine what kinds of interdependencies in its activities will benefit from coordination, and then to minimize the amount of coordination required by partitioning activities in such a way that a much lower rate of interaction, on a more leisurely time scale, is required between subunits at any level than is required within each subunit.' See similarly Blau and Scott 1963, pp. 183–5.
[61] Blau and Scott (1963, p. 184), building on Simpson (1959).
[62] Castells 2000.
[63] Baran's (1964, p. 1) initial RAND memo opens with the words, 'Let us consider the synthesis of a communication network which will allow several hundred major communication stations to talk with one another after an enemy attack.' For the fuller history see RAND (2020).
[64] Benkler 2006, p. 3.
[65] Benkler 2006, p. 10.

The story with the market is similar. The classic economic representation depicts the market as being composed of 'a collection of Leibnitzian monads ... hard, elastic little particles that bounce off each other without any other interaction, certainly without either responding to or influencing others' values'.[66] But this idealized image of a completely flat market structure, with no price-makers and only price-takers, contrasts sharply with what we know about concentration and power in most markets. Furthermore, the latter features seem to be increasing, if anything.[67]

The long and short of it is that, in the real world, coordination schemes are invariably an admixture of hierarchical command, market-style bargaining and network-style collaboration. The three elements complement one another. Each helps to compensate for the weaknesses of the other, making the hybrid more robust than any of the pure forms. That, in turn, confers a competitive advantage on those who organized in that way.

8.4 The Biases of Organization

'Organization', Schattschneider famously wrote, 'is the mobilization of bias'.[68] Unpacked, that observation involves two claims: first, that there is pre-existing bias or advantage of some sort or another; and second, that organizing around that bias or advantage both evokes and enhances it. Organization, understood as mobilization of bias, thus transforms one sort of advantage into another which is both more actionable and more durable.

One of the most conspicuous ways in which this occurs is in the organization of political systems. What policies can be enacted is, in part, a function of what political parties exist to promote them. Those, in turn, are a historical legacy—the product of some particular cleavage that was particularly salient at one point in time that got 'frozen' into the country's party structure.[69] Modern West European political parties were organized around the class differences rooted in manufacturing industries; and that party cleavage structure (and the policy biases built into it) persisted long after those industries had themselves

---

[66] Simon 2000, pp. 756, 750. A key assumption of perfect competition in the market is that: 'Every member of the society is to act as an individual only, in entire independence of all other persons.... And in exchanges between individuals, no interests of persons not parties to the exchange are to be concerned, either for good or for ill. Individual independence in action excludes all forms of collusion, all degrees of monopoly or tendency to monopoly....' (Knight 1921, pp. 67–9, quoted in Stigler 1957, p. 12).
[67] OECD 2018b.
[68] Schattschneider 1960, p. 71.
[69] Lipset and Rokkan 1967.

largely disappeared from the economy. Elsewhere, different cleavage structures got frozen into the political party system. In Northern Ireland, for example, the dominance of religious-based parties growing out of the 1921 partition of Ireland prevented the emergence of class-based parties such as predominated in the rest of the UK.[70]

Political decision rules can also introduce biases against certain outcomes and actors and in favour of others. If supermajorities are required, or if particular groups given a veto, certain outcomes may thereby be rendered politically impossible. Where special majority rules specify the status quo as the 'default winner' if no other option secures the requisite special majority, as typically they do, that biases the political system in favour of entrenched interests.[71] Similarly, if the political culture favours 'accommodation' over winner-take-all political competition, then radical change is once again effectively precluded.[72]

Organizational biases also shape what claims are made upon, and what inputs are fed into, the political system by lobby groups.[73] When Mancur Olson bemoaned the 'exploitation of the many by the few', he was pointing in part to the relative ease of organizing each group of people.[74] The rich and powerful are few, concentrated and aligned in their interests. Hence they are more easily organized, compared to the poor who are many, diverse, and dispersed. So, in addition to all their many other advantages, the rich and powerful enjoy an organizational advantage as well.

Organizational biases shape not only the political system but also the economy and society. Vertical monopolies are only the most dramatic example of organizational bias in the economy. The 'first-mover advantage' conferred upon a firm that organizes itself to occupy a particular market niche is another.[75] In some varieties of capitalism finance and production are more intertwined than others, and thanks to 'patient capital' firms are better able to cultivate job-specific skills in their more stable workforce in coordinated

---

[70] Rose 1971.
[71] Goodin and List 2006. Cf. Buchanan (2004) and Barry (1965, ch. 14).
[72] Lijphart 1968.
[73] Schattschneider's (1960, p. 71) particular interest, when coining the 'mobilization of bias' phrase, was in political agenda-setting and the way in which 'some issues are organized into politics while others are organized out'.
[74] Olson 1965, p. 35. In Trumbull's (2012, p. 3) succinct summary of this argument, 'The larger the number of individuals in a group, the harder the group will be to organize.... This coordination problem makes organizing diffuse interests a harder job than organizing concentrated interests.' Trumbull himself argues that these effects are outweighed by 'legitimacy' gains that come from being able to claim to represent large and diffuse constituencies. Another, different explanation is that sometimes the benefit of the policy being advocated are concentrated while its costs are dispersed. As Pareto (1906/1971, p. 379) observed long before, it is 'easier to put a protection[ist] measure into practice' when it 'provides large benefits to a small number of people, and causes a very great number of consumers a slight loss'.
[75] Kerin, Varadarajan, and Peterson 1992.

market economies (such as Germany's) than in liberal market economies (such as those of the US and UK). The former mode of organizing the economy advantages high-tech and service industries, the latter manufacturing industries.[76]

Organizational biases shape the social system as well. School systems powerfully sustain a society's status order. Elite schools recruit their students predominantly from elite groups, and in so doing certify and sustain their recruits' status as 'the chosen' ones.[77] Elite prep schools feed elite universities.[78] Within universities, elite social clubs further differentiate elite from non-elite members.[79] After university, elite connections are sustained by private clubs such as populate Pall Mall, where gentlemen who were 'at Oxford together' play on social connections for economic and political advantage.[80]

That is a good example of how advantage tends to build on itself. James Coleman remarks upon the way in which 'organization, once brought into existence for one set of purposes, can also aid others, thus constituting social capital available for use'.[81] That is the way the 'old boy network' works, as friendships forged 'on the playing fields of Eton' become the basis for economic deal-doing in the City of London and coalition-building in the halls of the Palace of Westminster.[82]

---

[76] Hall and Soskice 2001.
[77] Karabel 2005.
[78] When Franklin Delano Roosevelt matriculated at Harvard in September 1900, all but four of his 24 Groton classmates did likewise (Karabel 2005, p. 13; see further Michelman, Price, and Zimmerman 2022).
[79] Oxford's Bullingdon Club is perhaps the best known, counting two of its class of 1987 as recent UK Prime Ministers, David Cameron and Boris Johnson (Adams 2007).
[80] Reeves et al. 2017.
[81] Coleman 1988, p. S108.
[82] Mills 1956. Reeves et al. 2017. The 'playing fields of Eton' trope is from a quotation, attributed (probably apocryphally) to the Duke of Wellington to the effect that 'the battle of Waterloo was won on the playing fields of Eton'. In his essay, 'An Eton Boy', Matthew Arnold (1882) responded derisively: 'The aged Barbarian [i.e., Wellington] will ... mumble to us his story how the battle of Waterloo was won in the playing-fields of Eton. Alas! disasters have been prepared in those playing-fields as well as victories; disasters due to inadequate mental training—to want of application, knowledge, intelligence, lucidity.'

PART II
UNDERLYING DRIVERS

Previous chapters have explicated several specific mechanisms by which advantage, once produced, is perpetuated and exacerbated. Let us now stand back from those specifics to consider what more fundamental forces might drive those more specific mechanisms. Doubtless slightly different ones will be at work behind different mechanisms. Still, I think we can isolate two broad types of fundamental factors that underlie the more specific mechanisms.

Both sorts of underlying drivers to be discussed in this part of the book are 'structural', in the sense that they are rooted in features of the world within which people exercise their agency. Some of those drivers are *external* to the agent. They create opportunities for some, and obstacles for others, in exercising their will on the world. Those are the subject of Chapter 9. Other drivers are *internal* to the agent. The constraints that they impose frustrate some and facilitate others in exercising agency and having agency exercised upon them. Those are the subject of Chapter 10.

The point of isolating the drivers underlying the mechanisms that perpetuate advantage and disadvantage is, of course, to disrupt them or at least to dampen their effects. Neither the external nor the internal drivers that I identify can be eliminated altogether in most cases; and even where they can be, doing so would often be seriously undesirable in other respects. The most we can probably hope to do is to find some 'work-around' to evade their worst effects in terms of perpetuating advantage and disadvantage. In concluding, Chapter 11 will discuss various ways of working around each of the drivers of structural injustice identified in this part of the book.

9
External Opportunities
Scale Effects

The focus of this book, recall, is not so much on how advantage gets created in the first place but, instead, on how advantage once created gets perpetuated and expanded over time. Colloquially, the question is how it is that 'the rich get richer and the poor get poorer'.

Previous chapters have revealed many of the more specific mechanisms responsible. But what might they have in common? I shall argue that there are two fundamental sets of drivers, one rooted in the external world within which people exercise their agency, the other (discussed in the next chapter) internal to the agents themselves.

The fundamental external factors underlying the perpetuation of advantage are 'scale effects'. Some of those are located in processes of production (Section 9.1), others in processes of consumption (Section 9.2), yet others in processes of valuation (Section 9.3).

What is common across all of those 'scale effects', wherever they are found, is that 'bigger is better'. That is to say, they confer competitive advantages on bigger entities vis-à-vis smaller ones. By being associated with a bigger entity, in one way or another, people derive competitive advantage over people associated with smaller entities or with none at all. That competitive advantage is instrumental, in turn, in those people's obtaining consumption advantages as well.[1]

Furthermore, scale effects give rise to dynamics that further expand existing advantage.[2] If there are competitive advantages to being part of a bigger entity, people who are not currently part of it will have an incentive to associate themselves with it. As they do, the entity will become yet larger. And insofar as 'bigger is better' in terms of competitive advantage, those already

---

[1] In terms of the distinction made in Section 1.3 above.
[2] In terms of Section 2.2 above.

associated with the even-bigger entity will come to enjoy even greater competitive advantage owing to the new recruits.[3] Their advantage is thus not merely perpetuated but enhanced.

9.1 Scale Effects in Production

Finance offers one very straightforward way in which the 'rich get richer' as a result of scale effects. The rich have more to invest, and the more you invest the more you gain (over the long haul anyway) from investments.[4] Rentier 'coupon clippers' living off interest on their bonds is not merely socially inefficient.[5] It is also arguably unjust and, more to my present point, increasingly so over time. Investment income, if reinvested, accumulates and at an accelerating pace.[6] Compound interest is a prime example. Coupled with compounding is the tendency of more lucrative investments to be available to those with more to invest. In financial markets, to continue that example, you can get higher rates of interest if you are prepared to commit a larger sum; and high net-value investors get access to private equity investment vehicles that are unavailable to retail investors.[7] And of course capital markets and returns on equity and bonds are primary drivers of inequality via their contribution to growth in top incomes, as Piketty and his co-authors have shown.[8]

The classic case of scale effects in economics is in relation to production, however. Scale effects classically arise when cost per unit of producing something decreases as the number of units produced increases.[9] There are various reasons that this might occur. One is that there are large fixed costs (of building the factory for example) and low marginal costs (of producing each item

---

[3] Of course, at the limit, where everyone is associated with it, the size of the entity will cease to confer competitive advantage—there is no one left to have competitive advantage over.

[4] Kuznets (1955, p. 7) observes 'the concentration of savings in the upper-income brackets' and remarks that 'the cumulative effect of such inequality in savings would be the concentration of an increasing proportion of income-yielding assets in the hands of the upper groups—a basis for larger income shares of those groups and their descendants'.

[5] Thus, Marx (1844b/1959, p. 54) distinguishes between rentier and industrial capitalism. See further Stinchcombe 1998, p. 274.

[6] As Marx (1844b, p. 14) observes: 'the profit on capital is in proportion to the size of the capital. A large capital therefore accumulates more quickly than a small capital in proportion to its size, even if we disregard for the time being deliberate competition. Accordingly, the accumulation of large capital proceeds much more rapidly than that of smaller capital, quite irrespective of competition.'

[7] DiPrete and Eirich 2006, pp. 272–3. Barber and Goold 2007.

[8] Piketty, Saez, and Zucman 2018.

[9] With 'machine learning' that underpins the computer algorithms discussed in Section 10.2, benefits go up rather than costs coming down the larger the pool of 'training data' available from existing users (Posner and Weyl 2018, 224–30; Spiekermann et al. 2021).

within it).¹⁰ The larger the output of the factory, the more items there are over which to spread those fixed costs, and hence the less you need to charge for each. A factory with larger output can therefore undercut the price charged by a factory with smaller output. Another reason that unit cost might decrease as the volume increases might be that you are able to purchase inputs at discount when buying larger quantities. Yet another reason might be that the division of labour is more fully realized in the larger operation.¹¹

Economies of scale form the basis for the classical explanation for 'natural monopolies'.¹² A 'natural monopoly' exists, and only one firm finds it profitable to enter the market, wherever economies of scale exist over the entire range of market demand.¹³ Classic examples of such natural monopolies include gas and water supply, roads and railways, telephones and telegraphs.¹⁴ The classic policy response to natural monopolies involves either regulation or state-ownership.¹⁵

Economists are principally interested in the welfare effects of monopolies, calibrated in terms of the most socially efficient use of resources. Left to their own devices, monopolists undersupply and overcharge. Those are the inefficiencies that regulation or public ownership is supposed to remedy.

My concern here is more with distributional consequences. Those are two. First, unregulated monopolists themselves profit at the expense of the public, in the ways just described. Second, scale effects produce monopolies and then monopolies produce further scale effects; and the larger your market share, the larger the rents you can collect.

---

¹⁰ The same is true of producing information. 'Information is costly to *produce* but cheap to *reproduce*.' The 'production of an information good involves *high fixed costs* but *low marginal costs*. The cost of producing the first copy of an information good may be substantial, but the cost of producing (or reproducing) additional copies is negligible' (Shapiro and Varian 1999, p. 3; see similarly Arrow 1962b). The tendency towards monopolization often associated with such characteristics is avoided in information markets by suppliers personalizing their products and practicing price discrimination (Shapiro and Varian 1999, pp. 32–43). Such near-monopolies as we see in the information economy (Facebook, Twitter, etc.) are more due to network externalities (Shapiro and Varian 1999, ch. 7); more will be said about them in Section 9.3.1 below.

¹¹ Mill 1848/1965, bk 1, ch. 9, § 1; Sraffa 1926, p. 537; Arthur 1989.

¹² Sraffa 1926, pp. 540–3. More modern theories of natural monopoly are couched in terms of 'sub-additivity', of which economies of scale are only one special case (Baumol et al. 1982, p. xvi).

¹³ Mosca 2008. These monopolies are 'natural' in the sense that they derive from structural features of the economy rather than from a legal grant, such as Elizabeth I's 1599 grant to the East India Company of a monopoly on trade with the East (Mill 1848, bk 2, ch. 15, § 9) or earlier grants of monopolies to guilds (Letwin 1954). Opposition to de jure monopolies of that sort, led by Sir Edward Coke, resulted in the passage of the English Statute of Monopolies of 1624, 21 Jac. 1, c. 3, which outlawed the practice and laid the legal groundwork for granting time-limited patents to inventors.

¹⁴ The first pair is discussed by Mill, the second by Walras, the third by Ely (Mosca 2008, pp. 3223–4).

¹⁵ Mill (1848, bk 5, ch. 11, § 11, p. 957) says of natural or 'practical' monopolies, 'the state should either reserve to itself a reversionary property in such public works, or should retain, and freely exercise, the right of fixing a maximum of fares and charges'. See further: Pigou 1932, chs 20–2; Scitovsky 1971, p. 23; Joskow 2007; Wu 2009; Blackman and Srivastava 2011.

There are other monopolies of a more social sort, produced by legal fiat rather than some naturally occurring features of the production process or scale effects found there. While having a different source, those *de jure* monopolies confer analogous advantage on those who enjoy them compared to those who do not.

Examples abound. Lawyers enjoy a monopoly on representing other people in court proceedings. Licensed medical practitioners enjoy a monopoly on practising surgery in public hospitals. Anointed priests in many religions enjoy a monopoly on the performance of sacred rituals, and so on. In all those cases, monopoly powers are purely *de jure*. Instead of being fixed in the nature of the external world they are the product of civil or canon law.

Such monopoly status nevertheless confers advantages on the occupants of the professional role in question. In the first instance, that advantage is economic. The monopoly that they enjoy allows them to collect high rents.[16] But the advantage is social as well, conferring upon those enjoying that status something like a quasi-monopoly to pronounce authoritatively upon matters within their professional realm—and, through seepage, beyond. That seepage found in *de jure* monopolies is analogous to the second scale effect in natural economic monopolies. In both cases, the larger your market share the larger the rents you can collect.

Some of that seepage comes from their enjoying 'centrality' in larger social networks, as discussed in Section 4.2. Doctors and lawyers (and in some places also priests) are socially 'well connected', in the first instance to people with whom they directly relate in a professional capacity but also indirectly to other prominent people by virtue of that. Through those connections, they know and can do things that others cannot. And because of that, people who want to get certain sorts of things done come to them for advice and assistance well outside their professional remit. That is another source of advantage for those who enjoy such monopolies.

A further source of comparative advantage for those role occupants is 'seepage of trust'. I have already discussed the expectational advantages that derive from being trusted.[17] People who are certified (sometimes wrongly, of course) as being trustworthy in their professional roles often enjoy a 'halo effect' in being trusted beyond those roles. That is particularly true insofar as what is certified is taken to be, at least in part, commitment to the ethics of the profession and the larger character traits that that commitment betokens. It may well

---

[16] Weeden 2002.
[17] In Sections 4.5, 6.4, and 7.4.

be an erroneous extrapolation, but it is nevertheless a common one, to suppose that someone who manifests the right character traits to be a good doctor or lawyer or priest will also manifest the right character traits to be a good person more generally. If you trust that person for one purpose, you might be inclined to trust them more generally.

Beyond those very specific role occupants, much the same can be said about anyone who enjoys a position of status advantage as described in Section 3.1.1. Of course you might share the same status position with very many others—in which case you are not a monopolist in the sense that you occupy that position to the exclusion of all others, any more than do doctors, lawyers, and priests theirs. But in a status hierarchy there tend to be prerogatives exclusively reserved for those of a certain status. And from those special privileges and prerogatives—that 'monopoly', if you will—further advantages flow, directly or indirectly. Some of those advantages are in relation to processes of production, others are in relation to consumption, to which I now turn.

9.2 Scale Effects in Consumption

The economic analysis of the previous section turned on the effects of scale on the costs of producing and how that causes the already-advantaged to become even-more advantaged. Here I shall be concerned with the effects of scale when consuming, and I shall show that those also cause the already-advantaged to become even-more advantaged.

Some goods (or perhaps ways of consuming those goods) are such that the more of them you consume, the more of them you have to consume. The more of them you 'spend', the more you have to spend. Clearly, not all goods are like that—not by a very long shot.[18] Still, insofar as there are any important goods that display such a feature, they could have very important consequences. And as I have shown in Section 3.2, many 'positional goods' do display that property. The more you assert your authority and the more you exercise your power, the more authority or power you have—or are seen to have, which is in any case what really matters.

---

[18] Goodin 1990a. Marx (1859/1904, Appendix, sec. 2, p. 278) claims that it is always the case that 'production ... is at the same time consumption, and consumption is at the same time production'. But by that Marx means something both narrower and more general than the point here in view. He explains, 'in nutrition, e.g., which is but one form of consumption, man produces his own body; but it is equally true of every kind of consumption, which goes to produce the human being in one way or another' (p. 277).

An early recognition of this sort of phenomenon comes in John Bunyan's analysis of 'Christian love' in his 1678 allegory, *The Pilgrim's Progress*. There, the innkeeper Gaius poses a riddle to the pilgrims:

> A Man there was, tho some did count him mad,
> The more he cast away, the more he had.

'How can that be?'—that is the riddle. The answer, Gaius reveals, is that:

> He that bestows his Goods upon the Poor,
> Shall have as much again, and ten times more.[19]

That may not be literally true (although, as we are told, the Lord works in mysterious ways). But taking the allegorical reference to material goods as a reference to Christian love more generally, the message is that the more love you give the more you have to give.

That message cuts across the central teachings of economics in various ways. Economists advise us to arrange society in such a way as to make as few demands as possible on people's good will towards one another, which is inevitably in scarce supply. If we take Bunyan (and his contemporary heirs such as Richard Titmuss) seriously, we should do just the opposite.[20] More fundamentally, Bunyan's lesson calls into question the notion of scarcity more generally, at least with respect to a certain class of goods or to certain ways of using goods. Ordinarily, when you consume a good you use it up. Whatever you consume today is not available to you tomorrow. Not so, with goods of the sort Bunyan has in view.[21]

Those are interesting claims in their own right, of course. But my particular interest in this book is with how such goods might help to perpetuate, and indeed exacerbate, some people's advantage over others. The point to notice in that connection is that, with goods that grow with use, the more of those goods you have to start with the more additional goods you can create by using your initial stock.

Other goods are like that, but in ways different to that here in view. Take the case of capital for example: the more of it you have, the more you can produce with it. The more money you have to invest, the more lucrative your

---

[19] Bunyan 1678/1966, p. 357.
[20] Sir Dennis Robertson (1956, p. 154) posed the question, 'what does the economist economise?' His reply: 'love' (by which he meant 'good will' more generally). Hume (1742/1760) long before him had advised social engineers to be guided by the 'maxim that every man must be supposed a knave'. Cf. Titmuss 1973; Hirschmann 1984, pp. 93–5.
[21] Cornford 1972. Or if you use up those specific goods, in the process of using them up you create more of that same type of good. Think for example of a fast-breeder nuclear reactor, which produces more fuel than it consumes.

investments will be (ordinarily), as I already observed; or for another example, the more seed corn you have, the more you can plant and harvest next season. But the goods here in view are different, in that they (re)grow as the very result of *being consumed*. If you consume your corn today, in contrast, it will be unavailable to plant next year; and any capital that you use to finance current consumption will be unavailable to use for future production.

The phenomenon here in view is also different from 'learning by doing' models of skills acquisition.[22] The '10,000 hours rule' holds that excellence at any task is less a matter of native ability and much more the product of long hours of practice.[23] Whether or not that bolder 10,000-hour claim is correct, it is nonetheless the case that the most standard models within labour economics suppose that workers acquire human capital on-the-job over the course of their working lives, which explains why (within limits) older workers are more valued than younger ones.[24]

There is doubtless a positive feedback loop at work with these phenomenon as well. The longer you have been doing it, the better you are at doing it, so the more further improvement you will get out of another hour of doing it. That is another way in which the 'rich get richer'. But it is a different way from the one here in view. In 'learning-by-doing' models, the 'doing' is 'making an investment'—not undertaking an act of consumption.

What is distinctive about the goods, and ways of using goods, here in view is that they offer the opportunity to 'have your cake and eat it too'. That is to say, by the very act of consuming you produce more goods for you to consume. Here, instead of the ordinary trade-off between consumption and investment, with these goods consumption *is* investment. Anyone with access to these sorts of goods is therefore doubly advantaged. They have more to consume now, and by consuming them they will come to have more to consume in the future.

The only formal model to try to capture this process is Stigler and Becker's.[25] They take their lead from a passing comment by Alfred Marshall to the effect that the more good music you listen to the more you will come to appreciate good music. Stigler and Becker generalize that observation into the concept of 'consumption capital'. Their thought is that just as certain forms of human

---

[22] Arrow 1962a. 'Skills' is Hirschmann's (1984, pp. 93–5) take on Arrow's observation.
[23] Ericsson, Krampe, and Tesch-Römer 1993; Gladwell 2008. Kolers (2020) argues that there is a 'practice' element in moral development that is similar to that involved in athletes practising their sport.
[24] Mincer 1974; Heckman, Lochner, and Todd 2003. As Marx (1859, Appendix, sec. 2, p. 276) observed long before, 'The individual who develops his faculties in production, is also expending them, consuming them in the act of production....'
[25] Stigler and Becker 1977.

capital make you a more efficient producer, so too do other forms of human capital make you a more efficient consumer. That is to say, you derive more satisfaction from any given input the more consumption capital you have for processing such inputs.

They canvass several ways of coming by such consumption capital. Some of them are explicitly forms of 'learning by doing', in which effort is invested rather than anything being consumed. But at a certain point, which sometimes comes reasonably early, the effort itself becomes enjoyable in and of itself. Go back to Marshall's example of learning to appreciate classical music (or Chinese opera, for an example that is more striking, because more grating, to Western ears). Initially you may have to force yourself to listen to it, and you do that purely as an investment in learning to appreciate it. But at some point, listening becomes a pleasure, while still yielding dividends in terms of an ever-increasing capacity to appreciate the music in future. At that point, the double-dipping phenomenon here in view sets in. Investing has become a form of consuming, and consuming a form of investing. The rich get richer, as those who have spent a lot of music consumption capital listening to Chinese Opera come to have yet more music consumption capital.

Some of the examples from earlier chapters display something of the same characteristics. Take the example of trust, which has come up several times before.[26] 'Trust grows with use', in the sense that trust begets trust.[27] The more trusting and trustworthy you are, the more others can trust you in turn, and (since the same dynamic is at work on both sides of the dyad) the more warranted is your trust in them. That is the logic of 'confidence-building measures' that are used in international negotiations to de-escalate conflicts, for example.[28]

The same is true of power and the reputation for power. The law of anticipated reactions, already discussed, says that having a reputation for power helps you get what you want without the actual exercise of power or the expenditure of resources that that entails.[29] But it is equally true that the successful exercise of power builds your reputation for power. So your consuming resources in the exercise of power has the effect of enhancing your power. Engaging in full-on fights are only the most extreme version of this phenomenon.

---

[26] See Sections 4.5, 6.4, and 7.4.
[27] Dasgupta (1988, p. 64), building on an insight from Hirschmann (1984). Note that the way in which trust is 'used' is by being 'bestowed upon' or 'extended to' others—if not exactly 'consumed', it is at least 'given away'.
[28] Darilek 1992.
[29] See Sections 2.1 and Section 7.1 above.

For a more modest example, consider the case of gossip, where the same reputational dynamics are at work. As Gambetta observes, gossip is a resource that depletes by not being used.[30] Your reputation as a good gossip, and the power that that confers upon you socially, depends on your dispensing gossip early and often.

Sharing secrets makes them less secret, less uniquely yours, so that can be seen as a form of consumption. But if as a result of your sharing others share their secrets with you in return, you can end up knowing more secrets as a result.[31] Transactionally, that may look like a case of barter, trading my secret for yours. But relationally, the selective sharing of secrets among chosen others literally constitutes the gossip ring that you share.[32] 'Consuming' your secrets by sharing them causes you to have more secrets to share.

9.3 Scale Effects in Valuation

In Section 9.1 scale effects were shown to 'further advantage the already advantaged' by lowering the costs of production. Here I shall show that scale effects 'further advantage the already advantaged' by increasing the value of consumption in another way very different from that discussed in Section 9.2. There my focus was on goods that grow with use, and the further advantages that accrue to those who already have such goods as a result. Here my focus will be on goods that are more valuable the more people who already have them, and the further advantages that accrue to controllers and consumers of such goods.[33]

9.3.1 Scale Effects in Communication: Network Externalities

The goods in question are ones that display 'network externalities' of the sort already discussed at various points earlier in the book.[34] In the original

---

[30] Gambetta 1994, pp. 214–15.
[31] More precisely, the diminution in the value of secrets when shared may be offset by the greater number of such diminished-value secrets each knows.
[32] Williamson's (1985) notion of relational contracting has similar features.
[33] Describing this phenomenon, Shapiro and Varian (1999, p. 174) say that the 'fundamental economic characteristic' of networks is that 'the value of connecting to a network depends on the number of other people already connected to it'. They expand the term network to embrace 'virtual' ones, such as 'the network of Macintosh users, the network of CD machines, or the network of Nintendo 64 users' (p. 174); the driver there is largely the lock-in that comes from already owning lots of other products that have unique complementarities with one particular product line.
[34] Sections 4.2, 4.6, and 6.1.2.1.

example, having access to a telephone is more valuable the more other people who also have access to a telephone.[35] The same is obviously true of email and, indeed, of any other communication network or language system.[36] But as I shall proceed to show in Section 9.3.2, similar effects manifest themselves well beyond that particular sort of network.

In Section 9.1, scale effects in production lead to exclusionary outcomes as larger producers undercut the prices of smaller ones and drive them out of business. Scale effects in consumption that derive from network externalities have vaguely similar consequences, insofar as (if forced to choose) everyone prefers to be part of a larger network than a smaller one.

Why should anyone be forced to choose, however? Each network is more valuable to its users the more people are connected to it, after all. So why not welcome a new member into your network despite the fact (indeed, precisely because of the fact) that they are already part of some other network?

Insofar as admission to the network is controlled exclusively by the existing members of the network, that is precisely what should happen. But insofar as there are controllers of the network who derive some advantage (more advertising revenue, for example) from having more people connected to their network than to other networks, they will be tempted to admit people to their network only on condition that they foreswear all other network connections[37]—or to engineer 'lock-ins' that serve to ensure the same result.[38] And forced to choose only one network, people will invariably choose the largest one wherever network externalities are present.

That is one way in which the scale effects associated with network externalities further advantage the already advantaged. In the absence of external regulation, those who are in control of larger networks can drive competing networks out of business, pocketing whatever private benefits (advertising revenue, etc.) that derives from their providing the public good (the network).[39]

There is another way in which the scale effects associated with network externalities further advantage the already advantaged. People are more or less advantageously positioned in networks.[40] Networks encode categories

---

[35] First noticed by Antonio de Viti de Marco (1890); for a discussion see Mosca (2008, pp. 326–7).
[36] As discussed in Section 5.2 above.
[37] For example, when Nintendo overtook Atari as the dominant player in the home video game market in the late 1980s, 'every independent game developer [not only] paid royalties to Nintendo. They even promised not to make their games available on rival systems for two years following their release!' (Shapiro and Varian 1999, p. 178).
[38] Shapiro and Varian 1999, ch. 5.
[39] Shapiro and Varian (1999, p. 177) thus dub markets characterized by positive feedback in this was 'winner-take-all' markets.
[40] See Section 4.2 above.

that advantage some people over others.[41] As the scale effects associated with network externalities lead larger networks to drive out smaller ones, people who are advantaged in those ways by the former network gain further advantage over those who would have been advantaged by the latter becoming dominant.

9.3.2 Analogous Phenomena

The previous discussion has focused on network externalities in communication networks more specifically. But those are not the only sites at which such effects are felt. There are many other situations in which a good or service or connection is more valuable to you the more other people who also use or connect to it.

Economically, the adoption of new technologies often has the same dynamics. As Brian Arthur's classic paper on the topic explains:

> Modern, complex technologies often display increasing returns to adoption in that the more they are adopted, the more experience is gained with them, and the more they are improved. When two or more increasing-return technologies 'compete' then, for a 'market' of potential adopters, insignificant events may by chance give one of them an initial advantage in adoptions. This technology may then improve more than the others, so it may appeal to a wider proportion of potential adopters. It may therefore become further adopted and further improved. Thus a technology that by chance gains an early lead in adoption may eventually 'corner the market' of potential adopters, with the other technologies becoming locked out.[42]

Something similar occurs in the model of 'preferential attachment' discussed in Chapter 7. In the Hobbesian version of the story, what you are seeking is protection; and you prefer to put yourself under the protection of someone who already has more people under his protection, because having more people under his protection makes him better able to protect you (Section 7.1). If popularity is what you are seeking, and being friends with someone who is already popular makes you more popular, then you want to become the friend of people who already have more friends rather than fewer (Section 7.3). In both cases, attaching yourself to someone with more people already attached

---

[41] See Section 5.2 above.
[42] Arthur 1989, p. 116.

in preference to someone with fewer is not an objectively groundless subjective preference. Instead, it is objectively instrumental in helping to get you what you want, in terms of protection or popularity.

Those may seem to be very particular and perhaps atypical examples. But upon reflection the phenomenon can be seen to be actually quite ubiquitous. There are a great many situations in which having many second-degree neighbours (neighbours of neighbours) confers an advantage on you.[43] Consider very ordinary choices of which consumer product to buy. In Section 6.1.2.1, I offered the example of the choice between VHS and Betamax video recording technology. When deciding which to buy, you want (other things being equal) to buy the one that you expect most other people to buy, because there will be more video recordings available in that format than the other. Or again, when deciding which bank in which to open an account, you want (other things being equal) to open an account in one in which you expect many others to open accounts, because that ensures that there will be more branches of that bank and increases the probability that there will always be one conveniently near you wherever you are. Or when deciding which car to buy, you want (other things being equal) to buy one that you expect many others to buy, because that ensures that there will be more distributors with service departments and increases the likelihood of one near to you. Or in deciding which movie to watch, you want (other things being equal) to watch one that you expect many others will watch and want to talk about. In all of those perfectly ordinary consumer choices, you prefer (other things being equal) those products that many (if not literally the most, necessarily) others will also choose for perfectly rational reasons. Many other people choosing that product makes, in those various ways, that product more valuable to you in turn.

That has two consequences. One is for the producers: those already patronized by more people are more likely to attract yet more patrons, and hence the already-big get bigger (and hence richer) still. The other consequence is for consumers: patrons of larger and growing suppliers are advantaged over patrons of smaller and declining producers, as the products of the former become more valuable to patrons and the latter less so in consequence of their shifting market shares. At some point patrons of smaller and declining producers might have to bear the further costs of shifting to the increasingly dominant product, costs which those with the advantage of already using that product do not have to bear.

---

[43] There are of course many other situations of the opposite sort, where exclusivity confers an advantage on you.

10
Internal Constraints
Attention Scarcity

The 'scale effects' discussed in the last chapter are important external drivers of the perpetuation of advantage. They create opportunities for some people to seize and expand their advantages at the expense of others. But in addition to those external drivers, there are also important internal drivers of the perpetuation of advantage. The most important ones, I shall argue, derive from constraints on people's time and attention that lead them to employ various tools and shortcuts which almost inevitably work to the advantage of some people over others.

In Section 10.1, I shall discuss 'attention' as the most fundamentally scarce resource constraining our decision-making capacity. The internet, discussed in Section 10.2, provides perhaps the most striking example of that fact—and it also provides striking examples of biases being built into the tools and shortcuts employed to cope with the scarcity of attention. Building upon insights from that discussion, Section 10.3 shows how many of the mechanisms that earlier chapters showed perpetuating and expanding advantage are really, at root, devices for coping with the scarcity of time and attention. That is the fundamental driver underlying them.

10.1 Attention as a Scarce Resource

It is perhaps a platitude that 'information is important in providing a basis for action. But', as James Coleman rightly goes on to say, 'acquisition of information is costly. At a minimum, it requires attention, which is always in scarce supply.'[1] Nobel Laureate Herbert Simon, whose path-breaking work

---

[1] Coleman 1988, p. S104. Summarizing 'the main currents of psychological research', Crawford (2015, p. 11) writes that 'attention is a resource [such that] a person has only so much of it'. Economists have begun building models around that fact (Sims 2003; Lanham 2006, esp. ch. 2; Reis 2006; Falkinger 2007, 2008; Köszegi and Matejka 2020) and adducing empirical evidence of its economic consequences (DellaVigna 2009, pp. 348–53; Caplin et al. 2020). The basic insight has long been appreciated within economics, however. In his classic article on 'The general welfare in relation to problems of taxation

on decision-making interweaves economics, psychology, and artificial intelligence, elaborates:

> The human eye and ear are highly parallel devices, capable of extracting many pieces of information simultaneously from the environment and decoding them into their significant features. Before this information can be used by the deliberative mind, however, it must proceed through the bottleneck of attention—a serial, not parallel, process whose information capacity is exceedingly small. Psychologists usually call this bottleneck short-term memory, and measurements show reliably that it can hold only about six chunks (that is to say, six familiar items of information).[2]

Another way to put the same basic point is that of Nobel Laureate psychologist Daniel Kahneman: paying attention requires effort; the capacity to make such effort is, if not strictly fixed, at least certainly limited; so attending to some things rather than others involve the selective allocation of that scarce resource.[3]

In an 'information-rich world', both individuals and organizations can suffer 'information overload'.[4] Facts-on-file are importantly different from facts-at-our-fingertips, when it comes to making decisions on the basis of them.[5] Data, unanalysed, is of no use to us. To be useable, information must be attended to, processed, interpreted, and stored in some more accessible, compressed, and easily retrievable form.[6]

Sometimes paying attention to something is a voluntary act of will. Other times your attention is involuntarily seized, as when a car backfires nearby.[7]

---

and of railway and utility rates', for example, Hotelling (1938, p. 257) remarked, 'Another thing of limited quantity for which the demand exceeds the supply is the attention of people.' For other examples see Festré and Garrouste (2015).

[2] Simon 1985, p. 302. See further Simon 1969, ch. 3; see similarly Arrow 1974, p. 39; Baddeley 2012, p. 9; D'Esposito and Postle 2015; Dijksterhuis and Aarts 2010, pp. 470–1. In the panel discussion that followed an earlier presentation of this argument, Martin Shubik pointed out that members of the audience were having side conversations during Simon's presentation, and he said this was counterevidence to Simon's claim 'that man is a one-at-a-time, sequential, data-processing animal'. Simon tartly replied, 'The lesson I drew from Shubik's counterevidence was that clearly I was not saying enough per minute to load his channel!' (Simon 1971, pp. 56, 59).

[3] Kahneman 1973, p. 12 and chs 1–2 more generally.

[4] Simon 1971, pp. 42–4; 1960/1977, pp. 106 ff.

[5] Arrow 1974, p. 39.

[6] The 'bottleneck', as Simon (1969, p. 74) says, 'must lie in the small amount of rapid-access storage (so-called short-term memory) available and the time required to move items from the limited short-term store to the large-scale long-term store'.

[7] Kahneman 1973, pp. 3–4. Automobiles used to do that when gases accumulated in their tailpipes and the heat there caused them to explode—Millennials will just have to take my word for that or go watch an old movie.

The attention can pertain to external stimuli or internally generated information such as thoughts, decision rules, long term, or working memory.[8]

According to conventional accounts, 'Attention is focused mental engagement on a particular item of information. Items come into our awareness, we attend to a particular item, and then we decide whether to act.'[9] But more recent work suggests that all of that can sometimes occur without conscious awareness. The action is still volitional in some sense, but the person's goals rather than the person's consciousness are the drivers of attention and response. Implicit learning, evaluative conditioning and unconscious thought all work in that way.[10]

In paying attention to one thing, you fix your focus on it to the *exclusion* of some other things. Indeed, in his early work on the *Principles of Psychology* William James defines 'attention' as 'the taking possession by the mind, in clear and vivid form, of one out of what seem several simultaneously possible objects or trains of thought'. James adds, for emphasis, 'It implies withdrawal from some things in order to deal effectively with others....'[11] So attention is not only scarce but also selective, favouring some objects of attention over others.[12] Depending on how attention is distributed, that can favour some people, propositions, or positions over others—and persistently so insofar as the attention-directing factors remain the same over time.[13]

The need for attention can be reduced by shortcuts, routinized decision-making or the recurrence of familiar patterns.[14] As an interwar etiquette book writer said in introducing her subject,

> In a world complicated and chaotic, an established way of behaving simplifies our lives and soothes our nerves like a cool hand on a fevered brow.... It is a wonderful comfort to have islands of certainty to swim to when one plunges out from self into society.... The more we put recurring movements into form, the more mind we have left for spontaneous living that is refreshing and pleasant.[15]

---

[8] Chun et al. 2011.
[9] Davenport and Beck 2001, p. 20.
[10] Dijksterhuis and Aarts 2010.
[11] James 1890, pp. 403–4. For surveys of more recent philosophical and psychological work on the nature of attention see Watzl (2011a, b).
[12] Kahneman 1973, p. 12.
[13] That is particularly true as regards the way political attention is directed towards some problems and not others (Jones and Baumgartner 2005; Siegel 2022).
[14] Rationing the scarce resource of attention in some such ways is economically 'rational', although any given routine or shortcut may or may not be (Caplin, Dean, and Leahy 2018; Kohlhas and Walther 2021; Mackowiak, Matejka, and Wiederholt 2021; Morrison and Tabinsky 2021).
[15] Wilson (1937, pp. i, 2), quoted in Schlesinger (1946/1968, p. 68).

The same is true of the routines embodied in formal organizations that give them a competitive advantage. As Stinchcombe puts it, 'organizations are structures of coordinated callable routines, ... lying in wait for contingencies in which they are needed, so that the organization can be quickly mobilized to seize opportunities'; so 'they can act corporately faster than consensus can form' among unorganized actors, who are comparatively disadvantaged in consequence.[16]

By way of illustration, consider this example from De Groot's studies of perception among chess players. In the first experiment, he placed chess pieces on the board in positions taken from *actual* past chess games, let subjects view them for five seconds, then removed the pieces and asked subjects to place them back on the board where they had been. Chess grandmasters reconstructed the board almost perfectly, whereas amateur players got virtually all the positions wrong. In the second experiment, he placed the chess pieces on the board *randomly*. In that experiment, grandmasters were hardly better than amateurs at reconstructing the board. Having seen the pattern before in previous games seems to be what made all the difference.[17]

Insofar as we default to such shortcuts, routines, or familiar patterns in order to conserve scarce attention, however, something very much like status quo biases are built into our perceptual and information-processing systems.[18] We do the same things we have done before, or more easily perceive the same things we have perceived before, merely because we have done so before and the impact that that fact has on our own internal attention economy.[19] And those who have been previously advantaged by those shortcuts, routines, and familiar patterns will be advantaged time and again in consequence. That is the most fundamental way in which the scarcity of time and attention, and the mechanisms we use to cope with it, perpetuate social advantage.[20] In Section 10.3 below I shall show how a great many of the specific

---

[16] Stinchcombe 1998, pp. 284, 286; see further Stinchcombe 1990, ch. 2. On routines as attention-conserving shortcuts within organizations see further: Simon and March 1958; Cyert and March 1963; Nelson and Winter 1982.

[17] De Groot (1966), discussed in Simon (1969, pp. 86–7). See similarly Bordalo, Gennaioli, and Shleifer (2020).

[18] That is not to say there is literally 'no change over time' in these things (Feldman 2000); it is simply to say that change is relatively slow and costly compared to merely going with what we've got.

[19] March and Olsen (1984, p. 745) analyse incremental policy-making in public bureaucracies in these terms: 'The distribution of possible outcomes from a policy process ... result[s] from competition and bargaining over incremental adjustments in the current policy; the policy actually adopted is a draw from that distribution. This ... property of policymaking is not independent of institutional factors. Indeed, it seems a prototypic institutional characteristic. Policies, once adopted, are embedded into institutions. They are associated with rules, expectations, and commitments. By affecting attention and aspirations, they affect the future search behavior of political participants.' And as March and Olsen (1984, p. 740) emphasize, 'the allocation of attention' can be 'critical to the flow of events'.

mechanisms that previous chapters identified as contributing to the perpetuation of advantage are responses to the scarcity of time and attention in this way.

10.2 Lessons from the Internet

For a worked example of how biases might be built into our mechanisms for coping with attention scarcity, consider the case of the internet. That is an 'attention economy' *par excellence*. Indeed, the phrase was apparently first coined in relation to the internet, although of course the underlying ideas are much older.[21]

Not everything on the internet is free, to be sure. But it is amazing how much material there can be accessed without payment. Whereas we used to have to pay a thousand dollars for an encyclopaedia, we now consult websites offering the same information free of charge.[22] But of course it is not *really* 'free'. Rather, it is just a different business model. Free-to-use sites sell spots on their pages to advertisers, who hope that having caught our attention in that way we might buy their products; or the free-to-use sites sell information about our browsing patterns to marketers, who use that to better target their pitches to us in ways that will capture our attention.[23] Thus, free-to-use sites are actually renting or selling-on our eyeballs. That is perhaps the principal sense in which the internet is spoken of as an 'attention economy'. It is the user's attention that is bought and sold.[24]

Many bemoan this seizure of our attention as a diminution of our freedom— what, with apologies to Habermas, we might call a colonization of our lifeworld.[25] Having our attention hijacked by others is not just 'distraction', although it certainly is that and that is bad enough.[26] It is addictive, interfering

---

[21] By Goldhaber (1997), according to Festré and Garrouste (2015, p. 4).
[22] Shapiro and Varian 1999, pp. 19–20. They go on to remark, 'Commentators marvel at the amount of free information on the Internet, but it's not so surprising to an economist. The generic information on the Net— ... such as phone numbers, news stories, stock prices, maps and directories—are simply selling at marginal cost: zero' (p. 24).
[23] Fourcade and Healy 2017b; Fourcade and Kluttz 2020.
[24] Harris 2018; Wu 2016, 2019.
[25] Habermas 1987, p. 197; see further Jütten 2011. As Tristan Harris (2018, Q3178) put it in UK Parliamentary testimony, 'For a society to thrive, certain loops of attention have to exist. A parent has to be able to spend attention on their child; we have to spend attention on ourselves and in conversation with each other. We need to be present with each other. If attention does not go to those places, society would collapse: people do not believe in truth; kids do not get their developmental needs met— all those kinds of things. Technology companies are pointing their attention extraction machines at human minds, and they are sucking the attention out of all the places where it used to go.'
[26] Harris 2013, 2018; Eyal 2019.

with our rational agency.[27] Some say it is veritable 'attention serfdom'.[28] Such writers propose generalizing the right to privacy into a right of 'not being addressed' or a right to be 'forgotten'.[29] Economists propose taxing attention-seeking behaviour on the internet—in part for efficiency considerations of avoiding 'wasteful competition for scarce attention',[30] and in part 'with a view to restoring the property of attention to its rightful owners'.[31]

There is a second, deeper sense in which the internet is an attention economy. The internet has itself changed the nature of scarcity, what goods are scarce relative to demand for them. Before the internet, information was much more scarce, or anyway much less generally accessible. With the advent of the internet, that largely ceased to be true. There is now a plethora of information that is easily accessible—indeed, all-too-accessible. What is suddenly in short supply is time and attention to sift through and process all that newly available information. Herbert Simon famously anticipated this development back in 1971, writing:

> in an information-rich world, the wealth of information means a dearth of something else: a scarcity of whatever it is that information consumes. What information consumes is rather obvious: it consumes the attention of its recipients. Hence a wealth of information creates a poverty of attention....[32]

Here I shall be principally concerned with the 'coping strategies' that are employed to do that sifting. Search engines were developed to mechanically locate items posted on the internet containing words specified in the search terms. That was a useful first step. But of course in itself that was not sufficient to solve the problem of information overload, because for any remotely common search term returns thousands or indeed millions of results. So the crucial next step was the development of algorithms for ordering the search results so as to be maximally useful—which is to say, to display at the top of

---

[27] Eyal 2017. Castro and Pham 2020, pp. 7–9.
[28] Williams 2018, ch. 10. Nearly a century ago, Hotelling (1938, p. 257, emphasis added) similarly remarked, 'Attention is desired for a variety of commercial, political, and other purposes, and is obtained with the help of billboards, newspaper, radio, and other advertising. Expropriation of the attention of the general public and its commercial sale and exploitation constitute a lucrative business. From some aspects this business appears to be of a similar character to that of the *medieval robber barons*, and therefore to be an appropriate subject for prohibition by a state democratically controlled by those from whom their attention is stolen.'
[29] Crawford 2015, p. 8. Tran 2016.
[30] Falkinger 2008. See further Wu (2016, 2019).
[31] Hotelling 1938, p. 257.
[32] Simon 1971, p. 40. See similarly Williams 2018, ch. 3.

the list those that are most likely to meet the needs for which the search was being conducted.[33]

Zipf's 'principle of least effort'—better known today as Simon's principle of 'satisficing'—says that people continue searching only until a minimally acceptable ('good enough' or 'satisfactory') result is found, at which point they terminate their search.[34] Arguably, that is just a simple matter of rational 'maximization subject to constraints'—here, the constraints of time and attention.[35]

Clearly, users do approach the internet in just that way. It is a well-established 'law of surfing' that people sharply truncate their searches, more sharply the more items there are available to search. The mean number of pages visited in one surfing session is typically around three; the modal number is one.[36] Similarly when viewing the results delivered up by an internet search engine people 'satisfice' as well. Users of search engines typically do not look at anything beyond the first page of results—indeed, almost half of them do not get past the first item on the list.[37]

Owing to the scarcity of users' attention, therefore, the top results delivered by search engines are strongly privileged. Insofar as the search engine's algorithm allocates slots according to the number of previous hits on that page, a dynamic akin to 'preferential attachment' (as discussed in Section 7.3 above) is set off, as more and more new users view the page just because more previous ones have done so.[38]

But there are many other biases notoriously built into computer algorithms.[39] Some of them, once noticed, can easily enough be eradicated.[40] But

---

[33] Huberman and Wu 2008.
[34] Zipf 1949. Simon 1957, 1982. The 'law of least effort' was first posited by Ferrero (1894).
[35] Goodin 1999. See more generally Morton 2010, 2017. Cf. Simon 1999; Arrow 2003; Artinger, Gigerenzer, and Jacobs 2022.
[36] Huberman and Wu 2008, p. 488; Huberman et al. 1998.
[37] Huberman and Wu 2008, p. 488. Pass et al. (2006, table 4.7) find that only 14 per cent of users get beyond the first page of search results, and indeed that 45 per cent of them click only on the first result on the first page.
[38] Cho and Roy 2004; that is to say, algorithms bake in 'information cascades' of a familiar sort (Bikhchandani, Hirshleifer, and Welch 1992, 1998). That 'winner-takes-all' dynamic might be mitigated—but not completely eliminated—insofar as search engines increasingly 'personalize' searches according to a user's previous browsing patterns (Goldman 2006). Fortunato et al. (2006) report that the actual effects of search engines and search behaviour are more egalitarian than might be expected.
[39] Friedman and Nissenbaum 1996; Mehrabi et al. 2022. Herzog (2021a) argues explicitly that algorithms encode structural injustice.
[40] A classic case is a algorithm used by hospitals to estimate patients' care needs that used 'health costs' as a proxy for 'health needs', thus halving the number of black patients for extra care because blacks are more often uninsured and therefore have less spent on their health care (Obermeyer et al. 2019).

they must first be noticed. Machine learning is good at finding patterns; it is incapable of making sense of them, and for the same reason it is not good at 'explaining them away' and hence disregarding them as artefacts of something else that they should not be taking account of (perhaps even statistically, much less morally).[41]

Perhaps the most notorious case of bias in computer algorithms concerns racial disparities in the outputs of software used to assess a convict's risk of reoffending when making sentencing or parole decisions. A 2016 study examined more than 10,000 cases in one Florida jurisdiction using the COMPAS software to predict likely recidivism. That study showed that 'false positives' (being labelled a high risk of re-offending, but not actually subsequently reoffending) were almost twice as frequent for black as for white offenders.[42] Although that case has been much discussed, perhaps in that case the bias in the algorithm was more apparent than real, or perhaps it just reflected inevitable trade-offs among competing criteria of 'fairness'.[43]

There are, however, more pervasive ways in which biases can enter into algorithms. One is through biases in the 'training data' used in machine learning.[44] If police practices in the past have been racially biased—and compelling evidence suggests that they have[45]—then using police records to train an algorithm for allocating police resources will simply bake those biases into the results that the algorithm produces.[46]

Another way in which bias can enter into algorithms is through the assumptions that are programmed into them. Insofar as those who produce the labels attached to the training data are consciously or unconsciously biased in certain respects, and insofar as those biases affect the labels attached to the training data, the machine will in effect be learning to reproduce those biases.[47] As Congresswoman Alexandria Ocasio-Cortez remarked from a pulpit made famous by Martin Luther King, 'Algorithms are still made by human beings, and those algorithms are still pegged to basic human assumptions. They're just automated assumptions. And if you don't fix the bias, then you are just automating the bias.'[48]

---

[41] Fourcade and Healy 2013, 2017b, forthcoming. Mittelstadt et al. 2016.
[42] Angwin et al. 2016.
[43] Kleinberg, Mullainathan, and Raghavan 2017; Kleinberg et al. 2018; Hedden 2021; Eva 2022. Given that the base rate of re-offending differs among blacks and whites, the ratio of false-positives to false-negatives will inevitably be different even if the test is unbiased.
[44] Chandler 2017; Kleinberg et al. 2018.
[45] Knox, Lowe, and Mummolo 2020.
[46] Richardson, Schultz, and Crawford 2019.
[47] Feast 2019.
[48] Quoted in Hellman 2020, p. 813.

10.3 How Attention Scarcity Perpetuates Advantage

The internet is an attention economy *par excellence*. We have seen how the mechanisms for economizing on scarce attention resources there can lead to biases in our decision-making. Now I shall proceed to show that many of the mechanisms found to be perpetuating advantage in previous chapters can be seen to be responses to shortages of time, attention, and information as well.

Notice that those three shortages—of time, attention, and information—are all tightly connected. Attention is scarce in the sense that there are only so many things we can attend to at a time or within any period of time. Were we to devote more time to the task, we could attend to more components of that task.[49] And although other resources are sometimes required as well in order to obtain more information, time and attention is always required to do that—and sometimes time and attention are all that is required (because, for example, the information is already available to us and we just haven't processed it).

Among the various mechanisms for perpetuating advantage discussed in previous chapters, perhaps those most closely akin to the biased algorithms built into internet search engines are the coding categories and interpretive schema built into natural languages, as discussed in Chapter 5. Those, too, are mechanisms for imposing order on a vast array of otherwise unintelligible data—and in those cases, doing so in a socially mutually intelligible fashion. As with search engine algorithms, so too with social coding categories and interpretive scheme: they highlight some aspects of the data while obscuring other aspects. That in turn advantages some interpretations, and some people, over others.[50] And inevitably so.

Of course, no particular coding categories or interpretive schema were inevitable from the outset. But given the need to make sense of all that otherwise unintelligible data, it is inevitable that *some* coding categories and interpretive schema would be employed. And given the need to do make sense of it in a way that is socially mutually intelligible, it is inevitable that broadly the *same* coding categories and interpretive schema would be employed by many people. And once one particular set of coding categories and interpretive

---

[49] Whether that would do us any good in completing the task successfully depends crucially upon whether the task is 'decomposable' (Simon and Ando 1961; Fisher and Ando 1962; Simon 1969, pp. 209–29). If the task is such that all those components have to be attended to simultaneously, then saying that over time we could attend to all of them *seriatum* is of no assistance.

[50] That is how implicit cognition and stereotyping work, for example (Greenwald and Banaji 1995; Reskin 2003, p. 9; Davis 2016).

schema has become entrenched in a society it—and the biases built into it—are robust against change for those same reasons.⁵¹

What gives rise to the need for coding categories and interpretive schema is the same thing as gives rise to the need for search engine algorithms. Time and attention are scarce, relative to the amount of information available to be processed.

At various other points in my previous discussions, I depicted many of the mechanisms that helped to perpetuate advantage as nothing more than 'informational shortcuts'. When information—or time and attention to process it—is in short supply, people employ these shortcuts to help them make decisions that are 'good enough' for their purposes. Some people are advantaged, and others disadvantaged, in consequence—and insofar as the same shortcuts are recurringly employed, repeatedly so. That was not the main aim of those employing the shortcuts, however, or anyway not necessarily so. It may simply have been an unintended by-product of employing shortcuts to help them make decisions without devoting inordinate time and attention to the task.

Those who are well-placed with social networks enjoy advantage in just such a way, as Chapter 4 has shown. People have more experience of dealing with, and a better basis for assessing the trustworthiness of, those closely connected to them in social networks. When it comes to future mutually beneficial cooperative endeavours, trustworthy insiders are preferred to unknown outsiders.⁵² The latter may upon further inspection turn out to be equally trustworthy. But why expend scarce time and attention finding out, given that we already know we have 'good enough' cooperative partners within our existing network?

Reputation can work in much the same way, as Chapter 7 has shown. If we know that one person has a reputation for trustworthiness, and we do not know anything about the trustworthiness of others with whom we might cooperate instead, we will cooperate with the one reputed to be trustworthy. The others may be equally trustworthy. But why waste time and attention finding out, given that we already know that the one is reputed to be trustworthy enough for our purposes? Or, for another example, if we know that one person has a lot of followers, we will be inclined to want to follow that same person ourselves. Following someone else may be just as good for our purposes. But, again, why expend scarce time and attention finding out? Or, for a

---

⁵¹ Anderson 2012.
⁵² DiMaggio and Garip 2012.

final example, if we know that one person has a reputation for high status in some expertise-based network, we will be inclined to pay more attention to the views of that person compared to others. Those others may be just as expert, but once again why expend scarce time and attention finding out?[53]

---

[53] Notice in this connection the results of the following natural experiment involving an online discussion website. On that website, emails announcing new contributions ordinarily gave the names of all the authors. But during particularly busy periods only first authors' names were given, and the names of other authors were replaced by 'et al.' Sometimes 'et al.' masked the name of a well-known contributor on that website. When a famous author's name is hidden in that way the paper received much less feedback and was less likely to be published in improved, revised form than when the famous author's name was displayed (Simcoe and Waguespack 2011).

11
Interrupting Advantage

Although this book is motivated by a concern with structural injustice and how to overcome it, it has been minimally concerned with defining what structural injustice is or describing how it comes about in the first place. It has focused, instead, upon how the unfair advantage embodied in structural injustice is *perpetuated* over time.

Sometimes of course the unfair advantage is perpetuated by the same sorts of dastardly deeds of evil oppressors as created it in the first place. But those tend to be blatant and they are less effective for precisely that reason in the long term. This book—like Iris Marion Young's canonical discussion[1]—has focused on the more apparently innocent ways in which unfair advantage is insidiously perpetuated *without* the blatant intervention of any wrongful agency. Those are the ways in which injustice is said to be structural *instead of* agentic (in the familiar but misleading trope critiqued in Chapter 1).

The two preceding chapters have identified the internal and external drivers that underlie the various mechanisms that earlier chapters showed to be important in perpetuating unfair advantage. This concluding chapter is devoted to exploring what might be done to interrupt those underlying drivers and the more specific mechanisms to which they give rise.

To foreshadow, my conclusion will be that head-on attacks aimed at destroying those mechanisms will likely fail or anyway come at too high a cost all things considered, as I shall argue in Section 11.2. The best that can be done is probably to look, as I do in Section 11.3, for reasonable 'work-arounds' to moderate the workings of such mechanisms and soften their effects in perpetuating differential advantage.[2]

---

[1] Young 2011, esp. ch. 4.
[2] Although this book is motivated by a concern with unfair, unjust advantage, Chapter 1 announced that its focus would be (and in this chapter will continue to be) on advantage *simpliciter*, how it is perpetuated and how that can be interrupted. Furthermore, the sort of advantage this chapter will be looking for ways to disrupt is differential advantage—what Section 1.3 called 'comparative' rather than 'absolute' advantage.

11.1 Responding to Structural Injustice: The Standard Prescriptions

Iris Marion Young, the pre-eminent theorist of 'responsibility for structural injustice', advocates what she calls a 'social connection model of responsibility'. The basic thought underlying her model is that,

> because the particular causal relationship of the actions of specific individuals or organizations to structural outcomes is not possible to trace, there is no point in trying to seek redress from only and all those who have contributed to the outcome.... The point is not to compensate for the past, but for all who contribute to processes producing unjust outcomes to work to transform those processes.[3]

Those people, Young says, 'share a responsibility to organize collective action to transform those structures'.[4] Discharging that responsibility will, she says, involve 'vocal criticism, organized contestation, a measure of indignation, and concerted public pressure'.[5] It will involve 'public discussion and agitation ... [that] is productively disorderly, filled with passion and play....'[6]

11.1.1 Disruption, Then What?

As those quotations show, Young's analysis is long on 'who' and 'why'. It is also clear as to its ultimate goal of 'transforming unjust structures' and in its specific recommendations of tactics for disrupting them. Young's analysis is singularly silent, however, on two further questions of major importance. How, exactly, do those structures produce injustice? And what elements of them can and should be altered in order to stop them from cementing injustice into the social system?

Reformers of all stripes have a classic response to unfair structures: 'Disrupt them!'[7] Many different things may be meant by that. Standing back from

---

[3] Young 2011, p. 109. There are problems with Young's social connection model that I and others have elaborated elsewhere (Nussbaum 2011; Barry and Macdonald 2016; Goodin and Barry 2021; McKeown 2021; Sankaran 2021; Beck 2022; Gädeke 2021). But those issues are orthogonal—or anyway subsequent—to the question of whether and how each of the various mechanisms perpetuating advantage can and (all things considered) should be interrupted. The question of responsibility—'who should do so'—arises only further down the track.

[4] Young 2011, p. 184. Elsewhere Young (2000, p. 35) writes that 'organizing and political mobilization within formal democratic institutions and norms is usually the only realistic option for oppressed and disadvantaged people and their allies to improve social relations and institutions'.

[5] Young 2011, p. 150.

[6] Young 2000, p. 155.

[7] Hayward 2020; Wasow 2020; Jenkins 2021.

those details, however, 'disruption' typically means something like 'stopping them from working, at least for a time, through physical occupation of key sites or otherwise throwing metaphorical (or not so metaphorical) spanners in the works'. That's what Luddites did to the new machinery that was compromising their jobs in woollen mills in England. That's what Freedom Riders did during the civil rights movement through sit-ins at luncheon counters in the segregated American South. That's what trade unionists do by downing tools and going out on strike.

But such disruption can be sustained for only so long. Furthermore, as Saul Alinsky ruefully remarks, the Haves always possess more power than the Have-Nots, so the Have-Nots are unlikely to be able to install an alternative new order all on their own.[8] To succeed, they must employ a ju-jutsu move, turning the power of the status quo against itself. Sometimes it might amount to mere consciousness-raising: making the advantaged aware of their undeserved advantages and the unwarranted assumptions that implicitly underlie them. Maybe once they have been made aware of that the Haves (or enough of them) will rally to the side of the Have-Nots or anyway condescend to engage with them as moral equals in negotiating a new order.[9] More gently, the disruptions might serve as simple 'reminders of the fact that, because one participates unavoidably in unjust structures, one therefore bears a burden to work toward structural transformation'.[10] More robustly, threatening to continue disrupting things until their demands are met can be a way for the Have-Nots to hold the Haves to ransom.[11]

I do not deny the usefulness of disruptive politics.[12] That is a good way—it might often be the only way—for Have-Nots to get the attention of the Haves. But having got the attention of the Haves, the Have-Nots need something to say to them. They need to have some demands to put onto the table. The Have-Nots need an agenda, a programme, a practical scheme by which the

---

[8] Alinsky 1971, ch. 1.

[9] Hayward (2020) theorizes that strategy; Gandhi practised it.

[10] The 'basic function' of such reminders, Zheng (2018a, p. 12) says, 'is to redirect attention, to call upon an agent to stop and reflect on what else she ought to be doing'. And, conveniently from a strategic point of view, 'justification for [such] accountability practices does not depend on an answer to the question "Have you acted badly?" but merely on the fact that it is more or less always appropriate for us to be reminded of our burden'. But the psychological evidence remains mixed on whether 'attentional focus' actually attenuates implicit bias (Greenwald and Krieger 2006, p. 962).

[11] That can be particularly useful where—such as regards regulatory ones to ameliorate the perpetuation of advantages, discussed in Section 11.3.2—the active cooperation of the Haves is required. It can be particularly effective where the cooperation (active or passive) of the Have-Nots is required for outcomes that matter to the Haves.

[12] What Tilly and Tarrow (2015) call 'contentious politics'.

mechanisms that perpetuate unfair advantages might be overcome.[13] Setting out such a programme of proposed action is the goal of this chapter.

11.1.2 Collective Action: The Motivational Issue

Iris Marion Young is also insistent on a second point, which is that remedying structural injustice will inevitably require coordinated collective action. In one of the quotations at the beginning of this section, she says that the responsibility that her 'social connection model' lays upon people in respect of social injustice is to 'organize collective action to transform those [unjust] structures'. Elsewhere she is even more emphatic in insisting that that responsibility 'can be discharged *only* by joining with others in collective action.... No one of us can do this on our own.'[14] What Young there says will undoubtedly be true of a great many of the specific mechanisms to which earlier chapters have traced the perpetuation of unfair advantage—altering them will require the concerted action of many (perhaps a great many) people, and no one person can alter them alone.

Young is cagey about what, exactly, the collective action that she is calling for might actually involve. She gestures in various directions, saying for example that 'it involves enjoining one another to recognize collective relationships, debating with one another how to accomplish [the required] reorganization, and holding one another to account for what we are doing and not doing to undermine social injustice.'[15] Young adds that it 'must involve vocal criticism, organized contestation, a measure of indignation, and concerted public pressure'.[16] Young leaves the details vague and sketchy.[17] But that is as it should be, and my focus on the mechanisms by which structural injustice is perpetrated explains why: different sorts of collective actions are clearly going to be required to disrupt different ones of those mechanisms, each of which operates according to a logic that is to some not insignificant extent all its own.

What is less excusable in Young's classic analysis of how to respond to structural injustice is the failure to address the longstanding question of how to

---

[13] Thus, disruptions associated with acquisitions and mergers can lead to greater managerial representation of racial minorities and women precisely when, and because, schemes for precisely that had already been provided by 'regulators and advocates' before those disruptions occurred (Zhang 2021).
[14] Young 2011, p. 111, emphasis added.
[15] Young 2011, p. 153.
[16] Young 2011, p. 150. Beck (2019) usefully adds 'consumer boycotts' to the list, showing how they can help to overcome structural injustice.
[17] Piven and Cloward's (1979) fine-grained analysis of *Poor People's Movements* puts far more flesh on those bare bones. See also Jenkins 2021.

motivate people to undertake it. Convincing them that it is their moral responsibility to do so is a start. But it may well not be enough. There may be many barriers—some of them purely psychological—to people's acting upon their responsibility, even if they recognize that they have it, to eradicate structural injustice.[18]

Here I will focus instead upon another singularly rational reason that people may fail to be so motivated. If what people are morally responsible for is an outcome (altering a social structure that perpetuates injustice), and if no one person's contribution to the collective action will make all the difference to that structure's being altered (as is indisputably true for the vast majority of us), then there would seem to be no morally compelling reason for any of us to contribute to the requisite collective action. However deeply we internalize the moral principle at stake, there is simply nothing any one of us could do to achieve the outcome that it prescribes.[19]

Young largely sidesteps motivational questions in her own writings. Other theorists of structural injustice address it more directly, but without much success. One proposal, for example, is to say that overcoming structural injustice is the responsibility of the collective (the political community, and ultimately the state) rather than of individuals.[20] But that just pushes the motivational question back one step—how, especially in a democracy, can we get the state to act upon its responsibilities unless individual citizens are motivated to insist that it do so? Another option might seem to be to shift from the language of 'responsibilities' (i.e., to produce outcomes) to the language of 'duties' (i.e., to take specific actions, whether or not they produce any particular outcomes). But Young herself eschews that approach, insisting that it is crucial to her analysis that it be couched in terms of responsibilities rather than duties.[21]

Yet at the end of the day, it is precisely the latter sort of move towards which Young—rightly, in my view—gestures in sketching, very tentatively, how to motivate people to engage in collective action against structural injustice. She enjoins people to 'take a stand' against the injustice, even if their doing so (certainly individually and perhaps even collectively) is almost certain to prove quixotic.[22] Doing so is not only morally virtuous.[23] More to the present 'motivational' point, it can be sociologically irresistible—people want to 'be part'

---

[18] Smyth 2021.
[19] As commentators on Young's work have noticed. See, e.g., Marin 2017, pp. 1–4; and Sankaran 2021, p. 8.
[20] Parekh 2011.
[21] Young 2011, pp. 142–4. For further discussion see McKeown (2017).
[22] Young 2011, p. 76. Further elaborating this model, see Goodin and Barry (2021, pp. 345 ff.).
[23] Parfit 1984, p. 86; Nefsky 2017; Goodin 2018a.

of something that promises to change history for the better.[24] And of course if enough of them are individually motivated to act on that same virtuous thought, then collectively sufficiently many of them might well act in that way actually to achieve that desired social changes.[25]

We can, in that way, overcome the 'irrationality' motivational worry surrounding calls for collective action to overcome social injustice. But the further question remains. What, exactly, are we supposed to do in that direction? At what targets, exactly, should our collective action be directed? To those questions, we need to provide mechanism-specific answers, to which I now turn.

11.2 Head-on Attacks on Mechanisms Perpetuating Advantage

I shall address those questions in stages. First, in this section, I shall discuss what might be seen as 'head-on attacks' on mechanisms perpetuating advantage. These are designed either (i) to destroy the mechanisms themselves (Section 11.2.1), (ii) to render them redundant by reducing (*in extremis*, eliminating) the need for the mechanisms (Section 11.2.2) or (iii) to render them ineffectual by reducing (*in extremis*, eliminating) the differential advantages accruing from the mechanisms (Section 11.2.3). In a few cases those might at first glance look like promising strategies. Upon further inspection, however, those strategies generally seem to be either unlikely to work at all or, anyway, at a remotely reasonable cost. Having thus given up 'head-on attacks' on mechanisms that perpetuate advantage, I turn in Section 11.3 to 'work-around strategies' designed to ameliorate the perpetuation of advantage through the mechanisms I have been discussing.

11.2.1 Destroy the Mechanisms

One plan, as foreshadowed, would be to destroy the mechanisms by which advantage is created and perpetuated.[26] If new machines in the mills are enriching some while impoverishing others, destroy the machines: that was

---

[24] Hardin 1982, p. 42; Goodin 2022.
[25] See Goodin and Barry (2021, pp. 346–7) and sources cited therein.
[26] Sometimes the mechanisms are so interconnected that destroying one will cause all to crumble. Montesquieu had something like this in mind when writing: 'forasmuch as government is a structure composed of divers parts and members, joined and united together with so strict connection that it is impossible to stir so much as one brick or stone but the whole body will be sensible of it' (quoted in Ross 1901, p. 191).

the Luddite strategy at the turn of the nineteenth century in England.[27] If the accumulation of human capital is leading to persistent social inequality, exile the intellectuals out into the fields: that was the strategy of Mao's Cultural Revolution in mid-twentieth century China.[28]

Many (if not all) of the mechanisms that I have identified as perpetuating advantage could in principle be approached in this way. Scale effects perpetuating advantage could be prevented by breaking up large enterprises and networks, capping the size of factories, requiring workers to rotate among jobs frequently to prevent the accumulation of contacts and skills, and so on. The biases built into the mechanisms for overcoming the scarcity of attention could be eliminated flooding the environment with so much or such dubious information that those existing mechanisms are incapable of processing it, either at all or anyway correctly.[29] Reputations could be destroyed through deliberately planting false rumours. Expectations could be undercut by deliberately engineering unanticipatable outcomes. Coordination could be undermined by deliberately planting agents dedicated to subverting the organization at crucial nodes within it. Language can be subverted by persistent misuse that robs words of their meaning.[30]

I will not elaborate on these strategies, however, because they almost invariably come at such high social costs as to make them almost certainly unacceptable. At best, they would involve levelling down in a big way, destroying instruments that are valuable in absolute terms to a great many people (maybe literally all people) just because those instruments are comparatively more valuable to some than to others.[31] As I said in Section 5.1.1 à propos languages and the biases that they contain, even if they create a form of coordination with unequal rewards, everyone is better off being coordinated (however unequally, within broad limits) than not being coordinated at all.

---

[27] Thompson (1966, p. 554) quotes one contemporary source as reporting that the Luddites 'broke only the frames of such [owners] as have reduced the price of the men's wages; those who have not lowered the price, have their frames untouched; in one house, last night, they broke four frames out of six; the other two which belonged to masters who had not lowered their wages, they did not meddle with'.

[28] Moore 1985, pp. 203–4.

[29] Steve Bannon, President Trump's media guru and sometime campaign manager, famously described this, his preferred media strategy as 'flood the zone with shit' (Senior 2022). On 'information overload' as a strategy of political manipulation, see Goodin (1980, pp. 58–61). For a recent example of this practice, deployed for very different purposes, consider how during the 2020 COVID-19 pandemic a hacker disseminated computer code for swamping with false reports the website that Ohio had established for reporting people refusing to go back to work so they could be denied further unemployment benefits (Farzan 2020; Rose 2020).

[30] Orwell 1946.

[31] Maybe there is often a trade-off to be made between 'equity' and 'efficiency' (Okun 1975). My criticism of the 'destroy the mechanisms' strategy is that it leaves no room for trading one off for the other but, instead, gives absolute priority to 'equity'.

The same is true of a great many of the mechanisms that I have shown help to perpetuate advantage. Were we to cap the size of enterprises or networks, everyone would lose (albeit some more than others) from sacrificing the benefits that would otherwise ensue from the economies of scale in production or in networks. The mechanisms we use to limit demands on our inevitably scarce attention may be biased in their distributional consequences. But it would be very much more difficult (perhaps impossible) to negotiate our way through the world without some such mechanisms, any of which would contain biases of one sort or another.

11.2.2 Reduce the Need for the Mechanisms

If literally destroying the mechanisms responsible for perpetuating advantage is usually impossible or at least seriously inadvisable, what might we do instead? One thing would be to undermine those mechanisms by reducing the need for and hence reliance upon them.

But just how feasible is that strategy as applied to the two drivers that the previous two chapters have shown underlie many of the mechanisms at once? That strategy is basically inapplicable to scale effects of the sort discussed in Chapter 9 for one simple reason: scale effects work not by 'satisfying a need' but, rather, merely by 'providing a benefit'.[32] Larger producers are more cost-efficient, larger networks more communicatively useful, and so on. Those are undeniably benefits, but they do not remotely speak to 'needs'. We cannot undermine those mechanisms that work through scale effects by 'reducing the need' for them, because there is no need that they satisfy—merely a benefit that they confer. At most we might try to undermine those mechanisms by 'reducing their benefit'. That will be the subject of the next section.

When it comes to the second underlying driver—the scarcity of time and attention and the need for mechanisms to cope with it—there is a genuine need being served. Furthermore, that need derives from an obvious source. As Herbert Simon has already been quoted as saying, 'information' is what 'consumes the attention of its recipients'.[33] So one way to reduce the demands on our scarce attention is to reduce the information available to us. In one way, that seems like a terrible idea—assuming the information in question is true, relevant, and would be useful to us, provided only we had the time and attention to process it properly.

---

[32] Drawing a sharp distinction between those two things can be tricky however: cf. Frankfurt (1984) and Goodin (1985b).
[33] Simon 1971, p. 40. See further Section 10.2.

Not all information is like that, of course. Much of the 'information' we encounter on the internet is not really very informative at all. Rather, it is simply the consequence of a wasteful attention-seeking arms-race; and we would be better off if that counterproductive behaviour were suppressed.[34] Or, again, a fair bit of the 'information' that we encounter on the internet is deceptive, intentionally or otherwise, and we would be better off being shielded from it. The standard free-speech concern then arises, however: who is to determine which is which?[35] And more to the point of the present book, wouldn't any mechanism we establish for policing the internet in this regard inevitably contain biases that have the effect of advantaging some more than others—and persistently so, insofar as the same mechanism, with the same biases, operate continuously over time.[36] Furthermore, much information that we encounter on the internet, while true, is irrelevant to us. Finding the information that is relevant to us is the problem that search engines were designed to solve. But those search engines too inevitably contain certain biases and hence advantage some more than others—and persistently so, once again. And what is true of the internet is true well beyond it, of information suppressing or filtering strategies quite generally.

Another more promising strategy is to reduce the demands on our limited time and attention is through a division of labour. Insofar as the task for which the information is needed is 'decomposable' without (too much) cost into smaller subtasks, each of which could in principle be performed by a different person, then each of us could specialize in acquiring and processing the information for one of the subtasks and then simply pool our findings with those of trusted others who have done the same on the subtasks in which they specialize.[37] This is simply an individual-level informational analogue of division of labour within a firm, where decomposable tasks are entrusted to different branches of the firm and the results are then put together in the end.

The need for attention from each individual is thus reduced by pooling the efforts of multiple people. The problem to which that strategy gives rise is as Section 10.3 suggested. In deciding who you can trust to be a reliable partner in this way, your decisions are inevitably biased time and again in favour of those whom you know to be trustworthy—and against those who might actually be equally trustworthy, but about whom you know nothing. So if we are looking

---

[34] Perhaps through the imposition of taxes or charges, as suggested in Section 10.2.
[35] 'Who made you boss?' in Estlund's (2008, p. 40) terms. Howard 2021.
[36] The same questions arises with regards to the taxes Falkinger (2008) proposes to discourage excess information on the internet which is the product of an 'attention-seeking arms race' among those trying to sell us something. Who decides what information is of that sort and what is genuinely and usefully informative? And wouldn't whatever mechanism is established to make that determination to be subject to biases that advantage some over others, and persistently so over time?
[37] Simon and Ando 1961; Fisher and Ando 1962; Simon 1969, pp. 209–29.

for ways to overcome the perpetuation of advantage by undermining the need to devote time and attention to make decisions, this is not a good unbiased way to do that.

Looking to some of the more specific mechanisms that earlier chapters found to perpetuate advantage, there sometimes seems to be more scope for the 'reduce the need for them' strategy. Consider the case of language choice discussed in Section 5.1, for example. There we found that the biases contained in any given language were reinforced and perpetuated by the need for everyone to speak the same language. Once we all have translation and interpreter software installed on our computers and smartphones, we no longer need to speak the same language.[38] That frees us from the biases associated with any given language—but of course not from any biases that are common across all the languages that are known to our software or, of course, from any biases built into the translation programmes themselves.

For another example, recall my earlier discussions of employer hiring decisions. As I argued above, where individualized information was unavailable, employers can only make those hiring decisions on the basis of statistics pertaining to broad social categories (race, age, gender, whatever).[39] One can imagine that, with the growth of information technology, individualized information might become more readily available and more easily analysable. That would obviate the need to rely upon statistics about the social categories that may not accurately reflect the situation of the particular individual. But of course the computer software used to analyse all that individualized data may well contain biases of the sort discussed in Section 10.2.

Some biases are more objectionable than others, to be sure. Perhaps, for example, we would be less inclined to look unfavourably upon biases that did not work to the disadvantage of historically disadvantaged groups.[40] But to make that assessment, we obviously need to take account of whether or not a person is a member of one of the disadvantaged groups that we are trying to protect.[41] That takes us back to the sort of category-based assessment that we were trying to avoid in the first place, and the same problems arise here as before. What is true on average of people in the category is not necessarily true

---

[38] Chokkattu 2019.
[39] In Sections 5.2 and 6.1.
[40] This is the strategy of the US Supreme Court in subjecting to special scrutiny legislation that has a differential impact on 'suspect classifications', defined in terms of historical disadvantage (Stone 1938, fn. 4; Ackerman 1985). Blum (2004, pp. 278–9) extended that model to 'stereotypes' more generally, before subsequently registering some important cautions about it (Blum 2012).
[41] Indeed, advocates of 'algorithmic affirmative action' argue that computer algorithms can be made more fair by *including* information about a person's group identity (race, gender, etc.) rather than excluding it. See Dwork et al. 2012; Bent 2020; Hellman 2020.

of any one of them. Hence, whether any given person deserves to benefit from biases contained in the computer software in question on account of previous unfair disadvantages is a question that is not answerable merely by identifying the social category into which that person falls.

In short, it does not look as if 'reducing the need' for the mechanisms that perpetuate advantage would be a particularly promising general strategy. In some cases, that is because they answer to no 'need' but merely offer their users some 'benefit'. In other cases, that is because we can reduce the need for those mechanisms only by employing other mechanisms and strategies that themselves contain biases.

Those may well be different biases, and the advantages that they create (and, through their repeated use, perpetuate) may not be the same. There may well be much to be said for letting biases rotate, where we cannot avoid bias altogether. Still, undue advantages those will nonetheless be.

11.2.3 Reduce the Differential Advantages Conferred

When discussing the suggestion to destroy the mechanisms conferring differential advantage in Section 11.2.1, I concluded that that would typically come at too high a cost in terms of the absolute (even if differential) advantages that virtually everyone derived from them. One final suggestion would be to try somehow to reduce, not the advantages *tout court*, but rather the way in which the mechanisms *differentially* advantage some people over others.

In some of the cases discussed in previous chapters, that might be relatively straightforward. Consider scale effects in production, discussed in Section 9.1. Larger producers can produce each unit of output more cheaply than can smaller producers. That gives them a competitive advantage over smaller producers, enabling them to sell their products more cheaply. In the limiting case that gives rise to monopolies, which are good for the monopolists but which are in the end bad for everyone else, as monopolists hike up their prices once they have driven competitors out of business. Notice, however, that those further deleterious effects are not the automatic product of scale effects *per se*. Instead, they are the result of the rules governing market competition and the way in which those rules allow one party to appropriate all the proceeds of the scale effects. Those rules, obviously, can be restructured in ways that distribute the proceeds of the scale effects more equitably across the entire society. Public ownership of natural monopolies is one traditional way of doing that. Suitable regulation of privately-owned natural monopolies is another.

At the other extreme, reducing the differential advantages accruing from other of the mechanisms may be almost impossible to accomplish without extreme disruption. Consider for example Chapter 5's discussion of languages, coding categories or different conventions more generally. Of course different people would have been relatively more advantaged had we adopted different ones than we did. But once one has been adopted, with all of its in-built biases, altering the differential advantages that flow from those biases cannot be done without fundamentally altering the language, coding categories, or conventions themselves. That is just what it is for to have those biases 'built into' them.[42]

We can of course attempt to overcome in-built biases by fiddling at the margins—introducing a few new terms, categories or interpretations, for example, or repurposing some of the old ones.[43] What were originally terms of derision are embraced by their targets as badges of honour and rallying cries ('queer' by advocates of gay rights, for example, and 'SlutWalks' by opponents of rape culture).[44] If successful, such strategies would achieve the desired de-biasing at minimal cost to shared communicative and interpretive frameworks. That is what proponents of 'gender-neutral language' hope to accomplish, for example. Such strategies might suffice if the biases in view were merely incidental to the languages, categories of interpretive scheme in question. But if instead those are (as some say that indeed they are) saturated with bias, then such marginal tinkering will not suffice and wholesale replacement (with all its attendant disruptions) will instead be required for successful debiasing.[45]

In between those two extremes, there are many mechanisms such that we could, at least in principle, reduce the differential advantages flowing to different people from structural advantages and disadvantages without excessive broader disruptions. Take Chapter 3's positional advantages for example. In principle (how easy it might be in practice is another matter) we could certainly alter the differential advantages accruing to people occupying different positions in a status hierarchy or a formal organizational hierarchy.

A prime example here would be the remuneration that a firm pays to its chief executive officer compared to its median worker. That ratio has varied over time. In the US, for example, the realized earnings of the CEOs of the

---

[42] Maybe of course the biases were not really 'built into' them in this strong sense at all, and we could actually change those features without literally changing the language, categories, or conventions altogether. Still, for any biases that we would be remotely tempted to say are 'built into' them, such alterations are almost certain to be difficult and costly in various respects.

[43] As is commonly done, as Tarrow's (2013) extended history of the practice clearly shows.

[44] On the former see: Altman 1996; Seidman 1997; Smith 1998; Velasco and Paxton 2022. On the latter see: Valentini 2011; Mendes 2015.

[45] Or 're-biasing', as I have argued. On gender-neutral language reform and its limits, see: Spender 1985; Ehrlich and King 1992, 1994; and Cameron 1998, pt. 2.

350 largest companies was on average 320 times that of the median worker in their firms in 2019, up from 61 times what it was in 1989.[46] The ratio varies not only across time but also across countries, being substantially higher in Anglo-Saxon countries than Continental European ones for example.[47] There are various policy interventions for reducing that ratio, ranging from a general policy of high marginal tax rates on high incomes to more targeted policies such as higher corporate tax rates on companies with high ratios.[48] German marginal personal income tax rates on the highest incomes are more than 20 per cent higher than in the US. The overall economic performance of Germany compared to the US suggests that no catastrophic economic consequences would ensue from the US implementing similarly higher tax rates on high incomes.[49] That points to one clear way in which we could reduce the differential advantages and disadvantages accruing to people differently positioned in the status hierarchy of the economy, even while leaving the status hierarchy itself unchanged.

We could similarly reduce—indeed, we have already reduced—the differential political advantages and disadvantages accruing to people who are differently positioned in the social status hierarchy. Historically, people used to be able to vote in as many electorates as they owned property. In Sweden circa 1900, for example, rules permitted a person to have up to 100 votes (or two per cent of total ballots) in an urban district and up to 5000 (or 10 per cent of total ballots) in a rural district.[50] In Britain, one particular 'clergyman of the Church of England' is said to have 'contrived to vote in no fewer than forty different places' at one nineteenth-century General Election.[51] Such 'plural voters' constituted something like seven per cent of the UK electorate in 1911.[52] Those practices have now been outlawed, and each voter is entitled to vote in only one constituency.[53] People can still own property in multiple places, of course. The social hierarchy is in that sense unchanged. But the differential electoral power that they used to derive from such differential social status has now been erased.

---

[46] McGregor 2020.
[47] Marchese 2022. See more generally Atkinson, Piketty, and Saez 2011.
[48] On the former see Piketty 2003; Scheuer and Slemrod 2020; and Marchese 2022; on the latter see Mishel and Kandra 2021.
[49] The highest marginal personal tax rate in Germany is 45 per cent compared to 37 per cent in the US. For a comparison of their GDP growth rates see World Bank (2022).
[50] Reforms in 1907–1909 reduced both to 40; and equal and universal adult suffrage was introduced in 1918, putting an end to that practice altogether (Goldstein 1983, ch. 1).
[51] Shaw-Lefevre 1892, col. 1184.
[52] Blewett 1965, p. 46.
[53] Although the reforms often came surprisingly late—in the UK, for example, only with the Representation of the People Act of 1948.

11.3 Amelioration Strategies

The upshot of the previous section is that mounting head-on assaults on the mechanisms perpetuating advantage may not always, or even often, be a promising strategy. In a few cases that strategy might be feasible without intolerable costs; but those cases are the exceptions rather than the rule. Next, I shall consider a suite of strategies that leave in place the mechanisms and the differential advantages that accrue from them, and instead simply try to provide 'work-arounds' that mitigate their tendency to perpetuate differential advantage.

The concept of a 'work-around' comes from engineering, particularly in recent years information systems engineering. It refers to 'a means of avoiding or resolving a problem when the usual or most obvious solution is not feasible, possible or available'.[54] The general idea that I want to take away from that more technical literature is simply that 'when a path to a goal is blocked, people use their knowledge to create and execute an alternative path to that goal'.[55] Work-arounds may not be elegant.[56] Often they are (or anyway are expected to be) only temporary. But they are employed in a wide range of social settings to avoid blockages and inefficiencies in formal organizational rules and routines, with the aim of better achieving the organization's overall goals.[57]

There are fundamentally three types of strategies available for this purpose, corresponding to the three types of possible policy interventions to address distributional issues quite generally.[58] One is tax-and-transfer: in the cases of interest here, siphoning off some of the benefits from the mechanism in question and redistributing the proceeds to those disadvantaged by it (Section 11.3.1). A second is command-and control: regulate the mechanism in question in such a way as to mitigate its unwanted distributional impact (Section 11.3.2). A third is pluralism and competition: provide alternative mechanisms, each with its own distinctive distributional impact, to avoid people being locked into any particular one of them (Section 11.3.3).

---

[54] *Oxford English Dictionary*, qv. 'workaround'; it is also there described as a 'means of bypassing or resolving a technical difficulty when a system, procedure or mechanism fails to work' properly.
[55] Koopman and Hoffman 2003, p. 71.
[56] When they are not, they are often called a 'kluge': 'a fix that is awkward or clumsy but is at least temporarily effective' (Koopman and Hoffman 2003, p. 73; see further Marcus 2008).
[57] Azad and King (2012, pp. 366–8) give the example of ways that attending physicians and nurses have for circumventing rules that formally require prior approval of an infectious disease specialist before dispensing anti-microbial drugs, when that would seriously delay treatment of patients in urgent need of such drugs.
[58] This parsing blends insights from Dahl and Lindblom 1953; Lowi 1964; and Schultze 1977.

These strategies are all 'ameliorative' insofar they leave the basic mechanisms that perpetuate advantage untouched and instead merely strive to soften the effects of their workings.[59] Such strategies therefore constitute a less fundamental challenge to those mechanisms than do the strategies discussed in Section 11.2.

That will doubtless disappoint those who, in the spirit of Marx's *Critique of the Gotha Programme*, fetishize fundamentals.[60] They would complain that it 'treats the symptom rather than the disease'. My response would be to ask: 'What, exactly, is wrong with that?' If the treatment reliably and completely removes the symptom, and if the symptom is the only thing that bothers us about the disease, then 'merely' treating the symptom is a perfectly good response to the situation.

We might of course worry that the treatment for the symptom may not always be available or that it may not always work.[61] But by the same token, were we trying instead to treat the root cause of the disease, we would have to worry that that treatment might not always be available or that it might not always work (against a novel variant of the disease, for example).

Strategies attempting to ameliorate the effects of mechanisms that perpetuate structural injustice might be 'second-best' compared to strategies designed to eradicate those mechanisms altogether. Still, the former strategies may prove to be invaluable back-ups, insofar as the latter strategies are unavailable, unreliable, or unduly costly. Ameliorative strategies are well worth exploring, if only for that reason.

---

[59] A partial exception might be regulatory strategies discussed in Section 11.3.2 below which, depending on their details, might sometimes pose a more fundamental challenge to the workings of those structural mechanisms.

[60] Marx (1875/1972, pp. 388–9) criticizes social democrats for separating 'consideration and treatment of distribution [of means of consumption] as independent of the mode of production and hence the presentation of socialism as turning principally on distribution.... [I]t was in general a mistake to make a fuss about so-called *distribution* and put the principal stress on it. Any distribution whatever of the means of consumption is only a consequence of the distribution of the conditions of production themselves. The latter distribution, however, is a feature of the mode of production itself' (see similarly Cohen 1981). In her initial statement of her theory of structural injustice, Young (1990, pp. 3, 9) similarly says that 'instead of focusing on distribution, a conception of justice should begin with the concepts of domination and oppression.... Distributive injustices may contribute to or result from these forms of oppression, but none is reducible to distribution and all involve social structures and relations beyond distribution.'

[61] Or in the case of the first 'siphon off the benefits and redistribute them' strategy, we may worry that it would not always be implemented. An important part of the Marxian worry with distributional solutions is that they have to be implemented repeatedly, time and again, with the attendant risk that they might not be on some crucial occasion. While that may be a worry with the strategy discussed in Section 11.3.1, those discussed in Sections 11.3.2 and 11.3.3 are like structural solutions in being more once-and-for-all affairs.

11.3.1 Siphon Off the Benefits

Let us consider first the strategy of ameliorating a mechanism's distributional consequences, which would work by siphoning off some of the benefits from the mechanism and using those revenues to compensate people who are disadvantaged by that mechanism.[62] That strategy is akin to the welfare state's tax-transfer system by which cash is taken from the rich and redistributed to the poor.

Government tax-and-transfer policies can, with the right settings, seriously constrain inequalities in advantages that are calibrated in terms of money and what money can buy. I have already referred to the success of Continental-European, as compared to Anglo-Saxon, approaches to capping 'top incomes'.[63] There are various other policy instruments that governments can deploy, again with more or less success, to reduce income inequality more generally. Those range from flattening the 'pre-distribution' of market incomes, through taxing higher incomes progressively more, to making larger or more targeted transfer payments.[64] Likewise, there are various 'legislative interferences' that can reduce inequality in capital holdings. As Kuznets wrote long ago,

> These may be aimed at limiting the cumulation of property directly through inheritance taxes and other explicit capital levies. They may produce similar effects indirectly, e.g., by government-permitted or induced inflation which reduces the economic value of accumulated wealth stored in fixed-price securities or other properties not fully responsive to price changes; or by legal restriction of the yield on accumulated property, ... in the form of rent controls or of artificially low long-term interest rates maintained by the government to protect the market for its own bonds.[65]

Evidence suggests that, if all those sorts of policies are pursued effectively (as for example in the Nordic countries), inequalities in the post-government distribution of economic advantage can be held stable or even reduced somewhat over time.[66] But the evidence also suggests that only really major catastrophes—major wars, revolutions, the Black Death, and such like—can

---

[62] Sometimes taxes are used not for (re)distributional purposes, of course, but instead merely to disincentivize behaviour we want to discourage, as in the proposal discussed in Section 10.2 to tax attention-seeking on the internet.
[63] In Section 11.2.3.
[64] Joumard, Pisu, and Bloch 2012.
[65] Kuznets 1955, p. 9.
[66] Goodin et al. 1999; Piketty and Saez 2014; OECD 2019, pp. 98–9.

lead to really major reductions in the inequality of economic advantage.[67] In more ordinary times, government tax-and-transfer policies only reduce, but not eliminate, economic inequalities and the perpetuation of economic advantage.

Furthermore, according to the common critique, even those often modest accomplishments of tax-and-transfer policies can come at non-negligible cost to economic well-being. If too large a proportion of its benefits are taxed away, people might be disincentivized from engaging in the activity that would have produced those benefits. For a classic example, insofar as people are motivated to engage in paid labour only for its financial returns, they will work less the higher the marginal tax on labour income, and hence there will be less income to tax and less tax revenues available to transfer to the poor.[68] Likewise higher taxes on investment income may reduce investment and hence the investment income available to tax.

The same may be true of attempts to siphon off people's benefits from some of the mechanisms I have identified as perpetuating advantage. To the extent that people are prevented by the taxes from enjoying the benefits, they may cease engaging in the activities that generate the benefits that we had hoped to redistribute via the tax-transfer system. For an example from Section 9.1, if producers would only build a larger factory in order to benefit from the economies of scale resulting from greater output, taxing away those benefits deprives them of any incentive to enlarge their operations and generate those economies of scale. And that would be a bad outcome from the point of view of all those who would have benefited from the cheaper products that would have been produced by the larger factory.

There is an obvious second limitation to the tax-and-transfer style strategies for ameliorating the perpetuation of advantage. Cash taxes and transfers can obviously only affect distributions of cash and advantages linked to cash. Many of the advantages whose perpetuation worries us are not of that sort. Moralists insist that there are certain things that *should not* be bought and sold.[69] My point here is the more sociological one: there are, in any given society, certain things that *cannot* be bought and sold.[70] Taxes that siphon off financial benefits leave the distribution of those sorts of advantages untouched, as do transfers of financial benefits.

---

[67] Scheidel 2017; Alfani 2022; Jedwab, Johnson, and Koyama 2022.
[68] That is an important part of Okun's (1975) 'leaky bucket'. For a survey of the empirical evidence on labour supply effects see Moffitt (2002).
[69] Satz 2010; Sandel 2012.
[70] Tobin 1970. That might of course be sociologically true because people in that society have internalized the moral arguments and crafted their social norms around them.

A third limitation to the 'siphon off the benefits' strategy is that many of the advantages that worry us, unlike money, are non-transferable.[71] Take for example the advantages that accrue to someone from having accumulated human capital (Section 9.3). You can of course tax away the *income* derived from that human capital and transfer the monies thus raised to someone else. But you cannot literally redistribute one person's experience to another. Likewise with the advantage that a person enjoys from their reputation for reliability: you can of course tax-and-transfer part of *proceeds* from that reputation, but you cannot literally transfer the reputation itself to some other person (Section 7.4).

Sometimes you can, without changing the overall structure itself, replace one person with another at any given location within that structure. In a formal institutional hierarchy, for example, you can install a new person in the position formerly occupied by another (Section 3.1.2). Likewise, you can replace one person with another at any particular node in a communication network (Chapter 4). Different people would benefit, in consequence, from the advantages derived from that position in the institutional hierarchy or communication network. The point remains that the people in the advantageous positions—different though they may now be—are still differentially advantaged over those who not. And they are recurringly advantaged, the longer they remain in those positions. That, of course, is precisely the problem that we were trying to ameliorate.

Maybe rotating people in and out of positions of advantage might succeed in ameliorating that problem over time, if the rotation occurs rapidly enough and there are enough positions of advantage for everyone to enjoy one sooner or later. But insofar as the advantages from having once occupied the position enable one to accumulate further advantages subsequently, those who occupy the position earlier are advantaged over those who occupy it later.[72] And in any case, positions of advantage that are all that common are rarely all that advantageous.

Perhaps we should not mind differentially advantaging in that way people who were historically disadvantaged. Certainly we should not mind advantaging them instead of others (or more than others)—to some extent. But how much is enough, and how much would be too much? At some point their enjoying positions of advantage might lead them to have accumulated so many advantages that they come to be the 'new advantaged', despite their prior history of having once been disadvantaged. To avoid that, we need not only to

---

[71] Gheaus 2009.
[72] In ways described in Sections 1.2, 2.3, and 2.4.

have an answer to the question of 'how much is enough' but also some reliable mechanism for stopping them from continuing to reap advantages once that point has been reached. Rotating people out of the position of advantage, once that time comes, is fine so far as it goes—but that leaves untouched the further advantages that will continue to accrue to them from having once occupied those positions.

11.3.2 Regulate the Process

A second ameliorative strategy would be to try to regulate the process by which the mechanism in question works to perpetuate advantage. A classic case in point is the sort of regulations that are imposed upon the operation of natural monopolies created by scale effects in production (Section 9.1). But we could equally well imagine anti-discrimination or group defamation laws being deployed to restrict the ways in which language or coding categories disadvantage minority groups in society (Chapter 5). And we could address the sorts of mechanisms perpetuating organizational advantage discussed in Chapter 8 through regulations prohibiting forms of coordination that work to the egregious disadvantage of some segments of the community, just as anti-trust legislation prohibits 'combinations in restraint of trade'.[73]

Obviously, much detailed work would need to be done on how best to craft each of those sorts of regulations. But all attempts at regulation will be plagued by a similar difficulty. What Arthur Okun said of 'high tax rates' applies to regulations more generally: inevitably, they 'are followed by attempts of ingenious men to beat them as surely as snow is followed by little boys on sleds'.[74] Insofar as evasions would promptly and effectively undercut the effects of any regulation, the regulatory strategy in general is unpromising.[75]

11.3.3 Provide Alternative Mechanisms

A final strategy for ameliorating the effects of a mechanism perpetuating differential advantages is to create a multiplicity of such mechanisms, each with differing distributional impacts. Insofar as those alternative mechanisms all

---

[73] Prohibiting other sorts of coordinated collective action can of course be a way of perpetuating advantage, as when in the UK in the early nineteenth-century Combination Acts were enacted to prohibit employees from forming trade unions (Mill 1848/1965, vol. 3, bk 5, ch. 10, sec. 5; Goodin 2017).
[74] Okun 1975, p. 97.
[75] Parker and Nielsen 2017.

operate alongside one another, the distributional biases built into one might be at least partially offset by the differing distributional biases built into the others. A model of this might be the sort of 'women's networking' that was so warmly recommended by Second Wave feminists as a solution to problems facing females in the labour market.[76]

'Operating alongside one another' might mean either of two things, or a mixture of both. One is that each person uses only one of the mechanisms, but different people use different ones of them. The other is that each person uses all the mechanisms, if not literally simultaneously at least in quick succession. In the latter case, the differing biases built into the different mechanisms will tend to cancel one another at the level of each individual; in the former case, they will cancel one another only at the level of the population at large. Insofar as we worry only about the *overall* social impact of the mechanisms' biases, the latter might suffice. But insofar as the worry is at least in part about their interpersonal impact, something more like the former might be required.

Everyone using multiple mechanisms may not be possible, or anyway not without substantial cost. Take the case of language (Section 5.1). Language is supposed to be a means for people to communicate with one another, which requires that those people speak the same language. Different languages have different biases built into them. Everyone speaking multiple languages, each with differing biases, could in principle compensate for the biases built into any given language. In practice, however, there are clear limits to how many languages people can realistically be expected to master. In any case, one of the languages will almost always be the dominant one (because it is of higher status, spoken more widely, or whatever),[77] with detrimental consequences (in terms of health and human capital formation, among many other things) for those for whom the dominant language is not their first language (Section 5.1.2).

Or for another example, harking back to the Second Wave feminist recommendation just cited, consider the case of the advantages accruing to some people over others owing to their location in communication networks (Chapter 4). Different networks are structured differently, advantaging different individuals in this way. Where network externalities exist, the value to you of being part of any given network is a function of how many other people are

---

[76] Kanter 1977, pp. 282, see also pp. 181–6. The effectiveness of this strategy is suggested by the fact that 'women executives working in women-led firms earn 15–20% more in total compensation than women working in other firms, ceteris paribus. Women-led firms also hire proportionately more top women executives' (Booth 2009, p. 602).

[77] De Swaan 2001; Van Parijs 2011.

part of it; that gives you an incentive to part of the same network as everyone else.[78] But, as noted in Section 9.3.1, there is no reason in that logic to confine yourself to just *one* such network. From the user's perspective (as opposed to the perspective of the owner of the website or network) there is no reason in principle not to be a member of several networks. If you are, then the biases contained in any one network would be at least partially cancelled by the differing biases contained in the other networks to which you also belong. While that is perfectly possible in principle, in practice being a member of very many different communication networks will almost inevitably lead to communicative fragmentation and information overload. Given that your time and attention is scarce, the latter will lead you to adopt filtering mechanisms that contain their own biases (Chapter 10).

At the opposite extreme are cases in which there are multiple mechanisms but each person partakes of only one of them.[79] Perhaps the classic example of this is organizational: the introduction of 'countervailing power' of organized labour to offset the power of private owners in capitalist economies.[80] To counteract the biases introduced by one organization, create another organization with opposing biases and (ideally) equal power. Maybe the best way to do that is to try to find ways to let people self-organize without heavy organizational overheads, once they've been networked together in some minimal sense.[81] Multiculturalism might be seen as a manifestation of broadly the same strategy.

Multiculturalism might also be seen as a way of proliferating schema for interpreting the world (Section 5.3). The need for complete coordination—understood (naively) as everyone doing the same thing or at least complying with the same coordination scheme—is often exaggerated. True, there may be certain practical advantages in employing the same coding categories and interpretive schema as others around you (as discussed in Sections 5.2

---

[78] Discussed Sections 4.2, 4.6, 6.1.2.1, 7.3, and 9.3.1.

[79] Yang et al. (2019, p. 2033) show that women's rise to leadership positions turns heavily on their having different networks than men: 'Women with a network centrality in the top quartile and a female-dominated inner circle have an expected job placement level that is 2.5 times greater than women with low centrality and a male-dominated inner circle. Women who have networks that resemble those of high-placing men are low-ranking, despite having leadership qualifications comparable to high-placing women.'

[80] Galbraith (1952, 1954; cf. Stigler 1954) originally coined the term to apply to the power of large purchasers to extract price concessions from downstream suppliers, but it has been subsequently much expanded beyond that. The idea is extensionally equivalent to the later Dahl's 'polyarchy' (Dahl 1972), although in his earlier work he treated it instead as an aspect of a separate category of 'bargaining' (Dahl and Lindblom 1953, cf. chs 10–11 and 17).

[81] That strategy would rely on 'the strength of weak ties' (Granovetter 1973). The new management strategy of self-organizing work groups might be another model along the same lines (Pruijt 2003). Gaus (2021, pt 2) champions such self-organization as the linchpin of the Open Society more generally.

and 5.3 respectively). That may ease interpersonal communication and mutual understanding. But there can be social advantages in having alternative frameworks operating alongside one another as well. Progress in science, for example, is fostered by having competing laboratories set up on differing premises exploring alternative solutions to the same problem, such as finding a vaccine for a novel pathogen.[82] Within a single organization, different competing workgroups are often assigned the task of coming up with the best solution to one and the same problem.[83] So each group using just one of the many different mechanisms available might in principle work out well, at the overall group level.[84]

Still, that sort of balkanization can easily lead to ghettoization. Iris Young advocates giving people (particularly oppressed people) safe spaces in which they can enjoy 'differentiated solidarity'.[85] In principle that is all well and good, at least so long as is merely an option available for them to choose, rather than something that is imposed upon them.[86] In practice, however, 'differentiated solidarity' comes perilously close to 'separate but equal'—which as the US Supreme Court famously held is inherently in unequal when one of the separated groups is of a higher social status than the other.[87] Advantages and disadvantages flowing from people's differing positions in a status hierarchy (of the sort discussed in Section 3.1.1) are probably the hardest to address through this strategy.

11.4 Who Should Do What?

I promised at the outset of the book that enquiring into the mechanisms by which structural injustice is perpetuated, and how it might be overcome, would provide a more fine-grained analysis of who should do what in that

---

[82] Latour and Woolgar 1979; Kitcher 1990; Le et al. 2020.
[83] Franklin Roosevelt's administrative style was famously to put his advisors into competition with one another in just this way (Schlesinger 1958, p. 537; Dickinson 1996, p. 228).
[84] Competing interpretive schema might be thought of as 'alternative framings' of the situation. And as we know from studies of people looking at 'reversible images'—drawings that seen one way depict a rabbit and another way a duck, or an old woman and a young one—it is psychologically difficult for any given person to hold both framings in mind at the same time (Jastrow 1899; Toppino 2003; Long and Batterman 2012).
[85] Young 2000, ch. 6. See further Section 5.4 above.
[86] Schelling (1978, pp. 109–10) sketched a mathematical model of the advantages that could derive from splitting a population in these ways. Arguments for multiculturalism often echo this plea (Kymlicka 1995)—although of course if Kymlicka (1989; 1995, pp. 83–94) is right in thinking that culture provides a context for choice, then it is open to question to what extent culture can itself be a matter of choice.
[87] *Brown v. Board of Education*, 247 US 483 at p. 495 (1954), overturning *Plessey v. Ferguson*, 163 US 537 (1896). See further; Myrdal 1944; Trappenburg 2003.

regard. Having laid bare those mechanisms and the drivers underlying them, and canvassed various strategies for interrupting their workings, I am now in a position to address—if only still sketchily—that issue of 'responsibility for remedying structural injustice'.

The previous two sections have provided reasons for thinking that ameliorativist strategies are almost certainly to be preferred to head-on attacks on the mechanisms, some of which would most likely not work anyway and others of which would work only at an unacceptably high social cost. All those ameliorativist strategies (and all of the more dramatic ones as well, come to that) will ultimately require collective action of one sort or another to overcome structural injustice. That is just as the 'standard prescription' owing to Iris Marion Young and many following her has long claimed.[88] But the finer-grained analyses of mechanisms of structural injustice and how they might be overcome provided above now gives us a better grasp of *who* needs to undertake such collective action and *to what end*.

For example, if implementing the 'siphon off the and redistribute the benefits' strategy through the tax-transfer system, government officials responsible for raising and spending public revenue must ultimately be the ones responsible for implementing those policies. But getting those policies enacted in the first place requires political action—which in a representative democracy almost inevitably means the support of some of the main political parties. And getting political parties interested in the project almost inevitably requires persistent pressure from civil society, ideally organized in form (to ensure the pressure is persistent). Even though the organization itself may need to persist over time, its staff and supporters can come and go, just so long as there are enough of them 'on call' to weigh in at crucial moments as political exigencies require. And while political success might require that the cause enjoys diffuse support among at least a significant portion of the general public, that support need not be either universal or even particularly strong. All the same is true of ameliorative strategies for 'regulating the process'. In short, while the 'standard prescription' is correct in saying that 'collective action' will be required to overcome structural injustice in either of those ways, that collective action can in those cases be much more nimble and tightly targeted—and it can involve less intensive and less extensive cooperation across the community as a whole—than many of the standard hairshirt prescriptions often seem to imply.

---

[88] See Section 11.1.

The ameliorativist strategy of 'providing alternative mechanisms' might be different in that regard, depending on the details of the alternative mechanisms being envisaged. In building a 'women's employment network' or providing 'alternative interpretative schemes', some people will have to take the initiative and other people (potentially a great many others) will need to take part, typically in a much more modest way. But insofar as social diffusion rather than legislative enactment is envisaged as driving those alternative mechanisms, they require neither top-level 'political will' nor 'bureaucratic support' for their successful implementation. That effectively eliminates the need for certain sorts of collective action aimed at securing support in those quarters. Still, insofar as the alternative mechanisms in view rely instead on victims of structural injustice 'doing it for themselves', they require rather wider and deeper engagement across those communities than do the first two sorts of strategies.

11.5 Conclusion

In concluding, let me return to the larger issue of structural injustice that was the fundamental motivation for this book. The upshot of the discussion in this chapter, based on those that preceded it, is that we can now see why structural injustice is so very hard to overcome.

The mechanisms responsible for embedding and perpetuating some people's advantage over others all are, in one way or another, responses to external opportunities (created by scale effects of various sorts) and internal constraints (limited time and attention). To abandon those mechanisms would be to foreswear those opportunities for gains and put further strain on our scarce time and attention. Occasionally there may be scope for making the mechanisms in question work to the advantage of all (or anyway far more than they presently do). In any event, we should of course be prepared to sacrifice efficiency to justice, certainly at the margin and even some way beyond. But on the analysis offered in this book, we must resign ourselves to tinkering at the margins when trying to overcome many of the more important elements of structural injustice—which is not of course to say we should not do what we can in that regard.

That may seem like an unduly pessimistic conclusion. Pessimistic it certainly is—certainly more so than I had originally hoped, when first setting out to write this book. But upon reflection that conclusion, pessimistic though it is, seems singularly apt.

After all, we know it is *hard* to overcome structural injustice. What we need is to know why that is so. Looking closely at all the specific mechanisms by which advantage is perpetuated, and the fundamental drivers underlying them, helps us understand the sources of those difficulties. Any analysis purporting to show it is easy to overcome structural injustice would, sadly enough, simply not ring true to the phenomenon under investigation.[89]

---

[89] It bears emphasizing, for the benefit of those who might wrongly recall otherwise, that Iris Young, too, was similarly sanguine about the prospects of overcoming structural injustice. Here are her words: 'Changing structural processes that produce injustice must be a collective social project [yet s]uch collective action is difficult. It requires organization, the will to cooperate on the part of many diverse actors, significant knowledge of how the actions of individuals and the rules and purposes of institutions conspire to produce injustice, and the ability to foresee the likely consequences of proposed remedies. One or more of these conditions is often absent.... Usually the prospects for significant change [in social structures] are slim.... It would be nice if there were some means whereby well-organized agents interested in justice could institute changes in systems that once and for all would make justice happen. But it doesn't work that way' (Young 2011, pp. 153, 149–50). As noted in Section 11.1.2 above, Young nonetheless thinks that people should 'take a stand' against structural injustice even if doing so is likely to be futile, rather than because doing so holds out any great hopes of success. I concur with her in that judgement (Goodin and Barry 2021).

References

Aaronson, Daniel; Daniel Hartley; and Bhashkar Mazmuder. 2019. The effects of the 1930s HOLC 'redlining' maps. WP 2017-12, revised February 2019. Chicago: Federal Reserve Bank of Chicago. Available at <https://www.chicagofed.org/publications/working-papers/2017/wp2017-12>.

Abolafia, Mitchel Y. 1984. Structured anarchy: formal organization in the commodity futures markets. Pp. 129–50 in *The Social Dynamics of Financial Markets*, ed. Peter Adler and Patricia Adler. Greenwich, CT: JAI Press.

Acemoglu, Daron and James A. Robinson. 2008. Persistence of power, elites and institutions. *American Economic Review*, 98: 267–93.

Ackerman, Bruce. 1985. Beyond *Carolene Products*. *Harvard Law Review*, 98: 713–46.

Adams, Guy. 2007. Cameron's cronies: The Bullingdon Club's class of '87. *The Independent*, 13 Feb.; available at <https://www.independent.co.uk/news/uk/politics/camerons-cronies-the-bullingdon-clubs-class-of-87-436192.html>.

Adermon, Adrian; Mikael Lindahl; and Daniel Waldenström. 2018. Intergenerational wealth mobility and the role of inheritance: evidence from multiple generations. *Economic Journal*, 128: F482–F513.

Ager, Philipp; Leah Platt Boustan; and Katherine Eriksson. 2019. The intergenerational effect of a large wealth shock: white southerners after the Civil War. NBER Working Paper No. 25700, March 2019. Available at <https://www.nber.org/system/files/working_papers/w25700/revisions/w25700.rev0.pdf>.

Ager, Philipp; Leah Boustan; and Katherine Eriksson. 2021. The intergenerational effect of a large wealth shock: white southerners after the Civil War. *American Economic Review*, 111: 3767–94.

Akerlof, George. 1976. The economics of caste and of the rat race and other woeful tales. *Quarterly Journal of Economics*, 90: 599–617.

Alfani, Guido. 2022. Epidemics, inequality and poverty in preindustrial and early industrial times. *Journal of Economic Literature*, 60: 3–40.

Alinsky, Saul D. 1971. *Rules for Radicals*. New York: Random House.

Alkire, Sabina. 2006. Structural injustice and democratic practice. Pp. 47–61 in *Transforming Unjust Structures: The Capability Approach*, ed. Séverine Deneulin, Mathias Nebel, and Nicholas Sagovsky. Dordrecht: Kluwer.

Allen, David. 1983. New telecommunication services: network externalities and critical mass. *Telecommunication Policy*, 12: 257–71.

Allport, Gordon W. 1954/1979. *The Nature of Prejudice*. 25th anniversary edition. New York: Addison-Wesley; originally published 1954.

Almond, Douglas; Janet Currie; and Valentia Duque. 2018. Childhood circumstances and adult outcomes: Act II. *Journal of Economic Literature*, 56: 1360–446.

Alston, William P. 1989. *Epistemic Justification*. Ithaca, NY: Cornell University Press.

Altman, Dennis. 1996. Rupture or continuity? The internationalization of gay identities. *Social Text*, 48: 77–94.

Anderson, Cameron; John Angus D. Hildreth; and Laura Howland. 2015. Is the desire for status a fundamental human motive? A review of the empirical literature. *Psychological Bulletin*, 141: 574–601.

Anderson, Elizabeth. 2010. *The Imperative of Integration*. Princeton, NJ: Princeton University Press.

Anderson, Elizabeth. 2012. Epistemic justice as a virtue of social institutions. *Social Epistemology*, 26: 163–73.

Anderson, Elizabeth. 2014. A world turned upside down: hierarchies and a new history of egalitarianism. *Juncture*, 20: 258–61.

Anderson, Elizabeth. 2017. *Private Government: How Employers Rule Our Lives (and Why We Don't Talk about It)*. Princeton, NJ: Princeton University Press.

Anderson, Eric. 2006. Snow accumulation and ablation model – SNOW-17. Silver Spring, MD: Office of Hydrological Development, National Oceanic and Atmospheric Administration, National Weather Service. Available at <http://www.nws.noaa.gov/oh/hrl/nwsrfs/users_manual/part2/_pdf/22snow17.pdf>.

Angwin, Julia; Jeff Larson; Surya Mattu; and Luaren Kirchner. 2016. Machine bias. *ProPublica*, 23 May; available at <https://www.propublica.org/article/machine-bias-risk-assessments-in-criminal-sentencing>.

Applebome, Peter. 1986. The Hunts: a dynasty built on poker and oil. *New York Times*, 30 August; available at <https://www.nytimes.com/1986/08/30/business/the-hunts-a-dynasty-built-on-poker-and-oil.html>.

Aragon, Corwin and Alison M. Jaggar. 2018. Agency, complicity and the responsibility to resist structural injustice. *Journal of Social Philosophy*, 49: 439–60.

Archer, Margaret S. 1982. Morphogenesis versus structuration: on combining structure and action. *British Journal of Sociology*, 33: 455–83.

Arnold, David; Will Dobbie; and Crystal S. Yang. 2018. Racial bias in bail decisions. *Quarterly Journal of Economics*, 133: 1885–932.

Arnold, Matthew. 1882. An Eton boy. *Fortnightly Review*, 37 (June): 695–7.

Arrow, Kenneth J. 1962a. The economic implications of learning by doing. *Review of Economic Studies*, 29: 155–73.

Arrow, Kenneth J. 1962b. Economic welfare and the allocation of resources for invention. Pp. 609–26 in *The Rate and Direction of Inventive Activity: Economic and Social Factors*. Princeton, NJ: Princeton University Press for the National Bureau of Economic Research.

Arrow, Kenneth J. 1964. Control in large organizations. *Management Science*, 10: 397–408.

Arrow, Kenneth J. 1971. Some models of racial discrimination in the labor market. RAND Corporation research memorandum RM- 6253-RC. Santa Monica, CA: RAND Corporation. Available at <https://www.rand.org/content/dam/rand/pubs/research_memoranda/2009/RM6253.pdf>

Arrow, Kenneth J. 1974. *The Limits of Organization*. New York: Norton.

Arrow, Kenneth J. 2003. Is bounded rationality unboundedly rational? Some ruminations. Pp. 47–56 in *Models of a Man: Essays in Honor of Herbert A. Simon*, ed. Mie Augier and James G. March. Cambridge, MA: MIT Press.

Arrow, Kenneth J. and Ron Borzekowski. 2004. Limited network connections and the distribution of wages. Finance Economics Discussion Series 2004–41, Board Governors of the US Federal Reserve System. Available at <www.federalreserve.gov/pubs/feds/2004/200441/200441pap.pdf> or < https://ssrn.com/abstract=632321>.

Arthur, W. Brian. 1989. Competing technologies, increasing returns and lock-in by historical events. *Economic Journal*, 99: 116–31.

Artinger, Florian M.; Gerd Gigerenzer; and Perke Jacobs. 2022. Satisficing: integrating two traditions. *Journal of Economic Literature*, 60: 598–635.

Asch, Solomon E. 1951. Effects of group pressure upon the modification and distortion of judgements. Pp. 177–90 in *Groups, Leadership, and Men*, ed. Harold Guetzkow. Pittsburgh: Carnegie Press.

Asch, Solomon E. 1956. Studies of independence and conformity: a minority of one against a unanimous majority. *Psychological Monographs*, 70 (9) (# 416).

Ashforth, Blake E.; Glen E. Kreiner; Mark A. Clark; and Mel Fugate. 2007. Normalizing dirty work: managerial tactics for countering occupational taint. *Academy of Management Journal*, 50: 149–74.

Ásta. 2018. *Categories We Live By*. New York: Oxford University Press.

Ásta. 2019. Categorical injustice. *Journal of Social Philosophy*, 50: 392–406.

Astell, Mary and John Norris. 1695/2005. *Letters Concerning the Love of God*, ed. E. Derek Taylor and Melvyn New. Aldershot: Ashgate, 2005.

Atiyah, Patrick S. 1980. *Accidents, Compensation and the Law*. 3rd ed. London: Weidenfeld & Nicolson.

Atkinson, Anthony B.; Thomas Piketty; and Emmanuel Saez. 2011. Top incomes in the long run of history. *Journal of Economic Literature*, 49: 3–71.

Axelrod, Robert. 1981. Emergence of cooperation among egoists. *American Political Science Review*, 75: 306–18.

Axelrod, Robert. 1984. *The Evolution of Cooperation*. New York: Basic Books.

Azad, Bijan and Nelson King. 2012. Institutionalized computer workaround practices in a Mediterranean country: an examination of two organizations. *European Journal of Information Systems*, 21: 358–72.

Bachrach, Peter and Morton S. Baratz. 1963. Decisions and non-decisions: an analytic framework. *American Political Science Review*, 57: 632–42.

Baddeley, Alan. 2012. Working memory: theories, models and controversies. *Annual Review of Psychology*, 63: 1–29.

Bakhtin, Mikhail. 1984. *Rabelais and His World*, trans. Helene Iswolsky. Bloomington: Indiana University Press.

Bakker, Jan David; Stephan Maurer; Jörn-Steffen Pischke; and Ferdinand Rauch. 2021. Of mice and merchants: connectedness and the location of economic activity in the Iron Age. *Review of Economics and Statistics*, 103: 652–65.

Ballester, Coralio; Antoni Calvó-Armengol; and Yves Zenou. 2006. Who's who in networks. Wanted: the key player. *Econometrica*, 74: 1403–17.

Banaji, Mahzarin R. 2002. Stereotypes, social psychology of. Pp. 15100–4 in *International Encyclopedia of the Social and Behavioral Sciences*, ed. Neil Smelser and Paul Baltes. New York: Pergamon.

Banfield, Edward C. 1967. *The Moral Basis of a Backward Society*. New York: Free Press.

Barabási, Albert-László. 2002. *Linked*. Cambridge, MA: Perseus.

Barabási, Albert-László and Réka Albert. 1999. Emergence of scaling in random networks. *Science*, 286: 509–12.

Baran, Paul. 1964. *On Distributed Communications I: Introduction to Distributed Communications Networks*. RAND Memorandum RM-3420-PR. Santa Monica, CA: RAND Corporation. Available at <https://www.rand.org/pubs/research_memoranda/RM3420.html>.

Baran, Paul A. and Paul Sweezy. 1966. *Monopoly Capitalism*. New York: Monthly Review Press.

Barber, Felix and Michael Goold. 2007. The strategic secret of private equity. *Harvard Business Review*, 85 (9): 53–61.

Barjamovic, Gojko; Thomas Chaney; Kerem Cosar; and Ali Hortaçsu. 2019. Trade, merchants and the lost cities of the Bronze Age. *Quarterly Journal of Economics*, 134: 1455–503.

Barnes, Elizabeth. 2016. *The Minority Body*. Oxford: Oxford University Press.
Barry, Brian. 1965. *Political Argument*. London: Routledge & Kegan Paul.
Barry, Christian and Kate Macdonald. 2016. How should we conceive of individual consumer responsibility to address labour injustices? Pp. 92–118 in *Global Justice and International Labour Rights*, ed. Yossi Dahan, Hanna Lerner, and Faina Milman-Sivan. Cambridge: Cambridge University Press.
Barry, Christian and David Wiens. 2016. Benefiting from wrongdoing and sustaining wrongful harm. *Journal of Moral Philosophy*, 13: 530–52.
Barth, Frederik. 1967. Economic spheres in Darfur. Pp. 149–74 in *Themes in Economic Anthropology*, ed. Raymond Firth. London: Tavistock Publications.
Bask, Miia and Mikael Bask. 2015. Cumulative (dis)advantage and the Matthew Effect in life-course analysis. *PLoS ONE*, 10 (11): e0142447.
Basu, Kaushik. 2018. Markets and manipulation: time for a paradigm shift? *Journal of Economic Literature*, 56: 185–201.
Baugh, John. 2000. *Beyond Ebonics: Linguistic Pride and Racial Prejudice*. New York: Oxford University Press.
Baumol, William J.; John C. Panzar; and Robert D. Willig. 1982. *Constestable Markets and the Theory of Industry Structure*. New York: Harcourt Brace Jovanovich.
Beatty, Randolph P. and Jay R. Ritter. 1986. Investment banking, reputation and the underpricing of initial public offerings. *Journal of Financial Economics*, 15: 213–32.
Beauvoir, Simone de. 1955. *Privilèges*. Paris: Gallimard.
Beck, Valentin. 2019. Consumer boycotts as instruments for structural change. *Journal of Applied Philosophy*, 36: 543–59.
Beck, Valentin. 2022. Two forms of responsibility: reassessing Young on structural injustice. *Critical Review of International Social & Political Philosophy*, forthcoming; doi.rg/10.1080/13698230.2020.1786307.
Becker, Gary S. 1976. *The Economic Approach to Human Behavior*. Chicago: University of Chicago Press.
Becker, Gary S.; Scott Duke Kominers; Kevin M. Murphy; and Jörg L. Spenkuck. 2018. A theory of intergenerational mobility. *Journal of Political Economy*, 126: S7–S25.
Becker, Howard S. 1952. Social-class variations in the teacher–pupil relationship. *Journal of Educational Sociology*, 25: 451–65.
Becker, Howard S. 1974. Art as collective action. *American Sociological Review*, 39: 767–76.
Becker, Sascha O.; Yuan Hsiao; Steven Pfaff; and Jared Rubin. 2020. Multiplex network ties and the spatial diffusion of radical innovations: Martin Luther's leadership in the early Reformation. *American Sociological Review*, 85: 857–94.
Beckert, Jens. 2016. *Imagined Futures: Fictional Expectations and Capitalist Dynamics*. Cambridge, MA: Harvard University Press.
Beckert, Jens. 2022. Durable wealth: institutions, mechanisms and practices of wealth perpetuation. *Annual Review of Sociology*, 48: 233–55.
Beckert, Jens and Mark Lutter. 2009. The inequality of fair play: lottery gambling and social stratification in Germany. *European Sociological Review*, 25: 475–88.
Beeghly, Erin. 2015. What is a stereotype? What is stereotyping? *Hypatia*, 30: 675–91.
Beitz, Charles. 2018. Property and time. *Journal of Political Philosophy*, 26: 419–40.
Bell, Daniel. 1976. *The Cultural Contradictions of Capitalism*. New York: Basic Books.
Bénabou, Roland and Jean Tirole. 2002. Self-confidence and personal motivation. *Quarterly Journal of Economics*, 117: 871–915.
Bendix, Reinhard and Seymour Martin Lipset, eds. 1953. *Class, Status and Power: A Reader in Social Stratification*. Glencoe, IL: Free Press.

Benjamin, Beth A. and Joel M. Podolny. 1999. Status, quality and social order in the California wine industry. *Administrative Sciences Quarterly*, 44: 563–89.
Benkler, Yochai. 2006. *The Wealth of Networks: How Social Production Transforms Markets and Freedom*. New Haven, CT: Yale University Press.
Ben-Porath, Yoram. 1980. The F-connection: families, friends and firms in the organization of exchange. *Population and Development Review*, 6: 1–30.
Bent, Jason R. 2020. Is algorithmic affirmative action legal? *Georgetown Law Review*, 108: 803–53.
Bentham, Jeremy. 1838. Principles of the civil code. Vol. 1, pp. 297–364 in *Works*, ed. John Bowring. Edinburgh: William Tait. Available at <https://oll.libertyfund.org/titles/bentham-the-works-of-jeremy-bentham-vol-1>
Berger, Joseph; Bernard P. Cohen; and Morris Zeldich, Jr. 1972. Status characteristics and social interaction. *American Sociological Review*, 37: 241–55.
Bergmann, Barbara R. and David E. Kaun. 1967. *Structural Unemployment in the United States*. Volume 46, Economic Development Administration, US Department of Commerce. Washington, DC: Government Printing Office and Brookings Institution.
Berman, Harold J. 1983. *Law and Revolution: The Formation of the Western Legal Tradition*. Cambridge, MA: Harvard University Press.
Bernheim, B. Douglas. 1994. A theory of conformity. *Journal of Political Economy*, 102: 841–77.
Bernstein, Basil. 1959. A public language: some sociological implications of a linguistic form. *British Journal of Sociology*, 10: 311–26.
Bernstein, Basil. 1960. Language and social class. *British Journal of Sociology*, 11: 271–76.
Bernstein, Basil. 1971. *Class, Codes and Control*. London: Routledge & Kegan Paul.
Bernstein, Basil. 1981. Codes, modalities and the process of cultural reproduction: a model. *Language in Society*, 10: 327–63.
Bernstein, Lisa. 1992. Opting out of the legal system: extralegal contractual relations in the diamond industry. *Journal of Legal Studies*, 21: 115–57.
Berry, Jeffrey M. and Clyde Wilcox. 2018. *The Interest Group Society*, 6th edn. New York: Routledge.
Besen, Stanley M. and Joseph Farrell. 1994. Choosing how to compete: strategies and tactics in standardization. *Journal of Economic Perspectives*, 8: 117–31.
Besley, Timothy; Anders Jensen; and Torsten Persson. 2022. Norms, enforcement and tax evasion. *Review of Economics & Statistics*, forthcoming. doi.org/10.1162/rest_a_01123.
Bicchieri, Christina. 1990. Norms of cooperation. *Ethics*, 100: 838–61.
Bicchieri, Christina. 2006. *The Grammar of Society: The Nature and Dynamics of Social Norms*. New York: Cambridge University Press.
Biddle, B. J. 1986. Recent developments in role theory. *Annual Review of Sociology*, 12: 67–92.
Biggs, Michael. 2009. Self-fulfilling prophecies. Pp. 294–314 in *Oxford Handbook of Analytical Sociology*, ed. Peter Hedström and Peter Bearman. Oxford: Oxford University Press.
Bikhchandani, Suhil; David Hirshleifer; and Ivo Welch. 1992. A theory of fads, fashion, custom and cultural change as informational cascades. *Journal of Political Economy*, 100: 992–1026.
Bikhchandani, Sushil; David Hirshleifer; and Ivo Welch. 1998. Learning from the behavior of others: conformity, fads and informational cascades. *Journal of Economic Perspectives*, 12: 151–70.

Blackburn, Simon. 1998. Trust, cooperation and human psychology. Pp. 28–45 in *Trust and Governance*, ed. Valerie Braithwaite and Margaret Levi. New York: Russell Sage Foundation.

Blackman, Colin and Lara Srivastava, eds. 2011. *Telecommunications Regulation Handbook: Tenth Anniversary Edition*. Washington, DC: International Bank for Reconstruction and Development/World Bank, InfoDev and International Telecommunication Union.

Blackstone, William. 1765. *Commentaries on the Laws of England*. Oxford: Clarendon Press.

Blalock, Hubert M. Jr. 1991. *Understanding Social Inequality: Modeling Allocation Processes*. Newbury Park, CA: SAGE.

Blanes I Vidal, Jordi; Mirko Draca; and Christian Fons-Rosen. 2012. Revolving door lobbyists. *American Economic Review*, 102: 3731–48.

Blank, Rebecca M. 2005. Tracing the economic impact of cumulative discrimination. *American Economic Review (Papers & Proceedings)*, 95 (#2): 99–103.

Blank, Rebecca M.; Marilyn Dabady; and Constance F. Citro. 2004. *Measuring Racial Discrimination*. Washington, D.C.: National Research Council, National Academy of Sciences Press.

Blau, Peter M. 1960. Structural effects. *American Sociological Review*, 25: 178–93.

Blau, Peter and Otis Dudley Duncan. 1967. *The American Occupational Structure*. New York: Wiley.

Blau, Peter M. and W. Richard Scott. 1963. *Formal Organizations: A Comparative Approach*. London: Routledge & Kegan Paul.

Blaydes, Lisa and Christopher Paik. 2021. Trade and political fragmentation on the Silk Roads: the economic effects of historical exchange between China and the Muslim East. *American Journal of Political Science*, 65: 115–32.

Blewett, Neal. 1965. The franchise in the United Kingdom 1885-1918. *Past & Present*, 32: 27–56.

Blum, Lawrence. 2004. Stereotypes and stereotyping: a moral analysis. *Philosophical Papers*, 33: 251–89.

Blum, Lawrence. 2012. Moral asymmetry: a problem for the protected categories approach. *Lewis & Clark Law Review*, 16: 647–55.

Boissevain, Jeremy. 1968. The place of non-groups in the social sciences. *Man*, n.s., 3: 542–56.

Boissevain, Jeremy. 1974. *Friends of Friends: Networks, Manipulators and Coalitions*. Oxford: Blackwell.

Bolinger, Reneé Jorgensen. 2020. The rational impermissibility of accepting (some) racial generalizations. *Synthese*, 197: 2415–31.

Bonacich, Phillip. 1987. Power and centrality: a family of measures. *American Journal of Sociology*, 92: 1170–82.

Booth, Alison L. 2009. Gender and competition. *Labour Economics*, 16: 599–606.

Bordalo, Pedro; Nicola Gennaioli; and Andrei Shleifer. 2020. Memory, attention and choice. *Quarterly Journal of Economics*, 135: 1399–442.

Borgatti, Stephen P. 2005. Centrality and network flow. *Social Networks*, 27: 55–71.

Bortnick, S. M. and M. H. Ports. 1992. Job search methods and results: tracking the unemployed, 1991. *Monthly Labor Review*, 115 (#12): 29–35.

Bothner, Matthew S.; Richard Haynes; Wonjae Lee; and Edward Bishop Smith. 2010. When do Matthew Effects occur? *Journal of Mathematical Sociology*, 34: 80–114.

Bourdieu, Pierre. 1977a. The economics of linguistic exchanges. *Social Science Information*, 16: 645–68.

Bourdieu, Pierre. 1977b. *Outline of a Theory of Practice*. Cambridge: Cambridge University Press.
Bourdieu, Pierre. 1985. The social space and the genesis of groups. *Theory & Society*, 17: 723–44.
Bourdieu, Pierre. 1986. The forms of capital (trans. Richard Nice). Pp. 241–58 in *Handbook of Theory and Research for the Sociology of Education*, ed. John G. Richardson. New York: Greenwood Press.
Bourdieu, Pierre. 1991. *Language and Symbolic Power*, trans Gino Raymond and Matthew Adamson. Cambridge, MA: Harvard University Press.
Bowles, Samuel and Herbert Gintis. 1998. The moral economy of communities: structured populations and the evolution of pro-social norms. *Evolution and Human Behavior*, 19: 3.25.
Braddock, Jomills Henry II and James M. McPartland. 1987. How minorities continue to be excluded from equal employment opportunities: research on labor market and institutional barriers. *Journal of Social Issues*, 43: 5–39.
Bradley, F. H. 1876. My station and its duties. Pp. 98–147 in *Ethical Studies*, ed. Ralph G. Ross. Indianapolis, IN: Bobbs-Merrill, 1951.
Brandeis, Louis. 1914. *Other People's Money*. New York: Frederick A. Stokes.
Bratman, Michael. 1993. Shared intention. *Ethics*, 104: 97–113.
Bratman, Michael. 2007. *Structures of Agency*. Oxford: Oxford University Press.
Bratman, Michael. 2014. *Shared Agency: A Planning Theory of Acting Together*. Oxford: Oxford University Press.
Breed, Warren and Thomas Ktsanes. 1961. Pluralistic ignorance in the process of public opinion formation. *Public Opinion Quarterly*, 25: 382–92.
Brennan, Geoffrey; Lina Eriksson; Robert E. Goodin; and Nicholas Southwood. 2013. *Explaining Norms*. Oxford: Oxford University Press.
Brennan, Geoffrey and Alan Hamlin. 2004. Analytic conservatism. *British Journal of Political Science*, 34: 675–91.
Brennan, Geoffrey and Philip Pettit. 2004. *The Economy of Esteem*. Oxford: Oxford University Press.
Brennan, William. 2018. The code-switcher. *Atlantic Monthly*, 321 (#3: April): 18–20.
Brezis, Elise S. and Joël Cariolle. 2019. The revolving door, state connections and inequality of influence in the financial sector. *Journal of Institutional Economics*, 15: 595–614.
Brighouse, Harry and Adam Swift. 2006. Equality, priority and positional goods. *Ethics*, 116: 471–97.
Broome, John. 1990. Fairness. *Proceedings of the Aristotelian Society*, 91: 87–101.
Brown, Michael K. and David Wellman. 2005. Embedding the color line: the accumulation of racial advantage and disaccumulation of opportunity in post-civil rights America. *Du Bois Review*, 2: 187–207.
Brown, Vivienne. 2020. An intersubjective model of agency for game theory. *Economics & Philosophy*, 36: 334–54.
Brubaker, Rogers. 2015. Linguistic and religious pluralism: between difference and inequality. *Journal of Ethnic and Migration Studies*, 41: 3–32.
Buchanan, James M. 1965. An economic theory of clubs. *Economica*, 32: 1–14.
Buchanan, James M. 2004. The status of the *status quo*. *Constitutional Political Economy*, 15: 133–44.
Bunyan, John. 1678/1966. *Grace Abounding and The Pilgrim's Progress*, ed. Roger Sharrock. London: Oxford University Press, 1966.

Burger, Warren. 1971. Opinion of the US Supreme Court. *Griggs v. Duke Power Co.*, 401 US 424.
Burgess, Alexis; Herman Cappelen; and David Plunkett, eds. 2020. *Conceptual Engineering and Conceptual Ethics*. Oxford: Oxford University Press.
Burt, Ronald S. 1980. Models of network structure. *Annual Review of Sociology*, 6: 79–141.
Burt, Ronald S. 1982. *Toward a Structural Theory of Action*. New York: Academic Press.
Burt, Ronald S. 1992. *Structural Holes: The Social Structure of Competition*. Cambridge, MA: Harvard University Press.
Burt, Ronald S. 2000. The network structure of social capital. *Research in Organizational Behaviour*, 22: 345–423.
Burt, Ronald S; Martin Kilduff; and Stefano Tasselli. 2013. Social network analysis: foundations and frontiers on advantage. *Annual Review of Psychology*, 64: 527–47.
Bütikofer, Aline; Katrine V. Løken; and Alexander Willén. 2022. Building bridges and widening gaps. *Review of Economics & Statistics*, forthcoming. doi.org/10.1162/rest_a_01183.
Cai, Jing and Adam Szeidl. 2018. Interfirm relationships and business performance. *Quarterly Journal of Economics*, 133: 1229–82.
Cameron, David R. 1974. Toward a theory of political mobilization. *Journal of Politics*, 36: 138–71.
Cameron, Deborah, ed. 1998. *The Feminist Critique of Language*. 2nd edn. London: Routledge.
Caplin, Andrew; Dániel Csaba; John Leahy; and Oded Nov. 2020. Rational inattention, competitive supply and psychometrics. *Quarterly Journal of Economics*, 135: 1681–724.
Caplin, Andrew; Mark Dean; and John Leahy. 2018. Rational inattention, optimal consideration sets and stochastic choice. *Review of Economic Studies*, 86: 1061–94.
Carlana, Michela. 2019. Implicit stereotypes: evidence from teachers' gender bias. *Quarterly Journal of Economics*, 134: 1163–224.
Carmichael, Stokely [Kwame Ture] and Charles V. Hamilton. 1967. *Black Power: The Politics of Liberation in America*. New York: Random House.
Caro, Robert A. 1974. *The Power Broker: Robert Moses and the Fall of New York*. New York: Random House.
Castells, Manuel. 2000. Materials for an exploratory theory of the network society. *British Journal of Sociology*, 51: 5–24.
Castro, Clinton and Adam K. Pham. 2020. Is the attention economy noxious? *Philosophers' Imprint*, 20 (#17): 1–13.
Chambers, Clare. 2009. Each outcome is another opportunity: problems with the Moment of Equal Opportunity. *Politics, Philosophy & Economics*, 8: 374–400.
Chandler, Alfred D. Jr. 1977. *The Visible Hand: The Managerial Revolution in American Business*. Cambridge, MA: Harvard University Press.
Chandler, Anupam. 2017. The racist algorithm? *Michigan Law Review*, 115: 1023–45.
Chen, Maggie X. and Min Wu. 2021. The value of reputation in trade: evidence from Alibaba. *Review of Economics & Statistics*, 103: 857–73.
Chetty, Raj and Nathaniel Hendren. 2018. The impacts of neighborhoods on intergenerational mobility I: childhood exposure effects. *Quarterly Journal of Economics*, 133: 1107–62.
Chicago Mercantile Exchange (CME). 2019a. The art of hand signals. Pp. 100–7 in CME, *An Introduction to Futures and Options*. Available at <https://www.cmegroup.com/files/intro_fut_opt.pdf >.

Chicago Mercantile Exchange (CME). 2019b. *CME Rulebook.* Available at <https://www.cmegroup.com/rulebook/CME/>.
Chilton, Adam S. and Mila Versteeg. 2016. Do constitutional rights make a difference? *American Journal of Political Science*, 60: 575–89.
Cho, Junghoo and Sourashis Roy. 2004. Impact of search engines on page popularity. *WWW '04: Proceedings of the 13th International Conference on World Wide Web*, pp. 20–9; available at <https://oak.cs.ucla.edu/~cho/papers/cho-bias.pdf>.
Cho, Sumi; Kimberlé Williams Crenshaw; and Leslie McCall. 2013. Toward a field of intersectionality studies: theory, applications and praxis. *Signs*, 38: 785–810.
Chokkattu, Julian. 2019. Google Assistant can now translate speech through your phone. *Wired*, 13 Dec.; available at < https://www.wired.com/story/google-assistant-can-now-translate-on-your-phone/>.
Chouldechova, Alexandra. 2017. Fair prediction with disparate impact: a study of bias in recidivism prediction instruments. *Big Data*, 5 (2): 153–63.
Chun, Jennifer Jihye; George Lipsitz; and Young Shin. 2013. Intersectionality as a social movement strategy: Asian immigrant women advocates. *Signs*, 38: 917–40.
Chun, Marvin M.; Julie D. Golomb; and Nicholas B. Turk-Browne. 2011. A taxonomy of external and internal attention. *Annual Review of Psychology*, 62: 73–101.
Church of England. 1762. A catechism. Pp. 368–73 in *The Book of Common Prayer.* Cambridge: John Baskerville; originally published 1662. Available at <https://archive.org/details/bookcommonpraye00chur/page/n369/mode/2up >.
Churchland, Paul M. 1995. *The Engine of Reasoning, the Seat of the Soul: A Philosophical Journey into the Brain.* Cambridge, MA: MIT Press.
Ciepley, David. 2013. Beyond public and private: toward a political theory of the corporation. *American Political Science Review*, 107: 139–58.
Coase, R. H. 1937. The nature of the firm. *Economica*, 4: 386–405.
Codere, Helen. 1968. Money-exchange systems and a theory of money. *Man*, 3: 557–77.
Cohen, G. A. 1981. Freedom, justice and capitalism. *New Left Review*, 126: 3–16.
Cohen, G. A. 2013. Rescuing conservatism: a defense of existing value. Pp. 143–74 in *Finding Oneself in the Other*, ed. Michael Otsuka. Princeton, NJ: Princeton University Press.
Cohen, Stanley. 1980. *Folk Devils and Moral Panics.* Oxford: Martin Robertson.
Coleman, D. C. 1973. Gentlemen and players. *Economic History Review*, 26: 92–116.
Coleman, James S. 1984. Introducing social structure into economic analysis. *American Economic Review (Papers & Proceedings)*, 74 (2): 84–88.
Coleman, James S. 1988. Social capital in the creation of human capital. *American Journal of Sociology*, 94 (Supplement): S95–S120.
Coleman, James S. 1990. *Foundations of Social Theory.* Cambridge, MA: Harvard University Press.
Coleman, James S.; Elihu Katz; and Herbert Menzel. 1957. The diffusion of an innovation among physicians. *Sociometry*, 20: 253–70.
Collar, Anna. 2013. *Religious Networks in the Roman Empire: The Spread of New Ideas.* Cambridge: Cambridge University Press.
Collins, Randall. 1979. *The Credential Society: An Historical Sociology of Education and Stratification.* New York: Academic Press.
Collins, Stephanie. 2019. *Group Duties.* Oxford: Oxford University Press.
Cook, Karen. 1975. Expectations, evaluations and equity. *American Sociological Review*, 40: 372–88.

Cordes, Joseph J. and Robert S. Goldfarb. 1983. Alternative rationales for severance pay compensation under airline deregulation. *Public Choice*, 41: 351–69.

Cornford, James. 1972. The political theory of scarcity. Pp. 27–44 in *Philosophy, Politics & Society*, 4th series, ed. Peter Laslett, W.G. Runciman, and Quentin Skinner. Oxford: Blackwell.

Correll, Shelley J. and Stephen Benard. 2006. Biased estimators? Comparing status and statistical theories of gender discrimination. *Advances in Group Processes*, 23: 89–116.

Correll, Shelley J. and Cecila L. Ridgeway. 2003. Expectation states theory. Pp. 29–51 in *The Handbook of Social Psychology*, ed. John Delamater. New York: Kluwer.

Correll, Shelley J.; Cecilia L. Ridgeway; Ezra W. Zuckerman; Sharon Jank; Sara Jordan-Bloch; and Sandra Nakagawa. 2017. It's the conventional thought that counts: how third-order inference produces status advantage. *American Sociological Review*, 82: 297–327.

Crawford, Matthew B. 2015. *The World Beyond Your Head: On Becoming an Individual in an Age of Distraction*. Farrar, New York: Straus and Giroux.

Crenshaw, Kimberlé W. 1991. Mapping the margins: intersectionality, identity politics and violence against women of color. *Stanford Law Review*, 43: 1241–99.

Crenson, Matthew A. 1971. *The Un-politics of Air Pollution: A Study of Non-decisionmaking in the Cities*. Baltimore, MD: Johns Hopkins University Press.

Cressman, Ross and Yi Tao. 2014. The replicator equation and other game dynamics. *Proceedings of the National Academy of Sciences*, 111 (supp.3): 10810–17.

Cyert, Richard M. and James G. March. 1963. *A Behavioral Theory of the Firm*. Englewood Cliffs, NJ: Prentice-Hall.

D'Esposito, Mark and Bradley R. Postle. 2015. The cognitive neuroscience of working memory. *Annual Review of Psychology*, 66: 115–42.

Dahl, Robert A. 1972. *Polyarchy: Participation and Opposition*. New Haven, CT: Yale University Press.

Dahl, Robert A. and Charles E. Lindblom. 1953. *Politics, Economics and Welfare*. New York: Harper & Row.

Dahrendorf, Ralf. 1958/1968. Homo sociologicus. Pp. 19–87 in Dahrendorf, *Essays in Social Theory*. Stanford, CA: Stanford University Press; originally published 1958.

Dahrendorf, Ralf. 1968. *Essays in the Theory of Society*. Stanford, CA: Stanford University Press.

Dalton, Melville. 1959. *Men Who Manage*. New York: Wiley.

Dannefer, Dale. 2003. Cumulative advantage/disadvantage and the life course: cross-fertilizing age and social science theory. *Journal of Gerontology: Social Forces*, 58B: S327–37.

Darilek Richard E. 1992. The theory of confidence-building measures. Pp. 3–35 in *The De-escalation of Nuclear Crises*, ed. Joseph E. Nation. London: Macmillan.

Darity, William A. Jr. 2022. Position and possessions: stratification economics and intergroup inequality. *Journal of Economic Literature*, 60: 400–26.

Dasgupta, Partha. 1988. Trust as a commodity. Pp. 49–72 in *Trust: Making and Breaking Cooperative Relations*, ed. Diego Gambetta. Oxford: Blackwell.

Dasgupta, Partha. 1993. *An Inquiry into Well-being and Destitution*. Oxford: Clarendon Press.

Dasgupta, Partha and Debraj Ray. 1986/7. Inequality as a determinant of malnutrition and unemployment. *Economic Journal*, 96: 1011–34 and 97: 177–88.

Davenport, Lauren. 2020. The fluidity of racial classifications. *Annual Review of Political Science*, 23: 221–40.

Davenport, Thomas H. and John C. Beck. 2001. *The Attention Economy: Understanding the New Currency of Business.* Boston: Harvard Business Review Press.

David, Paul. 1985. Clio and the economics of QWERTY. *American Economic Review (Papers and Proceedings),* 75 (#2): 332–7.

Davidson, Donald. 1973-4. On the very idea of a conceptual scheme. *Proceedings and Addresses of the American Philosophical Association,* 47: 5–20.

Davidson, Donald. 1980. *Essays on Actions and Events.* Oxford: Clarendon Press.

Davis, Emmalon. 2016. Typecasts, tokens and spokespersons: a case for credibility excess as testimonial injustice. *Hypatia,* 31: 485–501.

Dawe, Alan. 1970. The two sociologies. *British Journal of Sociology,* 21: 207–18.

De Groot, Adriaan D. 1966. Perception and memory versus thought: some old ideas and recent findings. Pp. 19–50 in *Problem Solving: Research, Method, and Theory,* ed. B. Kleinmuntz. New York: Wiley.

De Long, J. Bradford. 1991. Did J.P. Morgan's men add value? An economist's perspective on financial capitalism. Pp. 201–36 in *Inside the Business Enterprise: Historical Perspectives on the Use of Information,* ed. P. Temlin. Chicago: University of Chicago Press. Available at <http://www.nber.org/papers/w3426.pdf>.

De Swaan, Abram. 2001. *Words of the World: The Global Language System.* Cambridge: Polity. <https://books.google.com.au/books?id=xjaXi6VGwfUC&printsec=frontcover&dq=de+swaan+words+of+the+world&hl=en&sa=X&ved=0ahUKEwilpMe8wtrgAhUFFHIKHSIqCA8Q6AEIKjAA#v=onepage&q=de%20swaan%20words%20of%20the%20world&f=false>

de Viti de Marco, Antonio. 1890. L'industria dei telefoni e l'esercizio di Stato. *Giornale degli economisti, serie seconda,* 1: 279–306.

Deats, Richard. 2005. *Mahatma Gandhi, Nonviolent Liberator: A Biography.* Hyde Park, NY: New City Press.

DellaVigna, Stefano. 2009. Psychology and economics: evidence from the field. *Journal of Economic Literature,* 47: 315–72.

Denning, Jeffrey T.; Richard Murphy; and Felix Weinhardt. 2022. Class rank and long-run outcomes. *Review of Economics and Statistics,* forthcoming; doi.org/10.1162/rest_a_01125.

Derber, Charles. 1978. Unemployment and the entitled worker: job-entitlement and radical political attitudes among the youthful unemployed. *Social Problems,* 26: 26–37.

Dermish, Ahmed; Christoph Kneiding; Paul Leishman; and Ignacio Mas. 2012. Branchless and mobile banking solutions for the poor: a survey of the literature. *innovations,* 6: 81–98.

Dickinson, Matthew J. 1996. *Bitter Harvest: FDR, Presidential Power and the Growth of the Presidential Branch.* Cambridge: Cambridge University Press.

Dieleman, Susan. 2015. Epistemic justice and deliberative democracy. *Hypatia,* 30: 794–810.

Dietsch, Peter. 2021. Money creation, debt and justice. *Politics, Philosophy & Economics,* 20: 151–79.

Dijksterhuis, Ap and Henk Aarts. 2010. Goals, attention and (un)consciousness. *Annual Review of Psychology,* 61: 467–90.

DiMaggio, Paul. 1997. Culture and cognition. *Annual Review of Sociology,* 23: 263–87.

DiMaggio, Paul and Filiz Garip. 2012. Network effects on social inequality. *Annual Review of Sociology,* 38: 93–118.

DiPrete, Thomas A. and Gregory M. Eirich. 2006. Cumulative advantage as a mechanism of inequality: a review of theoretical and empirical developments. *Annual Review of Sociology*, 32: 271–97.
Domina, Thurston; Andrew Penner; and Emily Penner. 2017. Categorical inequality: schools as sorting machines. *Annual Review of Sociology*, 43: 311–30.
Dotson, Kristie. 2014. Conceptualizing epistemic oppression. *Social Epistemology*, 28: 115–38.
Dougherty, Tom. 2020. Disability as solidarity: political not (only) metaphysical. *Philosophy & Phenomenological Research*, 100: 219–24.
Douglas, Mary. 1975. Self-evidence. Pp. 276–318 in *Implicit Meanings*. London: Routledge & Kegan Paul.
Doyle, Charles. 2017. Statute of limitations in federal criminal cases: an overview. Congressional Research Service Report RL31253. Available at <https://fas.org/sgp/crs/misc/RL31253.pdf>.
Drèze, Jean and Amartya Sen. 1989. *Hunger and Public Action*. Oxford: Clarendon Press.
Du Bois, William E. B. 1935. *Black Reconstruction: An Essay Toward a History of the Part which Black Folk Played in the Attempt to Reconstruct Democracy in America, 1860-1880*. New York: Harcourt, Brace.
Dumont, Louis. 1980. *Homo Hierarchicus: The Caste System & Its Implications*, trans. M. Sainsbury, L. Dumont, and B. Gulati. Chicago: University of Chicago Press.
Duxbury, Scott W. and Dana L. Haynie. 2021. Shedding a light on the shadows: endogenous trade structure and the growth of an online illegal market. *American Journal of Sociology*, 127: 787–827.
Dwork, Cynthia; Moritz Hardt; Toniann Pitassi; Omer Reingold; and Richard Zemel. 2012. Fairness through awareness. *ITCS '12: Proceedings of the 3rd Innovations in Theoretical Computer Science Conference*, pp. 214–26. Available at <https://arxiv.org/pdf/1104.3913.pdf>.
Dwyer, Rachel E. 2018. Credit, debt and inequality. *Annual Review of Sociology*, 44: 237–61.
Edgeworth, Francis Y. 1925. The pure theory of taxation. Vol. 2, pp. 100–16 in Edgeworth, *Papers Relating to Political Economy*. London: Macmillan.
Edsall, Thomas B. 2011. The trouble with that revolving door. *New York Times*, 18 Dec.; available at <https://campaignstops.blogs.nytimes.com/2011/12/18/the-trouble-with-that-revolving-door/>.
Eichengreen, Barry. 2011. *Exorbitant Privilege: The Rise and the Fall of the Dollar and the Future of the International Monetary System*. Oxford: Oxford University Press.
Ellickson, Robert C. 1991. *Order Without Law: How Neighbors Settle Disputes*. Cambridge, MA: Harvard University Press.
Elliott, James R. 2001. Referral hiring and ethnically homogeneous jobs. *Social Science Research*, 30: 401–25.
Elliott, Jay R. 2011. Stag hunts and committee work: cooperation and the mutualistic paradigm. *Review of Philosophy and Psychology*, 2: 245–60.
Elster, Jon. 1983. *Explaining Technical Change*. Cambridge: Cambridge University Press.
Elster, Jon. 1989. *Nuts and Bolts for the Social Sciences*. Cambridge: Cambridge University Press.
Elster, Jon. 2007. *Explaining Social Behavior: More Nuts and Bolts for the Social Sciences*. Cambridge: Cambridge University Press.
Elster, Jon. 2009. Norms. Pp. 195–217 in *Oxford Handbook of Analytical Sociology*, ed. Peter Hedström and Peter Bearman. Oxford: Oxford University Press.
Emerson, Ralph Waldo. 1882. *Works*. Boston: Houghton, Mifflin.

Emerson, Richard M. 1962. Power-dependence relations. *American Sociological Review*, 27: 31–41.
Epstein, Richard A. 1985. *Takings: Private Property and the Power of Eminent Domain.* Cambridge, MA: Harvard University Press.
Ericsson, Karl A.; Ralf T. Krampe; and Clemens Tesch-Römer. 1993. The role of deliberate practice in the acquisition of expert performance. *Psychological Review*, 100: 363–406.
Ehrlich, Susan and Ruth King. 1992. Gender-based language reform and the social construction of meaning. *Discourse & Society*, 3: 151–66.
Ehrlich, Susan and Ruth King. 1994. Feminist meanings and the (de)politicization of the lexicon. *Language in Society*, 23: 59–76.
Ermakoff, Ivan. 1997. Prelates and princes: aristocratic marriages, canon law prohibitions and shifts in norms and patterns of domination in the Central Middle Ages. *American Sociological Review*, 62: 405–22.
Esping-Andersen, Gøsta. 1985. *Politics Against Markets.* Princeton, NJ: Princeton University Press.
Estlund, David. 2008. *Democratic Authority.* Princeton, NJ: Princeton University Press.
Estlund, David. 2020. What's unjust about structural injustice? Paper presented to NYU Law School Colloquium in Legal, Political and Social Philosophy, 3 December 2020. Available at: <https://www.law.nyu.edu/sites/default/files/ESTLUND-DRAFT-Structural%20Injustice-NYU%20version%20Nov%202020_0.pdf>.
Eva, Benjamin. 2022. Algorithmic fairness and base rate tracking. *Philosophy & Public Affairs*, 50: 239–66.
Eyal, Nir. 2017. *Hooked: How to Build Habit-forming Products.* New York: Penguin.
Eyal, Nir. 2019. *Indistractable: How to Control Your Attention and Choose Your Life.* London: Bloomsbury.
Falkinger, Josef. 2007. Attention economies. *Journal of Economic Theory*, 133: 266–94.
Falkinger, Josef. 2008. Limited attention as the scarce resource in an information-rich economy. *Economic Journal*, 118: 1596–620.
Farzan, Antonia. 2020. Ohio wanted to strip benefits from people who didn't report to work during the pandemic. Hackers got in the way. *Washington Post*, 14 May; available at <https://www.washingtonpost.com/nation/2020/05/14/coronavirus-update-us/#link-2S7Q3X7DBVFP3CSYGXBFW4OQF4>.
Feast, Josh. 2019. 4 ways to address gender bias in AI. *Harvard Business Review*, 20 November; available at < https://hbr.org/2019/11/4-ways-to-address-gender-bias-in-ai>.
Feld, Scott L. 1991. Why your friends have more friends than you do. *American Journal of Sociology*, 96: 1464–77.
Feldman, Martha S. 2000. Organizational routines as a source of continuous change. *Organization Science*, 11: 611–29.
Feldstein, Martin. 1976. Compensating in tax reform. *National Tax Journal*, 29: 123–30.
Ferguson, Charles. 1959. Diglossia. *Word*, 15: 325–40.
Ferrero, Guillaume. 1894. L'inertie mentale et la loi du moindre effort. *Revue Philosophique de la France et de l'Étranger*, 37: 169–82.
Festré, Agnes and Pierre Garrouste. 2015. The 'economics of attention': a history of economic thought perspective. *OEconomia*, 5 (#1): 3–36.
Fine, Gary Alan. 1979. Small groups and culture creation: the idioculture of Little League baseball teams. *American Sociological Review*, 44: 733–45.
Fischhoff, Baruch; Paul Slovic; and Sarah Lichtenstein. 1978. Fault trees: sensitivity of estimated failure probabilities to problem representation. *Journal of Experimental Psychology: Human Perception and Performance*, 4: 330–44.

Fisher, Franklin M. and Albert Ando. 1962. Two theorems on *ceteris paribus* in the analysis of dynamic systems. *American Political Science Review*, 56: 108–13.

Fishkin, Joseph. 2014. *Bottlenecks: A New Theory of Equal Opportunity*. New York: Oxford University Press.

Fiske, Susan T. 1998. Stereotyping, prejudice and discrimination. Pp. 357–411 in *Handbook of Social Psychology*, ed. D. T. Gilbert, S. T. Fiske, and G. Lindzey. New York: McCraw-Hill.

Flåm, Sjur Didrik and Alf Erling Risa. 2003. Ability, self-confidence and search. *Journal of Institutional and Theoretical Economics*, 159: 439–56.

Fleurbaey, Marc and Vito Peragine. 2013. Ex ante versus ex post equality of opportunity. *Economica*, 80: 118–30.

Flückiger, Matthias; Erik Hornung; Mario Larch; Markus Ludwig; and Allard Mees. 2022. Roman transport network connectivity and economic integration. *Review of Economic Studies*, 89: 774–810.

Fogel, Robert W. 1994. Economic growth, population theory and physiology: the bearing of long-term processes on the making of economic policy. *American Economic Review*, 84: 369–95.

Fombrun, Charles. 1996. *Reputation: Realizing Value from the Corporate Image*. Boston: Harvard Business School Press.

Fombrun, Charles and Mark Shanley. 1990. What's in a name? Reputation building and corporate strategy. *Academy of Management Journal*, 33: 233–58

Ford, Thomas E. and Mark A. Ferguson. 2005. Social consequences of disparagement humor: a prejudiced norm theory. *Personality and Social Psychology Review*, 8: 79–94.

Fortunato, Santo; Alessandro Flammini; Filippo Menczer; and Alessandro Vespignani. The egalitarian effect of search engines. 2006. WWW2006, May 22–26, 2006, Edinburgh; available at <https://arxiv.org/pdf/cs/0511005.pdf>.

Fourcade, Marion and Kieran Healy. 2007. Moral views of market society. *Annual Review of Sociology*, 33, 285–311.

Fourcade, Marion and Kieran Healy. 2013. Classification situations: life-chances in the neoliberal era. *Accounting, Organizations and Society*, 38: 559–72.

Fourcade, Marion and Kieran Healy. 2017a. Categories all the way down. *Historical Social Research*, 42 (#1): 286–98.

Fourcade, Marion and Kieran Healy. 2017b. Seeing like a market. *Socio-Economic Review*, 15: 9–29.

Fourcade, Marion and Kieran Healy. Forthcoming. Rationalized stratification. *Social Stratification*, 5th edn, ed. David Grusky, Nima Dahir, and Claire Daviss. New York: Routledge.

Fourcade, Marion and Daniel N. Kluttz. 2020. A Maussian bargain: accumulation by gift in the digital economy. *Big Data & Society*, 7 (#1): article 2.

Frank, Andre Gundar. 1966. The development of underdevelopment. *Monthly Review*, 18 (4): 17–31.

Frank, Robert H. 2016. *Success and Luck: Good Fortune and the Myth of Meritocracy*. Princeton, NJ: Princeton University Press.

Frank, Robert H. and Philip J. Cook. 1995. *The Winner Take All Society*. New York: Free Press.

Frankfurt, Harry G. 1984. Necessity and desire. *Philosophy & Phenomenological Research*, 45: 1–13.

Franklin, J. Jeffrey. 2003. Anthony Trollope meets Pierre Bourdieu: the conversion of capital as plot in the mid-Victorian British novel. *Victorian Literature and Culture*, 31: 501–21.

Fraser, Nancy. 1992. Rethinking the public sphere: a contribution to the critique of actually existing democracy. Pp. 109–42 in *Habermas and the Public Sphere*, ed. Craig Calhoun. Cambridge, MA: MIT Press.
Freeman, Linton C. 1979. Centrality in networks: conceptual clarification. *Social Networks*, 1: 215–39.
Fretz, Stephan; Raphaël Parchet; and Frédéric Robert-Nicoud. 2022. Highways, market access and spatial sorting. *Economic Journal*, 132: 1011–36.
Freund, Daniel and Yannik Bendel. 2017. *Access All Areas: When EU Politicians Become Lobbyists*. Berlin: Transparency International EU.
Fricker, Miranda. 1999. Epistemic oppression and epistemic privilege. *Canadian Journal of Philosophy*, 29 (Supplement 1): 191–210.
Fricker, Miranda. 2007. *Epistemic Injustice: Power and the Ethics of Knowing*. Oxford: Oxford University Press.
Friedlaender, Christina. 2018. On microaggressions: cumulative harm and individual responsibility. *Hypatia*, 33: 5–21.
Friedman, Batya and Helen Nissenbaum. 1996. Bias in computer systems. *ACM Transactions on Information Systems*, July; available at <https://dl.acm.org/doi/10.1145/230538.230561>.
Friedman, Milton. 1962. *Capitalism and Freedom*. Chicago: University of Chicago Press.
Friedrich, Carl J. 1941. *Constitutional Government and Democracy*. Boston: Little, Brown.
Frohlich, Norman and Joe A. Oppenheimer. 1970. I get by with a little help from my friends. *World Politics*, 23: 104–20.
Frohlich, Norman; Joe A. Oppenheimer; and Oran R. Young. 1971. *Political Leadership and Collective Goods*. Princeton, NJ: Princeton University Press.
Fryer, Roland and Paul Torelli. 2005. An empirical analysis of 'acting white'. National Bureau of Economic Research Working Paper No. 11334. Available at <http://www.nber.org/papers/w11334>.
Furubotn, Eirik G. and Svetzar Pejovich. 1972. Property rights and economic theory: a survey of recent literature. *Journal of Economic Literature*, 10: 1137–62.
Gädeke, Dorothea. 2021. Who should fight domination? Individual responsibility and structural injustice. *Politics, Philosophy & Economics*, 20: 180–201.
Gais, Amy. 2020. The politics of hypocrisy: Baruch Spinoza and Pierre Bayle on hypocritical conformity. *Political Theory*, 48: 588–614.
Gal, Susan. 1987. Codeswitching and consciousness in the European periphery. *American Ethnologist*, 14: 637–53.
Gal, Susan. 1989. Language and political economy. *Annual Review of Anthropology*, 18: 345–67.
Galanter, Marc. 1974. Why the haves come out ahead. *Law and Society Review*, 9: 95–160.
Galanter, Marc. 1981. Justice in many rooms: courts, private ordering and indigenous law. *Journal of Legal Pluralism and Unofficial Law*, 13: 1–47.
Galbraith, John Kenneth. 1952. *American Capitalism: The Concept of Countervailing Power*. Boston: Houghton Mifflin.
Galbraith, John Kenneth. 1954. Countervailing power. *American Economic Review (Papers & Proceedings)*, 44 (#2): 1–6.
Galtung, Johan. 1969. Violence, peace and peace research. *Journal of Peace Research*, 6: 167–191.
Galtung, Johan. 1990. Cultural violence. *Journal of Peace Research*, 27: 291–305.
Gambetta, Diego. 1994. Godfather's gossip. *Archives Européenes de Sociologie*, 35: 199–223.

Gambetta, Diego. 1998. Concatenations of mechanisms. Pp.102–24 in *Social Mechanisms: An Analytical Approach to Social Theory*, ed. Peter Hedström and Richard Swedberg. Cambridge: Cambridge University Press.

Gambetta, Diego. 2009. Signalling. Pp.168–94 in *Oxford Handbook of Analytical Sociology*, ed. Peter Hedström and Peter Bearman. Oxford: Oxford University Press.

García-Jimeno, Camilo; Angel Iglesias; and Pinar Yildirim. 2021. Information networks and collective action: evidence from the Women's Temperance Crusade. *American Economic Review*, 112: 41–80.

Garfinkel, Alan. 1981. *Forms of Explanation: Rethinking the Questions in Social Theory*. New Haven, CT: Yale University Press.

Garfinkel, Howard. 1956. Conditions of successful degradation ceremonies. *American Journal of Sociology*, 61: 420–24.

Gaus, Gerald. 2021. *The Open Society and Its Complexities*. New York: Oxford University Press.

Gazdar, Gerald. 1979. Class, 'codes' and conversation. *Linguistics*, 17: 199–212.

Geertz, Clifford. 1962. The rotating credit association: a 'middle rung' in development. *Economic Development and Cultural Change*, 10: 241–63.

Geertz, Clifford. 1975. Common sense as a cultural system. *Antioch Review*, 33 (#1): 5–26.

Gellner, Ernest. 1983. *Nations and Nationalism*. Ithaca, NY: Cornell University Press.

Gendler, Tamar Szabó. 2011. The epistemic costs of implicit bias. *Philosophical Studies*, 156: 33–63.

Genovese, Eugene D. 1974. *Roll, Jordan, Roll: The World the Slaves Made*. New York: Vintage Books, Random House.

Gheaus, Anca. 2009. How much of what matters can we redistribute? Love, justice and luck. *Hypatia*, 24 (#2): 68–90.

Giddens, Anthony. 1984. *The Constitution of Society*. Cambridge: Polity.

Ginsberg, Ruth Bader. 2018. Opinion of the US Supreme Court. *McCoy v. Louisiana*, 138 S. Ct. 1500–11.

Ginsburgh, Victor and Shlomo Weber. 2020. The economics of language. *Journal of Economic Literature*, 58: 348–404.

Gladwell, Malcolm. 2008. *Outliers: The Story of Success*. Boston: Little, Brown.

Godden, Richard and Richard Maidment. 1980. Anger, language and politics: John F. Kennedy and the steel crisis. *Presidential Studies Quarterly*, 10: 317–31.

Goldhaber, Michael H. 1997. The attention economy and the net. *First Monday*, 2 (#4); available at <http://www.firstmonday.org/issues/issue2_4/goldhaber/>.

Goldhamer, Herbert and Edward A. Shils. 1939. Types of power and status. *American Journal of Sociology*, 45: 171–82.

Goldman, Eric. 2006. Search engine bias and the demise of search engine utopianism. *Yale Journal of Law & Technology*, 8: 188–200.

Goldstein, Robert J. 1983. *Political Repression in 19th Century Europe*. London: Routledge.

Gomez, Javiera Perez. 2022. Pushed to the edge of knowing: microaggression and self-doubt. *Journal of Applied Philosophy*, 39: 645–63.

González-Ricoy, Iñigo. 2022. Little republics: authority and the political nature of the firm. *Philosophy & Public Affairs*, 50: 90–120.

Goode, W. J. 1978. *The Celebration of Heroes: Prestige as a Control System*. Berkeley: University of California Press.

Goodin, Robert E. 1980. *Manipulatory Politics*. New Haven, CT: Yale University Press.

Goodin, Robert E. 1985a. Erring on the side of kindness in social welfare policy. *Policy Sciences*, 18: 141–56.

Goodin, Robert E. 1985b. The priority of needs. *Philosophy & Phenomenological Research*, 45: 615–25.
Goodin, Robert E. 1989. Theories of compensation. *Oxford Journal of Legal Studies*, 9: 56–75.
Goodin, Robert E. 1990a. De gustibus non est explanandum. Pp. 217–22 in *The Limits of Rationality*, ed. Karen S. Cook and Margaret Levi. Chicago: University of Chicago Press.
Goodin, Robert E. 1990b. Relative needs. Pp. 12–33 in *Needs and Welfare*, ed. Alan Ware and Robert E. Goodin. London: SAGE.
Goodin, Robert E. 1990c. Stabilizing expectations: the role of earnings-related benefits in social welfare policy. *Ethics*, 100: 530–53.
Goodin, Robert E. 1991. Compensation and redistribution. Pp. 143–77 in *Nomos XXXIII: Compensatory Justice*, ed. John W. Chapman. New York: New York University Press.
Goodin, Robert E. 1999. Rationality redux: reflections on Herbert Simon's vision of politics. Pp. 58–83 in *Competition and Cooperation: Conversations with Nobelists about Economics and Political Science*, ed. James Alt, Margaret Levi, and Elinor Ostrom. New York: Russell Sage Foundation Press.
Goodin, Robert E. 2000a. Institutional gaming. *Governance*, 13: 523–33.
Goodin, Robert E. 2000b. Trusting individuals vs trusting institutions: generalizing the case of contract. *Rationality & Society*, 12: 381–95.
Goodin, Robert E. 2001. Democratic wealth, democratic welfare: is flux enough? *New Political Economy*, 6: 67–79.
Goodin, Robert E. 2008. Clubbish justice. *Politics, Philosophy and Economics*, 7: 233–7.
Goodin, Robert E. 2009. The state of the discipline, the discipline of the state. Pp. 3–57 in Oxford *Handbook of Political Science*, ed. Goodin. Oxford: Oxford University Press.
Goodin, Robert E. 2010a. An epistemic case for legal moralism. *Oxford Journal of Legal Studies*, 30: 615–33.
Goodin, Robert E. 2010b. Global democracy: in the beginning. *International Theory*, 2: 175–209.
Goodin, Robert E. 2012a. Excused by the unwillingness of others. *Analysis*, 72: 18–24.
Goodin, Robert E. 2012b. *On Settling*. Princeton, NJ: Princeton University Press.
Goodin, Robert E. 2017. Acting in combination. *Philosophy & Public Affairs*, 45: 158–94.
Goodin, Robert E. 2018a. Constitutive responsibility: taking part, being part. *Analysis*, 78: 40–45.
Goodin, Robert E. 2018b. Emulation and the transformation of social norms. *Social Research*, 85: 53–72.
Goodin, Robert E. 2022. Cogs in collective action. Skytte Lecture, University of Uppsala, 30 September.
Goodin, Robert E. and Christian Barry. 2021. Responsibility for structural injustice: a third thought. *Politics, Philosophy & Economics*, 20: 339–56.
Goodin, Robert E. and Geoffrey Brennan. 2001. Bargaining over beliefs. *Ethics*, 111: 256–277.
Goodin, Robert E. and John Dryzek. 1980. Rational participation: the politics of relative power. *British Journal of Political Science*, 10: 273–92.
Goodin, Robert E.; Bruce Headey; Ruud Muffels; and Henk-Jan Dirven. 1999. *Real Worlds of Welfare Capitalism*. Cambridge: Cambridge University Press.
Goodin, Robert E. and Christian List. 2006. Special majorities rationalized. *British Journal of Political Science*, 36: 213–42.
Goodwin, Barbara. 1992. *Justice by Lottery*. Hemel Hempstead: Harvester Wheatsheaf.

Gopinath, Gita and Jeremy C. Stein. 2021. Banking, trade and the making of a dominant currency. *Quarterly Journal of Economics*, 136: 783–830.
Gould Roger V. 2002. The origins of status hierarchies: a formal theory and empirical test. *American Journal of Sociology*, 107: 1143–8.
Granovetter, Mark. 1973. The strength of weak ties. *American Journal of Sociology*, 78: 1360–80.
Granovetter, Mark. 1974/1995. *Getting a Job: A Study of Contacts and Careers*. 2nd edn. Chicago: University of Chicago Press; originally published 1974.
Granovetter, Mark. 1985. Economic action and social structure: the problem of embeddedness. *American Journal of Sociology*, 91: 481–510.
Greenwald, Anthony G. and Mahzarin R. Banaji. 1995. Implicit social cognition: attitudes, self-esteem and stereotype. *Psychological Review*, 102: 4–27.
Greenwald, Anthony G. and Linda Hamilton Krieger. 2006. Implicit bias: scientific foundations. *California Law Review*, 94: 945–67.
Grewal, David Singh. 2008. *Network Power: The Social Dynamics of Globalization*. New Haven, CT: Yale University Press.
Grice, H. Paul. 1975. Logic and conversation. Pp. 64–75 in *The Logic of Grammar*, ed. Donald Davidson and Gilbert Harman. Encino, CA: Dickenson Publishing Co.
Gumperz, John J. 1982. Conversational codeswitching. Pp. 59–99 in *Discourse Strategies*. Cambridge: Cambridge University Press.
Habermas, Jürgen. 1962/1989. *The Structural Transformation of the Public Sphere*, trans. Thomas Burger and Frederick Lawrence. Oxford: Polity; originally published 1962.
Habermas, Jürgen. 1987. *The Theory of Communicative Action*. Volume 2: A *Critique of Functionalist Reason*, trans. Thomas McCarthy. Boston: Beacon Press.
Hacker, Jacob S. and Paul Pierson. 2010. *Winner-Take-All Politics: How Washington Made the Rich Richer – and Turned Its Back on the Middle Class*. New York: Simon and Schuster.
Hale, Sarah Josepha. 1868. *Manners; or, Happy Homes and Good Society*. Boston: J. E. Tilton & Co.
Hall, Peter A. and David Soskice, eds. 2001. *Varieties of Capitalism*. Oxford: Oxford University Press.
Halliday, Daniel. 2016. Private education, positional goods and the arms race problem. *Politics, Philosophy & Economics*, 15: 150–69.
Halliday, Daniel. 2018. *Inheritance of Wealth: Justice, Equality and the Right to Bequeath*. Oxford: Oxford University Press.
Halliday, M. A. K. 1976. Anti-languages. *American Anthropologist*, 78: 570–84.
Hamdan, Jana. 2019. The impact of mobile money in developing countries. *DIW Roundup* 131. Berlin: Deutsches Institut für Wirtschaftsforschung.
Hardin, Curtis D. and Terri D. Conley. 2000. A relational approach to cognition: shared experience and relationship affirmation in social cognition. Pp. 3–17 in *Future Directions in Social Cognition*, ed. Gordon Moskowitz. Hillsdale, NJ: Erlbaum.
Hardin, Garrett. 1968. The tragedy of the commons. *Science*, 162: 1243–8.
Hardin, Russell. 1982. *Collective Action*. Baltimore, MD: Johns Hopkins University Press.
Hardin, Russell. 1983. Unilateral versus mutual disarmament. *Philosophy & Public Affairs*, 12: 236–54.
Hardin, Russell. 1991. Trusting persons, trusting institutions. Pp. 185–209 in *The Strategy of Choice*, ed. Richard J. Zeckhauser. Cambridge, MA: MIT Press.
Hardin, Russell. 1993. The street-level epistemology of trust. *Politics & Society*, 2: 505–29.
Hardin, Russell. 1995. *One for All*. Princeton, NJ: Princeton University Press.
Hardin, Russell. 2004. *Trust and Trustworthiness*. New York: Russell Sage Foundation.

Harel Ben Shahar, Tammy. 2018. Positional goods and the size of inequality. *Journal of Political Philosophy*, 26: 103–20.
Harris, Cheryl I. 1993. Whiteness as property. *Harvard Law Review*, 106: 1709–91.
Harris, Tristan. 2013. A call to minimize distraction and respect users' attention. Available at <https://idoc.pub/download/a-call-to-minimize-distraction-respect-users-attention-by-tristan-harris-d47e1096j7n2>.
Harris, Tristan. 2018. Oral evidence: fake news, HC 363. Presented to the Digital, Culture, Media and Sport Committee, UK House of Commons, 22 May 2018. Transcript available at <http://data.parliament.uk/writtenevidence/committeeevidence.svc/evidencedocument/digital-culture-media-and-sport-committee/fake-news/oral/83304.html>.
Harsanyi, John C. 1977. Rule utilitarianism and decision theory. *Erkenntnis*, 11: 25–53.
Hart, Herbert L. A. 1961. *The Concept of Law*. Oxford: Clarendon Press.
Haslanger, Sally. 1995. Ontology and social construction. *Philosophical Topics*, 23: 95–125.
Haslanger, Sally. 2000. Gender and race: (What) are they? (What) do we want them to be? *Nous*, 34: 31–55.
Haslanger, Sally. 2005. What are we talking about? The semantics and politics of social kinds. *Hypatia*, 20 (34): 10–26.
Haslanger, Sally. 2012. *Resisting Reality: Social Construction and Social Critique*. Oxford: Oxford University Press.
Haslanger, Sally. 2015. Social structure, narrative and explanation. *Canadian Journal of Philosophy*, 45: 1–15.
Haslanger, Sally. 2016. What is a (social) structural explanation? *Philosophical Studies*, 173: 113–30.
Haslanger, Sally. 2017. Culture and critique. *Proceedings of the Aristotelian Society, Supplement*, 91: 149–73.
Haslanger, Sally. 2018. What is a social practice? Pp. 231–47 in *Metaphysics: Royal Institute of Philosophy Supplement 82*, ed. Anthony O'Hear. Cambridge: Cambridge University Press.
Haslanger, Sally. 2019. Cognition as a social skill. *Australasian Philosophical Review*, 3: 5–25.
Haslanger, Sally. 2020. Going on, not in the same way. Pp. 230–60 in *Conceptual Engineering and Conceptual Ethics*, ed. Alexis Burgess, Herman Cappelen, and David Plunkett. Oxford: Oxford University Press.
Haugen, Einar. 1966. Dialect, language, nation. *American Anthropologist*, n.s., 68: 922–35.
Hay, Colin and David Richards. 2000. The tangled webs of Westminster and Whitehall: the discourse, strategy and practice of networking within the British core executive. *Public Administration*, 78: 1–28.
Hayward, Clarissa Rile. 2017. Responsibility and ignorance: on dismantling structural injustice. *Journal of Politics*, 79: 396–408.
Hayward, Clarissa Rile. 2020. Disruption: what is it good for? *Journal of Politics*, 82: 448–59.
Hayward, Clarissa Rile and Steven Lukes. 2008. Nobody to shoot? Power, structure and agency: a dialogue. *Journal of Power*, 1: 5–20.
Healy, Kieran. 2015. The performativity of networks. *Archives Européenes de Sociologie*, 56: 175–205.
Heath, Joseph. 2018. Mistakes were made: the role of catallactic bias in the financial crisis. *Midwest Studies in Philosophy*, 42: 229–47.
Heckman James J.; Lance J. Lochner; and Petra E. Todd. 2003. Fifty years of Mincer earnings regressions. IZA discussion paper no. 775, May 2003. NBER Work. Pap. 9732, Natl. Bur. Econ. Res., Inc. Available at <http://ideas.repec.org/p/nbr/nberwo/9732.html>.

Hedden, Brian. 2021. On statistical criteria of algorithmic fairness. *Philosophy & Public Affairs*, 49: 209–31.
Hedström, Peter. 1998. Rational imitation. Pp. 306–27 in *Social Mechanisms: An Analytical Approach to Social Theory*, ed. Peter Hedström and Richard Swedberg. Cambridge: Cambridge University Press.
Hedström, Peter and Peter Bearman, eds. 2009. *Oxford Handbook of Analytical Sociology*. Oxford: Oxford University Press.
Hedström, Peter and Richard Swedberg, eds. 1998a. *Social Mechanisms: An Analytical Approach to Social Theory*. Cambridge: Cambridge University Press.
Hedström, Peter and Richard Swedberg. 1998b. Social mechanisms: an introductory essay. Pp. 1–31 in *Social Mechanisms: An Analytical Approach to Social Theory*, ed. Hedström and Swedberg. Cambridge: Cambridge University Press.
Hedström, Peter and Petri Ylikoski. 2010. Causal mechanisms in the social sciences. *Annual Review of Sociology*, 36: 49–67.
Heinz, John P. and Edward O. Laumann. 1982. *Chicago Lawyers: The Social Structure of the Bar*. New York: Russell Sage Foundation.
Hellman, Deborah. 2018. Indirect discrimination and the duty to avoid compounding injustice. Pp. 105–22 in *Foundations of Indirect Discrimination Law*, ed. Hugh Collins and Tarunabh Khaitan. Oxford: Hart. Available at <https://papers.ssrn.com/sol3/papers.cfm?abstract_id=3033864 >.
Hellman, Deborah. 2020. Measuring algorithmic fairness. *Virginia Law Review*, 106: 811–66.
Hellman, Deborah S. 1997. Is actuarially fair insurance pricing actually fair – a case study in insuring battered women. *Harvard Civil Rights – Civil Liberties Law Review*, 32: 355–411.
Helper, Rose. 1969. *Racial Policies and Practices of Real Estate Brokers*. Minneapolis: University of Minnesota Press.
Hempel, Carl. 1952. *Fundamentals of Concept Formation in Empirical Science*. Chicago: University of Chicago Press.
Hernes, Gudmund. 1998. Real virtuality. Pp. 74–101 in *Social Mechanisms: An Analytical Approach to Social Theory*, ed. Peter Hedström and Richard Swedberg. Cambridge: Cambridge University Press.
Herzog, Lisa. 2021a. Algorithmic bias and access to opportunities. Ch. 12 in *Oxford Handbook of Digital Ethics*, ed. Carissa Véliz. Oxford: Oxford University Press.
Herzog, Lisa. 2021b. Global reserve currencies from the perspective of structural justice: distribution and domination. *Critical Review of International Social and Political Philosophy*, 24: 931–53.
Hicks, John R. 1941. The rehabilitation of consumers' surplus. *Review of Economics Studies*, 8: 108–16.
Hillier, Amy. 2005. Residential security maps and neighborhood appraisals: the Home Owners' Loan Corporation and the case of Philadelphia. *Social Science History*, 29: 207–33.
Hirsch, Fred. 1976. *Social Limits to Growth*. Cambridge, MA: Harvard University Press.
Hirschman, Albert O. 1970. *Exit, Voice and Loyalty*. Cambridge, MA: Harvard University Press.
Hirschman, Albert O. 1984. Against parsimony: three easy ways of complicating some categories of economic discourse. *American Economic Review (Papers and Proceedings)*, 74 (#2), 89–96.
Hirschman, Daniel. 2021. Rediscovering the 1%: knowledge infrastructures and the stylized facts of inequality. *American Journal of Sociology*, 127: 739–86.

Hirshleifer, Jack. 2001. *The Dark Side of the Force*. Cambridge: Cambridge University Press.
Hobbes, Thomas. 1651. *Leviathan*. London: Andrew Crooke.
Hobbes, Thomas. 1651/2012. *Leviathan*, ed. Noel Malcolm. Clarendon Edition of the Works of Thomas Hobbes. Oxford: Oxford University Press.
Hobbs, Allyson. 2014. *A Chosen Exile: A History of Racial Passing in American Life*. Cambridge, MA: Harvard University Press.
Hodas, Nathan O.; Farshad Kooti; and Kristina Lerman. 2013. Friendship paradox redux: your friends are more interesting than you. *Proceedings of the Seventh International AAAI Conference on Weblogs and Social Media*. Available at <https://www.aaai.org/ocs/index.php/ICWSM/ICWSM13/paper/viewFile/6136/6361>.
Hodgson, David H. 1967. *Consequences of Utilitarianism*. Oxford: Clarendon Press.
Hollis, Martin. 1977. *Models of Man: Philosophical Thoughts on Social Action*. Cambridge: Cambridge University Press.
Holzer, Henry J. 1987. Informal job search and black youth unemployment. *American Economic Review*, 77: 446–52.
Homans, George C. 1950. *The Human Group*. New York: Harcourt, Brace & World.
Homer. 1909. *The Iliad*, trans. Alexander Pope. London: Cassell.
Hong, Harrison; Jeffrey D. Kubik; and Amit Solomon. 2000. Security analysts' career concerns and the herding of earnings forecasts. *RAND Journal of Economics*, 31: 121–44.
Hornsby, Jennifer and Rae Langton. 1998. Free speech and illocution. *Legal Theory*, 4: 1–27.
Horowitz, Jonathan. 2018. Relative education and the advantage of a college degree. *American Sociological Review*, 83: 771–801.
Hotelling, Harold. 1938. The general welfare in relation to problems of taxation and of railway and utility rates. *Econometrica*, 6: 242–69.
Howard, Jeffrey W. 2021. Extreme speech, democratic deliberation and social media. Ch. 6 in *Oxford Handbook of Digital Ethics*, ed. Carissa Véliz. Oxford: Oxford University Press.
Huberman, Bernardo A. and Fang Wu. 2008. The economics of attention: maximizing user value in information-rich environments. *Advances in Complex Systems*, 11: 487–96.
Huberman, Bernardo A.; Peter L. T. Pirolli; James E. Pitkow; and Rajan M. Lukose. 1998. Strong regularities in World Wide Net surfing. *Science*, 280: 95–7.
Hume, David. 1739. *A Treatise of Human Nature*. London: John Noon.
Hume, David. 1742/1760. Of the independency of parliament. Part I, ch. 6 in *Essays, Literary, Moral and Political*. London: A. Millar, 1760; originally published 1742.
Hume, David. 1752/1760. Of the original contract. Part II, ch. 12 in in *Essays, Literary, Moral and Political*. London: A. Millar, 1760; originally published 1752.
Hume, David. 1777. *An Enquiry Concerning the Principles of Morals*. London: Cadell.
Hunzaker, M.B. Fallin and Lauren Valentino. 2019. Mapping cultural schemas: from theory to method. *American Sociological Review*, 84: 950–81.
Hwang, Jackelyn and Tyler W. McDaniel. 2022. Racialized reshuffling: urban change in the persistence of segregation in the twenty-first century. *Annual Review of Sociology*, 48: 137–419.
Ikonomou, Tess. 2022. Frydenberg lands Goldman Sachs gig. *Canberra Times*, 21 July; available at <https://www.canberratimes.com.au/story/7828859/frydenberg-lands-goldman-sachs-gig/?cs=14329>.
Ikuta, Jennie and Trevor Latimer. 2021. Aristocracy in America: Tocqueville on white supremacy. *Journal of Politics*, 83: 547–59.
Illies, Christian and Anthonie Meijers. 2009. Artefacts without agency. *The Monist*, 92: 420–40.

Ingram, Paul and Karen Clay. 2000. The choice-within-constraints new institutionalism and implications for sociology. *Annual Review of Sociology*, 26: 525–46.

International Commission of Jurists (ICJ). 2008. *Corporate Complicity & Legal Accountability*. Report of the International Commission of Jurists Expert Legal Panel on Corporate Complicity in International Crimes. Geneva: ICJ.

Inzlicht, Michael and Toni Schmader, eds. 2011. *Stereotype Threat: Theory, Process and Application*. New York: Oxford University Press.

Jackson, Kenneth T. 1985. *Crabgrass Frontier: The Suburbanization of the United States*. New York: Oxford University Press.

Jackson, Matthew O.; Brian W. Rogers; and Yves Zenou. 2017. The economic consequences of social-network structure. *Journal of Economic Literature*, 55: 49–95.

James, William. 1890. *The Principles of Psychology*. New York: Holt.

Jastrow, Joseph. 1899. The mind's eye. *Popular Science Monthly*, 54: 299–312.

Jedwab, Remi; Noel D. Johnson; and Mark Koyama. 2022. The economic impact of the Black Death. *Journal of Economic Literature*, 60: 132–78.

Jenkins, David. 2021. Understanding and fighting structural injustice. *Journal of Social Philosophy*, 52: 569–586.

Jenkins, Katharine. 2020. Ontic injustice. *Journal of the American Philosophical Association*, 6: 188–205.

Jevons, W. Stanley. 1875. *Money and the Mechanism of Exchange*. New York: Appleton.

Johnson, Glenn S. and Shirley A. Rainey. 2007. Hurricane Katrina: public health and environmental justice issues front and centered. *Race, Gender & Class*, 14: 17–37.

Jones, Bryan D. and Frank R. Baumgartner. 2005. *The Politics of Attention*. Chicago: University of Chicago Press.

Jones, Karen. 2012a. The politics of intellectual self-trust. *Social Epistemology*, 26: 237–51.

Jones, Karen. 2012b. Trustworthiness. *Ethics*, 123: 61–85.

Joskow, Paul L. 2007. Regulation of natural monopolies. vol. 2, pp. 1227–348 in *Handbook of Law and Economics*, ed. A. Mitchell Polinski and Steven Shavell. Amsterdam: North-Holland.

Joumard, Isabelle; Mauro Pisu; and Debbie Bloch. 2012. Tackling income inequality: the role of taxes and transfers. *OECD Journal: Economic Studies*, 2012 (#1): 37–70.

Jugov, Tamara and Lea Ypi. 2018. Structural injustice, epistemic opacity, and the responsibilities of the oppressed. *Journal of Social Philosophy*, 50: 7–27.

Jussim, Lee and Kent D. Harber. 2005. Teacher expectations and self-fulfilling prophecies: knowns and unknowns, resolved and unresolved controversies. *Personality and Social Psychology Review*, 9: 131–55.

Jütten, Timo. 2011. The colonization thesis: Habermas on reification. *International Journal of Philosophical Studies*, 19: 701–27.

Kahneman, Daniel. 1973. *Attention and Effort*. Englewood Cliffs, NJ: Prentice-Hall.

Kahneman, Daniel; Jack Knetsch; and Richard Thaler. 1990. Experimental test of the endowment effect and the Coase Theorem. *Journal of Political Economy*, 98: 1325–48.

Kahneman, Daniel; Paul Slovic; and Amos Tversky, eds. 1982. *Judgment under Uncertainty: Heuristics and Biases*. Cambridge: Cambridge University Press.

Kahneman, Daniel and Amon Tversky. 1979. Prospect theory: an analysis of decision under risk. *Econometrica*, 46: 263–91.

Kahneman, Daniel and Amos Tversky, eds. 2000. *Choices, Values and Frames*. Cambridge: Cambridge University Press.

Kant, Immanuel. 1784/1949. What is enlightenment? Pp. 132–9 in *The Philosophy of Kant*, trans. & ed. Carl J. Friedrich. New York: Random House, 1949; originally published 1784.

Kanter, Rosabeth Moss. 1977. *Men and Women of the Corporation*. New York: Basic.
Kantor, Brian. 1979. Rational expectations and economic thought. *Journal of Economic Literature*, 17: 1422–41.
Karabel, Jerome B. 2005. *The Chosen: The Hidden History of Admission and Exclusion at Harvard, Yale and Princeton*. Boston: Houghton Mifflin.
Katz, Michael and Carl Shapiro. 1985. Network externalities, competition, and compatibility. *American Economic Review*, 75: 424–40.
Kagan, Shelly. 2011. Do I make a difference? *Philosophy & Public Affairs*, 39: 105–41.
Kemeny, John G. and J. Laurie Snell. 1960. *Finite Markov Chains*. 2nd edn. New York: Van Nostrand.
Kemper, Theodore D. 1974. On the nature and purpose of ascription. *American Sociological Review*, 39: 844–53.
Kentikelenis, Alexander E. and Sarah Babb. 2019. The making of neoliberal globalization: norm substitution and the politics of clandestine institutional change. *American Journal of Sociology*, 124: 1720–62.
Kerin, Roger A.; P. Rajan Varadarajan; and Robert A. Peterson. 1992. First-mover advantage: a synthesis, conceptual framework and research propositions. *Journal of Marketing*, 56 (#4): 33–52.
Keynes, John Maynard. 1936/1964. *The General Theory of Employment, Interest and Money*. New York: Harcourt, Brace, 1936. Reprinted: London: Macmillan, 1964.
Kindleberger, Charles P. 1983. Standards as public, collective and private goods. *Kyklos*, 36: 377–96.
Kinsey, Alfred C.; Wardell B. Pomeroy; and Clyde E. Martin. 1948. *Sexual Behavior in the Human Male*. Philadelphia, PA: W.B. Saunders Company.
Kinsey, Alfred C.; Wardell B. Pomeroy; Clyde E. Martin; and Paul H. Gebhard. 1953. *Sexual Behavior in the Human Female*. Philadelphia, PA: W. B. Saunders Company.
Kitcher, Philip. 1990. The division of cognitive labor. *Journal of Philosophy*, 87: 5–22.
Kiviat, Barbara. 2019. The moral limits of predictive practices: the case of credit-based insurance scores. *American Sociological Review*, 84: 1134–58.
Kleinberg, Jon; Jens Ludwig; Sendhil Mullainathan; and Ashesh Rambachan. 2018. Algorithmic fairness. *AEA Papers and Proceedings*, 108: 22–7.
Kleinberg, Jon; Sendhil Mullainathan; and Manish Raghavan. 2017. Inherent trade-offs in the fair determination of risk scores. *Proceedings of the 8th Conference on Innovation in Theoretical Computer Science*, 43:1–23; available at <https://drops.dagstuhl.de/opus/volltexte/2017/8156/pdf/LIPIcs-ITCS-2017-43.pdf>.
Kleinfeld, Rachel and Elena Barham. 2018. Complicit states and the governing strategy of privilege violence: when weakness is not the problem. *Annual Review of Political Science*, 21: 215–38.
Knez, Marc and Colin Camerer. 1994. Creating expectational assets in the laboratory: coordination in 'weakest-link' games. *Strategic Management Journal*, 15 (Winter Special Issue): 101–19.
Knight, Frank. 1921. *Risk, Uncertainty and Profit*. New York: Houghton Mifflin.
Knoke, David. 1993. Networks of elite structure and decision making. *Sociological Methods and Research*, 22: 23–45.
Knox, Dean; Will Lowe; and Jonathan Mummolo. 2020. Administrative records mask racially biased policing. *American Political Science Review*, 114: 619–37.
Kohlhas, Alexandre N. and Ansgar Walther. 2021. Asymmetric attention. *American Economic Review*, 111: 2879–925.
Kolers, Avery. 2016. *A Moral Theory of Solidarity*. Oxford: Oxford University Press.

Kolers, Avery. 2020. Groundwork for the mechanics of morals. *Canadian Journal of Philosophy*, 50: 636–51.
Koopman, Colin. 2022. The political theory of data: institutions, algorithms and formats in racial redlining. *Political Theory*, 50: 337–61.
Koopman, Philip and Robert R. Hoffman. 2003. Work-arounds, make-work and kludges. *IEEE Intelligent Systems*, 18 (#6: Nov./Dec.): 70–5.
Korenman S. and S. Turner. 1996. Employment contacts and minority-white wage differences. *Industrial Relations*, 35: 106–22
Korpi, Walter. 1985. Power resources approach vs. action and conflict: on causal and intentional explanations in the study of power. *Sociological Theory*, 3 (#2): 31–45.
Korver-Glenn, Elizabeth. 2018. Compounding inequalities: how racial stereotypes and discrimination accumulate across the stages of housing exchange. *American Sociological Review*, 83: 627–56.
Kossinets, Gueorgi and Duncan J. Watts. 2009. Origins of homophily in an evolving social network. *American Journal of Sociology*, 115: 405–50.
Kőszegi, Botond and Filip Matejka. 2020. Choice simplification: a theory of budgeting and naive diversification. *Quarterly Journal of Economics*, 135: 1153–1207.
Kreps, David M. 1990. Corporate culture and economic theory. Pp. 90–143 in *Perspectives on Positive Political Economy*, ed. James Alt and Kenneth Shepsle. Cambridge: Cambridge University Press.
Kruks, Sonia. 2005. Simone de Beauvoir and the politics of privilege. *Hypatia*, 20 (#1): 178–205.
Kuhn, Thomas. 1962. *The Structure of Scientific Revolutions*. Chicago: University of Chicago Press.
Kukla, Rebecca. 2014. Performative force, convention and discursive injustice. *Hypatia*, 29: 440–57.
Kuran, Timur. 1991. Now out of never: the element of surprise in the East European revolution of 1989. *World Politics*, 44: 7–48.
Kuran, Timur. 1995. *Private Truths, Public Lies: The Social Consequences of Preference Falsification*. Cambridge MA: Harvard University Press.
Kuznets, Simon. 1955. Economic growth and income inequality. *American Economic Review*, 45: 1–28.
Kymlicka, Will. 1989. *Liberalism, Community and Culture*. Oxford: Clarendon Press.
Kymlicka, Will. 1995. *Multicultural Citizenship: A Liberal Theory of Minority Rights*. Oxford: Clarendon Press.
Kymlicka, Will and Alan Patten, eds. 2003. *Language Rights and Political Theory*. Oxford: Oxford University Press.
La Rochefoucauld, François de. 1664/2007. *Collected Maxims and Other Reflections*, trans. E. H and A. M Blackmore and Francine Giguère. Oxford: Oxford University Press; originally published 1664.
Laitin, David D. 2007. *Language Repertoires and State Construction in Africa*. Cambridge: Cambridge University Press.
Laitin, David D and Rajesh Ramachandran. 2016. Language policy and human development. *American Political Science Review*, 110: 457–80.
Landemore, Hélène and Isabelle Ferreras. 2016. In defense of workplace democracy: toward a justification of the firm-state analogy. *Political Theory*, 44: 53–81.
Landes, Xavier. 2015. How fair is actuarial fairness? *Journal of Business Ethics*, 128: 519–33.

Landry, Alysa. 2018. Paying to play Indian: the Dawes Rolls and the legacy of $5 Indians. *Indian Country Today*. Available at <https://indiancountrytoday.com/archive/paying-play-indian-dawes-rolls-legacy-5-indians >.
Lang, William W. and Leonard I. Nakamura. 1993. A model of redlining. *Journal of Urban Economics*, 33: 223–34.
Lanham, Richard A. 2006. *The Economics of Attention: Style and Substance in the Age of Information*. Chicago: University of Chicago Press.
Latour, Bruno. 1999. *Pandora's Hope*. Cambridge, MA: Harvard University Press.
Latour, Bruno and Steve Woolgar. 1979. *Laboratory Life*. Beverley Hills, CA: SAGE.
Laumann, Edward O. and John P. Heinz. 1982. *Chicago Lawyers: The Social Structure of the Bar*. New York: Russell Sage Foundation and American Bar Association.
Laumann, Edward O.; John P. Heinz; Robert L. Nelson; and Rebecca L. Sandefur. 2005. *Urban Lawyers: The New Social Structure of the Bar*. Chicago: University of Chicago Press.
Lazarsfeld, Paul F. and Robert K. Merton. 1954. Friendship as a social process: a substantive and methodological analysis. Pp. 18–66 in *Freedom and Control in Modern Society*, ed. Monroe Berger, Theodore Abel, and Charles H. Page. New York: Van Nostrand.
Lazarus, Jeffrey; Amy McKay; and Lindsey Herbel. 2016. Who walks through the revolving door? Examining the lobbying activity of former members of Congress. *Interest Groups and Advocacy*, 5: 82–100.
Le, Tung Thanh; Zacharias Andreadakis; Arun Kumar; Raúl Gómez Román; Stig Tollefsen; Melanie Saville; and Stephen Mayhew. 2020. The COVID-19 vaccine development landscape. *Nature Reviews: Drug Discovery*, 19: 305–6.
Lehmbruch, Gerhard. 1984. Concertation and the structure of corporatist networks. Pp. 60–80 in *Order and Conflict in Contemporary Capitalism*, ed. John H. Goldthorpe. Oxford: Clarendon Press.
Lepora, Chiara and Robert E. Goodin. 2013. *On Complicity and Compromise*. Oxford: Oxford University Press.
Leslie, Sarah-Jane. 2007. Generics and the structure of the mind. *Philosophical Perspectives*, 21: 375–403.
Letwin, William L. 1954. The English common law concerning monopolies. *University of Chicago Law Review*, 21: 355–5.
Lewis, David. 1969. *Convention*. Oxford: Blackwell.
Lewis, David. 1979. Scorekeeping in a language game. *Journal of Philosophical Logic*, 8: 339–59.
Liao, Shen-yi and Bryce Huebner. 2021. Oppressive things. *Philosophy & Phenomenological Research*, 103: 92–113.
Liebowitz, S. J. and Stephen E. Margolis. 1994. Network externality: an uncommon tragedy. *Journal of Economic Perspectives*, 8 (#2): 133–50.
Liebowitz, S. J. and Stephen E. Margolis. 1998. Network effects and externalities. Pp. 671–5 in *The New Palgrave Dictionary of Economics and the Law*, ed. Peter Newman. New York: Macmillan.
Lijphart, Arend. 1968. *The Politics of Accommodation: Pluralism and Democracy in the Netherlands*. Berkeley: University of California Press.
Lindblom, Charles E. 1965. *The Intelligence of Democracy*. New York: Free Press.
Lindblom, Charles E. 1977. *Politics and Markets*. New York: Basic.
Lindsay, A. D. 1924. The organisation of labour in the army in France during the war and its lessons. *Economic Journal*, 34: 69–82.
Linton, Ralph. 1936. *The Study of Man*. New York: Appleton-Century-Crofts.

Lippman, Walter. 1922/1997. *Public Opinion*. New York: Free Press; originally published 1922.

Lipset, Seymour Martin and Stein Rokkan, eds. 1967. *Party Systems and Voter Alignments*. New York: Free Press.

Lisle-Williams, Michael. 1984. Merchant banking dynasties in the English class structure: ownership, solidarity and kinship in the City of London, 1850–1960. *British Journal of Sociology*, 35: 333–62.

Lizardo, Omar. 2010. Beyond the antinomies of structure: Levi-Strauss, Giddens, Bourdieu and Sewell. *Theory and Society*, 39: 651–88.

Locke, John. 1689/1946. *Letter Concerning Toleration*. Pp. 125–67 in *John Locke, Second Treatise of Government*, ed. J. W. Gough. Oxford: Blackwell, 1946.

Long, Gerald M. and Jared M. Batterman. 2012. Dissecting perceptual processes with a new tri-stable reversible figure. *Perception*, 41: 1163–85.

Louis XIV. 1685. *Code Noir*. Translated as *The Black Code: Edict of the King Concerning the Enforcement of Order in the French American Islands from the Month of March 1685*. Available at <https://s3.wp.wsu.edu/uploads/sites/1205/2016/02/code-noir.pdf>.

Lourey, Glenn C. 1998. Discrimination in the post-civil rights era: beyond market interactions. *Journal of Economic Perspectives*, 12 (#2): 117–26.

Loury, Glenn. 2002. *The Anatomy of Racial Inequality*. Cambridge, MA: Harvard University Press.

Lowi, Theodore J. 1964. American business, public policy, case-studies and political theory. *World Politics*, 16: 676–715.

Lucas, Robert E. Jr. and Edward C. Prescott. 1971. Investment under uncertainty. *Econometrica*, 39: 659–68.

Luce, R. Duncan and Howard Raiffa. 1957. *Games and Decisions*. New York: Wiley.

Lundborg, Petter; Dan-Olof Rooth; and Jesper Alex-Petersen. 2022. Long-term effects of childhood nutrition: evidence from a school lunch reform. *Review of Economic Studies*, 89: 876–908.

Macaulay, Stewart. 1963. Non-contractual relations in business: a preliminary study. *American Sociological Review*, 28: 55–67.

Macaulay, Stewart. 1986. Private government. Pp. 445–518 in *Law and the Social Sciences*, ed. Leon Lipson and Stanton Wheeler. New York: Russell Sage Foundation.

Macaulay, Stewart. 1996. Organic transactions: contract, Frank Lloyd Wright and the Johnson Building. *Wisconsin Law Review*, 1996: 75–121.

Macaulay, Stewart. 2000. Relational contracts floating on a sea of custom? *Northwestern University Law Review*, 94: 775–804.

MacIntyre, Alasdair. 1999. Social structures and their threats to moral agency. *Philosophy*, 74: 311–29.

Mackie, Gerry. 1996. Ending footbinding and infibulation: a convention account. *American Sociological Review*, 61: 999–1017.

Mackowiak, Bartosz; Filip Matejka; and Mirko Wiederholt. 2021. Rational inattention: a review. *Journal of Economic Literature*, forthcoming. Available at <https://deliverypdf.ssrn.com/delivery.php?ID=135126090088118000111080029089029100084047065081011094098008114014097033007063120060047001090071098051014068036004089046120022080118085118022113110035077053102084100082005117073028108113031099008104112085110113100068009005121088119123&EXT=pdf&INDEX=TRUE>.

Mailer, Norman. 1968. *Miami and the Siege of Chicago: An Informal History of the Republican and Democratic Conventions of 1968*. New York: New American Library.

Maine, Henry Sumner. 1901. *Ancient Law*, 17th edn. London: John Murray.

Major, Brenda. 1987. Gender, justice and the psychology of entitlement. Pp. 124–48 in *Sex and Gender*, ed. Phillip Shaver and Clyde Hendrick. Beverley Hills, CA: SAGE.

Malone, Thomas W. and Kevin Crowston. 1994. The interdisciplinary study of coordination. *ACM Computing Surveys*, 26: 87–119.

Manne, Kate. 2020. *Entitled: How Male Privilege Hurts Women*. New York: Crown.

Manzini, Paola and March Mariotti. 2018. Competing for attention: is the showiest also the best? *Economic Journal*, 128: 827–44.

March, James G. and Johan P. Olsen. 1984. The new institutionalism: organizational factors in political life. *American Political Science Review*, 78: 734–49.

March, James G. and Johan P. Olsen. 2006. The logic of appropriateness. Pp. 689–708 in *Oxford Handbook of Public Policy*, ed. Michael Moran, Martin Rein, and Robert E. Goodin. Oxford: Oxford University Press.

March, James G. and Herbert A. Simon. 1958. *Organizations*. New York: Wiley.

Marchese, David. 2022. Interview: Thomas Piketty thinks America is primed for wealth redistribution. *New York Times Magazine*, 1 April; available at <www.nytimes.com/intractive/2022/04/03/magazine/thomas-pikett-interview.html>.

Marcus, Gary. 2008. *Kluge*. London: Faber & Faber.

Marin, Mara. 2017. *Connected by Commitment: Oppression and Our Responsibility to Undermine It*. New York: Oxford University Press.

Marmot, Michael G. 2004. *The Status Syndrome: How Social Standing Affects Our Health and Longevity*. New York: Henry Holt.

Marmot, Michael G. 2017. Amartya Sen Lecture: Capabilities, human flourishing and the health gap. *Journal of Human Development and Capabilities*, 18: 370–83.

Marmot, Michael G.; George Davey Smith; Stephen Stansfeld; Chandra Patel; Fiona North; Jenny Head; Ian White; Eric Brunner; and Amanda Feeney. 1991. Health inequalities among British civil servants: the Whitehall II study. *The Lancet*: 337: 1387–93.

Marschak, Jacob and Roy Radner. 1972. *Economic Theory of Teams*. New Haven, CT: Yale University Press.

Marsden, Peter V. 1987. Core discussion networks of Americans. *American Sociological Review*, 52: 122–31.

Marshall, Gordon; Adam Swift; and Stephen Roberts. 1997. *Against the Odds? Social Class and Social Justice in Industrial Societies*. Oxford: Clarendon Press.

Marshall, Thomas H. 1963. A note on 'status'. Pp. 220–9 in Marshall, *Class, Citizenship and Social Development*. Chicago: University of Chicago Press.

Martimort, David. 1997. A theory of bureaucratization based on reciprocity and collusive behavior. *Scandinavian Journal of Economics*, 99: 555–79.

Martin, Annette. 2021. What is white ignorance? *Philosophical Quarterly*, 71: 864–85

Martin, Karin A. 2009. Normalizing heterosexuality: mothers' assumptions, talk and strategies with young children. *American Sociological Review*, 74: 190–207.

Marx, Karl. 1844a/1975. Comments on James Mill *Éléments D'économie Politique*, trans. Clemes Dutt. Vol. 3, pp. 211–28 in Marx and Friedrich Engels, *Collected Works*. New York: International Publishers, 1975. Available at <https://marxists.architexturez.net/archive/marx/works/1844/james-mill/index.htm>.

Marx, Karl. 1844b/1959. *Economic and Philosophic Manuscripts of 1844*, trans. Martin Milligan and Dirk J. Struik. Moscow: Progress Publishers, 1959. Available at <https://www.marxists.org/archive/marx/works/download/pdf/Economic-Philosophic-Manuscripts-1844.pdf>.

Marx, Karl. 1859/1904. *Introduction to the Critique of Political Economy*, trans. N.i. Stone. Chicago: Charles H. Kerr & Co, 1904. Available at https://www.gutenberg.org/files/46423/46423-h/46423-h.htm.

Marx, Karl. 1875/1972. *Critique of the Gotha Programme*. Pp. 382–98 in *The Marx-Engels Reader*, ed. Robert C. Tucker. New York: Norton, 1972.

Marx, Karl and Friedrich Engels. 1845/1972. *The German Ideology*. Pp. 110–65 in *The Marx-Engels Reader*, ed. Robert C. Tucker. New York: Norton, 1972; originally written 1845.

Massey, Douglas. 2008. *Categorically Unequal: The American Stratification System*. New York: Russell Sage Foundation.

Mazrui, Ali A. 1972. *Cultural Engineering and Nation-building in East Africa*. Evanston, IL: Northwestern University Press.

McClure, Emma and Regina Rini. 2020. Microaggression: conceptual and scientific issues. *Philosophy Compass*, 15 (#4): e12659.

McCrain, Joshua. 2018. Revolving door lobbyists and the value of Congressional staff connections. *Journal of Politics*, 80: 1369–83.

McEwen, Craig A. and Bruce S. McEwen. 2017. Social structure, adversity, toxic stress and intergenerational poverty: an early childhood model. *Annual Review of Sociology*, 43: 445–72.

McGeer, Victoria. 2007. The regulative dimension of folk psychology. Pp. 137–56 in *Folk Psychology Re-assessed*, ed. Daniel D. Hutto and Matthew Ratcliffe. Dordrecht: Springer.

McGregor, Jena. 2020. Average CEO earnings soared to $21.3 million last year and could rise again in 2020 despite the coronavirus recession. *Washington Post*, 18 August; available at <www.washingtonpost.com/business/2020/08/18;corporate-executive-pay-increase>.

McIntosh, Peggy. 1988. White privilege and male privilege: a personal account of coming to see correspondences through work in Women's Studies. Wellelsey, MA: Wellesley Centers for Women. Available at <nationalseedproject.org/images/documents/White_Privilege_and_Male_Privilege_Personal_Account-Peggy_McIntosh.pdf>.

McIntosh, Peggy. 1998. White privilege and male privilege. Working Paper 189. Wellesley, MA: Wellesley Centers for Women. Available at <http://www.collegeart.org/pdf/diversity/white-privilege-and-male-privilege.pdf>.

McKeown, Maeve. 2021. Structural injustice. *Philosophy Compass*, 16 (#7): e12757.

McPherson, Miller; Lynn Smith-Lovin; and James M Cook. 2001. Birds of a feather: homophily in social networks. *Annual Review of Sociology*, 27: 415–44.

McPherson, Miller; Lynne Smith-Lovin; and Matthew E. Brashears. 2006. Social isolation in America: changes in core discussion networks over two decades. *American Sociological Review*, 71: 353–75.

Mehrabi, Ninareh; Fred Morstatter; Nripsuta Saxena; Kristina Lerman; and Aran Galstyan. 2022. A survey on bias and fairness in machine learning. *ACM Computing Surveys*, 54 (#6): article 115. Available at <https://arxiv.org/pdf/1908.09635.pdf >.

Mehta, Judith; Chris Starmer; and Robert Sugden. 1994. The nature of salience: an experimental investigation. *American Economic Review*, 84: 658–73.

Melamed, David; Christopher W. Munn; Brent Simpson; Jered Z. Abernathy; Ashley Harrell; and Matthew Sweitzer. 2020. Homophily and segregation in cooperative networks. *American Journal of Sociology*, 125: 1084–127.

Mendelberg, Tali. 2001. *The Race Card: Campaign Strategy, Implicit Messages and the Norm of Equality*. Princeton, NJ: Princeton University Press.

Mendes, Kaitlynn. 2015. *SlutWalk: Feminism, Activism and Media*. Houndmills: Palgrave Macmillan.

Merton, Robert K. 1948. The self-fulfilling prophecy. *Antioch Review*, 8: 193–210. Reprinted pp. 475–92 in Merton, *Social Theory and Social Structure* (New York: Free Press, 1968).
Merton, Robert K. 1968. The Matthew effect in science. *Science*, 159 (#3810): 56–63.
Merton, Robert K. 1988. The Matthew effect in science, II: Cumulative advantage and the symbolism of intellectual property. *Isis*, 79: 606–23.
Metcalfe, Bob. 2013. Metcalfe's Law after 40 years of Ethernet. *Computer*, 46 (#12): 26–31.
Meyer, Marco. 2018a. The ethics of consumer credit: balancing wrongful inclusion and wrongful exclusion. *Midwest Studies in Philosophy*, 42: 294–313.
Meyer, Marco. 2018b. The right to credit. *Journal of Political Philosophy*, 26: 304–26.
Michelman, Frank I. 1967. Property, utility, and fairness: comments on the ethical foundations of 'just compensation' law. *Harvard Law Review* 80: 1165–258.
Michelman, Valerie; Joseph Price; and Seth D. Zimmerman. 2022. Old boys' clubs and upward mobility among the educational elite. *Quarterly Journal of Economics*, 137: 845–909.
Miles, David. 2022. The half life of economic injustice. *Economics & Philosophy*, 38: 71–107.
Mileti, Dennis S. and Paul W. O'Brien. 1992. Warnings during disaster: normalizing communicated risk. *Social Problems*, 39: 40–57.
Milgrom, Paul, and Roberts, John. 1982. Predation, reputation and entry deterrence. *Journal of Economic Theory*, 27: 280–312.
Milgrom, Paul R.; Douglass C. North; and Barry R. Weingast. 1990. The role of institutions in the revival of trade: the Law Merchant, private judges and the Champagne fairs. *Economics & Politics*, 2: 1–23.
Mill, John Stuart. 1848/1965. *Principles of Political Economy*. Vols 2–3 in John Stuart Mill, *The Collected Works of John Stuart Mill*, ed. John M. Robson. Toronto: University of Toronto Press, 1965.
Mill, John Stuart. 1859/1977. *On Liberty*. Vol. 18, pp. 212–310 in John Stuart Mill, *The Collected Works of John Stuart Mill*, ed. John M. Robson. Toronto: University of Toronto Press, 1861/1977.
Mill, John Stuart. 1861/1977. *Considerations on Representative Government*. Vol. 19, pp. 371–557 in *The Collected Works of John Stuart Mill*, ed. John M. Robson. Toronto: University of Toronto Press, 1977.
Mill, John Stuart. 1869/1984. *The Subjection of Women*. Vol. 21, pp. 259–340 in John Stuart Mill, *The Collected Works of John Stuart Mill*, ed. John M. Robson. Toronto: University of Toronto Press, 1984.
Miller, Greg. 2011. Social scientists wade into the tweet stream. *Science*, 333: 1814–5.
Mills, C. Wright. 1956. *The Power Elite*. New York: Oxford University Press.
Mills, Charles W. 1997. *The Racial Contract*. Ithaca, NY: Cornell University Press.
Mills, Charles W. 2007. White ignorance. Pp. 11–38 *in Race and Epistemologies of Ignorance*, ed. Shannon Sullivan and Nancy Tuana. Albany: State University of New York Press.
Mincer, Jacob A. 1974. *Schooling, Experience, and Earnings*. New York: Columbia University Press.
Mishel, Lawrence and Jori Kandra. 2021. CEO pay has skyrocketed 1,322% since 1978. Economic Policy Institute Report, 10 April. Available at <www.epi.org/publication/ceo-pay-in-2020/>.
Mitford, Nancy, ed. 1956. *Noblesse Oblige: An Inquiry into the Identifiable Characteristics of the English Aristocracy*. London: Hamish Hamilton.
Mittelstadt, Brent Daniel; Patrick Allo; Mariarosaria Taddeo; Sandra Wachter; and Luciano Floridi. 2016. The ethics of algorithms: mapping the debate. *Big Data and Society*, 3 (#2: 1 December): 1–21.

Moav, Omer and Zvika Neeman. 2012. Saving rates and poverty: the role of conspicuous consumption and human capital. *Economic Journal*, 122: 933–56.

Moffitt, Robert A. 2002. Welfare programs and labor supply. Vol. 3, pp. 2393–430 in *Handbook of Public Economics*, ed. Alan J. Auerbach and Martin Feinstein. Amsterdam: Elsevier.

Mohr, Richard; Francesco Contini; and Patrícia Branco. 2022. Norm, normal and disruption: introductory notes. *Oñati Socio-Legal Series*, 12: 414–23.

Monge, Peter R. and Noshir S. Contractor. 2003. *Theories of Communication Networks*. Oxford: Oxford University Press.

Montesquieu, Charles de Secondat, Baron de. 1748/1949. *Spirit of the Laws*, trans. Thomas Nugent. New York: Haefner; originally published 1748.

Montgomery, John D. 1991. Social networks and labor-market outcomes: toward an economic analysis. *American Economic Review*, 81: 1408–18.

Moore, Barrington Jr. 1985. Authority and inequality under capitalism and socialism. *Tanner Lectures on Human Values*. Available at: <https://tannerlectures.utah.edu/_resources/documents/a-to-z/m/moore86.pdf>.

Moore, G. E. 1903. *Principia Ethica*. Cambridge: Cambridge University Press.

Morrison, William and Dmitry Taubinsky. 2021. Rules of thumb and attention elasticities: evidence from under- and overreaction to taxes. *Review of Economics & Statistics*, forthcoming; doi.org/101162/rest.a.01126.

Morton, Jennifer M. 2010. Toward an ecological theory of the norms of practical deliberation. *European Journal of Philosophy*, 19: 561–84.

Morton, Jennifer M. 2014. Cultural code-switching: straddling the achievement gap. *Journal of Political Philosophy*, 22: 259–81.

Morton, Jennifer M. 2017. Reasoning under scarcity. *Australasian Journal of Philosophy*, 95: 543–59.

Morton, Jennifer M. 2022. Resisting pessimism traps: the limits of believing in oneself. *Philosophy & Phenomenological Research*, 104: 728–46.

Mosca, Manuela. 2008. On the origins of the concept of natural monopoly: economics of scale and competition. *European Journal of the History of Economic Thought*, 15: 317–53.

Muldoon, Ryan; Chiara Lisciandra; Cristina Bicchieri; Stephan Hartmann; and Jan Sprenger. 2014. On the emergence of descriptive norms. *Politics, Philosophy & Economics*, 13: 3–22.

Munshi, Kaivan. 2019. Caste and the Indian economy. *Journal of Economic Literature*, 57: 781–824.

Murphy, Colleen. 2017. *The Conceptual Foundations of Transitional Justice*. Cambridge: Cambridge University Press.

Muth, John F. 1961. Rational expectations and the theory of price movements. *Econometrica*, 29: 315–35.

Myrdal, Gunnar. 1944. *The American Dilemma*. New York: Harper and Row.

Nee, Victor. 1998. Norms and networks in economic and organizational performance. *American Economic Review (Papers and Proceedings)*, 88 (#2): 85-9.

Nefsky, Julia. 2017. How you can help, without making a difference. *Philosophical Studies*, 174: 2743–67.

Nelson, Richard and Sidney Winter. 1982. *An Evolutionary Theory of Economic Change*. Cambridge, MA: Harvard University Press.

Neuhäuser, Christian. 2014. Structural injustice and the distribution of forward-looking responsibility. *Midwest Studies in Philosophy*, 38: 232–51.

Neustadt, Richard E. 1960. *Presidential Power*. New York: Wiley.

Newman, Mark; Albert-László Barabási; and Duncan J. Watts, ed. 2006. *The Structure and Dynamics of Networks*. Princeton, NJ: Princeton University Press.

Nicholson, Michael. 1972. *Oligopoly and Conflict: A Dynamic Approach*. Liverpool: Liverpool University Press.

Nix, Emily and Nancy Qian. 2015. The fluidity of race: 'passing' in the United States, 1880-1940. Working Paper 20828. Cambridge, MA: National Bureau of Economic Research. Available at <https://www.nber.org/system/files/working_papers/w20828/w20828.pdf>.

Nozick, Robert. 1972. Coercion. Pp. 101–35 in *Philosophy, Politics and Society*, 4th series, ed. Peter Laslett, W. G. Runciman, and Quentin Skinner. Oxford: Blackwell.

Nozick, Robert. 1981. *Philosophical Explanations*. Cambridge, MA: Harvard University Press.

Nussbaum, Martha C. 2011. Forward. Pp. ix–xxv in Iris Marion Young, *Responsibility for Justice*. Oxford: Oxford University Press.

Nuti, Alasia. 2019. *Injustice and the Reproduction of History: Structural Inequalities, Gender and Redress*. Cambridge: Cambridge University Press.

O'Gorman, Hubert J. 1975. Pluralistic ignorance and white estimates of white support for racial segregation. *Public Opinion Quarterly*, 39: 312–30.

O'Neill, John and Martin O'Neill. 2012. Social justice and the future of flood insurance. York: Joseph Rowntree Foundation. Available at: https://www.jrf.org.uk/report/social-justice-and-future-flood-insurance.

Obama, Michelle. 2020. Address to the Class of 2020. *Washington Post*, 7 June 2020; available at <https://www.washingtonpost.com/opinions/2020/06/07/michelle-obama-graduates-dont-ever-ever-let-anyone-tell-you-that-youre-too-angry/?arc404=true>.

Obermeyer, Ziad; Brian Powers; Christine Vogeli; and Sendhil Mullainathan. 2019. Dissecting racial bias in an algorithm used to manage the health of populations. *Science*, 355: 447–53.

Offord, Derek and Lara Ryazanova-Clarke. 2015. *French and Russian in Imperial Russia*. Edinburgh: Edinburgh University Press.

Okun, Arthur. 1975. *Equality and Efficiency: The Big Tradeoff*. Washington, DC: Brookings Institution.

Olick, Jeffrey K. 1998. What does it mean to normalize the past? Official memory in German politics since 1989. *Social Science History*, 22: 547–71.

Olson, Mancur Jr. 1965. *The Logic of Collective Action*. Cambridge, MA: Harvard University Press.

Olson, Mancur Jr. 1993. Dictatorship, democracy and development. *American Political Science Review*, 87: 567–76.

Oppenheimer, David B. 1993. Negligent discrimination. *University of Pennsylvania Law Review*, 141: 899–972.

Organisation for Economic Co-operation and Development (OECD). 2009. Revolving doors, accountability and transparency – emerging regulatory concerns and policy solutions in the financial crisis. GOV/PGC/ETH(2009)2. Paris: OECD. Available at <http://www.oecd.org/officialdocuments/publicdisplaydocumentpdf/?cote=GOV/PGC/ETH(2009)2&docLanguage=En>.

Organisation for Economic Co-operation and Development (OECD). 2018a. *A Broken Social Elevator? How to Promote Social Mobility*. Paris: OECD.

Organisation for Economic Co-operation and Development (OECD). 2018b. Market Concentration. DAF/COMP/WD(2018)46. Paris: OECD.

Organisation for Economic Co-operation and Development (OECD). 2019. *Society at a Glance 2019*: *OECD Social Indicators*. Paris: OECD.
Origgi, Gloria. 2018. *Reputation: What It Is and Why It Matters*, trans. Stephen Holmes and Noga Arikha. Princeton, NJ: Princeton University Press.
Orwell, George. 1949. *Nineteen Eighty-four*. London: Secker & Warburg.
Orwell, George. 1946. Politics and the English language. *Horizon*, 13 (#76: April): 252–65. Reprinted vol. 3, pp. 1–38 in *The Collected Essays, Journalism and Letters of George Orwell*, ed. Sonia Orwell and Ian Angus. London: Secker & Warburg, 1968.
Ostrom, Elinor. 1990. *Governing the Commons: The Evolution of Institutions for Collective Action*. New York: Cambridge University Press.
Ovid. 8. *Fasti*. Available in English translation at <https://www.poetryintranslation.com/PITBR/Latin/Fastihome.php>
Oye, Kenneth A., ed. 1986. *Cooperation Under Anarchy*. Princeton, NJ: Princeton University Press.
Padgett, John F. and Christopher K. Ansell. 1993. Robust action and the rise of the Medici, 1400-1434. *American Journal of Sociology*, 98: 1259–319.
Page, Scott E. 2006. Path dependence. *Quarterly Journal of Political Science*, 1: 87–115.
Page, William H. 2009. The Gary dinners and the meaning of concerted action. *SMU Law Review*, 62: 597–620.
Paluck, Elizabeth Levy and Michael Suk-Young Chew. 2017. Confronting hate collectively. *PS: Political Science & Politics*, 50: 990–2.
Paluck, Elizabeth Levy; Hana Shepherd; and Peter M. Aronow. 2016. Changing climates of conflict: a social network experiment in 56 schools. *Proceedings of the National Academy of Sciences*, 113: 665–73.
Papageorge, Nicholas W.; Seth Gershenson; and Kyung Min Kang. 2020. Teacher expectations matter. *Review of Economics and Statistics*, 102: 234–51.
Parekh, Serena. 2011. Getting to the root of gender inequality: structural injustice and political responsibility. *Hypatia*, 26: 672–89.
Pareto, Vilfredo. 1906. *Manual of Political Economy*, trans. Ann S. Schwier. New York: Augustus M. Kelley, 1971.
Parfit, Derek. 1984. *Reasons and Persons*. Oxford: Clarendon Press.
Parker, Christine and Vibeke Lehmann Nielsen. 2017. Compliance: 14 questions. Pp. 271–32 in *Regulatory Theory: Foundations and Applications*, ed. Peter Drahos. Canberra: ANU Press.
Parsons, Talcott. 1952. *The Social System*. London: Tavistock.
Pascal, Blaise. 1670. *Pensées*, introduction by T. S. Eliot. New York: E. P. Dutton, 1958.
Pass, Glen; Abdur Chowdhury; and Cayley Torgeson. 2006. A picture of search. *INFOSCALE '06: Proceedings of the First International Conference on Scalable Information Systems*, 29 May–1 June, Hong Kong; available at <https://dl.acm.org/doi/10.1145/1146847.1146848>.
Pateman, Carole. 1988. *The Sexual Contract*. Cambridge: Polity Press.
Pateman, Carole and Charles W. Mills. 2007. *Contract and Domination*. Cambridge: Polity.
Patterson, Orlando. 1982. *Slavery and Social Death: A Comparative Study*. Cambridge, MA: Harvard University Press.
Peale, Norman Vincent. 1952. *The Power of Positive Thinking*. New York: Prentice-Hall.
Pearson, Noel. 2014. Noel Pearson's eulogy for Gough Whitlam in full. *Sydney Morning Herald*, 5 November. Available at <https://www.smh.com.au/opinion/noel-pearsons-eulogy-for-gough-whitlam-in-full-20141105-11haeu.html>.

Peppard, Alan. 2008. Oil in the family. *Vanity Fair*, June; available at <https://www.vanityfair.com/news/2008/06/hunt200806>.
Perc, Matjz. 2014. The Matthew effect in empirical data. *Journal of the Royal Society Interface*, 11: 20140378.
Persad, Govind. 2015. Equality via mobility: why socioeconomic mobility matters for relational equality, distributive equality and equality of opportunity. *Social Philosophy & Policy*, 31 (#2): 158–79.
Petersen, Trond. 2009. Opportunities. Pp. 115–39 in *Oxford Handbook of Analytical Sociology*, ed. Peter Hedström and Peter Bearman. Oxford: Oxford University Press.
Peterson, Martin and Andreas Spahn. 2011. Can technological artefacts be moral agents? *Science and Engineering Ethics*, 17: 411–24.
Pew Research Center. 2014. Political polarization in the American public: how increasing ideological uniformity and partisan antipathy affects politics, comprises and everyday life. Available at <https://www.people-press.org/2014/06/12/political-polarization-in-the-american-public/>.
Phelps, Edmund S. 1972. The statistical theory of racism and sexism. *American Economic Review*, 62: 659–61.
Phillips, Damon J. and Ezra W. Zuckerman. 2001. Middle-status conformity: theoretical restatement and empirical demonstration in two markets. *American Journal of Sociology*, 107: 379–429.
Pierce, Chester. 1970. Offensive mechanisms. Pp. 265–82 in *The Black Seventies*, ed. Floyd B. Barbour. Boston: Porter Sargent.
Pierson, Paul. 2000. Path dependence, increasing returns, and the study of politics. *American Political Science Review*, 94: 251–67.
Pigou, Arthur C. 1932. *The Economics of Welfare*. 4th edn. London: Macmillan.
Piketty, Thomas. 2003. Income inequality in France, 1901-1998. *Journal of Political Economy*, 111: 1004–42.
Piketty, Thomas. 2020. *Capital and Ideology*. Cambridge, MA: Harvard University Press.
Piketty, Thomas and Emmanuel Saez. 2003. Income inequality in the United States, 1913-1998. *Quarterly Journal of Economics*, 118: 1–41.
Piketty, Thomas and Emmanuel Saez. 2014. Inequality in the long run. *Science*, 344: 838–43.
Piketty, Thomas; Emmanuel Saez; and Gabriel Zucman. 2018. Distributional national accounts: methods and estimates for the United States. *Quarterly Journal of Economics*, 133: 553–609.
Piper, Adrian. 1996. Passing for white, passing for black. Pp. 234–69 in *Passing and the Fictions of Identity*, ed. Elaine K. Ginsberg. Durham, NC: Duke University Press.
Piven, Frances Fox and Richard Cloward. 1979. *Poor People's Movements*. New York: Vintage.
Pocock, John G. A. 1957. *The Ancient Constitution and the Feudal Law*. Cambridge: Cambridge University Press.
Pocock, John G. A. 1971. *Politics, Language and Time*. New York: Atheneum.
Podolny, Joel M. 1993. A status-based model of market competition. *American Journal of Sociology*, 98: 829–72.
Podolny, Joel M. and Freda Lynn. 2009. Status. Pp. 498–520 in *Oxford Handbook of Analytical Sociology*, ed. Peter Hedström and Peter Bearman. Oxford: Oxford University Press.
Podosky, Paul-Mikhail Catapang. 2021. Privileged groups and obligation: engineering bad concepts. *Journal of Applied Philosophy*, 38: 7–22.

Podosky, Paul-Mikhail Catapang. 2022. Can conceptual engineering promote social justice? *Synthese*, 200 (#2): article 160.
Polanyi, Karl; Conrad M. Arensberg; and Harry W. Pearson, eds. 1957. *Trade and Market in Early Empires: Essays in History and Theory*. New York: Free Press.
Pool, Ithiel de Sola and Manfred Kochen. 1978/ 1979. Contacts and influence. *Social Networks*, 1: 5–51.
Posner, Eric A. and E. Glen Weyl. 2018. *Radical Markets*. Princeton, NJ: Princeton University Press.
Powell, Walter W. 1990. Neither market nor hierarchy: network forms of organization. *Research in Organizational Behavior*, 12: 295–6, 303–4.
Prentice, Deborah and Dale T. Miller. 1993. Pluralistic ignorance and alcohol use on campus: some consequences of misperceiving the social norm. *Journal of Personality and Social Psychology*, 62: 243–56.
Prosser, William and J. W. Wade. 1979. *Restatement (Second) of the Law of Torts*. 4th ed. St. Paul, MN: West, for the American Law Institute.
Pruijt, Hans. 2003. Teams between neo-Taylorism and anti-Taylorism. *Economic and Industrial Democracy*, 24: 77–101.
Przeworski, Adam. 2009. Conquered or granted? A history of suffrage extensions. *British Journal of Political Science*, 39: 291–321.
Radner, Roy. 1975. Satisficing. *Journal of Mathematical Economics*, 2: 253–62.
RAND Corporation. 2020. Paul Baran and the origins of the internet. Available at <https://www.rand.org/about/history/baran.list.html>.
Ransom, Roger L. and Sutch, Richard. 1977. *One Kind of Freedom: The Economic Consequences of Emancipation*. Cambridge: Cambridge University Press.
Rao, Hayagreeva. 1994. The social construction of reputation: certification contests, legitimation and the survival of organizations in the American automobile industry: 1895-1912. *Strategic Management Journal*, 15 (Winter Special Issue): 29–44.
Rawls, John. 1971. *A Theory of Justice*. Cambridge, MA: Harvard University Press.
Reeves, Aaron; Sam Friedman; Charles Rahal; and Magne Flemmen. 2017. The decline and persistence of the old boy: private schools and elite recruitment 1897 to 2016. *American Sociological Review*, 82: 1139–66.
Reiman, Jeffrey. 1989. *Justice and Modern Moral Philosophy*. New Haven, CT: Yale University Press.
Reiman, Jeffrey. 2012. The structure of structural injustice: thoughts on Iris Marion Young's *Responsibility for Justice*. *Social Theory and Practice*, 38: 738–51.
Reiman, Jeffrey. 2013. A moral equivalent of consent of the governed. *Ratio Juris*, 36: 358–77.
Reis, Ricardo. 2006. Inattentive consumers. *Journal of Monetary Economics*, 53: 1761–1800.
Reskin, Barbara F. 2000. The proximate causes of employment discrimination. *Contemporary Sociology*, 29: 319–28.
Reskin, Barbara F. 2003. Presidential Address: Including mechanisms in our models of ascriptive inequality. *American Sociological Review*, 68: 1–21.
Reskin, Barbara F. and Debra B. McBrier. 2000. Why not ascription? Organizations' employment of male and female managers. *American Sociological Review*, 65: 210–33.
Richardson, George B. 1972. The organization of industry. *Economic Journal*, 82: 883–96.
Richardson, Rashida; Jason M. Schultz; and Kate Crawford. 2019. Dirty data, bad predictions: how civil rights violations impact police data, predictive policing systems, and justice. *New York University Law Review*, 94: 192–233.

Richman, Barak D. 2006. How community institutions create economic advantage: Jewish diamond merchants in New York. *Law & Social Inquiry*, 31: 383–420.
Richman, Barak D. 2017. An autopsy of cooperation: diamond dealers and the limits of trust-based exchange. *Journal of Legal Analysis*, 9: 247–83.
Ridgeway, Cecilia L. 2014. Why status matters for inequality. *American Sociological Review*, 79: 1–16.
Rigney, Daniel. 2010. *The Matthew Effect: How Advantage Begets Further Advantage*. New York: Columbia University Press.
Riley, Emma. 2018. Mobile money and risk sharing against village shocks. *Journal of Development Economics*, 135: 43–58.
Rilinger, Georg. 2021. Who captures whom? Regulatory misperceptions and the timing of cognitive capture. *Regulation & Governance*, forthcoming; doi-org.virtual.anu.edu.au/10.1111/rego.12438.
Ringen, Stein. 1988. Direct and indirect measures of poverty. *Journal of Social Policy*, 17: 351–65.
Rini, Regina. 2019. How to take offense: responding to microaggression. *Journal of the American Philosophical Association*, 4: 332–51.
Rivera, Lauren A. 2012. Hiring as cultural matching: the case of elite professional service firms. *American Sociological Review*, 77: 999–1022.
Rivera, Mark T.; Sara B. Sonderstrom; and Brian Uzzi. 2010. Dynamics of dyads in social networks: assortative, relational and proximity mechanisms. *Annual Review of Sociology*, 36: 91–115.
Robertson, Dennis. 1956. What does the economist economise? Pp. 147–54 in Robertson, *Economic Commentaries*. London: Staples.
Rokkan, Stein and Derek Urwin, eds. 1982. *The Politics of Territorial Identity*. London: SAGE.
Rona-Tas, Akos. 2017. The off-label use of consumer credit ratings. *Historical Social Research*, 42: 52–76.
Rose, Janus. 2020. This script sends junk data to Ohio's website for snitching on workers. *Motherboard*, 9 May; available at <https://www.vice.com/en_us/article/wxqemy/this-script-sends-junk-data-to-ohios-website-for-snitching-on-workers>.
Rose, Richard. 1971. *Governing Without Consensus*. London: Faber & Faber.
Rose-Ackerman, Susan. 1998. Bribes and gifts. Pp. 296–328 in *Economics, Values and Organization*, ed. Avner Ben-Ner and Louis Putterman. Cambridge: Cambridge University Press.
Rosenthal, Robert and Lenore Jacobson. 1968. *Pygmalion in the Classroom: Teacher Expectations and Pupils' Intellectual Development*. New York: Holt, Rinehart and Winston.
Rosola, Martina and Federico Cella. 2020. Generics and epistemic injustice. *Ethical Theory and Moral Practice*, 23: 739–54.
Ross, Alan S.C. 1956. U and Non-U – an essay in sociological linguistics. Ch. 2 in *Noblesse Oblige*, ed. Nancy Mitford. London: Hamish Hamilton.
Ross, Edward Alsworth. 1897. Social control, IV: suggestion. *American Journal of Sociology*, 2: 255–63. New York: Macmillan. Reprinted in Ross 1901, pp. 146–95.
Ross, Edward Alsworth. 1901. *Social Control*. New York: Macmillan.
Roszak, Theodore. 1970. *The Making of a Counter Culture: Reflections on the Technocratic Society and Its Youthful Opposition*. London: Faber.
Rothman, Joshua. 2014. The origins of 'privilege'. *New Yorker*, 12 May; available at < www.newyorker.com/books/page-turner/the-origins-of-privilege>.

Rothstein, Richard. 2017. *The Color of Law: A Forgotten History of How Our Government Segregated America*. New York: Liveright/Norton.

Rousseau, Jean-Jacques. 1755/1973. *A Discourse on the Origin of Inequality*. Pp. 27–114 in *The Social Contract and Discourses*, trans. G. D. H. Cole. New ed. London: Everyman/Dent, 1973.

Rousseau, Jean-Jacques. 1762/1973. *The Social Contract*. Pp. 164–278 in *The Social Contract and Discourses*, trans. G. D. H. Cole. New ed. London: Everyman/Dent, 1973.

Roy, William G. 1997. *Socializing Capital: The Rise of the Large Industrial Corporation in America*. Princeton, NJ: Princeton University Press.

Royster, Deirdre A. 2003. *Race and the Invisible Hand: How White Networks Exclude Black Men from Blue-collar Jobs*. Berkeley: University of California Press.

Ruggie, John G. 2008. Corporations and human rights: a survey of the scope and patterns of alleged corporate-related human rights abuse. Report of the Special Representative of the UN Secretary-General on Business & Human Rights. UN Document A/HRC/8/5/Add.2, 23 May 2008. Available at < http://daccess-ods.un.org/TMP/2290393.85914803.html >.

Rydgren, Jens. 2009. Beliefs. Pp. 72–94 in *Oxford Handbook of Analytical Sociology*, ed. Peter Hedström and Peter Bearman. Oxford: Oxford University Press.

Ryle, Gilbert. 1931–1932. Systematically misleading expressions. *Proceedings of the Aristotelian Society*, 32: 139–70.

Saatcioglu, Argun and Thomas M. Skrtic. 2019. Categorization by organizations: manipulation of disability categories in a racially desegregated school district. *American Journal of Sociology*, 125: 184–260.

Salisbury, Robert H.; Paul Johnson; John P. Heinz; Edward O. Laumann; and Robert L. Nelson. 1989. Who you know versus what you know: the uses of government experience for Washington lobbyists. *American Journal of Political Science*, 33: 175–95.

Salmond, Anne. 1975. Mana makes the man: a look at Maori oratory and politics. Pp. 45–63 in *Political Language and Oratory in Traditional Society*, ed. Maurice Bloch. London: Academic Press.

Samuelson, Paul A. 1954. The pure theory of public expenditure. *Review of Economics and Statistics*, 36: 387–89.

Sandel, Michael. 2012. *What Money Can't Buy: The Moral Limits of Markets*. New York: Farrar, Straus and Giroux.

Sangiovanni, Andrea. 2018. Structural injustice and individual responsibility. *Journal of Social Philosophy*, 49: 461–83.

Sankaran, Kirun. 2021. 'Structural injustice' as an analytical tool. *Philosophy Compass*, 16 (#10): e12780.

Sartori, Giovanni. 1975. *The Tower of Babel*. Pittsburgh, PA: International Studies Association.

Satz, Debra. 2010. *Why Some Things Should Not Be for Sale: The Moral Limits of Markets*. Oxford: Oxford University Press.

Sauder, Michael; Freda Lynn; and Joel M. Podolny. 2012. Status: insights from organizational sociology. *Annual Review of Sociology*, 38: 267–83.

Saul, Jennifer, 2018. Dogwhistles, political manipulation and philosophy of language. Ch. 13 in *New Work on Speech Acts*, ed. Daniel Fogal, Daniel W. Harris, and Matt Moss. Oxford: Oxford University Press.

Say, Jean-Baptiste. 1821. *A Treatise on Political Economy*, trans. C. R. Prinsep. London: Longman, Hurst, Rees, Orme and Brown.

Schattschneider, E. E. 1960. *The Semisovereign People: A Realist's View of Democracy in America*. New York: Harcourt Brace.

Schauer, Frederick. 2003. *Profiles, Probabilities and Stereotypes.* Cambridge, MA: Harvard University Press.

Scheidel, Walter. 2017. *The Great Leveller: Violence and the History of Inequality from the Stone Age to the Twenty-First Century.* Princeton, NJ: Princeton University Press.

Schelling, Thomas C. 1958. Re-interpretation of the solution concept for 'non-cooperative' games. P-1385. Santa Monica, CA: RAND Corporation. Available at: <https://www.rand.org/content/dam/rand/pubs/papers/2006/P1385.pdf>.

Schelling, Thomas C. 1960. *The Strategy of Conflict.* Cambridge, MA: Harvard University Press.

Schelling, Thomas C. 1971. Dynamic models of segregation. *Journal of Mathematical Sociology,* 1: 143–86.

Schelling, Thomas C. 1978. *Micromotives and Macrobehavior.* New York: Norton.

Schelling, Thomas C. 1998. Social mechanisms and social dynamics. Pp. 32–44 in *Social Mechanisms: An Analytical Approach to Social Theory,* ed. Peter Hedström and Richard Swedberg. Cambridge: Cambridge University Press.

Scheuer, Florian and Joel Slemrod. 2020. Taxation and the superrich. *Annual Review of Economics,* 12: 189–211.

Schilke, Oliver and Gabriel Rossman. 2018. It's only wrong if it's transactional: moral perceptions of obfuscated exchange. *American Sociological Review,* 83: 1079–107.

Schlesinger, Arthur M. 1946/1968. *Learning How to Behave: A Historical Study of American Etiquette Books.* New York: Macmillan. Reprinted New York: Cooper Square Publishers, 1968.

Schlesinger, Arthur M. Jr. 1958. *The Coming of the New Deal.* Boston: Houghton Mifflin.

Schoeck, Helmut. 1969. *Envy,* trans. Der Neid. New York: Harcourt, Brace & World.

Schultze, Charles L. 1977. *The Public Use of Private Interest.* Washington, DC: Brookings Institution.

Schumpeter, Joseph A. 1950. *Capitalism, Socialism and Democracy.* 3rd edn. New York: Harper & Row.

Scitovsky, Tibor. 1971. *Welfare and Competition.* New edn. London: Allen & Unwin.

Scott, James C. 1986. *Weapons of the Weak: Everyday Forms of Peasant Resistance.* New Haven, CT: Yale University Press.

Scott, James C. 1998. *Seeing Like a State.* New Haven, CT: Yale University Press.

Seidman, Steven. 1997. *Difference Troubles: Queering Social Theory and Sexual Politics.* New York: Cambridge University Press.

Sen, Amartya. 1966. Labour allocation in a cooperative enterprise. *Review of Economic Studies,* 33: 361–71.

Sen, Amartya. 1977. Starvation and exchange entitlements: a general approach and its application to the Great Bengal Famine. *Cambridge Journal of Economics,* 1: 33–59.

Sen, Amartya. 1980. Equality of what? Vol. 1, pp. 196–220 in *Tanner Lectures on Human Values,* ed. Sterling McMurrin. Cambridge: Cambridge University Press.

Sen, Amartya. 1981. *Poverty and Famines.* Oxford: Clarendon Press.

Sen, Amartya. 1983. Poor, relatively speaking. *Oxford Economic Papers,* 35: 153–69.

Sen, Amartya. 1992. *Inequality Reexamined.* Oxford: Clarendon Press.

Senior, Jennifer. 2022. American Rasputin. *The Atlantic,* 6 June; available at <https://www.theatlantic.com/magazine/archive/2022/07/steve-bannon-war-room-democracy-threat/638443/>.

Sewell, William, Jr. 1992. A theory of structure: duality, agency and transformation. *American Journal of Sociology,* 98: 1–29.

Sewell, William, Jr. 2005. *Logics of History: Social Theory and Social Transformation.* Chicago: University of Chicago Press.
Shackle, G. L. S. 1943. The expectational dynamics of the individual. *Economica,* 10: 99–129.
Shagan, Ethan H. 2017. The emergence of the Church of England, c. 1520 to 1553. Vol. 1, pp. 28–44 in *The Oxford History of Anglicanism,* ed. Anthony Milton. Oxford: Oxford University Press.
Shapiro, Carl and Hal R. Varian. 1999. *Information Rules: A Strategic Guide to the Network Economy.* Boston: Harvard Business School Press.
Shaw, George Bernard. 1913. *Pygmalion.* Pp. 716–57 in *The Complete Plays of Bernard Shaw.* London: Odhams, 1934.
Shaw, George Bernard. 1928. *The Apple Cart.* Pp. 1009–43 in *The Complete Plays of Bernard Shaw.* London: Odhams Press, 1934.
Shaw-Lefevre, George. 1892. Plural Voting (Abolition) Bill (No. 42), Second Reading. *Hansard Parliamentary Debates (House of Commons),* 18 May, cols 1181-94.
Sherman, Nancy 2005. Of manners and morals. *British Journal of Educational Studies,* 53: 272–89.
Shiller, Robert J. 2019. *Narrative Economics.* Princeton, NJ: Princeton University Press.
Shubik, Martin. 1971. Games of status. *Behavioral Science,* 16: 117–29.
Siegel, Susanna. 2022. Salience principles for democracy. Pp. 235–66 in *Salience,* ed. Sophie Archer. New York: Routledge.
Silvermint, Daniel. 2018. Passing as privileged. *Ergo,* 5: 1–43.
Simcoe Timothy S. and Dave M. Waguespack. 2011. Status, quality, and attention: what's in a (missing) name? *Management Science,* 57: 274–90.
Simmel, Georg. 1922/1955. *The Web of Group Affiliations.* Pp. 125–95 in Simmel, *Conflict and the Web of Group Affiliations,* trans. Kurt H. Wolff and Reinhard Bendix. Glencoe, IL: Free Press, 1955; originally published 1922.
Simon, Herbert A. 1951. A formal theory of the employment relationship. *Econometrica,* 19: 293–305.
Simon, Herbert A. 1955. On a class of skew distribution functions. *Biometrika,* 42: 425–40.
Simon, Herbert A. 1957. *Models of Man.* New York: Wiley.
Simon, Herbert A. 1960/1977. *The New Science of Management Decision.* Rev. ed. Englewood Cliffs NJ: Prentice-Hall, 1977; originally published 1960.
Simon, Herbert A. 1969. *The Science of the Artificial,* 2nd edn. Cambridge, MA: MIT Press.
Simon, Herbert A. 1971. Designing organizations for an information-rich world. Pp. 37–72 in *Computers, Communication, and the Public Interest,* ed. Martin Greenberger. Baltimore, MD: Johns Hopkins Press.
Simon, Herbert A. 1982. *Models of Bounded Rationality.* 2 vols. Cambridge, MA: MIT Press.
Simon, Herbert A. 1985. Human nature in politics: the dialogue of psychology and political science [James Madison Lecture]. *American Political Science Review,* 79: 293–304.
Simon, Herbert A. 1991. Organizations and markets. *Journal of Economic Perspectives,* 5 (#2): 25–44.
Simon, Herbert A. 1999. The potlatch between economics and political science. Pp. 112–9 in *Competition and Cooperation: Conversations with Nobelists about Economics and Political Science,* ed. James Alt, Margaret Levi, and Elinor Ostrom. New York: Russell Sage Foundation Press.
Simon, Herbert A. 2000. Public administration in today's world of organizations and markets. *PS: Political Science & Politics,* 33: 749–56.

Simon, Herbert A. and Albert Ando. 1961. Aggregation of variables in dynamic systems. *Econometrica*, 29: 111–38.
Simpson, Richard L. 1959. Vertical and horizontal communication in formal organizations. *Administrative Science Quarterly*, 4: 88–96.
Sims, Christopher A. 2003. Implications of rational inattention. *Journal of Monetary Economics*, 50: 665–90.
Sinclair, Upton. 1906. *The Jungle*. New York: Doubleday.
Skyrms, Brian. 2001. The stag hunt. *Proceedings and Addresses of the American Philosophical Association*, 75 (#2): 31–41.
Skyrms, Brian. 2004. *The Stag Hunt and the Evolution of Social Structure*. Cambridge: Cambridge University Press.
Smith, Adam. 1776/1904. *The Wealth of Nations*, ed. Edwin Cannan. London: Methuen, 1904; originally published 1776.
Smith, Dinita. 1998. 'Queer theory' is entering the literary mainstream. *New York Times*, 17 Jan.; available at <https://www.nytimes.com/1998/01/17/books/queer-theory-is-entering-the-literary-mainstream.html>.
Smith, Holly. 1983. Culpable ignorance. *Philosophical Review*, 92: 543–71.
Smith, Leonie and Alfred Archer. 2020. Epistemic injustice and the attention economy. *Ethical Theory and Moral Practice*, 23: 777–95.
Smith, Olivia. 1984. *The Politics of Language, 1791-1819*. Oxford: Clarendon Press.
Smyth, Nicholas. 2021. Structural injustice and the emotions. *Res Publica*, 27: 577–92.
Solnick, Sara J. and David Hemenway. 2005. Are positional concerns stronger in some domains than in others? *American Economic Review (Papers & Proceedings)*, 95 (#2): 147–51.
Song, Seunghyun. 2022. Superseding structural linguistic injustice? Language revitalization and historically-sensitive dignity-based claims. *Critical Review of International Social and Political Philosophy*, 25: 347–63.
Sørensen, Aage B. 1979. A model and a metric for the process of status attainment. *American Journal of Sociology*, 85: 361–84.
Sørensen, Aage B. 1996. The structural basis of social inequality. *American Journal of Sociology*, 101: 1333–65.
Sparrow, Robert. 2021. How robots have politics. Ch. 10 in *Oxford Handbook of Digital Ethics*, ed. Carissa Véliz. Oxford: Oxford University Press.
Spender, Dale. 1985. *Man Made Language*. 2nd edn. Boston: Routledge & Kegan Paul.
Spiekermann, Kai. 2007. Translucency, assortation and information pooling: how groups solve social dilemmas. *Politics, Philosophy & Economics*, 6: 285–306.
Spiekermann, Kai. 2009. Sort out your neighbourhood: public good games on dynamic networks. *Synthese*, 168: 273–94.
Spiekermann, Kai; Adam Slavny; David V. Axelsen; and Holly Lawford-Smith. 2021. Big data justice: a case for regulating the global information commons. *Journal of Politics*, 83: 577–88.
Spinner-Halev, Jeff. 2012. *Enduring Injustice*. Cambridge: Cambridge University Press.
Sraffa, Piero. 1926. The law of returns under competitive conditions. *Economic Journal*, 36: 535–50.
Srinivas, M. N. 1956. A note on Sanskritization and westernization. *Far Eastern Quarterly*, 15: 481–96.
Stalnaker, Robert. 1973. Presuppositions. *Journal of Philosophical Logic*, 2: 447–57.
Stalnaker, Robert. 1999. *Context and Content*. Oxford: Clarendon Press.
Stalnaker, Robert. 2002. Common ground. *Linguistics and Philosophy*, 25: 701–21.

Stamberg, Susan. 2005. Many Katrina flooded homes had no insurance. National Public Radio, 9 Sept.; available at <https://www.npr.org/templates/transcript/transcript.php?storyId=4838689>.
Stanley, Jason. 2015. *How Propaganda Works*. Princeton, NJ: Princeton University Press.
Stanovich, Keith E. 1986. Matthew effects in reading: some consequences of individual differences in the acquisition of literacy. *Reading Research Quarterly*, 21: 360–407. Reprinted in *Journal of Education*, 189 (2009): 23–55.
Steele, Claude M. 2010. *Whistling Vivaldi, and Other Clues to How Stereotypes Affect Us*. New York: Norton.
Steele, Claude M. and Joshua Aronson. 1995. Stereotype threat and the intellectual test performance of African Americans. *Journal of Personality and Social Psychology*, 69: 797–811.
Stigler, George. 1954. Economists play with blocs. *American Economic Review (Papers & Proceedings)*, 44 (#2): 7–14.
Stigler, George and Gary Becker. 1977. De gustibus non est explanandum. *American Economic Review*, 67: 76–90.
Stigler, George J. 1957. Perfect competition, historically contemplated. *Journal of Political Economy*, 65: 1–17.
Stinchcombe, Arthur L. 1990. *Information and Organizations*. Chicago: University of Chicago Press.
Stinchcombe, Arthur L. 1991. The conditions of fruitfulness of theorizing about mechanisms in social science. *Philosophy of the Social Sciences*, 21: 367–88.
Stinchcombe, Arthur L. 1998. Monopolistic competition as a mechanism: corporations, universities and nation-states in competitive fields. Pp. 267–305 in *Social Mechanisms: An Analytical Approach to Social Theory*, ed. Peter Hedström and Richard Swedberg. Cambridge: Cambridge University Press.
Stokke, Andreas. 2017. Conventional implicature, presupposition and lying. *Proceedings of the Aristotelian Society (Supplement)*, 91: 127–47.
Stokke, Andreas. 2018. *Lying and Insincerity*. Oxford: Oxford University Press.
Stone, Deborah A. 1993. The struggle for the soul of health insurance. *Journal of Health Politics, Policy and Law*, 18: 287–317.
Stone, Harlan. 1938. Opinion of the Supreme Court. *United States v. Carolene Products Co.* 304 US 144.
Stone, Lawrence, 1958. The inflation of honours 1558-1641. *Past and Present*, 14: 45–70.
Strachey, Lytton. 1915. Voltaire and Frederick the Great. Reprinted pp. 167–99 in *Books and Characters: French and English*. New York: Harcourt, Brace, 2022.
Strauss, Claudia and Naomi Quinn. 1997. *A Cognitive Theory of Cultural Meaning*. Cambridge: Cambridge University Press
Strickland, James M. 2020. The declining value of revolving-door lobbyists: evidence from the American states. *American Journal of Political Science*, 64: 67–81.
Stryker, Robin. 2001. Disparate impact and the quota debates: law, labor market sociology and equal employment policies. *Sociological Quarterly*, 42: 13–46.
Sugden, Robert. 2003. The logic of team reasoning. *Philosophical Explorations*, 6: 165–81.
Sumner, William Graham. 1934. *Folkways: A Study of the Sociological Importance of Usages, Manners, Customs, Mores and Morals*. Boston: Ginn and Company.
Swift, Adam. 2004. Would perfect mobility be perfect? *European Sociological Review*, 20: 1–11.
Tarrow, Sidney. 2013. *The Language of Contention: Revolutions in Words, 1688-2012*. New York: Cambridge University Press.

Taylor, Ashley E. 2015. Solidarity: obligations and expressions. *Journal of Political Philosophy*, 23: 128–45.
Taylor, Michael. 1987. *The Possibility of Cooperation*. Cambridge: Cambridge University Press.
Teubner, Gunther. 2002. Hybrid laws: contitutionalizing private governance networks. Pp. 311–31 in *Legality and Community*, ed. Robert Kagan and Kenneth Winston. Berkeley, CA: Berkeley Public Policy Press.
Tharoor, Ishaan. 2014. Why Turkey's president wants to revive the language of the Ottoman Empire. *Washington Post*, 12 Dec.; available at <https://www.washingtonpost.com/news/worldviews/wp/2014/12/12/why-turkeys-president-wants-to-revive-the-language-of-the-ottoman-empire/?utm_term=.81dd66f186c0>.
Thévnot, Laurent. 2016. From social coding to economics of convention: a thirty-year perspective on the analysis of qualification and quantification investments. *Historical Social Research*, 41 (#2): 96–117.
Thierry, Guillaume; Panos Athanasopoulos; Alison Wiggett; Benjamin Dering; and Jan-Rouke Kuipers. 2009. Unconscious effects of language-specific terminology on preattentive color perception. *Proceedings of the National Academy of Sciences*, 106: 4567–70.
Thomas, William I. 1921/1966. Social types: immigrant roles. Reprinted pp. 182–91 in W. I. Thomas, *On Social Organization and Social Personality*, ed. Morris Janowitz. Chicago: University of Chicago Press, 1966.
Thomas, William I. and Dorothy S. Thomas. 1928. *The Child in America: Behavior Problems and Programs*. New York: Knopf.
Thompson, E. P. 1966. *The Making of the English Working Class*. New York: Vintage/Random House.
Tilcsik, András. 2021. Statistical discrimination and the rationalization of stereotypes. *American Sociological Review*, 86: 93–122.
Tilly, Charles. 1998. *Durable Inequality*. Berkeley: University of California Press.
Tilly, Charles. 2001. Mechanisms in political processes. *Annual Review of Political Science*, 4: 21–41.
Tilly, Charles and Robert E. Goodin. 2006. It depends. Pp. 3–32 in *Oxford Handbook of Contextual Political Analysis*, ed. Goodin and Tilly. Oxford: Oxford University Press.
Tilly, Charles and Sidney Tarrow. 2015. *Contentious Politics*. Oxford: Oxford University Press.
Timmermans, Stefan and Steven Epstein. 2010. A world of standards but not a standard world: toward a sociology of standards and standardization. *Annual Review of Sociology*, 36: 69–89.
Tirole, Jean. 1992. Collusion and the theory of organizations. Vol. 2, pp. 151–206 in *Advances in Economic Theory*, ed. Jean-Jacques Laffont. Cambridge: Cambridge University Press.
Titmuss, Richard M. 1973. *The Gift Relationship*. Harmondsworth: Penguin.
Tobin, James. 1970. On limiting the domain of inequality. *Journal of Law and Economics*, 13: 263–78.
Tocqueville, Alexis de. 1835/1966. *Democracy in America*, trans. George Lawrence, ed. J. P. Mayer and Max Lerner. New York: Harper & Row, 1966.
Toppino, Thomas C. 2003. Reversible-figure perception: mechanisms of intentional control. *Perception and Psychophysics*, 65: 1285–95.
Tran, Jasper. 2016. The right to attention. *Indiana Law Journal*, 91: 1023–62.
Trappenburg, Margo. 2003. Against segregation: ethnic mixing in liberal states. *Journal of Political Philosophy*, 11: 295–319.

Trumbull, Gunnar. 2012. *Strength in Numbers: The Political Power of Weak Interests*. Cambridge, MA: Harvard University Press.

Tsebelis, George. 2002. *Veto Players: How Political Institutions Work*. Princeton, NJ: Princeton University Press.

Tuck, Richard. 2016. Cartels and conspiracies. *Critical Review*, 28: 112–26.

Tuomela, Raimo. 2007. *The Philosophy of Sociality*. Oxford: Oxford University Press.

Tuomela, Raimo. 2013. *Social Ontology*. Oxford: Oxford University Press.

Turner, Bryan S. 1988. *Status*. Milton Keynes: Open University Press.

Ullmann-Margalit, Edna. 1977. *The Emergence of Norms*. Oxford: Clarendon Press.

Ullmann-Margalit, Edna and Sidney Morgenbesser. 1977. Picking and choosing. *Social Research*, 44: 757–85.

Urfalino, Philippe. 2014. The rule of non-opposition: opening up decision-making by consensus *Journal of Political Philosophy*, 22: 320–41.

US Federal Housing Administration. 1938. *Underwriting Manual: Underwriting and Valuation Procedure under Title II of the National Housing Act with Revisions to February 1938*. Washington, DC: Federal Housing Administration.

Useem, Michael. 2003. *The Inner Circle: Large Corporations and Business Politics in the US and UK*. New York: Oxford University Press.

Uslaner, Eric M. 2002. *The Moral Foundations of Trust*. Cambridge: Cambridge University Press.

Valentini, Jessica. 2011. SlutWalks and the future of feminism. *Washington Post*, 3 June; available at <https://www.washingtonpost.com/opinions/slutwalks-and-the-future-of-feminism/2011/06/01/AGjB9LIH_story.html>.

Van Parijs, Philippe. 2000. The ground floor of the world: on the socio-economic consequences of linguistic globalization. *International Political Science Review*, 21: 217–33.

Van Parijs, Philippe. 2004. Europe's linguistic challenge. *Archives Européennes de Sociologie*, 45: 113–54.

Van Parijs, Philippe. 2010. Linguistic justice and the territorial imperative. *CRISPP*, 13 (1: Mar): 181–202.

Van Parijs, Philippe. 2011. *Linguistic Justice for Europe and for the Rest of the World: The Rise of English as a Tool for Justice and a Source of Injustice*. Oxford: Oxford University Press.

van Wietmarschen, Han. 2021. What is social hierarchy? *Nous*. DOI.org/10.1111/nous.12387.

Veblen, Thorstein. 1899. *The Theory of the Leisure Class*. New York: Macmillan.

Velasco, Kristopher and Pamela Paxton. 2022. Deconstructed and constructive logics: explaining inclusive language change in queer nonprofits, 1998-2016. *American Journal of Sociology*, 127: 1267–310.

Verbeek, Peter-Paul. 2005. *What Things Do: Philosophical Reflections on Technology, Agency and Design*, trans. Robert P. Crease. University Park: Pennsylvania State University Press.

Viebahn, Emanuel. 2020. Lying with presuppositions. *Nous*, 54: 331–51.

Vrousalis, Nicholas. 2021. The capitalist cage: structural domination and collective agency in the market. *Journal of Applied Philosophy*, 38: 40–54.

Wagner, Peter. 1994. Dispute, uncertainty and institution in recent French debates. *Journal of Political Philosophy*, 2: 220–89.

Waldron, Jeremy. 1992. Superseding historic injustice. *Ethics*, 103: 4–28.

Walzer, Michael. 1983. *Spheres of Justice*. New York: Basic Books.

Wang, Jing. 2021. Between merchant network and memory work: Islamic cosmopolitanism along the Silk Road. *Asian Anthropology*, 20: 155–72.

Washington, George. 1775. Letter to Richard Henry Lee, 26 December 1775. Available at <https://founders.archives.gov/documents/Washington/03-02-02-0568>.
Washington, George. 1799. Letter to John Trumbull, 25 June 1799. Available at <https://founders.archives.gov/documents/Washington/06-04-02-0120>.
Washington, Marvin and Edward J. Zajac. 2005. Status evolution and competition: theory and evidence. *Academy of Management Journal*, 48: 82–296.
Wasow, Omar. 2020. Agenda seeding: how 1960s black protests moved elites, public opinion and voting. *American Political Science Review*, 114: 638–59.
Watzl, Sebastian. 2011a. The nature of attention. *Philosophy Compass*, 6: 842–53
Watzl, Sebastian. 2011b. The philosophical significance of attention. *Philosophy Compass*, 6: 722–33.
Weber, Eugen. 1976. *Peasants into Frenchmen: The Modernization of Rural France, 1870–1914*. Stanford, CA: Stanford University Press.
Weber, Max. 1922/1946. Class, status, party. Reprinted in Weber, *From Max Weber*, ed. H. H. Gerth and C. Wright Mills. Oxford: Oxford University Press, pp. 180–95; originally published 1922.
Weber, Max. 1946. *From Max Weber*, ed. H. H. Gerth and C. Wright Mills. Oxford: Oxford University Press.
Weber, Max. 1968. *Economy and Society*, ed. Guenther Roth and Claus Wittich. New York: Bedminster Press.
Wechsberg, Joseph. 1966. *The Merchant Bankers*. Boston: Little, Brown.
Weeden, Kim. 2002. Why do some occupations pay more than others? Social closure and earnings inequality in the United States. *American Journal of Sociology*, 108: 55–101.
Welch, Mary Scott. 1980. *Networking: The Great New Way for Women to Get Ahead*. New York: Harcourt Brace Jovanovich.
Wendt, Alexander E. 1987. The agent-structure problem in international relations theory. *International Organization*, 41: 335–70.
Wendt, Alexander E. 1999. *Social Theory of International Politics*. Cambridge: Cambridge University Press.
Western, Bruce; Deirdre Bloome; Benjamin Sosnaud; and Laura Tach. 2012. Economic insecurity and social stratification. *Annual Review of Sociology*, 38: 341–59.
White, Byron. 1991. Opinion of the US Supreme Court. *Arizona v. Fulminante*. 499 US 279.
White, Ismail K. and Chryl N. Laird. 2020. *Steadfast Democrats: How Social Forces Shape Black Political Behavior*. Princeton, NJ: Princeton University Press.
Whitworth, Joseph. 1841. A paper on an uniform system of screw threads. Ch. 2 in Whitworth, *Miscellaneous Papers on Mechanical Subjects*. London: Longman, Brown, Green, Longmans and Roberts, 1858. Available at <https://en.wikisource.org/wiki/Miscellaneous_Papers_on_Mechanical_Subjects>.
Whorf, Benjamin Lee. 1940/1956. Science and linguistics. Reprinted pp. 212–4 in *Language, Thought, and Reality*, ed. John B. Carroll. Cambridge, MA: Technology Press of Massachusetts Institute of Technology, 1956; originally published 1940.
Whyte, William Foote. 1943. *Street Corner Society*. Chicago: University of Chicago Press.
Wiedenbrüg, Anahí. 2021. Responsibility for financial crises. *American Journal of Political Science*, 65: 460–72.
Williams, Bernard. 1973. A critique of utilitarianism. Pp. 75–150 in J. J. C. Smart and Bernard Williams, *Utilitarianism, For and Against*. Cambridge: Cambridge University Press.
Williams, Bernard. 1981. *Moral Luck*. Cambridge: Cambridge University Press.

Williams, James. 2018. *Stand Out of Our Light: Freedom and Resistance in the Attention Economy.* Cambridge: Cambridge University Press.
Williamson, Oliver E. 1971. *Corporate Control and Business Behavior.* Englewood Cliffs, NJ: Prentice-Hall.
Williamson, Oliver E. 1975. *Markets and Hierarchies.* New York: Free Press.
Williamson, Oliver E. 1985. *The Economic Institutions of Capitalism: Firms, Markets, Relational Contracting.* New York: Free Press.
Wilson, Margery. 1937. *The New Etiquette: The Modern Code of Social Behavior.* New York: Frederick A. Stokes Co.
Wimmer, Andreas and Kevin Lewis. 2010. Beyond and below racial homophily: ERG models of a friendship network documented on Facebook. *American Journal of Sociology*, 116: 583–642.
Winner, Langdon. 1980. Do artifacts have politics? *Daedalus*, 109 (1: Winter): 121–36.
Wittgenstein, Ludwig. 1922. *Tractatus Logico-Philosophicus.* London: Kegan Paul.
Wolff, Jonathan and Avner de-Shalit. 2007. *Disadvantage.* Oxford: Oxford University Press.
Wollhiem, Richard. 1984. *The Thread of Life.* Cambridge: Cambridge University Press.
Woodward, C. Vann. 1955. *The Strange Career of Jim Crow.* New York: Oxford University Press.
World Bank. 2022. GDP growth (annual %) – Germany, United States 1961–2020. Available at: <https://data.worldbank.org/indicator/NY.GDP.MKTP.KD.ZG?locations=DE-US&name_desc=false>.
Wrong, Dennis H. 1968. Some problems in defining social power. *American Journal of Sociology*, 73: 673–81.
Wu, Tim. 2009. A brief history of telecommunications regulation. Vol. 5, pp. 95 ff. in *Oxford International Encyclopedia of Legal History*, ed. Stanley N. Katz. Oxford: Oxford University Press. Available at: <https://scholarship.law.columbia.edu/cgi/viewcontent.cgi?article=2462&context=faculty_scholarship>.
Wu, Tim. 2016. *The Attention Seekers.* New York: Knopf.
Wu, Tim. 2019. Blind spot: the attention economy and the law. *Antitrust Law Journal*, 82: 771–806.
Yang, Yang; Nitesh V. Chawla; and Brian Uzzi. 2019. A network's gender composition and communication pattern predict women's leadership success. *Proceedings of the National Academy of Science*, 116: 2033–8.
Young, H. Peyton. 1993. The evolution of conventions. *Econometrica*, 61: 57–84.
Young, Iris Marion. 1980. Socialist feminism and the limits of dual systems theory. *Socialist Review*, 51 (#51): 169–88.
Young, Iris Marion. 1990. *Justice and the Politics of Difference.* Princeton, NJ: Princeton University Press.
Young, Iris Marion. 2000. *Inclusion and Democracy.* Oxford: Oxford University Press.
Young, Iris Marion. 2006a. Katrina: too much blame, not enough responsibility. *Dissent* 53 (#1): 41–6.
Young, Iris Marion. 2006b. Taking the basic structure seriously. *Perspectives on Politics*, 4: 91–7.
Young, Iris Marion. 2011. *Responsibility for Justice.* Oxford: Oxford University Press.
Young, Iris Marion. 2012. Structural injustice and the politics of difference. Ch. 4 in *Social Justice and Public Policy: Seeking Fairness in Diverse Societies*, ed. Gary Craig, Tania Burchardt, and David Gordon. Bristol: Policy Press.

Yule, G. Udny. 1925. A mathematical theory of evolution, based on the conclusions of Dr. J. C. Willis, F. R. S. *Philosophical Transactions of the Royal Society of London, Series B*, 213: 21–87.

Zhang, Letian. 2021. Shaking things up: disruptive events and inequality. *American Journal of Sociology*, 127: 376–440.

Zheng, Robin. 2018a. Bias, structure and injustice: a reply to Haslanger. *Feminist Philosophical Quarterly*, 4 (#1): article 4.

Zheng, Robin. 2018b. What is my role in changing the system? A new model of responsibility for structural injustice. *Ethical Theory and Moral Practice*, 21: 869–85.

Zipf, George Kingsley. 1949. *Human Behavior and the Principle of Least Effort*. Reading, MA: Addison-Wesley.

Zucker, Linda G. 1986. Production of trust: institutional sources of economic structure, 1840-1920. *Research in Organizational Behavior*, 8: 53–111.

Zuckerman, Harriet. 1977. *Scientific Elite: Nobel Laureates in the United States*. New York: Free Press.

Index

Note: The following abbreviations have been used: 'f' indicates a figure; 'n' indicates a footnote.

A

Aaronson, Daniel 136n16
absolute advantage 14n62, 15, 16, 22n3, 26n17, 174n2
'absorbing Markov chains' 26n23, 55
Acemoglu, Daron 66n69
'achieved status' 39n14
activism *see* collective power/action
actuaries and actuarially-fair insurance 27n28, 87, 88n103, 98n18–20, 99n27, 115
Advanced Research Projects Agency (Defense Department) (United States) 145n63
advantage 1, 3, 5, 8, 9n44, 35, 68, 174n2
　attention scarcity 171n49–50, 172–3
　definition of 14n62
　expansion of 21, 25, 26n17, 26n19–22, 27n26, 27n28–9, 28, 29n33, 37n2
　general focus on 10n45, 11n47–9, 12n50, 12n52, 12n54, 13n57–9, 14
　initial advantage 12–13
　intergenerational transmission 16–18, 11n46, 31
　interrupting 51–3, 92–4, 174–98 *see also* amelioration strategies
　recreating of 31n41, 32n46, 33n48, 33n50, 37n2
　reducing differential advantages conferred 184, 185n42, 186n49–50, 186n53
　regulating processes 192n73, 196
　replication of 21, 29, 30n36–7, 31, 37n2
　responses to structural injustice 175n3–4, 176n10–12, 177n13, 177n16–17, 178, 179
　retaining advantage 21, 22n3, 23n5–9, 24n10, 25n14, 25n16, 28, 37n2
　types of 14–16
　unjust advantage 4, 10n45, 11n48
　see also coordination and organization; language; networks; position; reputation; social expectations and norms
'adverse possession' 14
aesthetic sensibilities 39
Afro-Americans 23n8, 102n38, *see also* black people, race
agency and agents 2, 3, 16, 91n121, 151
　social expectations and norms 113n90, 114n94, 114n99
　structures and 5n21, 6n22–3, 6n25–6, 7n28, 7n31, 8n35–6, 9n40–1, 9n43–4, 10
　temporally extended 113–4
Akerlof, George 129n62
algorithms 168, 169n38–40, 170, 171, 172, 183n41
Alinsky, Saul 176
Alkire, Sabina 131n4
Allport, Gordon 85n81
'altered' characteristics 24n10
amelioration strategies 187n54, 187n56–8, 188n59–60
　provision of alternatives 192, 193n76, 194n79–81, 195n83–4, 195n86, 197
　regulation of processes 192n73
　responsibility for remedying social injustice 195–7, 198n89
　'siphon off the benefits and redistribute them' strategy 188n61, 189n62, 190n68, 190n70, 191–2, 196, *see also* tax-and-transfer
American South 65, 66n67–70, 109, 138–9, 176
'ancestral positional advantage' 37n3
Anderson, Elizabeth 9n44

apartheid 112
Apple Cart, The (Shaw) 131
aristocracies 12n55, 32, 39n16, *see also* feudalism;
arms race
  attention-seeking 182
  educational 44
  see also positional goods
Arnold, Matthew 148n82
Arrow, Kenneth J. 63, 63–64n58
Arthur, Brian 161
Asch, Solomon 103
ascriptive characteristics 23n6, 24n10, 25, 30, 39n14, 129n62
'assortation' 129n60
Assurance Game 126, 133n8, 134f, 134n9, 136, 137, 139
Astell, Mary 95n3
'attention games' 44
attention scarcity 163n1, 164n2, 164n6–7, 165n13–14, 166n18–19, 167
  advantage and 171n49–50, 172–3, 180n29, 181, 183
  lessons from the internet 167n22, 167n25, 168n28, 169n34, 169n37–40, 170n43
authority 32, 40–1, 44n36, 45, 46, 48n57, 101n33, 138, 145, 155, *see also* social expectations and norms; status; status hierarchies
authoritarian advantage 40n23, 41, 43n26, 45, 46, 51
automobile industry 128
Azad, Bijan 187n57

B

'bandwagon' adoption models 100n30
Banfield, Edward C. 67n73
Bannon, Steve 180n29
Barnes, Elizabeth 93n133
Barry, Brian *xiii*
Barry, Christian *xiii*
'basic capabilities' model 14n63, 49n64
Basu, Kaushik 99n22
Becker, Gary 54n4, 157–8
Beck, Valentin 177n16
behavioural traits 129n62
Bentham, Jeremy 113n90, 114, 115n104
bequests 18, *see also* inheritance

Bergmann, Barbara R. 4n18
Bernstein, Basil 77n38, 78n43, 82n67
Besley, Timothy 110n80
'betweenness' 58n32
bias 27n28, 62n47, 69, 84, 85, 87n95, 88–90, 97n10, 163, 166167, 169, 170–72, 177, 180–1, 182–5, 193–4
  see also cognitive bias; discrimination; organizational bias; stereotypes
Blackburn, Simon 125n36
black people 1n4, 2n6, 27n28, 30, 94
  coding categories 85n86, 87n95
  labour markets 62n47, 63n54–5, 63n58
  position 40n21, 49n62
  see also Afro-Americans, race
blame 6, 8n36, 19n84, 20n85, 20n87,
  see also responsibility
Blau, Peter 39n15
Blum, Lawrence 183n40
Book of Common Prayer (Catechism) (Church of England) 40n17
Borzekowski, Ron 63n58
bottleneck short-term memory 164n6
'bottlenecks' (sociological) 18–19, 58n32
Bourdieu, Pierre 8n35, 31n41, 58n28, 68n77, 120
Bowles, Samuel 129n60
bribery 50–1
broadsheet newspapers 2
Brubaker, Rogers 75, 78, 79n46
brute force 41n26, 42, 43, 45, 47, 49
Bullingdon Club (Oxford University) 148n79
Bunyan, John 156
bureaucracies 2n5, 143n51, 166n19, 197, *see also* coordination and organization; heirarchies; institutions
Burt, Ronald S. 7n31, 58n32, 129n65
Bush, George W. 81

C

capitalist institutions 7n31, 13n55, 41, 51, 99n25, 147, 152n6, 194n80, *see also* market-style institutions
Carnival 95n5
'cascade' adoption models 100n30, *see also* information
caste 23n6, 31, 51, 54n5, 129n62
Catala, Amadine *xiii*

246 INDEX

categories *see* coding categories
'centrality' 58n29-31
chess players 166
Chicago Mercantile Exchange (CME) 126n46
Chilton, Adam S. 131n3
China 37n3, 39n16, 41, 52n77, 57, 59
'chokepoint power' 58n32-3, 59n35
City of London (stock exchange) 126n46
class 8n35, 11, 16, 31-2, 39, 52n77, 60, 77-9, 82, 84, 87n101, 101, 104n46, 105, 108, 146, 147
Class, Codes and Control (Bernstein) 78n43
Cloward, Richard 177n17
'clubbish justice' 130, 140
Code Noir (France) 109-10
coding categories 5, 17, 31, 35, 69, 93, 94, 95, 131-2, 171
 conferring advantage 81n62-3, 82n64-5, 82n67, 83n72, 84n75-6, 85n79-83, 85n85-6, 86n88, 86n93, 87n94-6, 87n98-101, 88n103
 interrupting advantage 183, 185, 192
 see also information; interpretive schema; language
coffeehouses (C18th) 2, 3
cognitive bias 89n114, 97n10
 coding categories 86, 87n94-5, 87n97
 interrupting advantage 183, 184, 185n42, 193, 194
'cognitive capture' 90n119
Coleman, James S. 129n60, 148, 163
collaborative corporate ventures 143n49, 144, 146
collective power/action 7n31, 93n133, 94n134
 interrupting advantage 177n16-17, 178, 179, 192n73, 196, 197, 198n89
command and control organization 142n43, 144n53, 146, 187
common sense 90n117
communism 51, 112
comparative advantage 14n62, 16, 18, 19n80, 22n3, 174n2
competitive advantage and resources 14-15, 28, 54, 151, 152n3

interrupting advantage 184, 187, 195n83-4
 position and 40, 42, 43n34-8, 44, 45n7, 47, 51, 52
 social expectations and norms 118, 119, 120n18, 121
'complex equality' 48
compound interest 152
conceptual mapping *xii*
'confidence-building measures' 158
conformism 103n41
Congress of Cardinals (Catholic Church) 42
Conley, Terri D. 90n120
constitutional rights 131n3
constitutive responsibility 20n85
'consumer boycotts' 177n16
consumerism 10, 190n70
'consumption resources' 14, 15n65-6, 42, 51, 54, 118, 119
 scale effects 151, 155n18, 156n20-1, 157n23-4, 158n27, 159n31-2, 162
contract law 135
conversational shorthand 79, 80n52
Cooperative Coordination Game 71f, 71n7, 72
coordination and organization 131n2-4, 132n6, 180
 biases of organization 146, 147n73-4, 148n78-9, 148n82
 formal/informal structures for 142n43, 143n44-5, 143n49, 143n51, 144n53, 145n60, 145n63, 146n66
 methods of coordination 135, 136n14-16, 137n17-18, 138, 139n25-6, 140n28, 140n31, 140n35, 141n36-8, 142
 varieties of coordination problems 132n7, 133f, 133n8, 134f, 134n9
Coordination Games 91
 language 70f, 71f, 71n4-5, 71n7, 72f, 72n8-9, 73n10
 varieties of coordination problems 132, 133f, 134f, 134n9, 135, 136, 137n18, 139n27
corporate networks 56n17, 57n22, 79n47
corporate rankings 128
'cosmic injustice' 7n28

cost-effective policy remedies 4
'countervailing power' 194n80
'courtly languages' 76–7
Crawford, Matthew B. 163n1
credit and debt markets 99n23–5
'credit ratings' 27n28, 99n23–4
Crenson, Matthew A. 119n11
Critique of the Gotha Programme (Marx) 188n60
Crowston, Kevin 132n7
Crusaders 52n77
cultural capital 8n35, 31n41
cultural codes 84–5
Cultural Revolution (China) 180
cultural systems 90n117
'cumulative advantage' 26n17–22, 27n26, 28n30

D

Dahl, Robert A. 142n43, 194n80
Dalton, Melville 143n51
Dasgupta, Partha 117n1
Davidson, Donald 82
debt peonage 2n6
decision-making 119n11, 141, 163, 164n2, 171, 182, 183
decomposable systems 145n60, 171n49, 182
defence 29n33
Defense Department (United States) 145n63
deference 39, 40n17, 41
'degradation ceremonies' 23n9
De Groot, Adriaan D. 166
de jure monopolies 153n13, 154
democracy 12, 41, 52, 168n28, 175n4
Democratic Party (United States) 102n38
descriptive norms and expectations 96, 97n10–13, 98n15, 98n18–20, 99n21–5, 99n27, 100n30, 101n32–3, 102n35–8, 103n41–2
    see also prescriptive norms and expectations
de-Shalit, Avner 14n63
'desire for status' 39n8
dialects 74, 75n22, 75n25
diamond exchanges 126, 129
'differentiated solidarity' 195
'disability' 93n133

disadvantage *xi*, *xii*, 1, 3, 5, 9n44, 14n63, 37, 49
    intergenerational transmission 16–18, 11n46
    labour markets 62n47, 63n54–5, 63n58, 64
    language and 78n41, 92n126
    modes of perpetuating advantage 25, 27n27, 29, 35
    networks 61, 62
    social expectations and norms 97, 99, 111
    see also advantage
Discourse on Inequality (Rousseau) 9
discrimination 19n84, 192
    gender 62, 78n42, 79, 110, 193n76, 194n79
    labour market 9n40, 62, 67
    perceptual 82n64, *see also* cognitive bias
    price 153n10, 194n80
    racial 27n28, 54n4, 62, 79n46, 87n95, 106–107, *see also* Jim Crow laws (American South)
    statistical 87, 97n10, 170n43, 183
    see also bias; stereotypes
disruption: structural injustice 175, 176n10–12, 177n13
distribution 188n60–1, 189n62, 190n68, 190n70, 191–2, 193
domestic abuse 98n20
double-dipping phenomenon 158
Duncan, Otis Dudley 39n15
Dwyer, Rachel E. 99n25

E

early-life developmental advantages 17–18, *see also* parents
economic markets 42, 51, 52n77, 83, 147–8, 163n1, 168
    scale effects 152n3–6, 152n9, 153n10, 153n12–13, 153n15, 154–5, 156n20–1
economic theory of teams 141n36
educational advantage 17, 27, 28n30, 86, 87, 98n15
    coordination and organization 148n78–9, 148n82

educational advantage (*Continued*)
  positional advantage 37n3, 39n16, 40n19, 40n21, 44, 51, 52
Eisenhower, Dwight 144
electoral competition 45, 186n53
Ellickson, Robert C. 140n31
Elster, Jon *xiii*
emancipation: slavery 2
'employment contracts' 39n14, 46, *see also* 'relational contracting'
end-use goods ('consumption resources') 43, 44, 45, 49, 54, 118, 119, 120
Engels, Friedrich 84n76
England 15n66, 32
English Acts of Apparel 52n77
English (language) 74, 76n30–31
English Statute of Monopolies (1624) 153n13
Equal Coordination Game 70f, 71n4–5, 72
essentialism 23
esteem 39, 97n12, 101n33, 121
ethnicity 1n4, 23, 27n27–8, 62, 136n14, 138–9
  language/coding categories/interpretive schema 78, 80–1, 85n86, 86
  social expectations and norms 96n6, 101, 105, 106–7
Eton 31, 148, *see also* segregation, educational; stratification
European Union 33
'evolution of pro-social norms' 129n60
'Expectation states theory' 97n10
exploitation 10, 85n83, 147n74, 168n28
'expressional solidarity' 94n134
external opportunities 151–2
  scale effects in consumption 155n18, 156n20–1, 157n23–4, 158n27, 159n31–2, 160
  scale effects in production 152n4–6, 152n9, 153n10, 153n12–13, 153n15, 154–5, 160, 162
  scale effects in valuation 159n33, 160n37, 160n39 161–2
  see also internal constraints

F
Facebook 58n27, 60n41, 153n10
fairness 12, 98n18, 98n20, 170n43
Falkinger, Josef 182n36
'false positives' 170
Falwell, Jerry 105
'family reputation' 17
'fault tree analysis' 83–4
Federal Home Loan Bank Board 136
Feld, Scott L. 123n27
Ferguson, Charles 77n38, 79n51
feudalism 9, 39, 48n57, 51, 108n67
financial advantage 32, 35, 73n10, 98n18–20, 99n21–5, 99n27, 152n3–6, 162
'financialized capitalism' 99n25
'first-mover advantage' 147
first-past-the-post (electoral system) 45
Fishkin, Joseph 48n58, 58n32
'flypaper' (sociological) 18–19
'focal points' theory 91n124, *see also* obvious solutions
formal coordination 135, 136n14–16, 137n17
formally organized competitive hierarchies 42, 47, 51
formal networks 68n77
Fortunato, Santo 169n38
France 15n66
Franklin, Benjamin 131n2
Fraser, Nancy 78n42
Frederick the Great (Prussia) 77
Freedom Riders 176
Freeman, Linton C. 58n32
free-to-use sites (internet) 167n22
French (language) 77
Fricker, Miranda 84
friendship networks 56n16, 60n41, 61, *see also* popularity
Frydenberg, Josh 56n17

G
Galanter, Marc 64n63, 65
Galbraith, John Kenneth 194n80
Galtung, Johan 5n21, 7n31, 8n37
Gambetta, Diego 67n73, 108n68, 119–20, 159
game theory 126, 139
games
  attention 44
  chess 166

INDEX 249

Coordination 70–3, 86, 91n124, 132–4, 136, 137, *see also* Cooperative Coordination Game, Equal Coordination Game 'Pure Coordination Game'; Unequal Coordination Game
Stag Hunt 133n8, *see also* Assurance Game
status 44n39
video 160n37
see also arms race; Assurance Game; Prisoner's Dilemma
Gandhi, Mahatma 5n20
Garfinkel, Howard 23n9
Gary, Elbert 141n37–38, 142n40
Gazdar, Gerald 79n51
Geertz, Clifford 90n117
gender *xii*, 23n6, 48, 49n62, 60, 62, 64, 78n41–2, 79n47, 86, 101, 105, 110, 112, 183, 185
 interrupting advantage 92, 185, 193n76, 194n79, 197
 social expectations and norms 101, 105, 110
generics 87n94, 87n98
Gephart, Richard 33n48
Germany 186n49
ghettoization 94, 137, 195, *see also* redlining; segregation
Gintis, Herbert 129n60
'global language' 73n10–11, 74
Goldman Sachs 56n17
Goodin, Robert E. 13n57
gossip networks 55, 56, 67n73
Gould, Roger V. 102n35, 120n18
Granovetter, Mark 54
graph theory 55n9, 56n18–19, 57, 58n27, 59, *see also* networks
Great Bengali Famine (1944) 15, 44
Greek (language) 82n64
'group conformism' 103n41

H
Habermas, Jürgen 2, 78n42, 167
Hale, Sarah Josepha 26n22
'hard drinking norm' 112, *see also* pluralistic ignorance
Hardin, Curtis D. 90n120
Hardin, Russell 67n74, 72n8
Harris, Tristan 167n25

Harsanyi, John C. 114n99
Hart, Herbert L. A. 106n57, 109
Haslanger, Sally 1n1, 6n23, 45n47, 85n80, 89n106, 89n112–13, 89n114, 90n117, 90n120
Haves/Have-Nots 176n10–12, 177n13
Haymarket Massacre 41
Hayward, Clarissa Rile 3n9, 176n9
Headey, Bruce *xiii*
health advantage 39n9, 76, 194, *see also* nutritional advantage
Hedström, Peter 97n13
Hemenway, David 43n35
hereditary monarchy 121n21
Herzog, Lisa 169n39
heterosexuality *see* sexuality
hierarchies 191
 coordination and organization 142n43, 143, 144, 145n60, 146
 formally organized competitive 42, 47, 51
 institutional 40n23, 41n24–5, 43, 45, 46, 51
 naked-power 41n26–8, 42, 47, 51
 see also status hierarchies
Hirsch, Fred *xiii*, 44, 49
Hirshleifer, Jack 119n10
Hobbes, Thomas 12n52, 21n2, 43n34, 76, 117, 118, 123, 135, 161
Hodas, Nathan O. 123n27
HOLC *see* Home Owner's Loan Corporation
home environment 27
Home Owner's Loan Corporation (HOLC) 136n14–16, 137n17
homogeneity 60n41, 61
homophily 60n41, 61, 78, 79n46, 129n63
homosexuality *see* sexuality
'horizontal cliques' 143n51
Hotelling, Harold 163n1, 168n28
housing markets 1n4, 27n28, 35, 136n14–16, 137n17
human capital 191, 193
Hume, David 9n41, 41n28, 98n19, 114
Hurricane Katrina 98n20
Hwang, Jackelyn 137n18
'hybrid networks' 67n75
'hyper-collective goods' 74n17

I

'ideological biases' *see* coding categories; interpretive schema; language
'ill will' 10
impersonal structures 2n5
'implicit bargaining' 140n28, 140n31, 146
implicit messaging 79, 80n52, 81
'income inequality' 189n62, 190n68, 190n70, 191–2
industry *see* production processes
informal networks 67, 68n77
information 153n10, 181–2
    attention scarcity 164, 168, 169n38, 171, 172
    transmitting networks 55n11, 56, 57n23, 66n71, 67n73–5, 68n77
    see also coding categories; interpretive schema; language
inheritance 8n35, 16–18, 120, 189, *see also* bequests; parents
initial advantage 12, 13n57–8
'instinctive Bayesianism' 67n74
institutional hierarchies 40n23, 41n24–5, 43, 45, 46, 51
institutions 1n1, 2n5, 7n31, 8n35. *see also* structures
insurance *see* actuaries and actuarially-fair insurance
'intellectual self-trust' 103n42
intentional actions 3, 6, 7n31, 8, 19n84, 31, 49n65, 59, 68, 84–5, 140, 142, 182
intergenerational transmission 16–18, 11n46, 31, *see also* bequests; inheritance; parents
interlocking directorates 2, 3
internal constraints
    attention as scarce resource 163n1, 164n2, 164n6–7, 165n13–14, 166n18–19, 167
    attention scarcity and advantage 171n49–50, 172–3
    lessons from the internet 167n22, 167n25, 168n28, 169n34, 169n37–40, 170n43
    see also external opportunities
internet 145n63, 180n29, 182n36
    attention scarcity 167n22, 167n25, 168n28, 169n34, 169n37–40, 170n43
interpersonal networks 54
interpersonal power 1, 2
interpretative schema 17, 31, 35, 69, 131–2, 171–2, 185
    conferring advantage 88n105, 89n106, 89n109, 89n112–14, 90n116–20, 91n121, 92n126, 93, 94, 95
    interrupting advantage 195n84, 197
    see also coding categories; information; language
interrupting advantage *see* advantage, interrupting
intrapersonal transmission 18
investment bankers 128
Italy 108n68
iterated games *see* game theory; games; repeat-play situations

J

James, William 82
Jensen, Anders 110n80
Jessop, Bob *xii*
Jevons, W. Stanley 50n71
'Jim Crow' laws (American South) 30, 109
Jütten, Timo *xiii*

K

Kahneman, Daniel 164
Kanter, Rosabeth 79
Kant, Immanuel 76
Kaun, David E. 4n18
Kemper, Theodore D. 40n18
Kennedy, John F. 140n35
Keynes, John Maynard 101n32
Kilduff, Martin 129n65
King, Nelson 187n57
Kinsey reports 112
'kluge' 187n54, 187n56–8
Kolers, Avery *xiii*, 157n23
Kooti, Farshad 123n27
Kreps, David 127, 128n54
Kukla, Rebecca 78n41
Kuznets, Simon 27n29, 189
Kymlicka, Will 195n86

L

labour markets 15n66, 17, 50, 83, 144n53, 157n23–4
    interrupting advantage 183, 185, 186n49–50, 197

networks 62n47, 63n54–55, 63n58, 64, 67, 193n76, 194n80–1
position 31, 35, 44
social expectations and norms 96, 97n10–11, 101, 110
Laird, Chryl N. 102n38
Laitin, David D. 75–6
language 17, 35, 88n105, 90n120, 93, 94, 95, 131–2
choice and advantage/disadvantage 73n11, 73n14, 74n17–19, 75n22, 75n25, 76
conventions as asymmetrical benefit 70f, 71f, 71n4–5, 71n7, 72f, 72n8–9, 73n10
gender-neutral 92, 185
interrupting advantage 180, 183, 185, 192, 193
manipulation of 69–70, 79n48, 79n50–1, 80n52, 80n57, 81
status marker 69, 76n30–1, 77n38, 78n41–3, 79n46–7
see also coding categories; information; interpretive schema
Latin (language) 76n31
'law of anticipated reactions' 23, 41n27, 45, 118, 119
'law of persons' 39n14
'law of surfing' 169n37, *see also* internet
'law of the jungle' 41
'learning by doing' 157, 158
legal norms 109n73, 110, 115, 138, 154
legal services networks 64n63, 65, 67
Lerman, Kristina 123n27
Leviathan (Hobbes) 76
Lewis, David 79n50, 80n52, 117n1, 137
Lewis, Kevin 60n41
Lindblom, Charles E. 142n43
Lindsay, A. D. 141n36
linguistic codes 84–5, 88n105
'linguistic injustice' 73n10–11, 78n41–2
Linton, Ralph 38n6
Lippmann, Walter 85n82
Lizardo, Omar 3n14
lobbyists 32, 33n48, 33n50, *see also* 'revolving door' lobbying
Locke, John 47
'logic of appropriateness' 46
'loss aversion' 24, 25, 29
'loss in transmission' 59

lotteries 12n50, 12n54, 52
Loury, Glenn 87n101
Luce, R. Duncan 72n8
Luddites 176, 180n27
Lukes, Steven 3n9

M
Macaulay, Stewart 126n48, 127
McBrier, Debra B. 64
McCrain, Joshua 33n50
McDaniel, Tyler W. 137n18
'machine learning' 152n9, 179
Maine, Henry Sumner 39n14, 109n73
'male privilege' 23n6
malnutrition (childhood) 16, 17n73
Malone, Thomas W. 132n7
Mandarin Chinese 74n19
Maori of Aotearoa (New Zealand) 48
March, James G. 166n19
market competition 47
market-style institutions 142, 143, 144, 146n66, 147n74, *see also* capitalist institutions
Mark,ov chain *see* 'absorbing Markov chains'
Married Women's Property Act (1870) 110
Marschak, Jacob 141n36
Marshall, Alfred 157, 158
Marshall, Thomas H. 38n6
Martimort, David 143n51
Marx, Karl 21n2, 50n69, 84n76, 99, 152n5–6, 155n18, 157n24, 188n60–1
'Matthew Effect' 21n2, 25, 26n17, 52
mechanisms xi–xii, xiii, 1, 4n16, 5, 8n35, 11, 16–19, 30, 35
head-on attacks on 179n26, 180n27, 180n29, 180n31, 181n32, 182n36, 183n40–1, 184, 185n42, 186n49–50, 186n53
provision of alternatives 192, 193n76, 194n79–81, 195n83–4, 195n86, 197
reducing need for 181, 182n36, 183n40–1, 184
Mendelberg, Tali 80–81
meritorious performance 12
Merton, Robert K. 21n2, 101n33
Metcalfe's Law 58n27
Miller, Greg 124n34
Mill, John Stuart 105n51, 106n58

Mills, Charles 83
Minority Body, The (Barnes) 93
mobile phone networks 57
modes of perpetuating advantage 21n1–2
   expanding advantage 21, 25, 26n17, 26n19–22, 27n26, 27n28–9, 28, 29n33, 33
   recreating advantage 21, 22, 31n41, 32n46, 33n48, 33n50
   replicating advantage 21, 22, 29, 30n36–7, 31, 33
   retaining advantage 21, 22n3, 23n5–9, 24n10, 25n14, 25n16, 33
money 50n69–71, 51
monopolies 146–7, 153n13, *see also de jure* monopolies; 'natural monopolies'; oligopolies
Montesquieu, Charles de Secondat, Baron de 52n77, 179n26
'Moral Majority' (organization) 105
moral norms 104n47, 105n49, 105n51
Muldoon, Ryan 96n8
multiculturalism 194, 195n86
mutual adjustment 139n25–7, 140n28, 140n31, 140n35, 141
mutual alignment 141n36–8, 142n
Myrdal, Gunnar 27n28, 96n6

N
naked-power hierarchies 41n26–8, 42, 47, 51
Native Americans 23n8
'naturalistic fallacy' 110n78
'natural monopolies' 153n12–13, 153n15, 154, 184, 192
Nature of Prejudice, The (Allport) 85n81
Nazi Germany 112n87
neighbourhoods 17–18
neoclassicism 54
neoliberal capitalism 51
network externalities
   distributional consequences of 57, 58n27, 68, 74, 100, 122n25
   external opportunities in communication 159–61, 159n33, 160n37, 160n39, 161
networks 5, 17, 33n50, 35, 54n1, 54n5, 55, 154, 172
   coordination and organization 142, 143, 145n63, 146
   construction *see* 'assortion'; homogeneity, homophily; 'horizontal cliques'
   distributional consequences of network externalities 57, 58n27, 68, 74, 100, 122n25
   homogeneity and homophily advantages 60n41, 61
   influence and preferential attachment 118, 122n25–6, 123n27–8, 124n29–35
   information and trust 56, 57n23, 66n71, 67n73–5, 68n77
   interrupting advantage 181, 191, 193n76, 194n79, 194n81
   nature of 55n9, 55n11, 55n14, 56n16–17
   network advantage in action 61n45, 62n47, 63n54–5, 63n58, 64n63, 65, 66n67–70
   power and advantage 57–60, 57n21–2, 58n27–33, 59n35–7, 60
Neustadt, Richard 144
'new advantaged' 191–2
Nintendo 160n37
nodes 56, 58n27, 58n30–1, 59n36–7, 60, *see also* networks; position
non-agentic forces 7n31, *see also* agents and agency; intentional actions; power, structural
'Non-contractual Relations in Business' (Macaulay) 126n48, 127
non-cooperative game theory 139n25
'non-decisions' 119n11
'normalization' 111, 112n84, 112n87
'normative authority' 138
norms *see* legal norms; moral norms; role norms; social expectations and norms
'norm substitution' 99n2
Northern Ireland 147
nouveau riche 24n10, 31, 32
Nozick, Robert 96n7
nutritional advantage 30, 49

O
Obama, Michelle *iii*
Ober, Josh *xiii*
observable characteristics 87, 127

'obvious' solutions 91–2, 92n126
Ocasio-Cortez, Alexandria 170
occupational advantages 31, 39n15, 41n25
Offe, Claus *xiii*
Okun, Arthur 192
'old boy's network' 56n16, 64, 148
'Old Time Gospel Hour, The' 105
oligopolies 2n8, 140, *see also* monopoly
Olsen, Johan P. 166n19
one-shot players 64, 65, *see also* repeat-play situations
'opportunity hoarding' 40n22
'opportunity pluralism' 48n58
oppression 1n1, 2n5, 18–19, 26, 89n112, 93n113, 94, 109, 132n6, 174, 175n4, 188n60, 195
organizational bias 146, 147n73–4, 148n78–9, 148n82
organizational structures 17, *see also* bureaucracies; coordination and organization
Origgi, Gloria 39n8
'Ottoman Turkish' (language) 77
Ovid 119–20

P
parents 11, 13n58, 14n63, 17–18, 32, 66, 167n25
Pareto, Vilfredo 147n74
Parsons, Talcott 38n6
Pascal, Blaise 121n21
'passing' 23n7–9
path dependency 3n15
patterns of outcomes 22n1, *see also* modes of perpetuating advantage
Pearson, Noel 122n22
perpetuating advantage *xi–xii*, 1, 4–8, 10–11, 13–14, 16–19, *see also* advantage; modes of perpetuating advantage
perpetuities, rule against 11n49
persisting injustice 1n4, 13n59, 14, 19
Persson, Torsten 110n80
Peterloo Massacre 41
Petersen, Trond 107n65
physical advantage 39
physical infrastructure 3, 9n42, 28
Pierce, Chester 26n22
Piketty, Thomas 83, 152
Pilgrim's Progress, The (Bunyan) 156

Piven, Frances Fox 177n17
'playing fields of Eton' 148n82
pluralism 187
'pluralistic ignorance' 112, 122n23, 138
'plural voters' 186n53
plutocracies 39
'polarization' 124n34
police services 170
policymaking 166n19
Political Action Committees 50
political advantage 32n46, 33n48, 33n50, 42
political communication 2
political mobilization 24, 25n14, 25n15
political systems 146, 147n73, 148, 196
Poor People's Movements (Piven and Cloward) 177n17
popularity 123n27, 162, *see also* friendship networks
position 37n2–3, 38, 185
  dynamics of positional-good competition 42, 43n34–8, 44, 45n47
  formally organized competitive hierarchy 42, 47, 51
  institutional hierarchy 40n23, 41n24–5, 43, 45, 46, 51
  language and 69, 76
  naked-power hierarchy 41n26–8 42, 47, 51
  nearly universal means 49n64–5, 50n66, 50n69–71, 51
  networks 57n21–2, 58n27–33, 59n35–7, 60, 61, 65, 67n73, 69
  separate spheres 37, 46, 47n52–3, 47n55, 48n57–8, 49n60, 49n62
  status hierarchy 38n4–6, 39n7–10, 39n14–16, 40n17–19, 40n21–2, 47, 48
  undoing positional advantage 38, 51, 52n77, 53
positional goods ('competition resources') 42, 43n34–8, 44, 45n47, 49, 52, 118, 155, *see also* arms race
power 1–2, 19n80, 21n2, 24–5, 32, 40, 46, 47, 48, 74, 84, 89n112, 90n119, 101n33, 106–107, 108, 109, 111–2, 120, 122n26, 131, 145, 146, 147, 158, 176, 186, 194n80

power (*Continued*)
    naked-power hierarchies 41n26–8, 42, 47, 51
    network advantage and 57n21–2, 58n27–33, 59n35–7, 60, 61n45, 66–7, 123
    reputation and 21n2, 117, 118n8, 119n9–11, 120n14, 155, 158, *see also* 'law of anticipated reactions'
    structural 3–4, 7n31, 8n34-5, 9–10, 24
'power law' 122n26, 124n30
preferential attachment 118, 121n19, 122n25–6, 123n27–8, 124n29–35, 161–2, 169
prescriptive norms and expectations 104n43–4, 104n46–7, 105n49, 105n51, 106n52, 106n57–8, 107n63, 107n65, 108n67–8, 109n73, 110
    see also descriptive norms and expectations
presidential nominations 102n36
'presumed practice dependence' 138
presupposition 79, 80n52
price setting 140n35, 141
'primary goods' 49n64–5, 50n66 *see also* universal means
primitive societies 39
'principle of least effort' 169n34
Principles of Psychology (James) 165n13
Prisoner's Dilemma 134f, 135, 137, 139n27
private clubs 130, 140–1, 148
'private government' 129n65, 130, 143
private languages 94
production processes 55–6, 57n22, 86n88, 181, 190, 192
    external opportunities 151, 152n4–6, 152n9, 153n10, 153n12–13, 153n15, 154–5, 160, 162
'professional' roles 108n67, 154–5
property 9, 23n6, 27n8, 110, 114, 115, 16, 138, 140, 153n15, 168, 186, 189
protection 161–2
psychological motivation: social expectations 100, 103n41–42
public goods 74n17, 130, 160
'public defenders' 108–9
'Pure Coordination Game' 132, 133f, 134, 136, 137n18

R

race *xii*, 9n43, 23, 24, 30, 60–3, 78n41, 80–1, 86, 87n96, 96n6, 101, 183,
    see Afro-Americans; black people; ethnicity; segregation
Race Card, The (Mendelberg) 80–1
racial discrimination 106–7
racial segregation 138–9
Radner, Roy 141n36
Raiffa, Howard 72n8
Ramachandran, Rajesh 75–6
RAND 145n63
Rational Expectations model 99n21
rationality: social expectations 100n30, 101n32–3, 102n35–8
Rawls, John 49n64–5, 50n66
'ready availability': friendship 60, 61
'reasonable expectations' 115
recidivism 87n96, 170n43
redlining 136–7
Reiman, Jeffrey 11n47
'relational contracting' 46, 126n48, *see also* employment contracts
reliability 125n36–7, 126n41–3, 126n45–6, 126n48, 127n51, 128n54, 129n60, 129n62–3, 129n65, 130
religious beliefs 47n55, 55n13, 147
Renaissance, The 58, 108n67
repeat-play situations 64n63, 65, 104, 124, 127n51, 139, 140n31
'replicator dynamics' 104
Republican National Convention (1968) 102n36
reputation 3n15, 5, 17, 35, 67n75, 117n1, 159
    attention scarcity 172, 173n53
    interrupting advantage 180, 191
    network influence/preferential attachment 121n19, 122n25–6, 123n27–8, 124n29–35
    position 39n8, 40n19, 52
    power and 117, 118n8, 119n9–11, 120n14
    reliability/trustworthiness 125n36–7, 126n41–3, 126n45–6, 126n48, 127n51, 128n54, 129n60, 129n62–3, 129n65, 130
    status position and 120n16, 120n18, 121n19, 121n21, 122n22–4

see also stereotypes
residential 'security' maps 136n14–16, 137n17
Reskin, Barbara F. 4n16, 64
resource expenditures 22–3, *see also* 'law of anticipated reactions'
'respected elder' 121, 122n22
responsibility *xi*, 6n23, 19–20, 19n84, 20n85, 20n87, 175–9, 195–7, 198n89, *see also* blame
'revolving door' lobbying 32n46, 56n17, *see also* lobbyists
Rilinger, Georg 90n119
Robertson, Sir Dennis 156n20
Robinson, James A. 66n69
robots 3n12
role norms 107n63, 107n65, 108n67–8, 109
Roman Catholic Church 76n30–1
Roman trade routes 55n14
Roosevelt, F.D. 148n78, 195n83
Ross, Alan S.C. 77n38
Ross, Edward Alsworth 104n43
Rossman, Gabriel 8n37
'rotating credit associations' 129n60
Rousseau, Jean-Jacques 9, 109
rule/act utilitarianism 114n99
'rule of law' 86n89
'rule of no-opposition' 102n37
Russia 77
Ryle, Gilbert 6n22

S
Saez, Emmanuel 83
salience 92, 146, 165, *see also* obvious solutions
Sangiovanni, Andrea 108n67
'Sanskritization' (Indian subcontinent) 23n6, 31
'satisficing': Simon's principle of 169n34
savings 12n50, 18, 27n29, 136, 152n4
scale effects 180, 181n32, 197
  consumption 155n18, 156n20–1, 157n23–4, 158n27, 159n31–2, 160
  production 152n4–6, 156n20–1, 157n23–4, 158n27, 159n31–2, 160, 192
  valuation 159n33, 160n37, 160n39, 161–2

Schattschneider, Elmer E. 146, 147n73
Schelling, Thomas C. 60, 71n7, 72n9, 91n124, 97n13, 106n52, 135, 195n86
Schilke, Oliver 8n37
schools *see* educational advantage; segregation, educational
science 88n105, 89, 195
  stratification system 52, 98n15, 101n33, 195
S. C. Johnson & Son 127
search engines: internet 168, 169n37–8, 171
second-degree neighbours 162n43
second languages 73n14, 74, *see also* linguistic justice
secrets 159n31
segregation 138
  residential 60, 136–7
  educational 40n21
  see also discrimination; race
self-fulfilling prophecies 27n28, 97n13, 98n15, 98n18–20, 99n21–5, 99n27, 100n30, 128
self-organizing work groups 194n81
'self-reinforcing causal circle' 122n24
Sen, Amartya 14n63, 15, 44, 49n64
separate spheres 46–9
sequential choice 100n30, 164n2
service networks 56
Sewell, William, Jr. 6n22, 89n113, 91n121, 108n67
sexuality 24n10, 105, 112, 185
Shackle, George L. 96n9
Shapiro, Carl 100n30, 159n33
shared norms/conventions 137n18, 138n20, 139, *see also* coordination and organization; Coordination Games; social expectations and norms
Shaw, George Bernard 77, 131
Shubik, Martin 44n39, 164n2
'Silk Roads' 55n14
Simmel, Georg 54
Simon, Herbert A. 132, 145n60, 163, 164n2, 164n6, 168, 181
simultaneous choice 100n30
'siphon off the benefits and redistribute them' strategy 188n61, 189n62, 190n68, 190n70, 191–2, 196
slavery 2, 24, 65, 66n67–70, 94, 144

Smith, Adam 21n2, 50n70, 66n71
social capital 57n21
'social cognition processes' 85n79, 85n81
'social connection model of responsibility' 175n3-4, 177
social esteem *see* esteem39, 97n12, 101n33, 121
social expectations and norms 3n15, 17, 35, 37, 95n1-5, 96n6-9, 180
   descriptive norms and expectations 96, 97n10-13, 98n15, 98n18-20, 99n21-5, 99n27, 100n30, 101n32-3, 102n35-8, 103n41-2
   prescriptive norms and expectations 104n43-4, 104n46-7, 105n49, 105n51, 106n52, 106n57-8, 107n63, 107n65, 108n67-8, 109n73, 110
   relations between descriptive/prescriptive norms 110n80, 111, 112n84, 112n87
   value of knowing 113n90, 114n94, 114n99, 115-116
   see also authority; legal norms; moral norms; normative authority
social media 123n27, 123n34
social norms 105, 106n52, 106n57-8, 107
social order 3, 19, 96n6, 135
social position and mobility 16, 19, 24n10, 25n14, 25n16, 31-2
social stability 95n3-4, 96n6
'social standing' *see* status
Solnick, Sara J. 43n35
sorting *see* 'assortition'; homogeneity, homophily; 'horizontal cliques'
South Africa 112
sporting competitions 42, 60, 112, 148n82, 157n23
stable expectations 115-16
'standardization' 85n85, 86
'statistical norms' *see* descriptive norms
Status
   games of, 44n39, *see also* positional goods
   honour and 31-2, 38, 39n7-8, 39n10-11
   languages as status marker 69, 76n30-1, 77n38, 78n41-3, 79n46-7
   reputation and 120n16, 120n18, 121n19, 121n21, 122n22-4

   social expectations and norms 101n33, 102n35, 107, 155
status hierarchies
   interrupting advantage 185, 186, 195
   position 38n4-6, 39n7-10, 39n14-16, 40n17-19, 40n21-2, 45, 47, 48, 51, 52
   see also hierarchies
'statutes of limitations' 14
steel industry 141n37-8, 142n40
Steele, Katie *xiii*
stereotypes 27n28, 85n79, 85n81, 85n82, 86n93, 87n94-6, 87n98, 87n100, 103n42, 183n40
   see also reputation
Stigler, George 157-8
Stinchcombe, Arthur L. *xiii*, 122n24, 166
stock markets 2n8, 44, 98, 99n21-2, 100, 126n46
Stone, Deborah A. 98n18
Strachey, Lytton 77
stratification, 4n16, 35, 38n4, 39n11, 41n25, 101n33, *see also* class
structural constraints 3n9, 3n14
structural holes 7n31, 58n32
structural injustice *xi-xii*, 1n3-4, 5, 3, 4, 5n21, 6n23, 7n31, 8-10, 11n47, 14, 19, 20n87, 26n19, 35, 37, 69, 73n11, 92, 93, 110,
   coordination and organization 131n4, 132n6
   responding to 174n2, 175n3-4, 176n10-12, 177n13, 177n16-17, 178, 179
   responsibility for 195-7, 198n89
'structural obfuscation' 8n37
structural power *see* power, structural
Structural Transformation of the Public Sphere, The (Habermas) 2
structural unemployment 4n18, *see also* unemployment
structural violence 8n37
structures: agency and 5n21, 6n22-3, 6n25-6, 7n28, 7n31, 8n35-6, 9n40-1, 9n43-4, 10
Sumner, William Graham 96n6
supply networks 55-6
Supreme Court (United States) 9n40, 9n43, 50n74, 195

Swedberg, Richard 97n13
Sweden 17n73, 18, 186n50

T

Tanasoca, Ana *xiii*
Tanzania 57
Tarrow, Sidney 176n12
Tasselli, Stefano 129n65
tax-and-transfer 187, 189, 190, 191, 196, *see also* amelioration strategies, 'siphon off the benefits and redistribute them' strategy
taxation 110n80, 186n49–50, 192, *see also* tax-and-transfer
Taylor, Ashley E. 94n134
teams 40n19, 90n117, 141n36, *see also* coordination and organization
technology adoption 100n30, 101n32–3, 161, 162, 183
telephones and telegraphs 55, 56, 58n27
temporally extended agency 113n90, 114n94, 114n99
'10, 000 hours rule' 157
Thierry, Guillaume 82n64
Third World 41–2
Thomas Theorem 104n44
Thomas, William I 107n63
Thompson, E.P. 180n27
Tiananmen Square massacre 41
Tilly, Charles *xiii*, 40n22, 85n83, 176n12
Tocqueville, Alexis de 12n55, 82
Tractatus Logico-Philosophicus (Wittgenstein) 82n65
trade associations 143
trading networks 55n14, 56
transaction cost economics 143n44
'transformed' advantage 31n41, 32n46
'triadic closure' 60n41
trials 9n43
Truman, Harry S. 144
Trumbull, Gunnar 147n74
trust-based network construction 128, 129n60, 129n62–3, 129n65, 130
trustworthiness 154–5, 158n27
  networks 66n71, 67n73–5, 68n77, 172, 182
  reputation 125n36–7, 126n41–3, 126n45–6, 126n48, 127n51, 128n54, 129n60, 129n62–3, 129n65, 130

Tsebelis, George 58n32
Turkey 77
Twitter 123n27, 124n34, 153n19

U

underlying drivers *see* external opportunities; internal constraints
Underwriting Manual (1938) 137n17
unemployment 4, 63n54, 115–16, 180n29
unemployment and sickness benefits 115–16, 180n29
Unequal Coordination Game 72f, 72n8–9, 86, 133f
United States 32, 33n48, 33n50, 145n63, 186n49, *see also* American South
universal means 49–51
unjust advantage *xi–xii*, 4, 10n45, 11n48
unwarranted reputation 120n14, 121, *see also* reputation
'upper-class'/'non-upper-class' languages 77n38, 78, 82, 104n46, *see also* class; language
Urfalino, Philippe 102n37
US Steel 140n35, 141n37–8, 142n40

V

valuation: external opportunities 151, 159n33, 160n37, 160n39, 161–2
value and disvalue 54n1, 58n33
Varian, Hal R. 100n30, 159n33
Versteeg, Mila 131n3
vertical monopolies 147
'veto power' 58n32
video recording technology 100, 101n32
Viti de Marco, Antonio de 58n27
Vrousalis, Nicholas 7n31

W

Walzer, Michael 48
Ward, Hugh *xii*
Washington, George 26n20, 29n33
wealth 151, 152n4, 152n6, 157, 162
Wealth of Nations, The (Smith) 50n70
Weber, Max 31–2, 37n3, 39n15, 101n33
Wendt, Alexander E. 6n26, 7n31
whalers 138
'white ignorance' 83
White, Ismail K. 102n38
Whiteness 23n8

White prejudice/discrimination 27n28, *see also* discrimination; segregation
'White privilege' 23n6, 30, 40n21, 62n47, 63n54, 63n58, *see also* discrimination; race; segregation
Whitlam, Gough 122n22
Whorf, Benjamin Lee 81–2
wills (legal) 109n73
Wimmer, Andreas 60n41
wineries (California) 29
'winner-take-all' competition 45, 147, 160n39, 169n38, *see also* first-past-the-post (electoral system)
wisdom 39
Wittgenstein, Ludwig 82n65
Wolff, Jonathan 14n63
'women's networking' 193n76, 194n79, 197, *see also* advantage, interrupting; gender; networks
'wonder-working power' 81
'work-arounds' 187n54, 187n56–8, *see also* amelioration strategies
workplace *see* labour markets
World War I 140, 141n36
World Wide Web 55n11, 56, 59, *see also* internet
Wright, Frank Lloyd 127
'wrongs': definition 6, 10, 14, 19–20

Y
Yang, Yang 194n79
Young, Iris Marion *xii*, 2n5, 6n23, 9n44, 20, 26n19, 37, 93n133, 111, 132n6
  interrupting advantage 174, 175n3–4, 177n16–17, 178, 195, 196, 198

Z
Zheng, Robin 176n10
Zipf, George Kingsley 124n30, 169n34
zoning *see* redlining; segregation, residential
Zuckerman, Harriet 26n21, 98n15, 101n33